Saint John Chrysostom

The Homilies of Saint John Chrysostom

Archbishop of Constantinople

Saint John Chrysostom

The Homilies of Saint John Chrysostom
Archbishop of Constantinople

ISBN/EAN: 9783337417284

Printed in Europe, USA, Canada, Australia, Japan

Cover: Foto ©Lupo / pixelio.de

More available books at **www.hansebooks.com**

THE

HOMILIES

OF

S. JOHN CHRYSOSTOM

ARCHBISHOP OF CONSTANTINOPLE

ON THE

EPISTLE OF S. PAUL THE APOSTLE

TO THE

HEBREWS

PUBLISHED AFTER HIS DECEASE

OXFORD:
JAMES PARKER AND CO.
AND RIVINGTONS
LONDON, OXFORD, AND CAMBRIDGE.
1877.

PRINTED BY THE SOCIETY OF THE HOLY TRINITY,
HOLY ROOD, OXFORD.

PREFACE.

This volume completes the series of S. Chrysostom's Homilies on the New Testament. Translated a quarter of a century ago by the Rev. T. Keble Vicar of Bisley, and revised with great labour in the use of the then existing editions by his brother, the Vicar of Hursley, it was thought best to delay the publication until Dr. Field had completed the long-delayed publication of the Greek Text. This appeared in 1862.

The editing of the text of S. Chrysostom's Homilies is attended with peculiar difficulties. Written sermons[a], if ever preached in those days, were the exception. Those which have been preserved to us have been generally taken down by some hearer. S. Augustine afterwards revised his, when brought to him for the purpose. In the case of S. Chrysostom's Homilies on the Acts of the Apostles, as well as of the present volume, there are two distinct texts still extant: that originally taken down by the short-hand writer, and another, when this had been polished and made neat at a subsequent time. Dr. Field's great labour then in the Greek text of the present volume had been to restore the older form of these Homilies. He had ample material, both in Greek MSS., in a Catena published not many years ago by our Dr. CRAMER, Principal of New Inn Hall, which

---

[a] See an animadversion of S. Cyril Alex. on those who committed to writing other people's sermons and thus preserved what might have been less deliberately uttered as though it had been thoroughly well weighed. De Ador. viii. t. i. 267. See also the constantly-occurring expressions in S. Augustine which belong to the natural extemporaneous delivery but which would be untrue in the delivery of written sermons. The Preface to the first volume of S. Augustine on S. John in this Library written by the Rev. H. Browne contains interesting details of S. Augustine's preaching. Fleury remarks of Atticus, Archbishop of Constantinople, in the beginning of the fifth century, just after S. Chrysostom's decease, "His sermons were indifferent, so that no one took the trouble to take them down in writing." Fleury, Eccles. Hist. xxii. 9 p.133 Oxford translation. The extract however which S. Cyril has preserved of Atticus (de recta fide ad Arcadiam Marinamque, repeated in his Apol. adv. Episcopos Orientales cap. 4) is eloquent and pious.

exhibit the older text (the former half of a second Catena, compiled by Niketas [b] Archbishop of Heraclea in Thrace in the eleventh century, and published by the same Dr. Cramer appears to use both); and, of yet more importance, in Latin versions.

Cassiodorus, an Italian, who lived about 150 years after S. Chrysostom, in the earlier part of his treatise, de Institutione Divinarum Litterarum cap. 8. (opp. t. ii. p. 543 ed. Rotom. 1679) in describing a volume of S. Paul's Epistles, in which 13 of the Epistles had a good commentary, goes on, "But in regard to the Epistle to the Hebrews which " S. John Bishop of Constantinople treated of in Greek in " 34 homilies, we have caused Mutianus, a most eloquent " man, to translate them into Latin, that the order of the " Epistles might not be unduly broken off."

To Cassiodorus then we owe the Latin version of Mutianus which has come down to us, and which, translated from the older form of text, has been a great assistance in the editing. It is often quoted in the footnotes. In p. 167 there is also given an extract from the 13th Homily by Facundus, an African Bishop, who lived about the same time with Mutianus, but who apparently translated the passage into Latin for himself.

The short-hand writer, who took down these Homilies and thus preserved them to us, is not unknown to us. It is S. Chrysostom's dearly-loved friend the Priest Constantine or Constantius [c]. For the title is, *Homilies of S. John Chrysostom Archbishop of Constantinople on the Epistle to the Hebrews, published after his decease from notes by Constantine Presbyter of Antioch.*

At the beginning of S. Chrysostom's exile in 404, when he was in Nicæa, in a Letter which he wrote to Constantius about a mission which he had set on foot at Phœnicia (Ep. 121 t. iii. pp. 721, 722 ed. Montf.), he begs him "not

[b] Dr. Cramer had published this from the Paris MS. Cod. Reg. 238 which contains the first half only: but the whole catena is extant in the Library of S. Ambrose at Milan (E. 63 part inf.)

[c] Montfaucon observes that the Manuscripts frequently interchange the name.

"to cease having a care for the Churches of Phœnicia and
"Arabia and the east, and to write to" S. Chrysostom "quite
"often, and tell him how many Churches had been built
"in a year and what holy men had gone into Phœnicia."
Soon after, Constantius seems to have asked leave of
S. Chrysostom to join him; for in his 13th letter to Olympias on arriving at Cocussus or Cucusus in Cappadocia, now
Goksyn, his bitter place of exile, S. Chrysostom says, (ib.
p. 594) " My Lord, the most pious priest Constantius,
"would fain have been here long ago, for he wrote to me
"begging that I would let him come." About this time,
perhaps while Constantius was on his actual journey to Cucusus, S. Chrysostom writes to him (Ep. 225 p. 724), grieved
at not having heard from him, and speaks of their great
love for each other and of Constantius' goodness to the
poor, the fatherless and widows: soon after he writes from
Cucusus to Elpidius bishop of Laodicea (Ep. 114 p. 656),
"the most reverend priests Constantius and Euethius are
"here with us." There are extant two Letters of Constantius, one of them to his mother, written while he was
companion of S. Chrysostom there (pp. 731 and 734). In
the course of this banishment S. Chrysostom writes (Ep.
123 pp. 663, 664) about this Phœnician mission to "the
"priests and monks in Phœnicia, who were instructing the
"Gentiles there," encouraging them in their work, and
saying that he had given orders that all their expenses
" in clothing, shoes and support of the brethren should be
"bountifully supplied," and adds that they will know about
his affairs from Constantius' letter. In a letter to Gerontius
(Ep. 54 p. 623) written during this exile about the mission
in Phœnicia, S. Chrysostom says that he had intrusted
Constantius to give Gerontius all he needed whether " for
"building or for the needs of the brethren."

To Constantius' piety we owe the preservation of these
Homilies. One very special value of them lies in the pious
fervent exhortation at the end of each, on Penitence, Almsgiving, or whatever S. Chrysostom had at the time chiefly
in mind, breathing forth words from a heart, filled with the
Love of God and that longed for his flock to partake it.

Hom. 1 on sin and Almsgiving
2 on high thoughts and on poverty and wealth
3 on God's gifts to each
4 on heathen practices at funerals
5 on temptation
6 on Heaven
7 on old age
8 on study of Scriptures
9 on Penitence and confession of our sins
10 on relieving distress
11 on Almsgiving and giving to beggars
12 on free-will and Penitence
13 on not postponing Baptism and on a right life
14 on Thought of GOD and earnest prayer
15 on sin-enslavement and on untimely laughter
16 on dwelling in Heaven
17 on worthily receiving Holy Communion
18 on the Might of Poverty
19 on the great Gain of loving one's neighbour
20 on slavery to possessions and on Thankfulness
21 on gossip
22 on seeking GOD, on His Protection and enduring Temptation
23 on the loss of GOD
24 on the acquirement of Virtue
25 on not caring for things of the world nor partaking with the covetous
26 on loyalty to GOD
27 on the might of Prayer and on minding us that we are sinners
28 value of Affliction and on simplicity of life and adornment of the soul
29 on the Peril of Luxury
30 on helping each other in way of salvation
31 on Penitence and keeping in mind our sins
32 on the Might of mercifulness to others
33 on the value of affliction, trial, poverty, and on Thankfulness
34 on using with intensity of mind and purpose, the Grace of the SPIRIT.

After the publication of Dr. Field's text (Bibliotheca Patrum Ecclesiae Catholicae Qui ante Orientis et Occidentis schisma floruerunt, tom vii. Oxonii 1862) the translation was again very carefully revised by that text by the Rev. Dr. BARROW, Principal of S. Edmund Hall: he also wrote heads for the present Preface. The headings were given (as far as could be done) in the MS. and many of them have been retained; others, fitting in less well with the printed page, seemed to need a little modification. For an occasional note enclosed in brackets, the son of the one remaining Editor of the Library is responsible.

P. E. PUSEY.

OXFORD, MAY 1877.

CORRIGENDUM.

p. 182 margin *for* Hab. ii. 14. *correct* Isa. xi. 9. and cancel note 1.

CONTENTS.

ARGUMENT.
Page 1.

HOMILY I.
Page 8.

HEB. i. 1, 2.

God, who at sundry times and in divers manners spake in times past unto the fathers by the Prophets, hath at the end of the days spoken unto us by His Son: whom He hath appointed heir of all things, by whom also He made the worlds.

HOMILY II.
Page 18.

HEB. i. 3.

Who being the brightness of His Glory and the express Image of His person, and upholding all things by the word of His power, when He had by Himself purged our sins.

HOMILY III.
Page 31.

HEB. i. 6—8.

And when He again bringeth in the First-Begotten into the world, He saith, And let all the angels of God worship Him. And of the angels He saith, Who maketh His angels spirits, and His ministers a flame of fire. But unto the Son He saith, Thy throne, O God, is for ever and ever.

HOMILY IV.
Page 47.
HEB. ii. 5—7.

For unto Angels He hath not put in subjection the world to come, whereof we speak. But one in a certain place testified, saying, What is man that Thou art mindful of him, or the son of man that Thou visitest him? Thou hast made him a little lower than the Angels.

HOMILY V.
Page 63.
HEB. ii. 16, 17.

For verily He taketh not hold of Angels, but of the seed of Abraham He taketh hold. Wherefore in all things it behoved Him to be made like unto His brethren.

HOMILY VI.
Page 76.
HEB. iii. 7—11.

Wherefore, as the Holy Ghost saith, To-day if ye will hear His voice, harden not your hearts, as in the provocation in the day of temptation in the wilderness, when your fathers tempted Me, proved Me, and saw My works forty years. Wherefore I was grieved with that generation, and said, They do alway err in their heart, and they have not known My ways. So I sware in My wrath, If they shall enter into My rest.

HOMILY VII.
Page 87.
HEB. iv. 11—13.

Let us labour therefore to enter into that Rest, lest any man fall after the same example of unbelief. For the word of God is quick [i. e. living] *and powerful, and sharper than any two-edged sword, and pierceth even to the dividing asunder of soul and spirit, and of the joints and marrow, and is a discerner of the thoughts and intents of the heart, neither is there any creature that is not manifest in His sight, for all things are naked and opened unto the eyes of Him with Whom we have to do.*

HOMILY VIII.
Page 100.
HEB. v. 1—3.

For every high priest taken from among men, is ordained for men in things pertaining to God, that he may offer both gifts and sacrifices for sins: who can have compassion on the ignorant and on them that are out of the way, for that he himself also is compassed with infirmity; and by reason hereof he ought, as for the people so also for himself to offer for sins.

HOMILY IX.
Page 114.
HEB. vi. 1—3.

Wherefore leaving the principles of the Doctrine of Christ, let us go on unto perfection, not laying again the foundation of repentance from dead works, and of faith towards God; of the doctrine of baptisms, and of laying on of hands: and of resurrection of the dead, and of eternal judgment. And this we will do, if God permit.

HOMILY X.
Page 127.
HEB. vi. 7, 8.

For the Earth which drinketh in the rain that cometh oft upon it, and bringeth forth herbs meet for them by whom it is dressed, receiveth blessing from God. But if it bear thorns and briars it is rejected, and nigh unto cursing, whose end is to be burned.

HOMILY XI.
Page 138.
HEB. vi. 13—16.

For when God made promise to Abraham, because He could swear by no greater, He sware by Himself, saying, Surely blessing I will bless thee, and multiplying I will multiply thee. And so after he had patiently endured, he obtained the promise. For men verily swear by the greater, and an oath for confirmation is to them the end of all strife.

HOMILY XII.
Page 150.
HEB. vii. 1—3.

For this Melchisedec, King of Salem, Priest of the most High God, who met Abraham as he was returning from the slaughter of the Kings, and blessed him: to whom also Abraham gave a tenth part of all; first being by interpretation King of Righteousness, and after that also King of Salem, which is, King of Peace, without father, without mother, without genealogy, having neither beginning of days, nor end of life, but made like unto the Son of God, abideth a Priest continually.

HOMILY XIII.
Page 160.
HEB. vii. 11—14.

If therefore perfection were by the Levitical priesthood (for under it the people have received the law); what further need was there that another priest should arise after the order of Melchisedec, and not be called after the order of Aaron? For the priesthood being changed, there is of necessity a change also of the law. For He of whom those things are spoken, pertained to another tribe, of which no man gave attendance at the altar. For it is evident that our Lord sprang out of Judah, of which tribe Moses spake nothing concerning priests.

HOMILY XIV.
Page 174.
HEB. viii. 1, 2.

Now of the things which we have spoken this is the sum. We have such an High Priest; who is set down at the right hand of the throne of the majesty in the heavens: a minister of the sanctuary and of the true tabernacle which the Lord pitched, and not man.

HOMILY XV.
Page 187.
HEB. ix. 1—5.

Then verily the first [covenant] had also ordinances of divine service, and a worldly Sanctuary. For there was a tabernacle made; the first, wherein was the Candlestick, and the Table, and the Shewbread; which is called the Sanctuary. And after the second veil, the tabernacle which is called the Holiest of all; which had the golden censer, and the Ark of the Covenant overlaid round about with gold, wherein was the golden pot that had manna, and Aaron's rod that budded, and the tables of the covenant; and over it the Cherubims of glory, shadowing the Mercy-seat, of which we cannot now speak particularly.

HOMILY XVI.
Page 198.
HEB. ix. 15—18.

And for this cause He is the Mediator of the New Testament, that by means of death for the redemption of the transgressions that were under the first Testament, they which are called might receive the promise of an eternal inheritance. For where a testament is, there must also of necessity be the death of the testator. For a testament is of force when men are dead, since it hath no force at all whilst the testator liveth. Whereupon neither was that first [testament] dedicated without blood.

HOMILY XVII.
Page 207.
Heb. ix. 24—26.

For Christ is not entered into the holy places made with hands, which are the figures of the true, but into Heaven itself, now to appear in the presence of God for us. Nor yet that He should offer Himself often, as the High Priest entereth into the Holy place every year with blood of others, for then must He often have suffered since the foundation of the world. But now, once, at the end of the world, hath He appeared to put away sin by the sacrifice of Himself.

HOMILY XVIII.
Page 218.
Heb. x. 8—18.

Above when He said, Sacrifice and offering, and burnt-offerings, and [offering] for sin, Thou wouldest not, neither hadst pleasure [therein], which are offered by the Law, then said He, Lo! I come to do Thy will, O God. He taketh away the first, that He may establish the second. By the which will we are sanctified, by the offering of the body of Jesus Christ, once for all. And every priest standeth daily ministering, and offering oftentimes the same sacrifices, which can never take away sins. But this [man] after He had offered one sacrifice for sins, for ever sat down on the right hand of God, from henceforth expecting till His enemies be made His footstool.

HOMILY XIX.
Page 226.
Heb. x. 19—23.

Having therefore, brethren, boldness to enter into the holiest by the blood of Jesus, by a new and living way which He hath consecrated for us, through the Veil, that is to say, His flesh, and having an High Priest over the house of God, let us draw near with a true heart, in full assurance of faith, having our hearts sprinkled from an evil conscience, and our bodies washed with pure water, let us hold fast the profession of our hope without wavering.

HOMILY XX.
Page 233.
HEB. x. 26, 27.

For if we sin wilfully, after we have received the knowledge of the truth, there remaineth no more sacrifice for sins, but a certain fearful looking for of judgment, and fiery indignation which shall devour the adversaries.

HOMILY XXI.
Page 243.
HEB. x. 32—34.

But call to remembrance the former days, in which after ye were illuminated, ye endured a great fight of afflictions; partly, whilst ye were made a gazing stock both by reproaches and afflictions, and partly whilst ye became companions of them that were so used. For ye had compassion on those who were in bonds, and took joyfully the spoiling of your goods, knowing that ye have for yourselves in heaven a better and an enduring substance.

HOMILY XXII.
Page 253.
HEB. xi. 3, 4.

Through faith we understand that the worlds were framed by the word of God; so that things which are seen were not made of things which do appear. By faith Abel offered unto God a more excellent sacrifice than Cain, by which he obtained witness that he was righteous, God testifying of his gifts; and by it he being dead yet speaketh.

HOMILY XXIII.
Page 264.
HEB. xi. 7.

By faith Noah, being warned of God of things not seen as yet, moved with fear, prepared an ark to the saving of his house; by the which he condemned the world, and became heir of the righteousness which is by Faith.

HOMILY XXIV.
Page 275.

HEB. xi. 13—16.

These all died in faith, not having received the promises, but having seen them afar off, and embraced them, and confessed that they were strangers and pilgrims on the earth. For they that say such things, declare plainly that they seek a country. And truly if they had been mindful of that country from whence they came out, they might have had opportunity to have returned. But now they desire a better country, that is, an heavenly; wherefore God is not ashamed to be called Their God, for He hath for them a city.

HOMILY XXV.
Page 285.

HEB. xi. 17—19.

By faith [Abraham] when he was tried offered up Isaac and he that had received the promises offered up his only-begotten son, of whom it was said, In Isaac shall thy seed be called: accounting that God was able to raise him up even from the dead; from whence also he received him in a figure.

HOMILY XXVI.
Page 296.

HEB. xi. 20—22.

By faith, concerning things to come Isaac blessed Jacob and Esau. By faith, Jacob when he was a dying blessed each of the sons of Joseph, and worshipped leaning on the top of his staff. By faith, Joseph when he died made mention of the departing of the children of Israel, and gave commandment concerning his bones.

HOMILY XXVII.
Page 309.

HEB. xi. 28—31.

By faith, he kept the Passover and the sprinkling of blood, lest he that destroyed the first-born should touch them. By faith, they passed through the Red sea, as by dry land;

which the Egyptians assaying to do, were drowned. By faith, the walls of Jericho fell down, after they had been compassed about for seven days. By faith, Rahab the harlot perished not with them that believed not, having received the spies with peace.

HOMILY XXVIII.
Page 320.
HEB. xi. 37, 38.

They wandered about in sheep-skins, in goat-skins, being destitute, afflicted, tormented (of whom this world was not worthy); wandering in deserts, and mountains, and dens, and caves of the earth.

HOMILY XXIX.
Page 339.
HEB. xii. 4—6.

Ye have not yet resisted unto blood, striving against sin. And ye have forgotten the exhortation which speaketh unto you as unto children, My son, despise not thou the chastening of the Lord, nor faint when thou art rebuked of Him. For whom the Lord loveth, He chasteneth: and scourgeth every son whom He receiveth.

HOMILY XXX.
Page 349.
HEB. xii. 11—13.

No chastisement for the present seemeth to be joyous, but grievous, nevertheless afterward it yieldeth the peaceable fruit of righteousness to them which have been exercised thereby. Wherefore lift up the hands which hang down, and the feeble knees: and make straight paths for your feet, lest that which is lame be turned out of the way, but let it rather be healed.

HOMILY XXXI.
Page 357.
HEB. xii. 14.

Follow peace with all men, and holiness without which no one shall see the LORD.

HOMILY XXXII.
Page 366.
HEB. xii. 18—24.

For ye are not come unto a fire that might be touched and that burned, and unto blackness, and darkness, and tempest, and the sound of a trumpet, and the voice of words, which voice they that heard entreated that the word should not be spoken to them any more. (For they could not endure that which was commanded, And if so much as a beast touch the mountain, it shall be stoned. And, so terrible was the sight, that Moses said, I exceedingly fear and quake.) But ye are come unto Mount Sion, and unto the city of the Living God, the Heavenly Jerusalem; and to myriads of Angels, in festive gathering, and to the Church of the first-born which have been enrolled in Heaven; and to God the Judge of all; and to the spirits of just men made perfect: and to JESUS *the Mediator of the New Covenant: and to the blood of sprinkling that speaketh better things than Abel.*

HOMILY XXXIII.
Page 376.
HEB. xii. 28, 29.

Wherefore we receiving a Kingdom that cannot be moved, let us have grace [or *gratitude*], *whereby we serve God acceptably with reverence and godly fear. For our God is a consuming fire.*

HOMILY XXXIV.
Page 387.
HEB. xiii. 17.

Obey them that have the rule over you, and submit yourselves. For they watch for your souls, as they that must give account, that they may do it with joy, and not with grief, for this is unprofitable for you.

HOMILIES

OF

S. JOHN CHRYSOSTOM

ARCHBISHOP OF CONSTANTINOPLE

ON THE

EPISTLE TO THE HEBREWS

PUBLISHED AFTER HIS DECEASE, FROM NOTES BY CONSTANTINE
PRESBYTER OF ANTIOCH.

THE ARGUMENT.

[1.] THE blessed Paul writing to the Romans, saith, (1) *Inasmuch then as I am the Apostle of the Gentiles, I magnify* Rom. xi. *mine office; if by any means I may provoke to jealousy them* 13, 14. *that are my flesh:* and again, in another place, *For He* Gal. ii. 8. *that wrought effectually in Peter to the apostleship of the circumcision, the same wrought effectually in me toward the Gentiles.* If therefore he were the Apostle of the Gentiles (for also in the Acts, God saith to him, *Depart; for* Acts xxii. *I will send thee far hence unto the Gentiles),* what had he 21. to do with the Hebrews? and why did he also write an Epistle to them?

And especially as besides, they were evil-disposed towards him; as is often from many places to be seen. For hear what James saith to him, *Thou seest, brother, how many* Ib. xxi. *thousands of Jews there are which have believed .... and* 20, 21. *these all have been informed of thee that thou teachest men to forsake the Law.* And oftentimes he had many disputings concerning this.

Thus (a person might enquire) considering that he was so
VOL. VII.   B

learned in the Law (for he was instructed in the Law at the feet of Gamaliel, and his zeal in the cause thereof was great), and that herein he was particularly able to confound them;—why did not God send him to the Jews? Because on this very account they had been made more vehement in their enmity against him. *For they will not endure thee,* saith God unto him. But, *Depart far off to the Gentiles, inasmuch as they will not receive thy testimony concerning Me.* Whereupon he himself saith, *Yea, Lord, they know that I imprisoned and beat in every synagogue them that believed on Thee; and when the blood of Thy martyr Stephen was shed, I also was standing and consenting unto his death, and kept the raiment of them that slew him.*

And this is the very thing which he says is a sign and argument of their not believing him. For thus it is: when a man starts off from any sort of people [1], if he be one of the least and of those who are nothing worth, he doth not much vex those from whom he is departed. But if he be among the distinguished or very earnest partizans, or those who sympathise with them, he exceedingly grieves and vexes them beyond measure; in that he especially overthrows their system, in the judgment of the many.

And besides this, there was something else in addition. What now might this be? That Peter and the others were with Christ, and also saw signs and wonders; but he having enjoyed none of these advantages, but being with Jews, all at once deserted, and became one of them. Which thing especially promoted our cause. For while they seemed to bear witness from mere favour, and a person might have said that in loving regret for their master, they testify these things: the special witness of the resurrection was of all men this man, who heard a voice only. For this cause thou seest them waging passionate war with him, and practising all for no other purpose than to slay him and raising seditions.

The unbelievers then on this account listened to him with evil dispositions, but the believers, what was their motive? Because in preaching to the Gentiles he was constrained to preach Christianity purely. And if haply he were found [doing it] even in Judæa, he cared not. For

[1] ἔθνους

Peter indeed and they that were with him, inasmuch as HEB. they had to preach in Jerusalem, where men's zeal was great, of necessity bade them keep the Law: whereas this man was quite at liberty. The converts too from the Gentiles were more in number than the Jews, inasmuch as they were without [a]. And this enfeebled the Law, and they had no longer so great reverence for it, although he preached all things purely. At least it is with respect to this that they seem to shame him by numbers, saying, *Thou* Acts xxi. *seest, brother, how many ten thousands of Jews there are* 20. *which are come together.* On this account they hated him and turned away from him, because *they have been in-* Ib. 21. *formed,* it saith, *concerning thee, that thou teachest men to forsake the Law.*

[2.] Why then, not being a teacher of the Jews, doth he send an Epistle to them? (And where abode those to whom he sent it? As it seems to me, in Jerusalem and Palestine.) How then doth he send them an Epistle? Just as he baptized, though to baptize was not his assigned duty. *For* (saith he) *I was not sent to baptize:* not however, 1 Cor. i. that he was forbidden, but he doth it, as somewhat over 17. and above his work.

And how could he fail to write to these, for whom he Rom. ix. was willing even to become accursed? Accordingly he 3. said [b], *Know ye that our brother Timothy is set at liberty;* Infra *with whom, if he come shortly, I will see you.* xiii. 23.

(For as yet he was not seized and imprisoned. Two years then he passed in prison at Rome. After this he was set free. Then having gone into the parts of Spain, he also perhaps saw the Jews. And then he returned to Rome, and then was slain by Nero. The Epistle to Timothy then was later [c] than this Epistle. For there he saith, *For I* 2 Tim. iv. *am now ready to be offered,* and there also he saith, *In my* Ib. 16. *first answer no man stood with me.*)

---

[a] The chosen people being *fewer than all people,* encircled on all sides by the heathen: see Mic. v. 7, 8.

[b] S. Chrys. introduces this as an instance of S. Paul's interest in the Hebrews: that he not only wrote to them, but also intended to visit them: and on that digresses to the events of his history and the relative date of the Epistles.

[c] πρεσβυτέρα, the word is elsewhere used in this sense by S. Chrysostom. See Mr. Field's notes. S. Chrys. often points out that the Ep. ii. to Timothy is the last of all S. Paul's Epistles. [Ben.]

ARGUMENT. The reason is that in many places they [the Hebrews] had to contend[d] [with persecution], as also he says in an Epistle to the Thessalonians, *Ye became followers of the Churches of Judea:* and writing to these very persons he says, *Ye took joyfully the spoiling of your goods.* Thou seest that *they* had to contend? And if men had thus treated the Apostles, not in Judea only, but also wherever they were among the Gentiles, what would they not have done to the believers?

1 Thess. ii. 14.
Infra x. 34.

For this cause, thou seest, he was very full of care for them. Thus, when he saith, *I go to minister to the saints which are in Jerusalem:* and again, when he exhorts the Corinthians to beneficence, and says that the Macedonians had already made their contribution, saying too, *If it be meet that I go* [&c], this is what he means.

Rom. xv. 25.
2 Cor. viii. 3.
1 Cor. xvi. 4.

And when he saith, *Only that we should remember the poor, which thing I was also forward to do*—this is what he means.

Gal. ii. 10.

And when he saith, *They gave to me and Barnabas the right hands of fellowship, that we should* [*go*] *to the Gentiles, and they to the Circumcision,*—this is what he means.

Ib. 9.

But this [was] not [done] with regard to the poor also who were there: but [it was ordered] so that in that respect we might be partakers in the doing kindness [to them]. For [we did] not so [apportion] the care for the poor, as we apportioned the preaching to each other, and that *we indeed should* [*go*] *to the Gentiles, and they to the circumcision.* And every where thou seest him using great care for them: as might be expected.

For in the other nations indeed, where there were both Jews and Greeks, no such thing took place. But there, inasmuch as they seemed still to have authority and independence, and to order many things by their own peculiar laws, the government not yet being established, nor entirely brought under the Romans, they, as might have been expected, exercised much tyrannical power. For if in other cities, as namely in Corinth, *they beat the Ruler of the synagogue before the Deputy's judgment seat, and Gallio cared for none of these things,* yet it was not so in Judea[c].

Acts xviii. 17.

[d] ἤθλησαν, see ἄθλησιν Heb. x. 32.
[e] i.e. in Judea, they beat and scourg-
ed, not through the indifference of the judge, but by their own authority.

You see at any rate that while in other cities they bring them to the magistrates, and need assistance from them and from the Gentiles: here, they took no care of this, but themselves assemble a council and put to death whomever they choose. HEB. (2)

In this way for instance they put Stephen to death, in this way they scourged the Apostles, not leading them before any rulers. In this way also they were about to put Paul to death, unless the chief captain had thrown himself upon them. For this took place while the priesthood was yet standing, as also the temple, the service, the sacrifices. Behold for example Paul himself on his trial before the High Priest, and saying, *I wist not that there is an High Priest*, and this in the presence of the Ruler[1]. For at that time they possessed great power. Consider then what sufferings they were likely to undergo, who dwelt in Jerusalem and Judea. Acts xxiii. 5. [1] i.e. before Lysias.

[3.] He then who prays to become accursed for those who were not yet believers, and who so ministers to the faithful, as to journey himself, if occasion required, and who every where took exceeding care of them; let us not wonder if he encourage and console them by letters also, and if when they are tottering and fallen he set them upright. For they were in one word worn down[f] by their manifold afflictions, and reduced to despair. And this he signifies near the end, saying, *Wherefore lift up the hands that hang down, and the feeble knees.* And again: *Yet a little while, he that shall come will come, and will not tarry;* and again, *If ye be without chastisement, ... then are ye bastards and not sons.* Infra xii. 12. Ib. x. 37. Ib. xii. 8.

For inasmuch as they were Jews, and (as others) were constantly told by their fathers, that they must expect both their good and their evil immediately and must live accordingly, whereas then the contrary took place, their good things being in hope and to come after death, their evils in hand; it was probable that although they had resolutely endured much, not a few of them would be fainthearted; —he discourses hereon.

[f] having lost their freshness and vigour like salted fish. See many instances of its use in this sense in Mr. Field's note on S. Chrys. on 1 Cor. Hom. xxviii. (p 255. A.) [see p. 390 O.T.]

ARGUMENT. These things however we will unfold at a fit opportunity. But at present we say that he could not choose but write to those, for whom he was used to take such anxious thought, the reason too being manifest, why he was not sent as an apostle to them; he was not hindered from writing.

Now that they were becoming faint-hearted, he signifies saying, *Lift up the hands that hang down and the feeble knees, and make straight paths.* And again, *For God is not unrighteous, to forget your work and your love.* For the soul being overtaken by many trials, was turned aside also from the Faith. Wherefore he exhorts them to *give heed to the things which they have heard,* and that there should not be *an evil heart of unbelief.* On this account also, in this Epistle particularly, he discourses much concerning Faith, and at the end after many [arguments] shews that to them [of old] also He promised their good things in hand, and yet gave nothing.

Infra xii. 12, 13.
Ib. vi. 10.

Ib. ii. 1.

Ib. iii. 12.

And beside these things, that they might not think themselves forsaken, he establishes two points, the one that they should bear nobly whatever befals them; the other, that they should assuredly expect their recompense. For surely He will not leave unrewarded Abel and the line of righteous persons following him.

And he draws his consolation from three arguments. First, from the sufferings of Christ: as He Himself also saith, *The servant is not greater than his Lord.* Next, from the good things laid up for them that believe. Thirdly, from the evils; and this point he enforces not from the future only (which would not be so persuasive), but also from what was past and had befallen their fathers. This Christ also doth, saying at one time, *The servant is not greater than his Lord;* and again, *There are many mansions with My Father.* He also denounces woes innumerable on them that believe not.

S. John xiii. 16.

Ib. xiv. 2.

And he makes much discourse both of the New and the Old Covenant. For indeed this same topic was very useful to him for the proof of the Resurrection. I mean lest they should utterly disbelieve Christ's resurrection, through His sufferings, he confirms it from the Prophets, and points out also, that the Jewish rites are not the really sacred ones, but ours. For the temple was still standing, and the sacrificial rites; therefore he saith, *Wherefore let us go forth without, bearing His reproach.* And this also was alleged against him : „If these things are a shadow, if these things „are an image, how is it that they have not given place, „or been withdrawn when the truth appeared—but these „[ancient rites] still flourish?" With respect to this also, he quietly and in a figure intimated that it would happen at the time that was close at hand. _{Heb.} _{Heb. xiii. 13.}

Moreover, that they had been for a long time in the Faith and in afflictions he declared, saying, *When for the time ye ought to be teachers,* and, *Lest there be ever in any of you an evil heart of unbelief,* and, *Ye became followers of them who through patience inherit the promises.* _{Ib. v. 12. Ib. iii. 12. Ib. vi. 12.}

HOMILY I.

HEB. i. 1, 2.

God who at sundry times and in divers manners spake in time past unto the fathers by the Prophets, hath at the end of the days[a] *spoken unto us by His Son: whom He hath appointed heir of all things, by whom also He made the worlds.*

(1)
Rom. v. 20.
[1.] TRULY, *where sin abounded, grace did much more abound.* This at least the blessed Paul intimates here also, in the very beginning of his Epistle to the Hebrews. For inasmuch as it was likely that they, afflicted, worn out as they had been by their evils, and judging of things thereby, would think themselves worse off than all other men,—he shews that herein they had rather been made partakers of greater grace, even very exceeding; arousing the hearer at the very opening of his discourse. Wherefore he saith, *God who at sundry times and in divers manners spake in times past unto the fathers by the Prophets, hath at the end of the days spoken unto us by His Son.*

Why did he [Paul] not oppose *himself* to *the prophets?* Certainly, he was much greater than they, inasmuch as a greater trust was committed to him. Yet he doth not so. What could be the reason? First, to avoid speaking great things concerning himself. Secondly, because his hearers

[a] ἐσχάτου τῶν ἡμερῶν. ἐσχάτων τ. ἢ. (in these last days) Sav. Ben. here and throughout the Homily. The former is considered to be the true reading of the Sacred Text. It is throughout the reading of S. Chrys. as is clear from his argument.

were not yet perfect. And thirdly, because he rather Heb. i. 1.
wished to exalt them, and to shew that their superiority
was great. As if he had said, What so great matter is it
that He sent prophets to our fathers? For to us [He has
sent] His own only-begotten Son Himself.

And well did he begin thus, *At sundry times and in divers
manners*, for he points out that not even the prophets themselves saw God; nevertheless, the Son saw Him. For the
expressions, *at sundry times and in divers manners* are the
same as "in different ways." *For I* (saith He) *have multiplied* Hos. xii.
visions, and used similitudes by the ministry of the Prophets. 10.
Wherefore the excellency consists not in this alone, that
to them indeed prophets were sent, but to us the Son; but
in that from among them no one saw God, but the Only-
begotten Son saw Him. He doth not indeed at once assert
this, but by what he saith afterwards he establishes it, when
he speaks concerning His human nature; *For to which of* ver. 5.
the Angels said He, Thou art My Son, and, *Sit thou on* ver. 13.
My right hand?

And look thou on his great wisdom. First he shews this
superiority from the prophets. Then having maintained
this as an acknowledged truth, he declares that to them
indeed He spake by the prophets, but to us by the Only-
begotten. Then [He spake] to them by Angels, and this again
he establishes, with good reason (for it is true that angels
also held converse with the Jews): yet even herein we have
the superiority, inasmuch as the Master [spake] to us, but
to them the servants, and prophets the fellow-servants.

[2.] Well also said he, *at the end of the days*, for by this
also he stirs them up and encourages them in their utter
despondency. For as he saith also in another place, *The* Phil. iv.
Lord is at hand, be careful for nothing, and again, *For now* Rom. xiii.
is our salvation nearer than when we believed: so also here. 11.
What then is it which he saith? That whoever has been
exhausted in the conflict, when he hears of the end thereof,
recovers his breath a little, knowing that it is the end indeed of his labours, but the beginning of his rest.

Hath in the end of the days spoken unto us in His Son.
Behold again he uses the saying, *in* [*His*] *Son* [1], for *through* [1] ἐν υἱῷ
the Son [2], against those who assert that this phrase is [2] διὰ τοῦ υἱοῦ

proper to the Spirit[b]. Dost thou see that the [word] *in* is *through?*

And the expression again, *In times past*, and this, *In the end of the days*, has some other hidden meaning. That when a long time had intervened, when we were on the edge of punishment, when the Gifts had failed, when there was no expectation of deliverance, when we were expecting to have less than all—then we have had more.

And see with what consideration he hath spoken it. For he said not, *Christ spake* (albeit it was He who did speak), but inasmuch as their souls were weak, and they were not yet able to hear the things concerning Christ, he saith, *God hath spoken by Him.* What meanest thou? did God speak through the Son? Yes. What then? Is it thus thou shewest the superiority? for here thou hast but pointed out that both the New and the Old [Covenants] are of One and the same: and that this superiority is not great. Wherefore he henceforth follows on upon this argument, saying, *He spake unto us by His Son.*

(Note, how Paul expresses it generally, and puts himself on a level with the disciples, saying, He spake *to us:* and yet He did not speak to him, but to the Apostles, and through them to the many. But he is lifting them [the Hebrews] up, declaring that He spake also to them. And as yet he doth not at all reflect on the Jews. For almost all to whom the prophets spake, were a kind of evil and polluted persons. But as yet the discourse is not of these: but hitherto of the gifts derived from God.)

Whom He appointed, saith he, *heir of all.* What means this *whom He appointed heir of all?* He is speaking here of the flesh [the human nature]. As He also saith in the second Psalm, *Ask of Me, and I will give Thee nations, for Thine inheritance.* For no longer is *Jacob the portion of the Lord*, nor *Israel His inheritance*, but all men: that is

[b] That is, the Macedonians or Pneumatomachi, who about the year 373 found great fault with S. Basil for using indifferently the two forms of doxology, sometimes μετὰ τοῦ Υἱοῦ σὺν τῷ Πνεύματι τῷ Ἁγίῳ, sometimes διὰ τοῦ Υἱοῦ ἐν τῷ Πνεύματι τῷ Ἁγίῳ. They said that the latter, by which they meant to imply inferiority in the Third Person especially, was the only proper form. This gave occasion to S. Basil's writing his Tract *De Spiritu Sancto*, in which he refutes them at large, proving among other things that ἐν is in Scripture often equivalent to σύν. c. 25. t. iii. 49. That ἐν is put for διὰ is also said by S. Chrys. Hom. on 1 Cor. i. 4 (p. 13 O.T.) and elsewhere.

to say, He hath made Him Lord of all: which thing Peter also said in the Acts, *God hath made Him both Lord and Christ.* But he has used the name *Heir*, thereby declaring two things: His proper sonship [1] and His indefeasible sovereignty.

HE.i.2-4.
Acts ii. 36.

[1] τὸ γνήσιον τῆς υἱότητος

Heir of all, that is, of all the world.

[3.] Then again he brings back his discourse to what had gone before. *By whom also He made the worlds* [*the ages*] [c]. (Where are those who say, There was [a time] when He was not?) (2)

Then, using degrees of ascent, he uttered that which is far greater than all this, saying,

ver. 3, 4. *Who being the brightness of His glory, and the express image of His person, and upholding all things by the word of His power, when He had by Himself purged our sins, sat down on the right hand of the Majesty on high; being made so much better than the Angels as He hath by inheritance obtained a more excellent name than they.*

O! the wisdom of the Apostle! or rather, not the wisdom of Paul, but the grace of the Spirit is the thing to wonder at. For he uttered not these things surely of his own mind, and in that way find his wisdom. (For whence could it be? From the knife, and the skins, or the workshop?) But it was of a divine energy. For his own understanding did not give birth to these thoughts, which was at the time we speak of so mean and slender as in no wise to surpass the baser sort; (for how could it, seeing it spent itself wholly on bargains and skins?) but the grace of the Spirit shews forth Its strength by whomsoever It will.

For just as one, wishing to lead up a little child to some lofty place, [a place] reaching up even to the top of Heaven, does this gently and by degrees, leading him upwards by the steps from below,—then when he has set him on high, and bidden him to gaze downwards, and sees him turning giddy and confused, and dizzy, taking hold of him, he leads him down to the lower stand, managing for him to take breath, then when he hath recovered it, leads him up again, and again brings him down;—just so did the blessed Paul likewise, both with the Hebrews and every where, having

[c] τοὺς αἰῶνας "the ages," "duration beyond time."

learnt it from his Master. For even He also did thus; sometimes He led His hearers up on high, and sometimes He brought them down, not generally allowing them to remain long.

See him, for example in this case too—by how many steps he had led them up, and placed them near the very summit of Religion, and then or ever they grow giddy, and dizziness seize them, how he leads them again lower down, and permitting them to take breath, says, *He spake unto us by His Son, whom He appointed Heir of all things* [d]. For the name of Son is so far common. For where it is understood of a true natural[1] [Son], He is far above all things: But however that may be, for the present he establishes by argument, that He is from above.

[1] γνήσιος

And see in what manner he says it: *Whom He appointed*, saith he, *heir of all things*. The phrase, *He appointed Heir*, is humble. Then he placed them on the higher step, subjoining, *by whom also He made the worlds*. Then on that which is higher still, and after which there is not another, *who being the brightness of His glory, and the express image of His person*. Truly he has led them to unapproachable light, to the very brightness itself. And before the [dizzy] darkness came over them, see how again he gently leads them down, saying, *and upholding all things by the word of His power, when He had by Himself effected the purifying of our sins, sat down on the right hand of the Majesty*. He does not simply say, *He sat down*, but *after the purifying, He sat down*, for he hath touched on the Incarnation, and his utterance is again lowly.

Then again having said some little by the way (for he saith, *on the right hand of the Majesty on high*), [he turns] again to what is lowly; *being made so much better than the angels, as He hath by inheritance obtained a more excellent name than they*. Henceforward then he treats in this passage of that which has respect to the flesh, since the phrase *being made better* doth not express His essence in respect

[d] That is for the moment S. Paul does not argue the dignity of Christ from the title " Son"—from His being the true Son of God, and therefore God, but condescending to the weakness of his hearers, at first uses the word in a general sense, and establishes His Divinity by other considerations.

of the Spirit ᵉ (for that was *begotten* not *made*) but in respect HEB.i.3,4.
of the flesh : for this was *made*.
Nevertheless the discourse here is not about the manner ᶠ
of existence. But just like John saying, *He that cometh* S. John i.
after me, is come to be before me, that is, higher in honour ¹⁵·
and esteem; so also in this place, *being made so much better
than the angels*—that is, higher in esteem and better and
more glorious.
*By how much He hath obtained by inheritance a more
excellent name than they.* Seest thou that he is speaking of
that which is according to the flesh? For this Name ᵍ, God
the Word ever had. He did not afterwards *obtain it by
inheritance*, nor did He afterwards become *better than the
Angels, when He had made purification of our sins;* but He
was ever *better*, and better without all comparison ¹. For ¹ ἀσυγ-
this is spoken of Him according to the flesh. κρίτως

So at least it is our way also, when we talk of man, to
speak things both high and low. Thus, when we say,
"Man is nothing," " Man is earth," " Man is ashes," we
denominate the whole from the worse part. But when we
say, " Man is an immortal animal," and " Man is rational,
and of kin to those on high," we denominate again the
whole from the better part. So also, in the case of Christ,
sometimes Paul discourseth from the less and sometimes
from the better; willing both to establish the economy,
and also to give instruction about the incorruptible nature.

[4.] Since then *He hath made purification of our sins*, (3)
let us continue pure; and let us admit no stain, but preserve the beauty which He hath implanted in us, and His
comeliness undefiled and pure, *not having spot or wrinkle* Eph. v.
27.

ᵉ κατὰ τὸ πνεῦμα is the reading
adopted by Mr. Field, following herein
an ancient Catena [compiled by Niketas Arch-Bishop of Heraclea in Thrace
who flourished in the 11th century]
which has preserved it: κατὰ τὸν
πατέρα is found in all other Mss. and
Editions, and was probably the reading in Mutianus' text, who translates
" essentiæ paternæ." Of the use of
πνεῦμα for the Divine Nature of the
Son, see many instances brought together in the note to the Oxford Translation of S. Athanasius against the
Arians,p. 196 d. [See also in Tertullian,
O.T. note H pp. 322 sqq.]
ᶠ φυσιώσεως, " communication of Being."cf.in 1 Cor.Hom.v.§4.p.56Oxf.Tr.
ᵍ That is the Name SON. The passage is thus rightly pointed by Mr.
Field in accordance with the addition
of the explanatory word " Son " in
[Niketas'] Catena (Supp). According
to the pointing of the other editions,
the translation would be, " For this
Name, (GOD THE WORD, He ever had."

Hom. 1. *or any such thing.* Even the smaller among sins are *a spot and a wrinkle,* such a thing, I mean, as Reproach, Insult, Falsehood.

Nay, rather not even are these small, but on the contrary very great: yea so great as to deprive a man of the very kingdom of Heaven. How, and in what manner? *He that calleth his brother fool, is in danger* (it saith) *of hell-fire.* But if he be so, who calls a man *fool,* which seems to be of all things the slightest, and rather mere children's talk; what sentence of punishment will not he incur, who calleth him malignant and crafty and envious, and casteth at him 10,000 other reproaches? What more thrilling to think of than this?

S. Matt. v. 22.

Now endure, I beseech you, what I say [h]. For if he that *doeth* aught *to one of the least, doeth it to Him,* and he that *doeth it not to one of the least doeth it not to Him,* how is it not the same also in the matter of good or evil speaking? He that reviles his brother, reviles God: and he that honours his brother, honours God. Train we therefore our tongue to speak good words. For *refrain,* it is said, *thy tongue from evil.* For God gave it not to this end, that we should speak evil, that we should revile, that we should calumniate one another; but to sing hymns to God withal, to speak those things which *give grace to the hearers,* things for edification, things for profit.

Ib. xxv. 40.
Ib. 45.

(1)
Ps.xxxiv. 13.

Eph. iv. 29.

Hast thou spoken evil of such a man? what is thy gain, entangling thyself in mischief together with him? for thou hast obtained the character of a slanderer. For there is not any, no not any evil, which stops at him that suffers it, but it includes the doer also. As for instance, the envious person seems indeed to plot against another, but himself first reaps the fruit of his sin, wasting and wearing himself away, and being hated of all men. The cheat deprives another of his money; yea and himself too of men's good will: and causes himself to be evil spoken of by all men. Now a reputation is much better than money, for the one it is not easy to wash out, whereas it is easy to gain possession of the other. Or rather, the absence of the one

[h] comp. Heb. xiii. 22. It seems as if the hearers were shewing themselves surprised at the severity of what he was saying.

doth no hurt to him that wanteth it; but the absence of HEB.i.3,4. the other makes you reproached and ridiculed, and an object of enmity and warfare to all.

The passionate man again first punishes and tears himself in pieces, and then him with whom he is angry.

Just so the evil speaker disgraces first himself and then him who is evil-spoken of: or, it may be, even this hath proved beyond his power, and while he departs with the credit of a foul and detestable kind of person, he doth but procure for the other more abundant love. For when a man having a bad name given him, doth not requite the giver in the same kind, but with praise and admiration, he doth not in effect praise the other, but himself. For I before observed that, as calumnies against our neighbours first touch those who devise the mischief, so also good works done towards our neighbours, gladden those who do them, before those to whom they are done, the parent either of good, or evil, justly reaping the fruit of it first himself. And just as water, whether it be brackish or sweet, whilst it fills the vessels of those who resort to it, at the same time lessens not the fountain itself which sends it forth; so surely also, both wickedness and virtue, from whatever person they proceed, prove either his joy or his ruin.

So far as to the things of this world. But the things of that world what speech may recount, either the goods or the evils? there is none. For as to the blessings, they surpass all thought, not speech only. For their opposites, they are indeed expressed in terms familiar to us. For fire, we read, is there, and darkness, and bonds, and a worm that never dieth.

But this represents not only the very things which are spoken of, but other too more intolerable. And to convince thee, consider at once this first: I mean, if it be fire, how is it also darkness? seest thou how that fire is more intolerable than this? for it hath no light. If it be fire, how is it for ever burning? Seest thou how it is more intolerable than this fire? for it is not quenched. Yea, therefore is it called unquenchable. Let us then consider how great a misery it must be, to be for ever burning, and to be in darkness, and to utter unnumbered groanings, and to gnash the teeth, and not even to be heard. For if here any

16 Make friends of the mammon of unrighteousness.

Hom. 1. one of those ingenuously brought up, should he be cast into prison, speaks of the mere ill savour, and the being laid in darkness, and the being bound with murderers, as more intolerable than any death: think what it is when we are burning with all the murderers of the whole world, neither seeing nor being seen, but in so vast a multitude thinking that we are alone. For the darkness and gloom doth not allow our distinguishing even those who are near to us, but each will feel as if he were the only person thus suffering. Moreover, if darkness of itself afflicteth and terrifieth our souls, how then will it be when together with the darkness there are likewise so great pains and burnings?

Wherefore I entreat you to be ever revolving these things with yourselves, and to submit to the pain of the words, that we may not have the things to undergo as our punishment. For assuredly, all these things shall be, and those whose doings have deserved those chambers of torture no Ps. xlix. man shall rescue, not father, nor mother, nor brother. *For* 7 LXX. *a brother redeemeth not*, it saith, *shall a man redeem?* though he have much confidence, though he have great power with God, since it is He Himself who rewards every one according to his works, and upon these depends our chance of salvation or punishment.

S. Luke xvi. 9. Let us make then to ourselves *friends of the mammon of unrighteousness*, that is: Let us do works of mercy; let us exhaust our possessions upon them, that so we may exhaust that fire: that we may quench it, that we may have boldness there. For there also it is not they who receive us, but our own work: for that it is not simply our having them for friends which can save us, we may learn from what is added. For why did He not say, *Make to yourselves friends, that they may receive you into their everlasting habitations*, but added also the manner? in that, when He saith, *of the mammon of unrighteousness*, He points out that we must make friends of them by means of our possessions, shewing that friendship as such will not protect us, unless we have good works, unless we spend righteously the wealth unrighteously gathered.

Moreover, this our discourse, of Almsgiving I mean, will be suitable not for the rich only, but also for the needy.

The least gifts from a good disposition avail. 17

Yea even if there be any person who supporteth himself Heb.i.3,4.
by begging, even to him this word appertains. For there is
no one, so poverty-stricken, however exceeding poor he may
be, as not to be able to provide *two mites*. It is therefore S. Luke
possible that a person giving a small sum from small means, xxi. 2.
should surpass those who have large possessions and give
more; as that widow did. For not by the measure of what
is given, but by the means and willingness of the givers is
the extent of the Alms-deed estimated. In all cases the
will is needed, in all, a right disposition; in all love towards
God. If with this we do all things, though having little
we give little, God will not turn away His face, but will
receive it as great and admirable: for He regards the will,
not the gifts: and if He see that to be great, He assigneth
His votes and judges accordingly, and maketh them partakers of His everlasting benefits.

Which may God grant us all to obtain, by the grace and
mercy of our Lord Jesus Christ, with whom to the Father
together with the Holy Ghost, be glory, power, honour,
now and for ever, and world without end Amen.

HOMILY II.

HEB. i. 3.

Who being the brightness of His Glory and the express Image of His person, and upholding all things by the word of His power, when He had by Himself purged our sins.

(1) [1.] EVERYWHERE indeed a reverential mind is requisite, but especially when we say or hear anything of God: Since neither can tongue speak nor thought[1] hear anything suitable to our God. And why speak I of tongue or thought[1]? For not even the understanding[2] which far excels these, will be able to comprehend anything accurately, when we desire to utter aught concerning God. For if *the peace of God surpasseth all understanding*, and *the things which are prepared for them that love Him have not come up into the heart of man*; much more He Himself, the God of peace, the Creator of all things, doth by a wide interval exceed our power of estimating. We ought therefore to receive all things with faith and reverence, and when our discourse[3] fails through weakness, and is not able to set forth with accuracy the things which are spoken, then especially to glorify God, for that we have such a God, surpassing both our thought and our conception[4]. For many of our conceptions[5] about God, we are unable to express, as also many things we express, but have not strength to conceive of them. As for instance:—That God is everywhere, we know; but how, we no longer understand[6]. That there is a certain incorporeal power the cause of all our good things, we know: but how it is or what it is, we know not. Lo! we speak, and do not understand. I said, That He is everywhere, but I do not understand it. I said, That He is without beginning, but I do not under-

[1] διάνοια οὖς Sav. Ben. in both places
[2] ὁ νοῦς
Phil. iv. 7.
1 Cor. ii. 9.
[3] λόγος
[4] τὴν ἔννοιαν, τὸν λόγον Sav. Ben.
[5] ὧν νοοῦμεν
[6] νοοῦμεν

stand it. I said, That He begat from Himself, and again Heb. i. 3. I know not how I shall understand it. And some things there are which we may not even speak— as for instance, my thought conceives[1] but cannot utter.

[1] νοεῖ ἡ διάνοια

And to shew thee that even Paul is weak and doth not put out his illustrations with exactness; and to make thee tremble and refrain from searching too far, hear what he says, having named Him Son and Creator, *Who being the brightness of His Glory, and the express image of His person.*

This we must receive with reverence and clear of all incongruities. *The brightness of His glory,* saith he. But observe in what reference he understands this, and so do thou receive it :—that One is of the Other[a] : that This is without passion : that the Other is not made either the greater, or the less, since there are some, who from the illustration derive certain strange things. For, say they, *the brightness* is not substantial[2], but hath its being in another. Now do not thou, O man, so interpret it, neither be thou sick of the disease of Marcellus[b] and Photinus[c]. For he hath a remedy for thee close at hand, that thou fall not into that imagination, nor doth he leave thee to be hurried down into that fatal malady. And what saith he?

[2] ἐνυπόστατον

And the express image of His person [or *subsistence*[d]] : that is, just as He [the Father] is personally subsisting, and is in need of nothing[3], so also the Son. For he saith this here, indicating the undeviating similitude[4] and the peculiar Impress of the Prototype, that He [the Son] is in subsistence by Himself.

[3] Sav. Ben. add πρὸς ὑπόστασιν
[4] ἀπαράλλακτον

For he who said above, that *by Him He made all things* here assigns to Him absolute authority. For what doth

[a] ὅτι ἐξ αὐτοῦ, that He [Christ] is of Him [the Father].
[b] Marcellus Bishop of Ancyra lapsed towards Sabellianism, holding, as it seems, virtually at least, that our Lord is not a Person eternally distinct from the Father, but, a Manifestation of the Father, lasting from the Incarnation to the Judgment. His views are anathematised in 1 Conc. Constantinop. Canon 1.
[c] Photinus Bp. of Sirmium, who had been Deacon under Marcellus, and carried his theory out, maintaining our Lord to have had no distinct existence before His Birth of Mary. Socr. E.H. 2. 29. His doctrine too was condemned at Constantinople, ubi sup.
[d] ὑποστάσεως. S. Chrys. understands the word to mean here neither "substance" nor "Person," but, if we may use such a word, "substantiality," or "substantive existence," which in speaking de Divinis we call "Personality." see below page 22 note h.

20   *S. Paul guards one illustration by means of another.*

HOM. 2.   he add? *And upholding all things by the word of His power;* that we might hereby infer not merely His being the express image of His Person, but also His governing all things with authority.

See then, how he applies to the Son that which is proper to the Father. For for this cause he did not say simply, *and upholding all things,* nor did he say, *by His power,* but, *by the word of His power.* For much as just now we saw him gradually ascend and descend; so also now, as by steps, he goes up on high, then again descends, and saith, *by whom also He made the worlds.*

Behold how here also he goes on two paths, by the one leading us away from Sabellius, by the other from Arius, yea and on another (so to say), that He [Christ] should not be accounted unoriginated [e], which he does also throughout, nor yet alien from God. For if, even after so many [arguments], there are some who assert that He is alien, and assign to Him another father, and say that He is at variance with Him;—had Paul not declared these things, what would they not have uttered?

How then does he this? When he is compelled to heal, then is he compelled also to utter lowly things: as for instance, *He appointed Him* (saith he) *heir of all things,* and *by Him He made the worlds.* But that He might not be in another way dishonoured, he brings Him up again to absolute authority and declares Him to be of equal honour with the Father, yea, so equal, that many thought the Father to be the same [with the Son].

Supra ver. 2.

And observe thou his great wisdom. First he lays down the former point and secures it with accuracy. And when this is demonstrated, that He is the Son of God, and not alien from Him, he thereafter speaks out securely all the high sayings, as many as he will. I mean, because any high speech concerning Him, led many into the notion just mentioned, he first sets down what is humiliating and then securely mounts up as high as he pleases. And having said,

[e] ἄναρχον. On this third heresy respecting the Holy Trinity, see S. Greg. Naz. Orat. ii. 37; xx. 6; in both which places it is, as here, mentioned as the third form of error with Sabellianism and Arianism. See also Bp. Bull, Def. Fid. N. iv. 1. 8. The mention of this is not found in the Common text, in which the whole passage is recast.

whom He appointed heir of all things, and that *by Him He* Heb. i. 3.
made the worlds, he then adds, *and upholding all things by
the word of His power.* For He that by a word only governs
all things, could not be in need of any one, for the producing all things.

[2.] And to prove this, mark how again going forward, (2)
and laying aside the *by whom,* he assigns to Him absolute
power. For after he had effected what he wished by the
use of it, thenceforward leaving it, what saith he? *Thou* Infra
Lord in the beginning hast laid the foundation of the earth, ver. 10.
and the heavens are the works of Thine hands. Nowhere
is there the saying *by whom,* or that *by Him He made the
worlds.* What then? were they not made by Him? Yes,
but not, as thou sayest or imaginest, 'as by an instrument:'
nor as though He would not have made them unless the
Father had reached out a hand to Him. For just as He
judgeth no man, and is said to judge by the Son, in that He S. John
begat Him to be judge; so also, to create by Him, in that v. 22.
He begat Him [to be] Creator. And if the Father be the
original cause of Him, in that He is Father, much more of
the things which have been made by Him. When therefore he would shew that He is of Him, he speaks of
necessity in that lowly strain. But when he would utter
high things, Marcellus takes a handle, and Sabellius; avoiding however the excess of both, he holds on a middle [way].
For neither does he dwell on the humiliation, lest Paul
of Samosata should obtain a standing place; nor yet does
he for ever abide in the high sayings, and shew on the
contrary His abundant nearness; lest Sabellius rush in
upon him. He names Him *Son,* and immediately Paul of
Samosata comes on him, saying that He is a son, as men
in general are. But he gives him a fatal wound, by calling
Him *Heir.* Still, with Arius, he is importunate. For the
saying, *He appointed Him heir,* they both keep hold of: the
former one simply saying, it comes of weakness; the other
still presses objections, endeavouring to support himself
by the clause which follows. For by saying, *by Whom
also He made the worlds,* he strikes backwards the impudent
Samosatene: while Arius still seems to be strong. Nevertheless see how he again smites him likewise, saying again,

22 The Son Express Image *of the Father's Personality.*

Hom. 2. *who being the brightness of His glory.* But behold! again springs on us Sabellius, with Marcellus, and Photinus: but on all these also he inflicts one blow, saying, *and the express image of His person and upholding all things by the word of His power.* Here again he wounds Marcion too [f]; not very severely, but however he doth wound him, yea, through the whole of this Epistle he is fighting against them.

But the very thing which he said, *the brightness of the glory,* hear thou Christ Himself saying, *I am the Light of the world.* And with this intent does he [the Apostle] use the word *brightness,* pointing out how that also was said in this sense as *Light of Light.* Nor is it this alone which he points out, but also that He hath enlightened our souls, and hath Himself notified the Father. By *the brightness* too he indicated the nearness of the Being [of the Father and the Son [g]]. Observe the subtlety of his expressions. He hath taken one essence and subsistence to indicate two subsistences. Which thing he also doth in regard to the knowledge of the Spirit[1]; for as he saith that the knowledge of the Father is one with that of the Spirit, as being indeed one, and in nought varying from itself: so in this place also he hath taken hold of one certain [thing] whereby to express the subsistence of the Two[h].

And he adds that He is *the express Image.* For the express Image [of any thing] is in one sense Another[2], compared with its Prototype: howbeit not Another in all respects, but as to having separate subsistence. Since here also the term, *express image,* indicates there being no variation from that whereof it is the *express image;* its similarity in all respects. When therefore he calls Him both Form[3], and express Image, what can they say? "Yea, saith he, man is also called an Image of God[4]." What then! is

S. John viii. 12.

[1] Cf. for. sitan 1 Cor. ii. 10,.. 12.

[2] ἄλλος τις

[3] Phil. ii. 6. see below.

[4] εἰκόνος εἰκὼν, Ben.: εἰκών. (only) Sav.

[f] Because Marcion, holding the Creation to be evil, denied the Son's preserving Power.

[g] καὶ διὰ τοῦ ἀπαυγάσματος τῆς οὐσίας τὴν ἐγγύτητα ἔδειξεν. Sav. and Ben. read διὰ δὲ τοῦ ἀ. τὸ ἴσον ἐσήμανε τῆς οὐσίας, καὶ τὴν πρὸς τὸν πατέρα ἐγγύτητα. "By &c. he indicated the equality of His Substance and His nearness to the Father."

[h] εἰς τὴν τῶν δυὸ ὑπόστασιν. Sav. and Ben. read ἑ. τ. τ. δ. ὑποστάσεων δήλωσιν, "whereby to shew the two Subsistencies." Mr. Field says that the old translation of Mutianus in some degree confirms this latter reading, which is easier. The word ὑπόστασιν in the singular is used in the sense of "Personality," as above p. 19 note d.

he so [an image of Him] as the Son is? No (saith he) but Heb. i. 3. because the term, image, doth not shew resemblance. And yet, in that man is called an Image, it sheweth resemblance, as in man. For what God is in Heaven, that man is on earth, I mean as to dominion. And as he hath power over all things on earth, so also hath God power over all things which are in heaven and which are on earth. But otherwise, man is not called *Express image*, he is not called Form: which kind of phrase declares the substance or rather substance and similarity in substance. Therefore just as *the form of a slave* expresses no other thing than a Phil. ii. 6, 7. man without variation [1] [from human nature], so also *the form of God* expresses no other thing than God. ¹ ἀπαράλλακτον

Who being (saith he) *the brightness of His glory.* See thou what Paul is doing. Having said, *Who being the brightness of His glory*, he added again, *He sat down on the right hand of the Majesty*: what names he hath used, no where finding a name for the Substance. For neither *the Majesty*, nor *the Glory* setteth forth the Name, Which he wishes to say, but is not able to find a name. For this is what I said at the beginning, that oftentimes we think some things, and supra p. 19. are not able to express [them]: since not even the word God is a name of substance, nor is it at all possible to find a name of that Substance.

And what marvel, if it be so in respect of God, inasmuch as not even in respect of an Angel, could any one find a name expressive of his substance? Perhaps too, neither in respect of the soul. For this name [soul] doth not seem to me to be significative of the substance thereof, but of breathing. For one may see that the same [thing] is called both Soul and Heart and Mind: for, saith he, *Create in me a* Ps. li. 10. *clean heart, O God*, and one may often see that it [the soul] is called spirit.

And upholding all things by the word of His power. Tell me, *God said* (it is written), *Let there be light:* "the Gen. i. 3. Father, saith one [i], commanded, and the Son obeyed?" (3) But behold here He also makes by [His] Word. For (saith he), *And upholding all things*—that is, governing;

---

[1] This is an heretical objection, as is expressed by the reading in the editions of Sav. and Ben.

Hom. 2. He holds together what [otherwise] would fall to pieces; For, to hold the world together, is no less a thing than making it, but rather yet greater (if one must say what is even wonderful). For the one is to bring forward something out of non-existence: but the other, when things which have been made are about to fall back into non-existence, to hold and fasten them together, utterly at variance as they are with each other: this is indeed great and wonderful, and a certain proof of exceeding power.

Then shewing the easiness, he said, *upholding:* (he did not say, governing[1], from the figure of those who simply with their finger move any thing, and cause it to go round.) Here he shews both the mass of the creation to be great, and that this greatness is nothing to Him. Then again he shews [that] the [work is] without labour, saying, *By the word of His power.* Well said he, *By the word.* For since, with us, a word is accounted to be [somewhat] naked and bare, he shews that with God it is not so. But, in what way *He upholdeth by [His] word,* he hath not further added: for neither is it possible to know. Then he added concerning His majesty: for thus John also did: having said that *He is God,* he brought in the handy-work of the Creation. For the same thing which the one indirectly expressed, saying, *In the beginning was the Word,* and *All things were made by Him,* this did the other also declare by *the Word,* and in saying *by whom also He made the worlds.* Thus he also sets Him forth both as a Creator, and as being before all ages. What then? when concerning the Father the prophet saith, *Thou art from everlasting and to everlasting,* and concerning the Son, that He is before all worlds [ages], and the maker of them all—what can they say? Nay rather, when the very thing which was spoken of the Father,—*He which was before the worlds,*—this one may see spoken of the Son also? And that which one saith, *He was life,* pointing out that whereby He preserves His creation, that Himself is the Life of all things,—so also saith this other, *and upholding all things by the word of His power:* not as the Greeks [do], depriving Him, as much as in them lies, both of Creation itself, shutting up His power, and of Providence to reach only as far as to the Moon.

[1] κυβερνῶν

S. John i. 1.

Ib. 1, 3.

Ps. xc. 2.

S. John i. 4.

By His own self (saith he) *having made purification of our* Heb. i. 3.
sins. Having spoken concerning those marvellous and great
matters, those which are most above us, he proceeds to
speak also afterwards concerning His solicitude for men.
For it is true indeed that the former expression also was
universal, viz. *and upholding all things :* nevertheless this is
much greater, for it is also universal: for, for His part, *all*
men believed. As John also, having said, *He was life,* and so
pointed out His providence, saith again, and *He was light.*

By Himself, saith he, *having purged our sins, He sat down
on the right hand of the Majesty on high.* He here setteth
down two very great proofs of His solicitude for us, first
the *cleansing us from our sins,* then the doing it *by His own
self.* And in many places, thou seest him making very much
of this, I mean, not only of our reconciliation with God,
but also of its being accomplished through the Son. For
the gift which was truly great, was made even greater by
being through the Son.

For[1] in saying, *He sat on the right hand,* and, *having by* [1] γὰρ om.
Himself purged our sins,—though he had put us in mind of S.
the Cross, he quickly added the mention of the resurrection and ascension. And see thou his unspeakable wisdom:
he said not, "He was commanded to sit down" but *He
sat down.* Then again, lest thou shouldest think that He
standeth, he subjoins, *For to which of the angels said He
at any time, Sit thou on My right hand.*

He sat (saith he) *on the right hand of the Majesty on
high.* What is this *on high?* Doth he enclose God in place?
Away with such a thought! but just as, when he saith, *on the
right hand,* he described Him not as having figure, but [only]
shewed His equality of dignity with the Father; so, in
saying *on high,* he did not enclose Him there, but expressed
the being higher than all things, and having ascended up
above all things. That is, He attained even unto the very
throne of the Father: as therefore the Father is on high,
so also is He. For the *sitting together* implies nothing
but equality of dignity. But if they say, that He said,
Sit Thou, we may ask them, What then? did He say [this]
to Him standing? Moreover, he said not that He commanded, nor that He enjoined, but that *He said:* for no

Hom. 2. other reason, than to hinder thee from thinking Him without origin and without cause. For that this is why he said it, is evident from the place of His sitting. For had he intended to signify inferiority, he would not have said, *on the right hand*, but on the left hand.

ver. 4. *Being made*, saith he, *so much better than the angels, as He hath by inheritance obtained a more excellent name than they.* The *being made*, here, is instead of being declared, as one may say. Then also from what does he reason confidently? From the Name. Seest thou that the name Son is wont to declare true and proper relationship? And indeed if He had not been a true Son (and "true" is nothing else than "of Him"), how were it that he reasons confidently from this? For if He be Son only by grace, He not only is not *more excellent than the angels*, but is even less than they. How? Because righteous men too were called sons; and the name son, if it be not a genuine son, doth not avail to shew the "excellency." When too he would point out that there is a certain difference between creatures and their maker, hear what he saith:

ver. 5. *For to which of the Angels said He at any time, Thou art My Son, to-day have I begotten thee. And again, I will be to Him a Father, and He shall be to Me a Son?* For these things indeed are spoken with reference also to the flesh: [viz.] this, *I will be to Him a Father, and He shall be to Me a Son*—while this ᵏ, *Thou art My Son, this day have I begotten Thee*, expresses nothing else than " from

¹ ὤν [the time] that God is." For just as He is said to be¹, from the time present (for this befits Him more than any other), so also the [word] *To-day* seems to me to be used in this place with reference to the flesh. For when He hath taken hold of it, thenceforth he speaks out all boldly. For indeed the flesh partakes of the high things, just as the Godhead of the lowly. For He who disdained not to become man, and did not decline the reality, how should He have declined the expressions?

ᵏ Sav. and Ben. omit the words σή-
μερον....σε, and for ἐξ οὗ ἐστιν ὁ θεός.
ὥσπερ γὰρ have ἐξ αὐτοῦ ἐστιν· ὥσπερ δέ,
so that the passage runs; "but this,
'Thou art My Son,' expresses nothing
else than that He is of Him. And just
as &c."... The corrector seems to have
misapprehended the meaning of ἐξ οὗ
in this place.

Seeing then that we know these things, let us be ashamed of nothing, nor have any high thoughts. For if He Himself being God and Lord and Son of God, did not decline to take the form of a slave, much more ought we to do all things, though they be lowly. For tell me, O man, whence hast thou high thoughts? from things of this life? but these or ever they appear, run by. Or, from things spiritual? nay, this is itself one spiritual excellency,—to have no high thoughts. HEB. i. 5. (4)

Wherefore then dost thou cherish high thoughts? because thou goest on aright? hear Christ saying, *When ye have done all things, say, we are unprofitable servants, for we have done that which it was our duty to do.* S. Luke xvii. 10.

Or because of thy wealth hast thou high thoughts? Dost thou not see those before thee, how they departed naked and desolate? did we not come naked into life, and naked also shall depart? who hath high thoughts on having what is another's? for they who will use it to their own enjoyment alone, are deprived of it however unwillingly, often before death, and at death certainly. But (saith one) while we live we use them as we will. First of all, one doth not lightly see any man using what he hath as he will. Next, if a man do even use things as he will, neither is this a great matter: for the present time is short compared with the ages without end. Art thou high-minded, O man, because thou art rich? on what account? for what cause? for this befalleth also robbers, and thieves, and man-slayers, and effeminate, and whoremongers, and all sorts of wicked men. Wherefore then art thou high-minded? Since if thou hast made meet use of it, thou must not be high-minded, lest thou profane the commandment: but if unmeet, this should make thee above all shrink into thyself, for having become a slave of money and goods, and being overcome by them. For tell me, if any man sick of a fever should drink off much water, which for a short space indeed quencheth his thirst, but afterwards kindleth the flame, ought he to be high-minded? And what, if any man have many cares without cause, ought he therefore to be high-minded? tell me, wherefore? because thou hast many masters? because thou hast ten thousand cares? because many will

Hom. 2. flatter thee? [Surely not.] For thou art even their slave. And to prove that to thee, hear this. The other affections which are within us, are in some cases useful. For instance, Ecclus. i. 22. Anger is often useful. For (saith he) *unjust wrath shall not be innocent:* wherefore it is possible for one to be justly S. Matt. v. 22. in wrath. And again, *He that is angry with his brother without cause, shall be in danger of hell.* Again for instance, emulation, desire, [are useful] : the one when it hath reference to the procreation of children, the other when he directs his emulation to excellent things. As Paul Gal. iv. 18. 1 Cor. xii. 31. also saith, *It is good to be zealously affected in a good thing alway,* and, *Covet earnestly the best gifts.* Both therefore are useful : but an insolent spirit is in no case good, but is always an unprofitable and hurtful thing.

(5) However, if a man must be proud, [let it be] for poverty, not for wealth. Wherefore? Because he who can live upon a little, is far greater and better than he who cannot. For tell me, supposing certain persons called to the Imperial City, if some of them should need neither beasts, nor slaves, nor umbrellas, nor lodging-places, nor sandals, nor vessels, but it should quite suffice them to have bread, and to take water from the wells,—while others of them should say, ' unless ye give us conveyances, and a soft bed, we cannot ' come ; unless also we have many followers, unless we may ' be allowed continually to rest ourselves, we cannot come, ' nor unless we have the use of beasts, unless too we may ' travel but a small portion of the day—and we have need ' of many other things also :' whom should we admire? those or these? plainly, these who require nothing. So also in this case : some need many things for their journey through this life ; others, nothing. So that if it were at all right to be proud, those who are so for poverty would have the better right.

" But the poor man (saith one) is ever despicable." Not he, but those who despise him. For why do not I [in my turn] despise those who know not how to admire what they ought? Why, if a person be a painter, he will laugh to scorn all who jeer at him, so long as they are uninstructed; nor doth he regard the things which they say, but is content with his own testimony. And shall we hang ourselves on the opinion of the many? Therefore, we are despicable Heb. i. 5. when men despise us for our poverty, and we despise them not, nor call them miserable.

And I say not how many sins are produced by wealth, and how many good things by poverty. But rather, neither wealth nor poverty is excellent in itself, but through those who use it. The Christian shines out approved, in poverty rather than in riches. How? He will be less arrogant, more sober-minded, graver, more equitable, more considerate: but he that is in wealth, hath many impediments to these things. Let us see then what are the doings of the rich man, or rather, of him who useth his wealth amiss. Such an one practiseth rapine, fraud, violence. Men's unseemly loves, unholy unions, witchcrafts, poisonings, all their other horrors,—wilt thou not find them produced by wealth? Seest thou, that in poverty rather than in wealth the pursuit of virtue is less laborious? For do not, I beseech thee, imagine, that because rich men suffer not punishment here, therefore they do nothing amiss. Since if it were easy for a rich man to suffer punishment, thou wouldest surely have found the prisons filled with them. But among its other evils, wealth hath this also, that he who possesseth it, transgressing in unpunished wickedness, will never be stayed from doing so, but will receive wounds without remedies, and no man will put a bridle on him.

Moreover if a man please he will find that even for pleasure, the means which poverty affords us are more abundant. How? Because it is freed from cares, from hatred, fighting, contention, strife, from evils out of number.

Therefore let us not follow after wealth, nor be for ever envying those whose possessions are great. But let those of us who have wealth, use it aright; and those who have not, let us not therefore be vexed, but for all things give thanks unto God, because He enableth us to receive with little labour the same return with the rich, or even (if we will) a greater: and from small means we shall have great gains. For so he that brought the two talents, was admired and honoured equally with him who brought the five. Now why? Because he was entrusted with [but] two talents, yet he accomplished all his own part, and brought in what

Hom. 2. was entrusted to him, double. Why then do we make haste to have much entrusted to us, when we may by a little reap the same fruits, or even greater? when the labour indeed is less, but the reward much more abundant? For more easily will a poor man part with his own, than a rich man who hath many and great possessions. What, know ye not, that the more things a man hath in his grasp, the more he setteth his love upon? Therefore, lest this befal us, seek we not after wealth, nor let us be impatient of poverty, nor make haste to be rich: and let those of us who have [riches] so use them as Paul commanded. *(They that have,* saith he, *as though they had not, and they that use this world as not abusing it:)* that we may obtain the good things promised. And may it be granted to us all to obtain them, by the grace and mercy of our Lord Jesus Christ, with whom to the Father together with the Holy Ghost, be glory, power, honour, now, and for ever, and world without end. Amen.

1 Cor. vii. 29, 31.

HOMILY III.

Heb. i. 6—8.

And when He again bringeth in the First-Begotten into the world, He saith, And let all the angels of God worship Him. And of the angels He saith, Who maketh His angels spirits, and His ministers a flame of fire. But unto the Son He saith, Thy throne, O God, is for ever and ever.

[1.] Our Lord Jesus Christ calls His coming in the flesh, an [exodus or] going out: as for instance when He saith, *The sower went out to sow*. And again, *I went out from the Father, and am come*. And in many places one may see this. But Paul calls it an [eisodus or] coming in, saying, *And when again He bringeth in the First-Begotten into the world*, meaning by this Bringing in, His taking on Him our flesh.

Now why have they ordered their expressions thus? The things signified [thereby] are manifest, and in what respect it is [thus] said. For Christ on His part calls it a Going out, and justly; for we were out from God. For just as in royal palaces, prisoners and those who have offended the king, stand without, and he who desires to reconcile them, does not bring them in, but himself going out discourses with them, until having made them meet for the king's presence, he may bring them in, so also Christ hath done. Having come out to us, that is, having taken flesh, and having discoursed to us of the King's messages, so He brought us in, having cleansed us from our sins, and reconciled us. For this cause he calls it a Going out.

But Paul names it a Coming in, from the metaphor of those who come to an inheritance and receive any portion

(1)

S. Matt. xiii. 3.
S. John xvi. 28.

or possession. 'For his saying, *but when again He bringeth in the First-Begotten into the world*, means this, 'when he putteth the world into His hand.' For He then obtained possession of the whole thereof, when also He was made known. He saith not these things concerning God The Word, but concerning that which is according to the flesh. For if according to John, *He was in the world, and the world was made by Him:* how is He *brought in*, otherwise than in the flesh?

And, saith he, *let all the angels of God worship Him.* Whereas he is about to say something great and lofty, he prepares it beforehand, and makes it acceptable, in that he represents the Father as *bringing in* the Son. He had said above, that *He spake to us not by prophets but by His Son;* that the Son is superior to angels; yea and he establishes this from the name [SON]. And here, in what follows, from another fact also. What then may this be? From worship. And he shews how much greater He is, as much as is a Master than a slave; just as any person introducing another into a house straightway commands those who have the care thereof to do him reverence; [so] saying in regard to that which is after the Flesh, *And let all the Angels of God worship Him.*

Is it then Angels only? No; for hear what follows next: *And of His Angels He saith, Which maketh His angels spirits, and His ministers a flame of fire: but of the Son, Thy Throne, O God, is for ever and ever.*

Behold, the very greatest difference! that they are created, but He uncreated. While of His angels He saith, Who *maketh;* wherefore of the Son did he not say "Who maketh?"

And if you mark it, he might have expressed the difference as follows: *Of His Angels He saith, Who maketh His Angels Spirits, but of the Son,* 'The Lord created Me:' 'God hath made Him Lord and Christ.' But neither was that first word spoken concerning the Son, nor this latter concerning God The Word, but concerning that which is after the flesh. For when he desired to express the true difference, he no longer included angels only, but the whole ministering power which is above. Seest thou how he

distinguishes, and with how great clearness, between crea- Heb. i. 9.
tures and Creator, ministers and Lord, the Heir and true
Son, and slaves?
[2.] *But unto the Son he saith, Thy throne, O God, is
for ever and ever.* Behold a symbol of Regal Dominion.
A sceptre of righteousness is the sceptre of Thy kingdom.
Behold again another symbol of Royalty.

Then again with respect to His human nature (ver. 9)
*Thou hast loved righteousness and hated unrighteousness,
wherefore God, even Thy God, hath anointed Thee.*

What is, *Thy God?* Why, after that he hath uttered a
great word, he again qualifieth it. Here both Jews, and
the followers of Paul of Samosata, and the Arians, and
Marcellus, and Sabellius, and Marcion receive a blow from
him. How? The Jews, by his indicating two Persons and
God and Man [a]; the other Jews [b], I mean the followers
of Paul of Samosata, by thus discoursing concerning His
eternal existence, and uncreated essence: for by way of
distinction, against the word, *He made,* he set, *Thy throne,
O God, is for ever and ever.* Against the Arians there is
both this same again, and also that He is not a slave; but
if a creature, He is a slave. And against Marcellus and the
others, that these are two Persons, distinguished in reference to their subsistence [c]. And against the Marcionites,
that the Godhead is not anointed, but only the Manhood.

Next he saith, *Above Thy fellows.* But who are these
His *fellows* other than men? that is Christ received *not the* S. John
Spirit by measure. Seest thou how with the doctrine con- iii. 34.
cerning His uncreated nature he always joins also that of (2)
the *Economy?* what can be clearer than this? Didst thou
see how that what is created and what is begotten are not
the same? For otherwise he would not have made the distinction, nor in contrast to the word, *He made* [&c], have
added, *But of the Son He said, Thy throne, O God, is for*

---

[a] δυὸ πρόσωπα δεικνὺς, καὶ Θεὸν καὶ ἄνθρωπον. That is *both* two distinct Persons in the Godhead, and also the Divine and human natures of the Christ. The Corrector would seem to have understood it "two Persons, both God and man"; the common texts read δυὸ τὸν αὐτὸν δεικνὺς, κ. θ. κ. ἀ.

"shewing the same [Person] to be two, both God and man."
[b] Sav. and Ben. omit Ἰουδαίους. The teaching of Paul of Samosata was regarded as closely connected with Judaism, and he and his followers were called Jews.
[c] κατὰ τὴν ὑπόστασιν, see above, p. 19.

Hom. 3. *ever and ever.* Nor would he have called the name, *Son, a more excellent Name,* if it is a sign of the same thing. For where is the excellence? for if that which is created, and that which is begotten be the same, and they [the Angels] were made, what is there [in Him] *more excellent?*

Lo! again ὁ Θεὸς, *God,* with the Article [d].

[3.] And again he saith: (ver. 10-12) *Thou Lord in the beginning hast laid the foundation of the earth, and the heavens are the works of Thine hands. They shall perish, but Thou shalt endure, and they all shall wax old as a garment, and as a vesture shalt Thou fold them up, and they shall be changed; but Thou art the same and Thy years shall not fail.*

Lest when thou hearest the words, *and when He bringeth in the First-Begotten into the world;* thou shouldest think it to be as it were a Gift afterwards super-added to Him; this he both corrected above by anticipation, and again further corrects, saying, *in the beginning:* not now, but from the very first.

See again he inflicts a mortal wound both on Paul of Samosata and also on Arius, in applying to the Son the things which relate to the Father. And withal he has also intimated another thing by the way, greater even than this. For surely it is the transfiguration of the world which he hath incidentally pointed out, saying, *they shall wax old as a garment, and as a vesture Thou shalt fold them up and they shall be changed.* Which thing also he saith in the Epistle to the Romans, that He shall transfigure the world. And shewing the facility thereof, he adds, as if a man should fold up a garment so shall He both fold up and change it. But if He with so much ease works the transfiguration and the creation to what is better and more perfect, needed He another for the inferior creation? How far doth your shamelessness go? At the same time too this is a very great consolation, to know that things will not be as they are, but they all shall receive change, and all shall be altered, but He Himself remaineth ever existing, and living infinitely: *and Thy years,* he saith, *shall not fail.*

see Rom. viii. 21.

[d] The Ben. editor observes that it had been said that ὁ θεός with the article is used in Scripture only of the Father, and that S. Chrys. here as in other places argues that it is used of the Son.

[4.] ver. 13. *But to which of the Angels said He at any time,* Heb.i.14. *Sit thou on My right hand until I shall have made thine enemies thy footstool?* Behold, again he encourages them, inasmuch as their enemies were to be worsted, and their enemies are the same also with Christ's.

This again belongs to Sovereignty, to Equal Dignity, to Honour and not weakness, that the Father should be angry for the things done to the Son. This belongs to His great Love, and honour towards the Son, as of a father towards a son. For He that is angry in His behalf how is He a stranger to Him? Which very thing he saith also in the second Psalm, *He that dwelleth in heaven shall laugh* Ps.ii.4,5. *them to scorn, and the Lord shall have them in derision. Then shall He speak unto them in His wrath, and vex them in His sore displeasure.* And again He Himself saith, *Those* S. Luke *that would not that I should reign over them, bring hither* xix. 27. *before Me, and slay them.* For that they are His own words, hear also what He saith in another place, *How often would I* Ib. xiii. *have gathered thy children together, and ye would not! Be-* 34, 35. *hold, your house is left desolate.* And again, *The kingdom* S. Matt. *shall be taken from you, and shall be given to a nation bring-* xxi. 43. *ing forth the fruits thereof.* And again, *He that falleth upon* Ib. 44. *that stone shall be broken, but on whomsoever It shall fall, It will grind him to powder.* And besides, He who is to be their Judge in that world, much more did He Himself repay them in this. So that the words *Till I make thine enemies thy footstool* are expressive of nothing but honour towards the Son.

ver. 14. *Are they not all ministering spirits, sent forth to minister for them who shall be heirs of salvation?* What marvel (saith he) if they minister to the Son, when they minister even to our salvation? See how he lifts up their minds, and shews that the honour which God has for us is great, inasmuch as He has assigned to Angels who are above us this ministration on our behalf. As if one should say, for this purpose (saith he) He employs them; this is the office of Angels, to minister to God for our salvation. This therefore is an angelical work, to do all for the salvation of the brethren: or rather it is the work of Christ Himself, for He indeed saves as Lord, but they as servants. And we though servants are yet Angels' fellow-servants. Why gaze ye so earnestly on the Angels (saith he)? they are servants of the Son of God, and are sent many ways for our sakes, and minister to our salvation. And so they are partners in service with us.

Consider ye how he ascribes no great difference to the kinds of creatures. And yet the space between angels and men is great; nevertheless he brings them down near to us, all but saying, For us they labour, for our sake they run to and fro: on us, as one might say, they wait. This is their ministry, for our sake to be sent every way.

(3) And of these examples as the Old [Testament] is full, so also is the New. For when Angels bring glad tidings to the shepherds, or to Mary, or to Joseph; when they sit at the sepulchre, when they are sent to say to the disciples, *Ye men of Galilee, why stand ye gazing up into heaven*, when they release Peter out of the prison, when they discourse with Philip, consider how great the honour is; when God sends His Angels for ministers as to friends, when to Cornelius [an Angel] appears, when [an Angel] brings forth all the apostles from the prison, and says, *Go, stand and speak in the temple to the people the words of this life;* and to Paul himself also an Angel appears. Dost thou see that they minister to us on God's behalf, and that they minister to us in the greatest matters? wherefore Paul saith, *All things are yours, whether life or death, or the world, or things present, or things to come.*

Well then the Son also was sent, but not as a minister, nor as one discharging a task, but as a Son, Only-Begotten, and having the same will with the Father. Rather indeed, He was not *sent:* for He did not pass from place to place, but took on Him flesh: whereas these change their places, and leaving those in which they were before, come thereafter to others in which they were not.

And by this again he incidentally encourages them, saying, What fear ye? to us Angels are ministering.

[5.] And now having spoken concerning the Son, both what related to the Economy, and to His power as Creator, and to His sovereignty, and having pointed out His co-equal dignity, and that as absolute Master He ruleth not men

only but also the powers above, he next gives them exhor- Heb. ii. 3.
tation, having made out his argument, that we ought to
give heed to the things which have been heard. ch. ii. 1.
*Wherefore we ought to give more earnest heed to the things
which we have heard.* Why *more earnest?* Here he meant
more earnest than to the Law: but he suppressed the actual
expression of it, and yet makes it plain in the course of
reasoning, not in the way of counsel, nor of exhortation.
For so it was better.

ver. 2, 3. For *if the word spoken by Angels* (saith he) *was
stedfast, and every transgression and disobedience received
a just recompense of reward; how shall we escape if we
neglect so great salvation, which at the first began to be
spoken to us by the Lord, and was confirmed unto us by
them that heard Him?*

Why ought we to *give more earnest heed to the things
which we have heard?* were not those former things of
God, as well as these? Either then he meaneth *more
earnest* than [to] the Law, or *very earnest;* not making
comparison, God forbid. For since, on account of the
long space of time, they had a great opinion of the Old
Covenant, but these things had been despised as yet new,
he proves (more than his argument required) that we
ought to give attention to these rather. How? By saying
in effect, Both these and those are of God, but not in a
like manner. And this he shews us afterwards: but for
the present he treats it somewhat superficially, but afterwards more clearly, saying; *For if that first covenant had* Infra viii.
been faultless, and many other such things: *for that which* 7.
decayeth and waxeth old is ready to vanish away. But as Ib. 13.
yet he ventures not to say any such thing in the beginning
of his discourse, nor until he shall have first occupied and
possessed his hearer by his fuller [arguments.]

Why then ought we *to give more earnest heed? Lest at
any time,* saith he, *we should leak away*—that is, lest at
any time we should perish, lest we should fall off. And
here he points out the grievousness of this falling off, in
that it is a difficult thing for that which hath leaked out
to return again, inasmuch as it hath happened through
wilful negligence. And he took this form of speech from

the Proverbs. For, saith he, *my son [take heed] lest thou leak away,* shewing both the easiness of the fall, and the grievousness of the ruin. That is, our disobedience is not without danger. And while by his mode of reasoning he points out that the chastisement is greater, yet again he leaves it in the form of a question, and not in his conclusion. For indeed this is to make one's discourse inoffensive, when one does not in every case of one's own self infer the judgment, but leaves it in the power of the hearer to give his own sentence: and this would render them more open to conviction. And both the prophet Nathan doth it in the Old [Testament], and in Matthew Christ, saying, *What will He do to the husbandmen* of that vineyard? so compelling them to give out their sentence themselves: for this is the most complete victory.

Next, when he had said, *For if the word which was spoken by Angels was stedfast*—he did not add, much more that by Christ: but letting this pass, he said what is less, *How shall we escape, if we neglect so great salvation?* And see how he makes the comparison. *For if the word which was spoken by Angels,* saith he. There, *by Angels,* here, *by the Lord*—and there *a word,* but here, *salvation.*

Then lest any man should say, Thy sayings, O Paul, are they Christ's? he proves their credibility, both from his having heard it all of Him, and from its being now spoken by God; since not merely a voice is wafted, as in the case of Moses, but signs are done, and facts bear witness.

[6.] But what is this, *For if the word spoken by Angels was stedfast?* For in the Epistle to the Galatians also he saith to this effect, *Being ordained by angels in the hand of a Mediator.* And again, *Ye received a law by the disposition of Angels, and have not kept it.* And in every place, he saith it was given by angels. Some indeed say that Moses is signified; but it is not reasonable. For here he says Angels in the plural: and the Angels too which here he speaks of, are those in Heaven. What then is it? Either he means the Decalogue only (for there Moses spake, and God answered him),—or that angels were present, God disposing them in order,—or that he speaks thus in regard of all things said and done in the old Covenant, as if Angels had been partakers in them. But how is it said in another place, *The Law was given by Moses,* and here *by Angels?* For it is said, *And God came down in thick darkness*ᵉ.

For if the word spoken by angels was stedfast. What *was stedfast?* True, as one may say; and faithful in its proper season; and all the things which had been spoken came to pass. Either this is his meaning, or that they prevailed, and the threatenings were coming to be accomplished. Or by *the word* he means injunctions. For apart from the Law, Angels sent from God enjoined many things: for instance at Bochim, in the Judges, in [the history of] Sampson. For this is the cause why he said not "the Law" but *the word.* And he seems to me haply rather to mean this, viz., those things which are committed to the management of angels. What shall we say then? The angels who were entrusted with the charge of the nation were then present, and they themselves made the trumpets, and the other things, the fire, the thick darkness.

And every transgression and disobedience, saith he. Not this one and that one, but *every* one. Nothing (saith he) remained unavenged, but *received a just recompence of reward,* i.e. punishment. Why now spake he thus? Such is the manner of Paul, not to make much account of his phrases, but indifferently to put down words of evil sound, even in matters of good meaning. As also in another place he saith, *Bringing into captivity every thought to the obedience of Christ*ᶠ. And again he hath put *the recompence* for punishment¹, as here he calleth punishment *reward. If it be a righteous thing,* saith he, *with God to recompense tribulation to them that trouble you, and to you who are troubled rest.* That is, justice was in no degree violated, but God went forth in its behalf, and caused the penalty to come round on them that had sinned, though not all their sins are made manifest, but only where the express ordinances were trangressed.

How then shall we, saith he, *escape if we neglect so great*

Heb. ii. 3.
S. John i. 17.
Exod. xix. 16, 20.

Judg. ii. 1. xiii. 3.

Exod. xix. 16.

2 Cor. x. 5.
¹ Rom. i. 27.
² Thess. i. 6, 7.

ᵉ This last clause seems unconnected as it stands here. If there were MS. authority one should be glad to transfer it a few lines lower, after, The management of Angels: τὰ διὰ τῶν ἀγγέλων οἰκονομηθέντα, or to place here the words *What shall we say,* down to *thick darkness.*

ᶠ See S. Chrys. on the passage, 2 Cor. x. 5 [p. 242 O.T.]. The expression *captivity* was the "word of evil sound."

40   *The greatness of our salvation. Attested by* GOD.

Hom. 3. *salvation!* Hereby he signified, that that other salvation was no great thing. Well too did he add the word *So great.* For not from wars (saith he) will He now rescue us, nor bestow on us the earth and the good things that are in the earth, but it will be the dissolution of death, the destruction of the Devil, the kingdom of Heaven, everlasting life. For all these things he hath briefly expressed, by saying, *if we neglect so great salvation.*

[7.] Then he subjoins what makes it all credible. *Which at the first began to be spoken by the Lord:* that is, had its beginning from the very fountain itself. It was not a man who brought it over [g] into the earth, nor any created power, but the Only-Begotten Himself.

And was confirmed unto us by them that heard [*Him*]. What is *confirmed?* It was believed [h], or, it came to pass. For (saith he) we have the earnest [i]; that is, it hath not been extinguished, it hath not ceased, but it is strong and prevaileth. And the cause is, the Divine power works therein. It means they who heard from the Lord, themselves confirmed us. This is a great thing and trustworthy:
S. Luke i. 2. which also Luke saith in the beginning of his Gospel, *As they delivered unto us, which from the beginning were eyewitnesses and ministers of the Word.*

How then was it confirmed? what if those that heard were forgers? saith some one. This objection then he overthrows, and shews that the grace was not human. If they had been forgers, God would not have borne witness to them; for he subjoined (ver. 4.) *God also bearing witness with them.* They indeed also bear witness, and God beareth witness too. How doth He bear witness? not by word or by voice (though this also would have been worthy of belief): but how? *By signs, and wonders, and divers miracles.*

[g] lit, *ferried* it over: διεπόρθμευσεν, the word is specially applied to messages between earth and Heaven, by Pseudo-Dionys. Areop. de Celesti Hierarchia, c. 15. 6. "The Angels are called Winds, to express their rapid power of making things, how it reaches almost to all things without time; and the motion in the manner of those who ferry over, from above downwards, and again from the lower parts up the steep, both drawing out the things of secondary order towards that loftier height, and moving those of the first order to come forth in the way of sympathy and care for their inferiors."

[h] ἐπιστεύθη. Dunæus suggested ἐπιστώθη, *it was accredited,* but there is no MS. authority for the change.

[i] S. Chrys. seems to have had in view 2 Cor. i. 21, 22, where "confirming" is connected with "the earnest of the Spirit."

(Well said he, *divers miracles*, declaring the abundance of Heb.ii.4.
the gifts: which was not so in the former dispensation,
neither so great signs and so various.) That is, we did not
believe them simply, but through signs and wonders:
wherefore we believe not them, but God Himself.

*And by portionings of the Holy Ghost, according to His
own will.*

What then, if wizards also do signs, and the Jews said
that He *cast out devils through Beelzebub?* But they do not S. Luke
such kind of signs: therefore said he *divers miracles:* for xi. 15.
those others were not miracles, [or powers [1]], but weakness [1] δυνάμεις
and fancy, and things altogether vain. Wherefore he said,
by portionings of the Holy Ghost according to His own will.

[8.] Here he seems to me to intimate another thing (5)
also. For it is likely there were not many there who had
gifts, but that these had failed, upon their becoming rather
slothful. In order then that herein also he might comfort
them, and not leave them utterly to fall, he referred all to
the will of God. He knows (he says) what is expedient, and
for whom, and apportions His grace accordingly. Which
kind of thing also he does in the Epistle to the Corinthians, saying, *God hath placed every one of us, as He willed.* 1 Cor.xii.
And again, *The manifestation of the Spirit is given to every* 18.
man to profit withal. Ib. 7.

According to His will. He intimates that the gift is
according to the will of the Father. But oftentimes on
account of their unclean and slothful life many have not
received a gift, and sometimes also those whose life is good
and pure have not received one. Why, I pray you? Lest
they might be made haughty, that they might not be
puffed up, that they might not grow more negligent, that
they might not be more excited. For if even without any
gift, the mere consciousness of a pure life be sufficient to
lift a man up, much more when the grace is added also.
Wherefore to the humble, to the simple, it was rather
given, and especially to the simple: for it is said, *in simpli-* Acts ii.
city and gladness of heart. Yea, and hereby also he rather 46.
urged them on, and gave them a spur, if they were growing
negligent. Inasmuch as the humble man, and he who

imagines no great things concerning himself, becomes more earnest when he has received a gift, in that he has obtained what is beyond his deserts, and thinks that he is not worthy thereof. But he who thinks he hath done any thing very well, reckoning the matter to be his due, is even puffed up. Wherefore God dispenseth this for [men's] good: which one may see taking place also in the Church: for one man hath the word of teaching, another hath not power so much as to open his mouth. Let not this man (he says) be grieved because of this. For *to every man the manifestation of the Spirit is given to profit withal.* For if a man that is an householder knoweth what he will entrust, and to whom, much more God, who is acquainted with the mind of men, *who knoweth all things or ever they come into being.* One thing only is worthy to be grieved for, Sin: there is nothing else.

Say not thou, Wherefore have I not riches? or, If I had, I would give to the poor. Thou knowest not, if thou hadst them, whether thou wouldest not be more covetous. For now indeed thou sayest these things, but being put to the trial thou wouldest be different. Since also when we have satisfied ourselves, we think that we are able to fast; but when we have gone without a little space, other thoughts come into us. Again, when we are out of the way of drunkenness we think ourselves able to master our appetite, but no longer so, when we are caught by it.

Say not thou, Wherefore had I not the gift of teaching? or, If I had had it, I should have edified innumerable souls. Thou knowest not, if thou hadst it, whether it would not be to thy condemnation,—whether envy, whether indolence would not have disposed thee to hide thy talent. Well then, thou art now free from all these, and though thou give not *the portion of meat,* thou art not called to account: but then, thou wouldest have been responsible for souls innumerable.

[9.] And besides, neither now art thou without God's gift. Shew thou in that which is little, what manner of person thou wouldst have been, if thou hadst had the other. *For if* (saith he) *ye prove not faithful in that which is little, how shall any one give you that which is great?*

Give such proof as did the widow; she had two farthings[1], Heb. ii.4.
and she cast in all, whatsoever she was possessed of. [1] ὀβολοὺς

Dost thou seek riches? shew that thou art above minding the few things, that I may trust thee also concerning the many things. But if thou art not even above these, much less wilt thou be above the other.

Again, in speech, shew that thou canst use as may be requisite exhortation and counsel. Thou hast not external eloquence, thou hast not store of thoughts: but nevertheless these common things thou knowest. Thou hast a child, thou hast a neighbour, thou hast a friend, thou hast a brother, thou hast kinsmen. And though publickly before the Church, thou art not able to draw out a long discourse, to these thou canst give exhortation in private. Here, there is no need of rhetoric, nor of discourses long drawn out: shew thou in these, that if thou hadst skill of speech, thou wouldest not have neglected it. But if in the small matter thou art not in earnest, how shall I trust thee concerning the great?

For, to prove that this is what every man can do, hear what Paul saith, how even to lay people he hath committed this charge; *Edify*, saith he, *each one of the other, as also ye do.* And, *Comfort ye one another with these words.* 1 Thess. v. 11. Ib. iv. 18. God knoweth how He should distribute to every man. Art thou better than Moses? hear how he shrinks from the hardship. *Am I*, saith he, *able to bear them? for Thou saidst to me, Take them up, as a nursing-father would take up the sucking-child.* Num. xi. 12. What then did God? He took of his spirit and gave unto the others, shewing that neither when he bare them was the gift his own, but of the Spirit. If thou hadst had the gift, thou wouldst perchance[k] have been lifted up, perchance wouldst thou have been turned out of the way. Thou knowest not thyself as God knoweth thee. Let us not say, To what end is that? on what account is this? When God dispenseth, let us not call Him to account: for this [is] of the uttermost impiety and folly. We are slaves, and slaves far apart from our Master, knowing not even the things which are before us.

[10.] Let us not then busy ourselves about the counsel

[k] πολλάκις see Mr. Field's note.

of God, but whatsoever He hath given, this let us guard, though it be small, though the very last, and we shall be altogether approved. Or rather, none of the gifts of God is small: art thou grieved because thou hast not the gift of teaching? Then tell me, whether, thinkest thou, is the greater, to have the gift of teaching, or the gift of driving away diseases? doubtless this latter. But what? tell me; doth it not seem to thee a greater thing to give eyes to the blind than even to drive away diseases? But what? tell me; doth it not seem to thee a greater thing to raise the dead than to give eyes to the blind? What again, tell me; doth it not seem to thee a greater thing to effect this by shadows and napkins, than to do it by a word? Tell me then, which wouldst thou? raise the dead with shadows and napkins, or have the gift of teaching? Doubtless thou wilt say the former, to raise the dead with shadows and napkins.

(6) If then I should shew to thee, that there is another gift far greater than this, and that thou dost not receive it when it is in thy power to receive it, art not thou justly deprived of those others? Yea and this gift not one or two, but all may have. I know that ye open wide your mouths and are amazed, at being to hear that it is in your power to have a greater gift than raising the dead, and giving eyes to the blind, doing the same things which were done in the time of the Apostles. And haply it appears to you even past belief.

What then is this gift? charity. Nay, believe me; for the word is not mine, but Christ's, speaking by Paul. For what saith he? *Covet earnestly the best gifts: and yet shew I unto you a more excellent way.* What is this, *yet more excellent?* What he meaneth is of this kind. Some Corinthians were inclined to have high thoughts about their gifts, and they who had tongues, the least gift, were puffed up against the rest. He saith therefore, Do ye by all means desire gifts? I shew unto you a way of gifts not merely excelling but far more excellent. Then he saith, *Though I speak with the tongues of Angels, and have not charity, I am nothing. And though I have faith so as to remove mountains, and have not charity, I am nothing.*

Hast thou seen the gift? Covet earnestly this gift. This is greater than raising the dead. This is far better than all the rest together. And that it is so, hear what Christ Himself saith, discoursing with His disciples, *Hereby shall all men know that ye are My disciples.* And shewing in what respect, He mentioned not the miracles, but what? *If ye have love one with another.* And again He saith to the Father, *Hereby shall they know that Thou hast sent Me, if they be one.* And He said Himself to His disciples, *A new commandment I give to you, that ye love one another.* Such an one therefore is more venerable and glorious than those who raise the dead; with reason. For that indeed is wholly of God's grace, but this, of thine own earnestness also. This is of one who is a Christian indeed: this shews the disciple of Christ, the crucified, the man that hath nothing common with earth. Without this, not even martyrdom can be of any avail.

Heb. ii. 4.

S. John xiii. 35.

Ib. xvii. 21.

Ib. xiii. 34.

And as a proof, see this plainly. The blessed Paul took two of the topmost virtues, or rather three; namely those which consist in miracles, those in knowledge, those in life. And without this those, he said, are nothing. And how these are nothing, I will say. *Though I give my goods to feed the poor,* saith he, *and have not charity, I am nothing.* For it is possible not to be charitable even when one feeds the poor and exhausts one's means.

1 Cor. xiii. 3.

[11.] And indeed these things have been sufficiently declared by us, in the place concerning Charity[1]: and thither we refer the readers. Meanwhile, as I was saying, let us zealously seek the Gift, let us love one another: and we shall need nothing else for the perfect acquisition of virtue, but all will be easy to us without violent labours and we shall do all perfectly with much diligence.

'But see, even now,' it is said, 'we love one another. For one man hath two friends, and another three.' But this is not to love for God's sake, but for the sake of being beloved. But to love for God's sake hath not this as its principle of Love; but such an one will be disposed towards all men as towards brethren; loving those that are of the same faith as being genuine brothers; Heretics and Hea-

---

[1] His Homily on 1 Cor. xiii. 3. [pp. 444 sqq. O.T.] is referred to.

then and Jews, brothers indeed by nature, but vile and unprofitable, pitying and wearing himself out for them and shedding tears. Herein we shall be like unto God if we love all men, even our enemies; not, if we work miracles. For even God we regard with admiration when He worketh wonders, yet much more, when He sheweth love towards man, when He is long-suffering. If then even in God that Love is worthy of much admiration, much more in men is it evident that this rendereth us admirable.

This then let us zealously seek after: and though we may be not able to drive away a fever, we shall be no way inferior to Paul and Peter and those who have raised innumerable dead. But without this Love, though we should work greater miracles even than the Apostles themselves, though we should expose ourselves for the faith to dangers innumerable: there will be to us no profit from any. And these things not I say, but he, the very nursling of Charity, knoweth these things. To him then let us be obedient; for thus we shall be able to attain to the good things promised, of which may we all be made partakers, by the grace and mercy of our Lord Jesus Christ, with whom to the Father and also to the Holy Ghost, be the glory, now and for ever and world without end. Amen.

HOMILY IV.

II Heb. ii. 5—7.

For unto Angels He hath not put in subjection the world to come, whereof we speak. But one in a certain place testified, saying, What is man that Thou art mindful of him, or the son of man that Thou visitest him ? Thou hast made him a little lower than the Angels.

[1.] I COULD have wished to know for certain whether any of you hear with suitable attention the things that are said, whether we are not casting the seeds by the way-side: for in that case I should have made my instructions with more cheerfulness. For we shall speak, though no one hear, for the fear which is laid on us by our Saviour. For, saith He, testify thou to this people; even if they hear not, thou shalt thyself be guiltless. If however I had been persuaded of your earnestness, I should have spoken not for fear only, but should have done it with pleasure also. For now indeed, even if no man hear, even if my work, so long as I fulfil my own part, brings no danger, still the trouble [I take] is not attended with pleasure. For what profit is it, when though I be not myself open to blame, no one is benefited? If on the other hand any were likely to be attentive, the advantage we shall receive, will not be so much from avoiding punishment ourselves as from your progress. *see Ezek. iii. 19.*

How then shall I know this? Having taken notice of some of you, those [I mean] who are not very attentive, I shall question them privately, when I meet them. And if I find that they retain any of the things that have been spoken (I say not all, for this would not be very easy for you), but even if [they retain] a few things out of many, it is plain I should have no further doubts about the rest. And indeed we ought, without giving notice beforehand, to have attacked you when off your guard. However it will be pretty well, even if in this way I should be able to attain my purpose. Nay rather, even as it is, I can attack you when you are off your guard. For that I *shall* question you, I have forewarned you; but *when* I shall question you I do not as yet make evident. For perhaps it may be to-day; perhaps to-morrow, perhaps after twenty or thirty days, perhaps after fewer, perhaps after more. Thus has God also made uncertain the day of our death. Nor hath He allowed it to be clear to us, whether it shall befal us to-day, or to-morrow, or after a whole year, or after many years; that through the uncertainty of the expectation we may through all time keep ourselves firm in virtue. And that we shall indeed depart, He hath said,—but when, He hath not yet said. Thus too I have said that I shall question you, but I have not added when, wishing you always to be thoughtful.

And let no man say, I heard these things four or five weeks ago, or more, and I cannot retain them. For I wish the hearer to retain them in such a way as to have his recollection perpetual and not apt to fade, nor yet that he should reject with scorn what is spoken. For I wish you to retain them, not, in order to tell them to me, but to have profit yourselves; and this is that which is to me the matter of serious interest. Let no one then say this.

[2.] However, I must now begin with what follows in the epistle. What then is set before us to speak on to-day?

For not to angels, saith he, *did He put in subjection the world to come* [1], *whereof we speak.* Is he then discoursing concerning some other world? no; but concerning this. For, on this account he added *whereof we speak,* that he might not allow the mind to wander away in search of some other. In what sense then does he call it *the world to come?* Exactly as he also says in another place, *Who is the figure of him that was to be* [2], when he is speaking about Adam and Christ in the Epistle to the Romans; calling Christ according to the flesh *Him that was to be* in respect

[1] τὴν μέλ-λουσαν
Rom. v. 14.
[2] τοῦ μέλ-λοντος

of the times of Adam (for [then] He was to be). So now Heb.ii.8. also, since he had said, *but when He bringeth in the First-begotten into the world:* that thou mightest not suppose that he is speaking of another world, it is made certain from many other considerations and from the very fact itself of his saying *to come.* For the world was to be, but the Son of God ever was. This world then which was about to exist, He put in subjection not to Angels but to Christ. For that this is said with reference to the Son (he means) is evident: for surely no one would assert the other alternative, that it was said in reference to Angels.

Then he brings forward another testimony also and says, *but one in a certain place testified, saying.* Wherefore did he not mention the name of the prophet, but concealed it? Yea, and in other testimonies also he doth this: as when he saith, *but when He bringeth in again the First-Begotten* supra i. 6, *into the world, He saith, And let all the angels of God wor-* 5, 7, 10. *ship Him. And again, I will be to Him a Father. And of the Angels He saith, Who maketh His angels spirits. And, Thou, Lord, in the beginning hast laid the foundations of the earth:*—so also here he saith, *but one in a certain place testified saying.* And this very thing (I conceive) is the act of one that conceals himself, and shews that they were well acquainted with the Scriptures; his not setting down [I mean] the name of him who uttered the testimony, but introducing it as familiar and obvious.

What is man that Thou art mindful of him, or the son of man that Thou visitest him ? Thou madest him a little lower than the angels: Thou crownedst him with glory and honour[a]. (ver. 8.) *Thou hast put all things in subjection under his feet.*

Now although these things were spoken of human nature (2) generally, they would nevertheless apply more properly to Christ according to the flesh. For this, *Thou hast put all things in subjection under his feet,* belongs to Him rather than to us. For the Son of God visited us when we were nothing: and after having assumed what was derived from us[1], and united it to Himself, He became higher than all. [1] τὸ ἐξ ἡμῶν

---

[a] S. B. add καὶ κατέστησας αὐτὸν ἐπὶ τὰ ἔργα τῶν χειρῶν σου. This clause is omitted from the text of the Epistle by Critical editors of the New Testament, and is not commented on by S. Chrysostom.

For, saith he, *in that He hath put all things in subjection under Him, He left nothing not put under Him: but now we see not yet all things put under Him.*

What he means is to this effect. Since he had said, *Until I have made Thine enemies Thy footstool*—and it was likely that they would still be grieved, so then after this having inserted a few things parenthetically, he added this testimony in confirmation of the former. For that they might not say, How is it that He hath put His enemies under His feet, when we have suffered so much? he sufficiently hinted at it in the former place indeed (for the word *until* shewed, not what should take place immediately, but in course of time) but here he followeth it up. For do not suppose (saith he) that because they have not yet been made subject, they are not being made subject: for that they must be made subject, is evident; for, for this cause was the prophecy spoken. *For*, he says, *in that He hath put all things under Him, He left nothing not put under Him.* How then is it that all things have not been put under Him? Because they are hereafter to be put under Him.

If then all things must be made subject to Him, but have not yet been made subject, do not vex, nor trouble thyself. If indeed when the end were come, and all things were made subject, thou wert still suffering these things, with reason wouldst thou repine: *But now we see not yet all things put under Him.* The King has not yet clearly gained the mastery. Why then art thou troubled when suffering affliction? the preaching [of the Gospel] hath not yet prevailed over all; it is not yet time that they should be altogether made subject.

[3.] Then again there is another consolation; if indeed He who is hereafter to have all put in subjection under Him, hath Himself also died and submitted to sufferings innumerable. (ver. 9.) *But,* saith he, *we see Him who was made a little[2] lower than the angels, even Jesus, for the suffering of death*—then [come] the good things again,—*crowned with glory and honour.* Seest thou, how all things apply to Him? For the [expression], *a little* [lower], would rather suit Him, who was only three days in Hades, but not our-

selves who are for a long time in corruption. Likewise HEB.ii.9.
also the [expression] *with glory and honour* will suit Him
much more than us.

Again, he puts them in mind of the Cross, thereby effecting
two things; shewing His solicitude [for them] and persuading
them to bear all things nobly, looking to their Master. For
(he would say) if He who is worshipped of Angels, for thy
sake endured to have a little less than the Angels, much
more oughtest thou who art inferior to the angels, to bear
all things for His sake. Then he shews that the Cross is
glory and honour, just as He Himself also always calls it
saying, *That the Son of Man should be glorified;* and, *the* S. John
Son of Man is glorified. If then He calls what [He suffered] xi. 5.
for His servants' sake *glory*, much more shouldest thou what Ib. xii. 23.
[thou sufferest] for thy Lord.

Seest thou the fruit of the Cross, how great it is? fear
not the matter: for it seemeth to thee indeed to be dismal,
but it brings forth good things innumerable. From these
considerations he shews the benefit of trials. Then he says,
*That He by the grace of God should taste death for every
man.*

That by the grace of God, saith he. And He indeed
because of the grace of God towards us suffered these things.
He who spared not His Own Son, he saith, *but delivered Him* Rom. viii.
up for us all. Wherefore? He did not owe us this, but has 32.
done it of grace. And again in the Epistle to the Romans
he saith, *Much more the grace of God, and the gift by grace* Ib. v. 15.
*which is of one man Jesus Christ, hath abounded unto the
many.*

*That by the grace of God He should taste death for every
man*, not for the faithful only, but even for the whole world:
for He Himself indeed died for all; But what if all have
not believed? He hath fulfilled His own [part.]

Moreover he said in strict propriety of expression *taste
death for every man*, he did not say *die*. For as if He really
was tasting it, when He had spent a little time therein, He
immediately arose.

By saying then *for the suffering of death*, he signified real
death, by saying that [He was made] *superior to angels*, he
declared the resurrection. For just as a physician though

noways obliged to taste the victuals prepared for the sick man, yet in his solicitude for him tastes first himself, that he may persuade the sick man with confidence to venture on the food, so since all men were afraid of death, in persuading them to take courage against death, He tasted it also Himself though He was not obliged. *For*, saith He, *the prince of this world cometh and findeth nothing in Me.* So both the words *by grace* and *should taste death for every man*, establish this.

[4.] ver. 10. *For it became Him, for whom are all things, and by whom are all things, in bringing many sons unto glory, to make the Captain of their salvation perfect through sufferings.* In this place he is speaking of the Father. Seest thou how again he applies the [expression] *by whom*[1] to Him? which he would not have done, had it been [an expression] of inferiority, and only applicable to the Son. And what he says is to this effect. He has done what is worthy of His love towards mankind, in shewing His First-born to be more glorious than all, and in setting Him forth as an example to the others, like some noble wrestler that surpasses the rest.

The Captain of their salvation, that is, the Cause of their salvation. Seest thou how great is the space between? He also is a Son, and we are sons; but He saves, we are saved. Seest thou how He both brings us together and then separates us; *bringing*, saith he, *many sons unto glory:* here he brings us together,—*the Captain of their salvation,* again he separates.

To make perfect through sufferings. It follows then that sufferings are a perfecting, and a cause of salvation. Seest thou that to suffer affliction is not the portion of those who are utterly forsaken; if indeed it was by this that God first honoured His Son, by leading Him through sufferings? And in very deed His having taken on Him our flesh and suffered what He did suffer, is a far greater thing than making the world, and bringing it out of non-existence. This indeed also is [a token] of His lovingkindness to man, but the other is a far greater. And [the Apostle] himself also pointing out this very thing, says, *That in the ages to come He might shew forth the exceeding riches of His good-*

ness, He both raised us up together, and made us sit together in the heavenly places in Christ Jesus. [He.ii.11. Eph.ii.6.]

For, saith he, *it became Him for whom are all things and by whom are all things in bringing many sons to glory, to make the Captain of their salvation perfect through sufferings.* For (he means) it became Him who taketh tender care [of all], and brought all things into being, to give up [His] Son for the salvation of the rest, the One for the many. However he did not express himself thus, but, *to make perfect through sufferings*, shewing that he who suffers for any one, not merely profits *him*, but himself also becomes more glorious and more perfect. Yea, and this too he says in reference to the faithful, giving them encouragement by the way: for even Christ was glorified at the time when He suffered. But when I say, He was glorified, do not thou suppose that an acquisition of glory was made by Him: for that He ever had, even that of [His] nature, and acquired nothing in addition.

[5.] *For*, saith he, *both He that sanctifieth, and they who are sanctified, are all of one, for which cause He is not ashamed to call them brethren.* Behold again how he brings [them] together, honouring them and comforting them, and making them brethren of Christ, in this respect that they are *of one*[1]. Then again carefully guarding himself and shewing that he is speaking of that which is according to the flesh, he introduces, *For He who sanctifieth*, [i. e.] Christ, *and they who are sanctified*, ourselves. Dost thou see how great is the space that intervenes[2]? He sanctifies, we are sanctified. And above he said, *the Captain of their salvation. For there is one God, of whom are all things*[b]. [1 Cor. viii. 6.]

[1] ἐξ ἑνὸς
[2] τὸ μέσον

For which cause He is not ashamed to call them brethren. Seest thou how again he shews the superiority? For by saying, *He is not ashamed*, he shews that the whole comes not of the nature of the thing, but of the loving affection of Him who was *not ashamed*, [yea] of His great humility. For though we be *of one*, yet He sanctifieth and we are sanctified: and great is the space between[3]. Moreover *He is*

[3] τὸ μέσον

---

[b] This citation is to be connected with *they are of one*, the intervening words "Then again ... salvation," being introduced parenthetically.

of the Father, as a genuine Son, that is, of His substance; *we*, as created, that is, brought out of non-existence, so that the space between us is great. Wherefore he says, *He is not ashamed to call them brethren,* (ver. 12) *saying, I will declare Thy name unto My brethren.* For when He clothed Himself with flesh, He clothed Himself also with the brotherhood, and at the same time came in the brotherhood therewith.

This however he brings forward naturally. But this other, (v. 13) *I will put my trust in Him,* what does it mean? for what follows this is also [introduced] naturally. *Behold, I and the children which God hath given Me.* For as here He shews Himself a Father, so before, a Brother. *I will declare Thy name unto My brethren,* He saith.

And again he indicates the superiority and the great interval [between us], by what follows: (ver. 14) *Since then the children,* he saith, *are partakers of flesh and blood* (thou seest where he saith the likeness is? in reference to the flesh), *in like manner He also Himself took part of the same.* Let all the Heretics be ashamed, let those hide their faces who say that He is come in appearance and not in reality. For he did not say, *He took part of these* only, and then say no more; and yet even had he said thus, it would have been sufficient, but he asserted something else which is greater, by adding the [words] *in like manner,* not in appearance, he means, or by an image (since in that case *in like manner* is not preserved) but in reality; shewing [thereby] the brotherhood.

[6.] Next he sets down also the cause of the economy [1]. *That through death,* he saith, *He might destroy him that had the power of death, that is, the Devil.*

In these words he points out the wonderful circumstance, that by that whereby the devil prevailed, by this same was he overcome, and the very thing which was his strong weapon against the world, [namely], Death, by this Christ smote him. In this he exhibits the greatness of the conqueror's power. Thou seest how great good death hath wrought.

ver. 15. *And should deliver them,* saith he, *who through fear of death were all their life-time subject to bondage.* Wherefore (he means) do ye shudder? why do you fear him that hath been brought to nought? No longer is he terrible, but has been trodden under foot, hath been utterly despised; vile he is and of no account. ^{He.ii.15.} ^{2 Tim. i. 10.}

But what is *through fear of death were all their life-time subject to bondage?* He either means this, that he that is afraid of death is a slave, and submits to all things rather than die. Or this, that all men were slaves of death and were held under his power, because he had not yet been done away. Or that men spent their lives in continual terror, ever expecting that they should die; and being afraid of death, could have no sense of pleasure, while this terror was present with them. For this he hinted at in saying, *All their life-time.* In these words, he shews that those that are afflicted, that are harassed, that are persecuted, that are deprived of country and of substance and of all other things, spend their lives more sweetly and more like free-men than they of old time who were in luxury, who suffered no such afflictions, who were in continual prosperity, if indeed these *all their life-time* were under this fear and were slaves; while the others have been freed from this terror, and laugh at that which they shudder at. For in fact it is just the same thing as if, when a captive was on the point of being led away to death, and in continual expectation of it, one should feed him up with abundant dainties (something such as this was Death of old). But now as if some one taking away that fear together with the dainties were to promise that the man should wrestle [for a prize], and propose the combat on such conditions as to lead him no longer to death, but to a kingdom. Of which number wouldst thou have wished to be—those who whilst they are fed up in the prison-house, are every day looking for their sentence, or those who contend much and labour willingly, that they may crown themselves with the diadem of the kingdom? Seest thou how he has raised up their soul, and made them elated? He shews too, that not death alone has been put an end to, but that thereby he also who is ever shewing that war against us in which there is no truce, I mean the Devil, hath been brought to nought; since he that fears not death is out of reach of the Devil's power. For if *skin for skin, yea all things a man would give* ^{Job ii. 4.}

for his life—when any one has determined to disregard even this, of what henceforward will he be the slave? He fears no one, he is in terror of no one, he is higher than all, and more like a freeman than all. For he that disregards his own life, much more [doth he disregard] all other things. And when the Devil finds a soul such as this, he will not be able to accomplish in it any of his works. For what? tell me, shall he threaten the loss of property, and degradation, and banishment from one's country? But these are small matters to him who *counteth not even his life dear* unto him, according to the [pattern of the] blessed Paul. Thou seest that in casting out the tyrannical power of death, he at the same time overthrew also the strength of the Devil. For he who has learnt to dwell on innumerable deep truths concerning the resurrection[1], how should he fear death? how should he shudder any more?

[Acts xx. 24.]

[1] μυρία φιλοσοφεῖν

[7.] Wherefore be ye not grieved, saying, why do we suffer such and such things? for in this war the victory becomes more glorious. And it would not have been glorious, unless by death He had destroyed death; but the most admirable thing is this, that He conquered him by the very means by which he was strong, shewing in every point the abundance of His means, and the excellence of His contrivances. Let us not then give up the gift which has been bestowed on us. *For we*, he saith, *have received not a spirit of cowardice, but a spirit of power, and of love, and of a sound mind.* Let us stand then nobly, laughing death to scorn.

[Rom. viii. 15. 2 Tim. i. 7.]

(5) But [I pause] for it comes over me to groan bitterly [at the thought of] what Christ hath raised us up to, and to what we have brought ourselves down. For when I behold the wailings in the public places, the groanings over them which depart out of [this] life, the howlings, all the other unseemly behaviour, believe me, I am ashamed before those heathen, and Jews, and heretics who see it, yea, and indeed before all who for this cause laugh us to scorn. For whatever I may afterwards say, I shall talk to no purpose, when philosophizing concerning the resurrection. Why, I ask? because the heathen do not attend to what is said by me, but to what is done by you. For they will say at once,

'when will any of these [fellows] be able to despise death, He.ii.15. 'when he is not able even to see another dead?'

Beautiful are the things spoken by Paul, beautiful and worthy of Heaven, and of the love of God to man. For what does he say? *And He shall deliver them who through fear of death were all their life-time subject to bondage.* But ye do not allow these things to be believed, contending against them by your deeds. And yet God had caused many things to be done, building a wall [as it were] against this [error], that He might take away this evil custom. For tell me, what mean the bright torches? do we not attend them forth as [victorious] champions? and what [mean] the hymns? do we not glorify God, and give thanks that at last He has crowned the departed one, that He has freed him from his labours, that He has taken him out of uncertainty, and has him with Himself? is it not for this that there are Hymns? is it not for this that there is Psalmody? all these are the acts of persons that are in joy. *For*, it is said, *is any merry?* S. James *let him sing psalms.* But to these things the heathen give v. 13. no heed. For (one will say) do not tell me of him who is philosophical[c] when he is out of the affliction, for this is nothing great or surprising;—shew me a man who in the very affliction itself is philosophical, and then I will believe the resurrection.

And indeed, that women engaged in the affairs of this life[1] should act thus is no ways surprising. And yet indeed [1] Βιωτικὰς this too is sad; for from them also is the same philosophy required. For which cause Paul also says, *But concerning* 1 Thess. *them which are asleep, I would not have you ignorant, that* iv. 13. *ye sorrow not even as the rest who have no hope.* He wrote not this to solitaries, nor to those [who had resolved to remain] in perpetual virginity, but to women and men engaged in the world[2]. But however this is not so sad. [2] κοσμι-But when any man or woman, professing to be crucified κοσμικοῖς to the world, in the one case tears his hair, in the other shrieks violently—what can be more unseemly than this?

Believe me when I say if things were done as they ought to have been, such persons must needs be excluded for a

---

[c] The word includes the ideas of being patient, as well as of thinking and speaking deep things.

<small>Hom. 4.</small> long time from the thresholds of the Church. For those who are indeed worthy of being grieved for, are these who are still in fear of death and shudder at it, who have no faith at all in the resurrection.

'But I do not disbelieve the resurrection (saith one) but I 'long after his society.' Why then, tell me, when he goes from home, and that for a long absence, dost not thou do the same? 'Yea, but I do weep then also (she says) and 'mourn as I long after him.' But that is the conduct of those that really long after their associates, this that of one who despairs of his return.

<small>Ps. cxvi. 7.</small> Think, what thou singest on that occasion, *Return unto thy rest, O my soul, for the Lord hath dealt bountifully with* <small>Ib. xxiii. 4.</small> *thee.* And again, *I will fear no evils, for Thou art with me.* <small>Ib. xxxii. 7.</small> And again, *Thou art my refuge from the affliction which encompasseth me.* Think what these Psalms mean. But thou dost not give heed, but art become drunken from thy grief.

Consider carefully the funeral lamentations of others at least, that thou mayest have a remedy in thine own case. *Return, O my soul, to thy rest, for the Lord hath dealt bountifully with thee.* Tell me, sayest thou that the Lord hath dealt bountifully with thee, and weepest? Is not this a play? is it not mere acting? For if indeed thou really believest the things thou sayest, thy sorrow is superfluous: but if thou art in sport and acting a part, and thinkest them to be fables, why dost thou also sing psalms? why dost thou even endure the persons that present themselves? why dost thou not drive away the singers? But this would be the act of madmen. And yet the other is much more [so].

For the present, then, I advise you: but as time goes on, I shall treat the matter more seriously: for indeed I am greatly afraid that by this practice some grievous disease may also make its way into the Church.

The case of the wailings then we will hereafter correct. And meanwhile I charge and testify, both to rich and poor, both to women and men.

May God indeed grant that you all depart out of life unwailed, and according to the fitting rule fathers now grown old may be attended to their graves by sons, and mothers by daughters, and grand-children, and great grand-children, in a green old age, and that untimely death may in no case occur. May this then be, and this I pray myself, and I exhort the prelates and all of you to beseech God for each other, and to make this prayer in common. But if (which God forbid, and may it never happen) any bitter death should occur, bitter, I mean, not in its nature (for henceforth there is no bitter death, for it differs not at all from sleep), but bitter in regard of your disposition, if it should happen, and any should hire these mourning women, believe me when I say (I speak not without meaning[1] but as I have resolved, let him who will, be angry), that person we will exclude from the Church for a long time, as we do the idolater. For if Paul calls *the covetous man an idolater*, much more [would he so call] him who brings in the practices of the idolaters over a believer. HE.ii.15.

[1] ἄλλως

Eph.v.5.

For, tell me, for what cause dost thou invite presbyters, and the singers? Is it not to afford consolation? is it not to honour the departed? Why then dost thou insult him? and why dost thou make him a public show? and why dost thou make game as in a play? We come, discoursing of the things concerning the resurrection, instructing all, even those who have not yet been smitten, by the honour shewn to him, to bear it nobly if any such thing should befal themselves: and dost thou bring those who overthrow our [teachings] as much as in them lieth? What can be worse than this ridicule and mockery? what more grievous than this inconsistency?

(6)

[8.] Be ye influenced by shame and reverence: but if ye will not, we cannot endure the bringing in upon the Church of practices so destructive. For, it is said, *them that sin rebuke before all*. And as to those miserable and wretched women, we through you forbid them[d] ever to introduce themselves into the funerals of the faithful, lest we should oblige them in good earnest to wail over their own evils, and teach them not to do these things in the ills of others, but rather to weep for their own misfortunes. For an affec-

1 Tim. v. 20.

---

[d] The hired wailers were heathens and not present: S. Chrys. hints at having some corporal punishment inflicted on them.

^{Hom. 4.} tionate father too, when he has a disorderly son, not only advises him not to draw near to the wicked, but puts them in fear also. Behold then, I advise you, and those women through you, that you do not invite such persons, and that they do not present themselves. And may God grant that my words may produce some effect, and that my threat may avail. But if (which God forbid) we should be disregarded, we have no choice henceforward but to put our threat into execution, chastising you by the laws of the Church, and those women as befits them.

Now if any man is obstinate and contemptuous, let him hear Christ saying even now, *If any one trespass against thee, go, tell him his fault between thee and him alone;* but if he will not be persuaded, *take with thee one or two.* But if even so he speak contrary, *tell it to the Church, but if he shall also refuse to hear the Church, let him be unto thee as a heathen man and a publican.* Now if when a man trespasses against me, and will not be persuaded, [the Lord] commands me thus to turn away from him, judge ye in what light I ought to hold him who trespasses against himself, and against God. For do not you yourselves condemn us when we come down so gently upon you?

^{S. Matt. xviii. 15.}
^{Ib. 16.}
^{Ib. 17.}

If however any man disregard the bonds which we inflict, let Christ again instruct him, saying, *Whatsoever ye shall bind on earth shall be bound in heaven; and whatsoever ye shall loose on earth shall be loosed in heaven.* For though we ourselves be miserable and good for nothing and worthy to be despised, as indeed we are; yet are we not avenging ourselves nor shielding ourselves from anger, but are anxious for your salvation.

^{Ib. 18.}

Be influenced by reverence, I beseech you, and respect. For if a man bear with a friend when he attacks him more vehemently than is right, ascertaining his object, and that he does it with kind intention, and not out of insolence; much more [should he bear with] a teacher when rebuking him, and a teacher who does not even himself say these things as of authority, nor as one in the position of a ruler, but in that of a kindly guardian. For we do not say these things as wishing to exhibit our authority, (for how could we, we who pray that we may never come to the actual trial of them?) but grieving and lamenting for you. HE.ii.15.

Forgive me then, and let no man disregard the bonds of the Church. For it is not a mere man who binds, but Christ who has given unto us this authority, and makes men lords of this so great dignity. For ourselves indeed wish to have largely used this power for loosing; or rather, we wish to have no need even of that, for we wish that there should not be any bound among us—we are not so miserable and wretched [as that] even though we be extreme good-for-nothings. If however we be compelled [so to act], forgive us. For it is not of our own accord, nor wishing it, but rather out of sorrow for you that are bound that we put these chains around you. But if any man despise these chains, the time of judgement will come quickly, which shall teach him. And what comes after I do not wish to speak of, lest I should wound your minds. For in the first place indeed we do not wish to be brought into this necessity; but if we are so brought, we fulfil our own part, we cast the chains around the sinners. And if any man burst through them, I have done my part, and am henceforth free from blame, and thou wilt have to give account to Him who commanded me to bind.

For neither, when a king is sitting in public, if any of the guard who stand beside him be commanded to bind one of the attendants, and to put the chains around [him], and he should not only thrust this man away, but also break the bonds in pieces, is it the guard who suffers the insult, and not much more the King who gave the order. For if He claim as His own, the things which are done to the faithful, much more will He feel as though He were Himself insulted when he is insulted who has been appointed to teach.

But God grant that none of those who are over this Church should be driven to the necessity of [inflicting] these bonds. For as it is an excellent thing not to do amiss, so is it profitable to endure reproof. Let us then endure to be rebuked, and earnestly endeavour not to do amiss; and if we should do amiss let us bear to be reproved. For as it is an excellent thing not to be wounded, but, if this should happen, to apply the remedy to the wound, so also in this case.

But God forbid that any man should need such remedies as these. *But we are persuaded better things of you, and things that accompany salvation, though we thus speak.* We have however discoursed more vehemently for the sake of greater security. For it is better that I should be suspected by you of being a harsh and severe, and self-willed person, than that you should do things not approved of God. But we trust in God, that this reproof will not be unserviceable to you, but that ye will be so changed, that these discourses of mine may be devoted to encomiums on you and in praises: that we may all be counted worthy to attain to those good things, which God hath promised to them that love Him in Christ Jesus our Lord, with Whom to the Father and also to the Holy Ghost be glory, might honour now and for ever and world without end. Amen.

HOMILY V.

HEB. ii. 16, 17.

For verily He taketh not hold of Angels, but of the seed of Abraham He taketh hold[1]. *Wherefore in all things it behoved Him to be made like unto His brethren.*

[1 marg. of E. V.]

[1.] PAUL wishing to shew the great kindness of God towards man, and the Love which He had for the human race, after saying: *Forasmuch then as the children were partakers of blood and flesh, He also Himself likewise took part of the same*—follows up the subject in this passage. For do not thou regard carelessly what is spoken, nor think this to be merely a slight [matter], His taking on Him the flesh derived from us. He granted not this favour to Angels; *For verily He taketh not hold of Angels, but of the seed of Abraham.* What is it that he saith? He took not on Him an Angel's nature but man's. But what is *He taketh hold of?* He did not (he means) grasp that other nature, that of angels, but our's. But why did he not say, 'He took on Him', but used this expression, *He taketh hold of?* It is derived from the figure of persons pursuing those who turn away from them, and doing every thing to overtake them as they flee, and to take hold of them as they are bounding away. For when human nature was fleeing from Him, and fleeing far away *(for we were far off)*, He pursued after and overtook us. He shewed that He has done this only out of kindness for man, and love, and tender solicitude. As then when he saith, *Are they not all ministering spirits, sent forth to minister for them who shall be heirs of salvation*— he shews His extreme interest in behalf of human nature,

(1)

Supra ver. 14.

Eph. ii. 13.

Supra i. 14.

and that God makes great account of it, so also in this place he sets forth the far higher degree of it by a comparison, For he saith, *He taketh not hold of angels.* For in very deed it is a great and a wonderful thing, and full of amazement that the flesh [derived] from us should sit on high, and be adored by Angels and Archangels, by the Cherubim and the Seraphim. For myself having oftentimes thought upon this, I am amazed at it, and imagine to myself great things concerning the human race. For I see that the introductions are great and splendid, and that the earnest care which God has on behalf of our nature, is large.

Moreover he said not "of men (simply) He taketh hold," but being desirous to exalt them [the Hebrews] and to shew that their race is great and honourable, he says, *but of the seed of Abraham He taketh hold.*

Wherefore it behoved [*Him*] *in all things to be made like unto His brethren.* What is this, *in all things?* He was born (he means) was brought up, grew, suffered all things which it was necessary [He should suffer], at last He died. This is, *in all things to be made like unto His brethren.* For after he had discoursed much concerning His majesty and the glory on high, he then begins to discourse concerning the dispensation. And consider with how great power [he doth this]. How he represents Him as having a very earnest desire *to be made like unto us:* which was a sign of much solicitude. For having said above, *Inasmuch then as the children were partakers of flesh and blood, He also Himself in like manner took part of the same;* in this place also he says, *in all things to be made like unto His brethren.* Which is all but saying, He that is so great, He that is *the brightness of His glory*, He that is *the express image of His person*, He that *made the worlds*, He that *sitteth on the right hand of the Father*, even He was willing and earnestly desirous to become our brother in all things, and for this cause did He leave the angels and the other powers, and come down to us, and took hold of us, and wrought innumerable good things. He destroyed Death, He cast out the devil from his tyrannical power, He freed us from slavery: not by brotherhood alone did He honour us, but also in other ways beyond number. For He was willing also to become our High Priest with the Father: for he He. ii. 18. adds,

[2.] *That He might become a merciful and faithful High Priest in things pertaining to God.* For this cause (he means) He took on Him our flesh, only for Love to man, that He might have mercy upon us. For neither is there any other cause of the economy, but this alone. He saw us, I mean, cast on the ground, perishing, tyrannized over by Death, and He had compassion on us. *To make reconciliation,* he saith, *for the sins of the people.*

That He might be a merciful and faithful High Priest. What is [the meaning of] *faithful?* True, Able. For the Son is a faithful High Priest, able to deliver from their sins those whose High Priest He is. In order then that He might offer a sacrifice which should be able to purify us, for this cause He has become man.

Accordingly he added, *in things pertaining to God,*—that is, for the sake of things in relation to God. We were become altogether enemies to God, (he would say) condemned, degraded, there was none who should offer sacrifice for us. He saw us when we were in this condition, and He had compassion on us, not appointing an High Priest for us, but Himself becoming a High Priest. In what sense He was *faithful,* he added [viz.], *to make reconciliation for the sins of the people.*

ver. 18. For, he saith, *in that He hath suffered Him-* (2) *self being tempted, He is able to succour them that are tempted.* This is altogether low and mean, and unworthy of God. *For in that He hath suffered Himself,* saith he. It is of Him who was made flesh that he is speaking in this place, and it was said for the full assurance of the hearers, and on account of their weakness. That is (he would say) He went through the very experience of the things which we have suffered; *now* He is not ignorant of our sufferings; not only does He know them as God, but as man also He has become acquainted with them, by the trial wherewith He was tried; He suffered much, He knows how to sympathize with those that suffer. And yet God is incapable of suffering: but in this place he is relating what belongs to the Incarnation, as if he had said,

Hom. 5. Even the very flesh of Christ suffered many terrible things. He knows what tribulation is; He knows what temptation is, not less than we who have suffered, for He Himself also has suffered.

(What then is this, *He is able to succour them that are tempted?* It is as if one should say, He will stretch forth His hand with great eagerness, He will be sympathizing.)

[3.] For inasmuch as they wished for something great, and to have an advantage over the [converts] from the Gentiles, he points out that they have an advantage in this respect, in doing which he was not hurting those from the Gentiles at all. In what respect now is this? Because of them is the salvation, because He took hold of them first, because from that race He assumed flesh. *For,* he saith, *He taketh not hold of angels, but of the seed of Abraham He taketh hold.* Hereby he both gives honour to the Patriarch, and shews also what *the seed of Abraham* is. He reminds them of the promise which was made to him, which saith, *To thee and to thy seed will I give this land;* shewing the nearness [of the relationship] by the very least thing, in that they were *all of one.* But that nearness was not great: [so] he comes back to this other, and thenceforward dwells upon the dispensation which was after the flesh, and says, Even the mere willing to become man was a proof of great solicitude and love; but now it is not this alone, but there are also the undying benefits which are bestowed on us through Him, for, he saith, *to make reconciliation for the sins of the people.*

Gen. xiii. 15.

Wherefore said he not, of the world, instead of *the people?* for He bare away the sins of all. Because thus far his discourse was concerning [the Hebrews] themselves. Since the Angel also said to Joseph, *Thou shalt call His name* JESUS, *for He shall save His people.* For this too ought to have taken place first, and for this purpose He came, to save them and then through them the rest, although the contrary came to pass. This also the Apostles said at the first, *To you* [*God*] *having raised up His Son, sent* [*Him*] *to bless you:* and again, *To you was the word of this Salvation sent.* Here he shews the noble birth of the Jews, in saying, *to make reconciliation for the sins of the people.* For a while

S. Matt. i. 21.

Acts iii. 26.
Ib. xiii. 26.

he speaks in this way. For that it is He Himself who forgives the sins of all men, He declared both in the case of the paralytic, saying, *Thy sins are forgiven;* and also in that of Baptism: for He saith to the disciples, *Go ye and make disciples of all the nations, baptizing them in the Name of the Father, and of the Son, and of the Holy Ghost.* Heb.iii.3. S. Mark ii. 5. S. Matt. xxviii.19.

[4.] But when Paul has once begun to treat of the flesh, he proceeds to utter all the lowly things, without any fear: for see what he says next:

Ch. iii. 1, 2. *Wherefore, holy brethren, partakers of a heavenly calling, consider the Apostle and High Priest of our confession,* Jesus Christ, *who is faithful to Him that appointed [or made] Him, as also Moses [was faithful] in all His house.*

Being about to place Him before Moses in comparison, he directed his discourse to the law of the high-priesthood; for they all had a high esteem for Moses: moreover, he is already before-hand casting down the seeds of the superiority. Well then he begins from the flesh, and goes up to the Godhead, where there was no longer any comparison. He began by assuming for a time their equality from the flesh [from His Human nature], and says, *as also Moses in all His house:* nor does he at the beginning shew His superiority lest the hearer should start away, and straightway stop his ears. For although they were believers, yet nevertheless they still had strong feeling of conscience as to Moses. *Who was faithful,* saith he, *to Him that made Him*—made [Him] what? *Apostle and High-priest.* He is not speaking at all in this place of His Essence, nor of His Godhead; but so far concerning human dignities [only].

As also Moses in all His house, that is, either among the people, or in the temple. In this place however he uses the expression *in His house,* just as one might say, concerning those in the household; even as some guardian and steward of a household, so was Moses to the people. For in that by *house* he means the people, he added, *whose house we are;* that is, we are in His creation. Then [comes] the superiority. infra ver. 6.

ver. 3. For *this man was counted worthy of greater glory than Moses,* (Again [he is speaking] of the Flesh,) inasmuch as he who constructed¹ [the house] hath more honour ¹ κατασκευάσας *than the house;* [Moses] himself also (he means) was of the house. (Moreover he did not say, For this one was a servant, but the Other a master, but he covertly intimated it.) If the people were the house and himself again was of the people, it follows that he also was of the household. For so also we are accustomed to say, such an one is of such an one's house [or household]. For here he is speaking of a house, not of the temple, for the temple was not constructed by God but by men. But He that made[e] him [is] God. Moses he means. And see how he covertly shews the superiority. *Faithful*, he says, *in all His house*, being himself also of the house, that is, of the people. The builder has more honour than the house, yet he did not say "the artificer hath more honour than his works," but *he that constructed the house, than the house.* ver. 4. *But he that constructed all things is God.* Thou seest that he is speaking not about the temple but about the whole people.

ver. 5. *And Moses indeed [was] faithful in all His house, as a servant, for a testimony of those things which were to be spoken.* Here is also another point of superiority, that [which is derived] from the Son and the servants. You see again that by the appellation of The Son, he intimates genuineness of relationship. (ver. 6.) *But Christ as a Son over His own house.* Perceivest thou how he separates the thing made and the maker, the servant and the son? Moreover He indeed enters into His Father's property as an owner, but the other as a servant.

Whose house are we [i. e.], God's [house], *if we hold fast the confidence and the glorying of the hope firm unto the end.* In this place again he encourages them to stand nobly, and not to fall: for we shall be the *house* of God (he saith), as Moses was, *if we hold fast our confidence and our glorying firm unto the end.* He however (he would say) that is distressed in his trials, and who falls, doth not glory: he that is ashamed, he that hideth himself, does not have confidence, he that is perplexed doth not glory.

And then he also commends them saying, *if we hold fast the confidence and the glorying of the hope firm unto the end,*

---

[e] ποιήσας. Referring to what is implied in ver. 2. that Moses was faithful to Him that made him.

implying that they had even made a beginning; but that Heb.iii.5. there is need of the end; and [it is necessary for them] not simply to stand, but to have their hope firm *in full assurance of faith*, without being shaken from their position by their trials.

[5.] And be not thou astonished, that the [words] *Himself being tempted* are spoken more after the manner of men. For if of the Father, who was not made flesh, the Scripture saith, *The Lord looked down from heaven, and beheld all the sons of men*, that is, accurately acquainted Himself with all things; and again, *I will go down, and see whether they do altogether according to the cry of them*; and again, *God cannot endure the evil ways of men*, [saith] the divine Scripture, shewing forth the greatness of His wrath: much more of Christ, who even suffered in the flesh, are these things said. For inasmuch as many men consider experience more to be relied on than any thing else for [the attainment of] knowledge, he wishes to point out that He that has suffered knows what human nature suffers.

Whence[1] *holy brethren* (he saith *whence* instead of "for this cause"), *partakers of an heavenly calling*—(seek nothing here, if ye have been called yonder—yonder is the reward, yonder the recompence. What then?) *Consider the Apostle and High Priest of our confession, Christ Jesus, who was faithful to Him that made Him, as also Moses* [was faithful] *in all His house.* (What is *who was faithful to Him that made Him?* it is, well disposed towards Him, protecting what belongs to Him, not allowing them to be lightly carried away, *as also Moses in all His house*) that is, know who your High Priest is, and how great He is, and ye will need no other consolation nor encouragement. Now he calls Him *Apostle,* on account of His having been *sent,* and *high priest of our confession,* that is of the Faith. This One also was entrusted with a people, as the other with the command and guardianship of a people, but a greater one, and upon higher grounds.

For a testimony of those things which shall be spoken. What meanest thou? Doth God receive the witness of man? Yes, certainly. For if He call to witness heaven and earth and hills (saying by the prophet, *Hear, O heaven, and* Is. i. 2.

supra ii. 18.

Ps. xiv. 2.

Gen. xviii. 21. Ib. vi. 5 (?)

[1] ὅθεν

give ear, O earth, for the Lord hath spoken, and *Hear ye ravines ᶠ, foundations of the earth, for the Lord hath a controversy with His people)* much more men; that is, that they may be witnesses, when [these] themselves [the Jews] are shameless.

ver. 6. *But Christ as a Son.* The one takes care of the property of another, but this One of His own. *And the glorying of the hope.* Well said he *of the hope.* For since the good things were all in hope, and yet we ought so *to hold it fast,* as even now to glory as for things which had already come to pass: for this cause he says, *the glorying of the hope.*

And adds, *hold it, firm unto the end.* For *by hope we have been saved;* if therefore *we have been saved by hope, and are waiting with patience,* let us not be grieved at the things that are present, nor seek already those that have been promised afterwards; *For* (saith he) *hope which is seen is not hope.* For since the good things are great, we cannot receive them here in this transitory life. With what object then did He even tell us of them beforehand, when He was not about to give them here? In order that by the promise He might refresh our souls, that by the engagement He might strengthen our zeal, that He might anoint [preparing us for our contests] and stir up our mind. For this cause then all these things were done.

(4) [6.] Let us not then be disturbed, let no man be disturbed, when he seeth the wicked prospering. The recompence is not here, either of wickedness or of virtue; and if in any instance there be [here a recompence] of wickedness or of virtue, yet is it not according to desert, but merely as it were a taste of the judgment, that they who believe not the resurrection may yet even by things that happen here be brought to their senses. When then we see a wicked man abounding in wealth, let us not be cast down; when we see a good man in affliction, let us not be troubled. For yonder are the crowns, yonder the punishments.

ᶠ S. Chrys. had mentioned hills (βουνοί) as called to witness by God: in the verse preceding this (Micah vi. 1) occur the words, "let *the hills* hear Thy voice"; and this verse itself runs "Hear ye hills" (βουνοί) according to the Alexandrine MSS. of the LXX. or "ye mountains" (ὄρη according to the Vatican) "the judgment of the Lord, and ye ravines," &c.

Yea and in another point of view, it is not possible either that a bad man should be altogether bad, but he may have some good things also: nor again that a good man should be altogether good, but he may also have some sins. When therefore the wicked man prospers, know thou that it is for evil on his own head. For, for this cause does he receive his recompence in this life, that having here received the reward of those few good things, he may hereafter be entirely punished yonder. And happy is he most of all who is punished here, that having put away all his sins, he may depart approved, and pure, and without having to be called to account. And this is what Paul teacheth us when he says, *For this cause many [are] weak and sickly among you, and a good many sleep.* And again, *I have delivered such an one to Satan.* And the prophet saith, *for she hath received of the Lord's hand her sins double;* and again David, *Behold mine enemies that they are multiplied above the hairs of my head*[g]*, and [with] an unjust hatred have they hated me: and forgive Thou all my sins.* And again another: *O Lord, our God, give peace unto us; for Thou hast rendered all things to us again.* Heb.iii.6.
1 Cor. xi. 30.
Ib. v. 5.
Is. xl. 2.
Ps. xxv. 19.
Ib. 18.
Is. xxvi. 12.

These however are [the words] of one shewing that good men receive here the punishments due for their sins. But where are the wicked [mentioned] who receive their good things here, and there are utterly punished? Hear Abraham saying to the rich man, *Thou didst receive good things,* and *Lazarus evil things.* What sort of good things? For in this place by saying *thou receivedst*[1], and not thou "hadst given[2]," he shews that it was according to what was due to him that each was treated, and that the one was in prosperity, and the other in adversity. And he saith, *Therefore he is comforted* here (for thou seest him pure from sins) *and thou art tormented.* Let us not then be perplexed when we see sinners well off here; but when we ourselves are afflicted, let us rejoice. For this very thing is paying off the penalty[3] of sins. S. Luke xvi. 25.
[1] ἀπέλαβες
[2] ἔλαβες
[3] ἔκτισις

[7.] Let us not then seek relaxation: for Christ promised tribulation to His own disciples: and Paul saith, *All who* 2 Tim. iii. 12.

---

[g] The words "above the hairs of my head" are part of another Psalm, xl. 12, or lxix. 4.

will live godly in Christ Jesus, shall suffer persecution. No noble-spirited wrestler, when in the lists [1], seeks for baths, and a table full of victuals and wine. This is not the conduct of a wrestler but of an effeminate sluggard. For the wrestler contendeth with dust, with oil, with the heat of the sun's ray, with much sweat, with pressure and constraint. This is the season for the contest and for fighting, therefore also for being wounded, and for being made bloody, and for being in pain. Hear what the blessed Paul saith, *So fight I, not as one that beateth the air.* Let us consider that our whole life is engaged in combats, and then we shall at no time seek rest, at no time shall we feel it strange when we are afflicted: no more than a boxer feels it strange, when he is engaged in combat. Another season is the season for repose. It is by tribulation we must be made perfect.

And even if there is not any persecution, nor tribulation, yet are there other afflictions which befal us every day. And if we do not endure these, we should scarcely endure those [other]. *There hath no temptation taken you*, it is said, *but such as is common to man.* Let us then pray indeed to God that we may not come into temptation; but if we have come into it, let us bear it nobly. For that indeed is the part of prudent men, not to throw themselves upon dangers, but this latter of men of noble spirit and true philosophers. Let us not then lightly cast ourselves upon [dangers], for that is rashness; nor yet if led into them, and called by circumstances, let us give in, for that is cowardice. But if indeed the Gospel [2] call us, let us not decline the trial; but in a simple case, when there is no reason, nor need, nor necessity which calls us in connection with religion, let us not run to [trials]. For this is mere display, and useless ambitiousness. But should any of those things which are injurious to religion occur, then even if it be necessary to endure ten thousand deaths, let us in no respect decline the trial. Challenge not trials, when thou findest the things that concern religion succeed as thou desirest. Why drawest thou needless dangers upon thyself which bring no advantage?

These things I say, because I wish you to observe the

Hom. 5.
[1] σκάμματα

1 Cor. ix. 26.

Ib. x. 13.

What courage

What rashness

what cowardice
[2] κήρυγμα

what display

laws of Christ who commands us to *pray that we enter not into temptation*, and commands us to *take up the cross and follow Him*. For these things are not opposed to one another, nay on the contrary they are exceedingly in harmony. Do thou be so prepared as is a valiant soldier, be continually in thine armour, sober, watchful, ever expecting the enemy: do not however breed wars, for this is not [the act] of a soldier but of a mover of sedition. But if on the other hand the trumpet of religion call thee, go forth immediately, and make no account of thy life, and enter with great zeal into the contests, break thou the phalanx of the adversaries, bruise the face of the Devil, set up thy trophy. If however religion be in no wise suffering, and no one laying waste our doctrines (those I mean which relate to the soul), nor compel us to do anything displeasing to God, do not thou interfere needlessly. Heb.iii.6. S. Matt. xxvi. 41. Ib. xvi. 24.

The life of the Christian must be full of bloodsheddings; I say not in shedding that of others, but in being prepared to shed his own. Let us then pour out our own blood, when it is done for the sake of Christ, with as great readiness of mind, as one would pour out water (for the blood which circulates around the body is water), and let us put off our flesh with as much good temper, as one even would a garment. And this shall we do, if we be not bound to riches, if not to houses, if not to affections, if we be detached from all things. For if they who live this life of [earthly] soldiers bid farewell to all things, and whithersoever war calls them there present themselves, and make journeys, and endure all things with ready mind; much more ought we, the soldiers of Christ, so to have prepared ourselves, and to set ourselves firm against the war of the passions.

[8.] There is no persecution now, and God grant that one may never arise: nevertheless another war there is, that of the desire of money, of envy, of the passions. Paul describing this war, saith, *We wrestle not against flesh and blood*. This war is ever at hand. For this cause he wishes us to stand ever armed. For in that he does wish us to stand ever armed, he says, *Stand, having girded yourselves about*. Which itself also belongs to the time present, and expresses that we ought ever to be armed. For great is the Eph. vi. 12. Ib. 14.

war through the tongue, great that through the eyes; this then we must keep down—great [too] is that of the lusts.

For this cause he begins at that point to arm the soldier of Christ: for *stand*, saith he, *having your loins girt about*, and he added *with truth*. Why *with truth?* Because lust is a mockery and a lie: wherefore the prophet saith, *My loins are filled with mockings*. The thing is not pleasure, but a shadow of pleasure. *Having your loins*, saith he, *girt about with truth;* that is, with true pleasure, with temperance, with orderly behaviour. For this cause he gives this advice, knowing the unreasonableness of sin, and wishing that all our members should be hedged round; for *unjust anger*, it is said, *shall not be guiltless*.

Moreover he wishes us to have around us a breastplate and a buckler. For wrath is a wild beast which easily springs forth, and we shall have need of walls and fences innumerable, to overcome, and to restrain it. And for this cause God has built this part [of our body] with bones, as with a kind of stones, more than any other part, placing them as a support around it, so that wrath might not at any time, having broken or cut through, easily injure the whole man. For it is a fire (it is said) and a great tempest, and no other part of the body could endure this violence. And the sons of the physicians too say that for this cause the lungs have been spread under the heart, so that the heart being itself [put] into something soft and tender, by beating as it were into a sort of sponge, may continually be rested, and not [by striking] against what is resisting and hard, [I mean] the sternum, receive hurt through the violence of its beatings. We have need therefore of a strong breastplate, so as to keep this wild beast alway quiet.

We have need also of an helmet; for since the reasoning faculty is there, and from this it is possible for us either to be saved, when what is right is done, or it is possible for us to be ruined—for this cause he says, *the helmet of salvation*. For the brain is indeed by nature soft and tender; and for this cause it is itself also covered above with the scull, as with a kind of shell. And it is to us the cause of all things both good and evil, according as it determine what is fitting, or what is not so. Yea and our feet too and our hands need armour, not these hands, nor these feet, but as before those of the soul—the former by being employed about what is right, the latter, that they may walk where it behoves [them]. Thus then let us thoroughly arm ourselves, and we shall be able to overcome our enemies, and to wreathe ourselves with the crown in Christ Jesus our Lord, with whom to the Father and also to the Holy Ghost be glory, might, honour, now and for ever and world without end. Amen.

Heb.iii.6.

HOMILY VI.

Heb. iii. 7—11.

Wherefore, as the Holy Ghost saith, To-day if ye will hear His voice, harden not your hearts, as in the provocation in the day of temptation in the wilderness, when your fathers tempted Me, proved Me, and saw My works forty years. Wherefore I was grieved with that generation, and said, They do alway err in their heart, and they have not known My ways. So¹ I sware in My wrath, If they shall enter into My rest.

[1.] PAUL, having treated of hope, and having said that *We are His house, if we hold fast the confidence and the rejoicing of the hope firm unto the end;* next shews that we ought to look forward with firmness, and this he proves from the Scriptures. But do you be attentive, because he has expressed this in a manner somewhat difficult and not readily to be comprehended. And therefore we must first make our own statements, and after we have briefly made you acquainted with the whole argument, then direct our discourse to the actual words of the Epistle. For you will no longer have need of us, if you have once understood the scope of the Apostle.

His discourse was concerning Hope, and that it behoves us to hope for the things to come, and that for those who have toiled and suffered here there will assuredly be some reward and fruit and refreshment. This then he shews from the prophet; and what saith he? *Wherefore as the Holy Ghost saith, To-day if ye will hear His voice, harden not your hearts, as in the provocation, in the day of temp-*

¹ as

(1) supra ver. 6.

tation in the wilderness: *when your fathers tempted Me,* Heb.iii.7. *proved Me, and saw My works forty years. Wherefore I was grieved with that generation, and said, they do alway err in their heart, and they have not known My ways. So*[1] *I sware in My wrath, If they shall enter into My rest.*

[1] as

He says that they are *three* rests: one, that of the Sabbath, in which God rested from His works; the second, that of Palestine, into which when the Jews had entered they would be at rest from that their great affliction and labours; the third, that which is Rest indeed, the kingdom of Heaven; which those who obtain, do indeed rest from their labours and troubles. Of these three then he makes mention in this place.

And with what object did he mention the three, when he is treating of the one only? That he might shew that the prophet is speaking concerning this one. For he was not speaking (saith he) concerning the first. For how could he be speaking of what had taken place long before? Nor yet again concerning the second, that in Palestine. For how could he? for he says, *They shall not enter into My rest.* It remains therefore that it be this third.

[2.] But it is necessary also to lay before you the history, to make the argument more clear. For when after they had come forth out of Egypt, and had accomplished a long journey, and had received proofs innumerable of the power of God, both in Egypt, and in the Red Sea, and in the wilderness, they determined to send spies thoroughly to search out the nature of the land; and these went and returned back, admiring indeed the country, and saying that it abounded in excellent fruits, yet that nevertheless it was a country of strong and invincible men: and the ungrateful and senseless Jews, when they ought to have called to mind the former mercies of God, and how when they were hemmed in in the midst of so many Egyptian armies, He rescued them from their perils, and made them masters of their enemies' spoils; and in the wilderness clave the rock, and bestowed on them that abundance of waters, and gave them the manna, and the other wonderful things which He had wrought; [when they ought, I say, to have remembered this,] and to have trusted in God, they considered none of

cf. Acts vii. 36.

these things, but being struck with terror, just as if nothing had taken place, they said, we wish to go back again into Egypt, *for God hath brought us out hither* (it is said) *to slay us, with our children and wives.* God therefore being angry that they had so quickly cast off the memory of all that had been done, sware that that generation, which had said these things, should not enter into the Rest; and they all perished in the wilderness. When David then (he means) speaking at a later period, and after these events, after that generation of men, said, *To-day, if ye will hear His voice, harden not your hearts,* that ye may not suffer the same things which your forefathers did, and be deprived of the Rest; he evidently [said this] on the supposition of there being some [future] rest. For if they had received their Rest (he says) why does He again say to them, *To-day if ye will hear His voice harden not your hearts,* as your fathers did? What other rest then is there, except the kingdom of Heaven, of which the Sabbath was an image and type?

[3.] Next having set down the whole testimony (and this is, *To-day if ye will hear His voice, harden not your hearts, as in the provocation in the day of temptation in the wilderness, when your fathers tempted Me, proved Me, and saw My works forty years. Wherefore I was grieved with that generation, and said, They do alway err in their heart, and they have not known My ways. So I sware in My wrath, If they shall enter into My rest,* he then adds:

ver. 12. *Take heed, brethren, lest there be in any of you an evil heart of unbelief in departing from the Living God.* For from hardness unbelief ariseth: and as in bodies, the parts that have become callous and hard do not yield to the hands of the physicians, so also souls that are hardened yield not to the word of God. For it is probable besides that some even disbelieved as though the things which had been done were not true.

On this account he says, *Take heed lest there be in any of you an evil heart of unbelief in departing from the Living God.* For since the argument from things future is not so persuasive as that from the past, he reminds them of the history, in which they had wanted faith. For if your fathers (saith he) because they did not hope as they ought to have hoped, suffered these things, much more will you [suffer]. HE.iii.15. Since to themselves also is this word addressed: for, *To-day* (saith he) is "ever," so long as the world lasts.

[4.] ver. 13. *Wherefore exhort ye one another daily, while it is called to-day.* That is, edify one another, raise yourselves up: lest the same things should befal you. *Lest any one of you be hardened by the deceitfulness of sin.* Seest thou that sin produces unbelief? for just as unbelief is the parent of an evil life, so also a soul, *when it is come into a depth of evils, becometh contemptuous*[1], and having become contemptuous it endures not even to believe, in order thereby to free itself from fear. For *they said* (saith one), *The Lord shall not see, neither shall the God of Jacob consider.* 'And again, *Our lips are our own who is Lord over us?* and again, *Wherefore hath the wicked man provoked God to wrath?* and again, *The fool hath said in his heart, there is no God; they are corrupt and become abominable in their doings. There is no fear of God before his eyes, for he was deceitful before Him, to find out*[2] *his iniquity and to hate.* Yea and Christ also says this very same thing, *Every one that doeth evil, hateth the light and cometh not to the light.*

(2)
Prov. xviii. 3.
[1] καταφρονεῖ
Ps. xciv. 7.
Ib. xii. 4.
Ib. x. 13.
Ib. xiv. 1.
Ib. xxxvi. 1, 2.
[2] τοῦ εὑρεῖν
S. John iii. 20.

Then he adds, (ver. 14) *For we have been made partakers of Christ.* What is this, *We have been made partakers of Christ?* We share in Him (he means); we were made One, we and He—since He is the Head and we the body, *fellow-heirs and of the same body; we are one body, of His flesh and of His bones.*

Eph. iii. 6.
Rom. xii. 5.
Eph. v. 30.

If we hold fast the beginning of our confidence [or, the principle of our subsistence[a]] *stedfast unto the end.* What is *the principle of our subsistence?* The faith by which we were made to subsist, and have been brought into being and were made substantial, as one may say.

[5.] Then he adds, (ver. 15) *When it is said*[3], *To-day if ye hear His voice, harden not your hearts, as in the provocation.* This is a transposition[4], *when it is said To-day if ye hear His voice, harden not your hearts.* [It must be read thus:]

[3] ἐν τῷ λέγεσθαι in its being said
[4] καθ' ὑπερβα-τον

(Ch. iv. 1, 2.) *Let us fear lest a promise being left us of*

---

[a] ἀρχὴν τῆς ὑποστάσεως. S. Chrys. understands ὑπόστασις in its prior sense, as "subsistence," "subsisting," "being brought into real existence."

entering into His rest, any of you should seem to come short of it; for to us hath the Gospel been preached[b] *as well as unto them, when it is said, To-day if ye hear His voice* (for *To-day* is "at every time [1]".)

Then [he adds] *but the word of hearing did not profit them, as they were not mixed*[c] *by faith with them that heard.* How was it that it did not profit [them]? Then wishing to alarm them, he shews this very thing by what he says:

(ch. iii. 16—19) *For some when they had heard did provoke, howbeit not all that came out of Egypt by Moses: And with whom was He grieved forty years? Was it not with them that had sinned, whose carcases fell in the wilderness? And to whom sware He that they should not enter into His rest, but to them that believed not? So* [2] *we see, that they could not enter in because of unbelief.* After again repeating the testimony, he subjoins also the question, by doing which he makes the argument clear. For he said (he repeats), *To-day if ye hear His voice, harden not your hearts, as in the provocation.* Of whom does he speak (saith he) [as] having been hardened? of whom [as] not believing? is it not of the Jews?

Now what he says is to this effect. They also heard, just as we hear: but no benefit resulted to them. Do not suppose then that by *hearing* what is proclaimed [in the Gospel] ye will be profited; seeing that they also heard, but derived no benefit because they did not believe.

Caleb then and Joshua, inasmuch as they agreed not with those who did not believe, escaped the vengeance that was sent forth against them. And see how admirably he said, not They did not agree, but, *they were not mixed*— that is, they stood apart, without creating any factious divisions when all the other had one and the same mind. In this place it seems to me that a faction too is hinted at[d].

[1] δεί

[2] And

---

[b] That is, these words are addressed to us as well as to them.

[c] συγκεκραμένους. Sav. and Ben. have συγκεκραμένης (i.e. ἀκοῆς). The received text of the New Testament has συγκεκραμένος, "the word not being mixed." Lachmann [& Tisch.] read συγκεκερασμένους, which is the reading of some MSS. of S. Chrys.

[d] αἰνίττεσθαι. That is, is indirectly condemned, by the contrast of the conduct of Caleb and Joshua. S. Chrys. reverses the expression of the Epistle, and says, "Caleb and Joshua were not mixed with the unbelievers," when the Apostle had said, "the unbelievers were not mixed with them."

[6.] (ch. iv. 3) For *we who have believed,* saith he, *shall* HEB.iv.9. *enter into rest.* He subjoined that from which this becomes evident, *as He said, as I sware in My wrath, if they shall enter into My rest: although the works were finished from the foundation of the world.* This however tends to shew not that we shall enter in, but that they did not enter in. What then? Up to this point he is labouring to shew that just as that [first] rest does not hinder another rest from being spoken of, so neither does this [second exclude] that of Heaven. Up to this point he wishes to point out that they [the Israelites] did not attain to the rest. For because this is what he means he says, (ver. 4, 5) *For he spake in a certain place concerning the seventh day on this wise, And God rested on the seventh day from all His works. And in this place again, If they shall enter into My rest.* Thou seest how that first rest doth not hinder this other rest also from being?

ver. 6, 7. *Seeing then it remaineth* (saith he) *that some must enter therein, and they to whom it was first preached entered not in because of unbelief: again he limiteth a certain day, saying in David, To day, after so long a time; as it has been said before*[e]. But what is it that he means? *Seeing then* (he would say) that *some must* certainly *enter in,* and *they did not enter in.* And that it behoves that [men] *enter in,* and that *some must enter in,* let us hear from what this is clear. Because after so many years (he saith) David again saith: *To-day if ye will hear His voice, harden not your hearts,* (ver. 8) *For if Joshua had given them Rest he would not have spoken of another day after that.* It is evident, that he says these things, on the view that some persons are to attain some recompence.

[7.] ver. 9. *There remaineth therefore a Sabbath Rest*[1] *for the people of God.* Whence [does this appear]? from his giving the exhortation, *Harden not your hearts:* for if there were no Sabbath Rest, these exhortations would not have been given. Neither would they have been exhorted not to do the same things [with the Jews] lest they should suffer the same things, unless they were about to suffer the

[1] σαββατισμὸς

---

[e] προείρηται. This is the correct reading of the sacred text Heb. iv. 7: for which the common editions have εἴρηται "it is said."

same. But how were they who were in possession of Palestine about to suffer the same things [i.e. exclusion from the Rest] unless there were some other Rest?

(3) And well did he conclude the argument. For he said not Rest but *Sabbath-keeping;* calling the kingdom *Sabbath-keeping,* by the appropriate name, and that which they rejoiced in and were attracted by. For just as, on the Sabbath He commands that men abstain from all evil things; and that those things which relate to the Service of God alone should be done, which things the Priests were wont to accomplish, and whatever things are profitable to the soul, and nothing else; so also [will it be] then. However he did not say thus himself, but what [said he]? ver. 10. *For he that hath entered into his rest, he also hath ceased from his own works, as God [did] from His.* As God (saith he) ceased from His works, so he that hath entered into His rest [hath ceased]. For since his discourse to them was concerning rest, and they were desirous to hear when this would be, he concluded the argument with this.

[8.] And [he said] *To-day*[f], that they might never at any time be without hope. *Exhort one another daily,* he saith, [*while it is called to-day,*] that is, even if a man have sinned, as long as it is *To-day,* he has hopes: let no man then despair so long as he lives. Above all things indeed, he says, *let there not* ever *be* [such a thing as] *an evil heart of unbelief.* But even suppose there should be, let no man despair, but let him recover himself; for as long as we are in this world, the *To-day* hath [its] season. But in this place he means not unbelief only but also murmurings: *whose carcases,* he says, *fell in the wilderness*[g].

Then that none may suppose that they will simply be deprived of rest only, he adds the mention of punishment also, saying (ch. iv. 12) *For the Word of God is living, and powerful; and sharper than any two-edged sword, and pierceth even to the dividing asunder of soul and spirit, and of the joints and marrow: and is a discerner of the thoughts and intents of the heart.* Here he is speaking of Hell and

---

[f] S. Chrys. returns here to ch. iii. 13 connecting the *To-day if ye hear His voice harden not your heart,* with *Exhort one another daily while it is called To-day:* as he had said "to-day is at every time."

[g] The words of the Apostle ch. iii. 17. are those of Numb. xiv. 29 &c. where murmuring is the sin specified.

of the punishment [in store for the wicked]. *It pierceth* (he saith) *into the secrets of our heart, and cutteth asunder the soul.* Here it is not the falling of carcases nor, as in the former case, the being deprived of a country, but of a heavenly kingdom; and being delivered to an everlasting hell, and to undying punishment and vengeance. He.iii.14.

(ch. iii. 13) *But exhort*[h] *one another.* Observe the gentleness and mildness [of the expression]: he said not 'Rebuke', but *Exhort.* Thus ought we to bear ourselves towards those who are distressed by tribulation. This he says also in writing to the Thessalonians, *Warn them that are unruly,* but in speaking of the feeble-minded, not so, but what? *Comfort the feeble-minded, support the weak, be patient toward all men;* that is, Do not cease to hope; do not despair. 'For he that does not encourage one who is straitened by affliction, makes him more hardened. 1 Thess. v. 14.

[9.] *Lest any of you,* he saith, *be hardened by the deceitfulness of sin.* He means either the deceit of the devil (for it is indeed a deceit, not to look for the things to come, to think that what we are and what we do will not be brought to account, and that we shall not suffer punishment for the things which we have done here, nay, that there will not ever be a resurrection), or in another sense insensibility [or] despairing is a deceit. For to say, What is there left [for me]? I have sinned once for all, I have no hope of recovering myself, is a deceit.

Then he suggests hopes to them, saying, (ver. 14) *We have been made partakers of Christ;* All but saying, He that so loved us, He that counted us worthy of so great things, as to make us His Body, will not suffer us to perish in neglect. Let us consider (he says) of what we have been thought worthy: we and Christ are One: let us not then distrust Him. And again, he hints at that which had been said in another place, that *If we suffer, we shall also reign with Him.* For this is [implied in] *We are made partakers,* we partake of the same things whereof Christ also partakes. 2 Tim. ii. 12.

He encouraged them from the good things; *for we are,* saith he, *partakers of Christ.* Then, again, from gloomy

---

[h] παρακαλεῖτε. The word includes the idea of comforting and encouraging as well as of exhorting.

ones (ch. iv. 1) *Let us fear, lest at any time a promise being left us of entering into His Rest, any of you should seem to come short of it.* For that is manifest and confessed.

(ch. iii. 9) *They proved Me,* saith He, *and saw My works forty years.* Thou seest that it is not right to call God to account, but whether He defend [our cause] or not, to trust Him? For against those [of old] he now brings this charge, that *they tempted God.* For he that will have absolute proof either of His power, or of His providence, or of His tender care, does not yet believe, that He is either powerful or kind to man. This he insinuates in writing to these [Hebrews] also, who probably wished, even already, in their trials, to obtain the experimental proof and positive evidence of His power and His providential care for them. Thou seest that in all cases the provocation and the angering arises from unbelief.

What then saith he? (ch. iv. 9) *There remaineth therefore a Sabbath-Rest for the people of God.* And see how he has summed up the whole argument. *He sware,* saith he, to those former ones, *that they should not enter into* the *Rest,* and they did not enter in. Then long after their time discoursing to the Jews, he saith, *Harden not your hearts,* as your fathers [did], shewing that there is another Rest. For of Palestine we have not to speak: for they were already in possession of it. Nor can he be speaking of the seventh [day]; for surely he was not discoursing about that which had taken place long before. It follows therefore that he hints at some other, that which is Rest indeed.

(4) [10.] For that is indeed Rest, where *pain, sorrow and sighing are fled away:* where there are neither cares, nor labours, nor agony, nor fear stunning and shaking the soul; but only that fear of God which is full of delight. There there is not, *In the sweat of thy face thou shalt eat thy bread,* nor any *thorns and thistles,* no longer, *In sorrow thou shalt bring forth children, and to thy husband shall be thy desire and he shall rule over thee.* All is peace, joy, gladness, pleasure, goodness, meekness. There is not there jealousy, nor envy, no sickness, nor this death of the body, nor that other of the soul. There is no darkness nor night; all [is] day, all light, all things are bright. It is not

possible to be weary, it is not possible to be satiated: ever HEB.iv.9. shall we continue with a desire of good things [1].

Would you that I should also give you some image of [our] condition there? It is impossible. But yet, so far as it is possible, I will try to give you some image of it. Let us look up into the heaven, when without any intervening cloud it shews forth its crown [of stars]. Then when we have dwelt long on the beauty of its appearance, let us think that we too shall have a pavement, not indeed such [as this], but as much more beautiful as is a roof of gold than those of clay, and [let us think] on that which is beyond it again, the higher roof; then on the Angels, the Archangels, the infinite multitude of unbodied powers, the very palace of God itself, the Throne of the Father.

But language is too weak (as I said) to set forth the whole. Experience is necessary, and the knowledge which [cometh] by experience. Tell me, how was it (think you) with Adam in Paradise? This [heavenly] life is far better than that, as much as heaven [is better] than earth.

[11.] But however let us search after another image still. If it so happened that he who now reigns was master of the whole world, and yet was troubled neither by wars nor by cares, but was honoured only and lived delicately; and had large tributes, and on every side gold flowed in to him, and he was looked up to, what feelings do you think he would have, if he saw that all the wars in all parts of the world had ceased? Some thing such as this will it be. But rather I have not even yet arrived at that image [which I seek]; therefore I must search after another too.

Imagine then, I pray you; for just as some royal child, so long as he is in the womb, has no sense of any thing, but should it happen that he suddenly came forth from thence, and ascended the royal throne, [and] not gradually, but all at once received possession of all things. So is it as regards this [present] and that [future] state. Or, if some captive, having suffered evils innumerable, should be caught up at once to the royal throne.

But not even thus have I attained to the image exactly. For here indeed whatever good things a person may obtain

---

[1] [The insatiate yet satisfied;
The full yet craving still.
Rhythm of Bernard de Morlaix, translated by Dr. Neale, p. 15.]

HOM. 6. even shouldst thou say the empire itself, during the first day indeed his desires are in full vigour, and for the second too, and the third, but as time goes on, he continues indeed to have pleasure, but not so great. For of whatever kind [the pleasure] be, it always ceases from our being accustomed to it. But yonder not only is it not diminished, but it even increases. For imagine how great a thing it is, that a soul after departing thither, should never any more look for an end of those good things, no, nor yet change, but increase, and life that has no end, and life set free from all danger, and from all despondency and anxiety, full of cheerfulness and blessings innumerable.

For if when we go out into a plain, and there see the soldiers' tents fixed with curtains, and the spears, and helmets, and bosses of [their] bucklers glittering, we are raised above the earth in wonder and admiration; but if we also chance to see the Emperor himself running in the midst or even riding with golden armour, we think we have every thing; what thinkest thou that [it will be] when thou seest the everlasting tabernacles of the saints pitched in heaven?

S. Luke xvi. 9. (for he saith, *They shall receive you into their everlasting tabernacles*) when thou seest each one of them beaming with light above the rays of the sun, not from brass and steel, but from that glory the gleamings of which the eye of man cannot behold? And this indeed with respect to the human beings [that are there]. But what, if one were to speak of the thousands of Angels, of Archangels, of Cherubim, of Seraphim, of thrones, of dominions, of principalities, of powers, whose beauty is inimitable, passing beyond all understanding?

But [I pause]; for to what point shall I go without checking myself in pursuing what cannot be overtaken? *For*

1 Cor. ii. 9. *neither hath eye seen*, he saith, *nor ear heard, neither hath entered into the heart of man, the things which God hath prepared for them that love Him.* Therefore nothing is more pitiable than those who miss, nor anything more blessed than those who attain. Let us then be [of the number] of the blessed, that we may attain to the everlasting good things that are in Christ Jesus our Lord with whom to the Father and also the Holy Ghost be glory might honour now and for ever and world without end. Amen.

HOMILY VII.

Heb. iv. 11—13.

Let us labour therefore to enter into that Rest, lest any man fall after the same example of unbelief. For the word of God is quick [i. e. *living*] *and powerful, and sharper than any two-edged sword, and pierceth even to the dividing asunder of soul and spirit, and of the joints and marrow, and is a discerner of the thoughts and intents of the heart, neither is there any creature that is not manifest in His sight, for all things are naked and opened unto the eyes of Him with Whom we have to do.*

[1.] FAITH is indeed a great thing and bringeth salvation, and without it, it is not possible to be saved at any time. It is not however of itself sufficient to accomplish this, but there is need of a right conversation also. Wherefore for this cause Paul also exhorts those who had already been counted worthy of the mysteries; saying, *Let us labour to enter into that Rest.* *Let us labour* (saith he) on the view that Faith is not sufficient, but that the life also ought to be added thereto, and that our earnestness be great; for there is need indeed of much earnestness too in order to go up into Heaven. For if they who had suffered so great distress in the Wilderness, were not counted worthy of [the promised] land, and were not able to attain [that] land, inasmuch as they murmured and inasmuch as they committed fornication: how shall we be counted worthy of Heaven, if we live neglectfully and indolently? We then have need of much earnestness.

And observe, the punishment does not extend to this only, the not entering in (for he said not, *Let us labour*

(1)

to enter into the *Rest*, lest we fail of [attaining] so great blessings) but what most of all arouses men, this he added. Of what kind then is this? *Lest any man fall, after the same example of unbelief.* What means this? It means that we should have our mind, our hope, our expectation, yonder, that we fail not in like manner [as they did]. For that [otherwise] we shall fail, the example shews, *lest* [&c.] *after the same*, saith he.

[2.] In the next place, lest when thou hearest [the words] *after the same* [*example*], thou shouldest think that the punishment is the same, hear what he adds; *For the Word of God is living and powerful, and sharper than any two-edged sword, and pierceth even to the dividing asunder of soul and spirit, and of the joints and marrow, and is a discerner of the thoughts and intents of the heart.* In these words he shews that He Himself, the WORD of God, wrought those former things also, and lives and has not been quenched.

Do not then when thou hearest of the WORD, think of it lightly. For *He is sharper*, saith he, *than a sword.* Observe His condescension; and hence consider why the prophets also needed to speak of brand[1] and bow and sword[2]. *If ye turn not*, saith one, *He will whet His sword, He hath bent His bow and made it ready.* For if now, after so long a time, and after their being perfected [a], He cannot smite [men] down by the name of the WORD alone, but needs these expressions in order to shew the superiority [arising] from the comparison [of the Gospel with the law]: much more then [of old].

Piercing, saith he, *even to the dividing asunder of soul and spirit.* What is this? He hinted at something more fearful. Either that He divides the spirit from the soul, or that He pierces even through incorporeal [substances], not as a sword, only through bodies. Here he shews, that the soul also is punished, and that the most inward things are thoroughly searched out.

[He is *a sword*] piercing wholly through the whole man. *And is a discerner of the thoughts and intents of the heart, neither is there any creature that is not manifest in His sight.* In these words did he most of all terrify them. For

[1] μάχαιραν
[2] ῥομφαίαν
Ps. vii. 12.

[a] μετὰ τελείωσιν, *i.e.* by Baptism.

do not (saith he) be confident if ye still stand fast in the Faith, but yet without full assurance. He judges the inner heart, for there He passes through, both in punishing and in searching out. ^{He.iv.13.}

And why speak I of men? saith he. For even if thou speak of Angels, of Archangels, of the Cherubim, of the Seraphim, even of any *creature* whatsoever: all things are laid open to that Eye, all things are clear and manifest; there is nothing which is able to escape it; *All things are naked and opened unto the eyes of Him, with whom we have to do.*

But what is *opened*[1]? [It is] a metaphor from the skins which are drawn off from the victims. For just as in that case, when a man has killed them, and has drawn aside the skin from the flesh, he lays open all the inward parts, and makes them manifest to our eyes; so also do all things lie open before God. And observe, I pray thee, how he constantly needs corporeal images; which arose from the weakness of the hearers. For that they were weak, he shewed evidently, when he said that they were *dull*, and *had need of milk, not of strong meat. All things are naked*, saith he, *and laid open before the eyes of Him, with whom we have to do.* [1] τετρα-χηλισμέ-να

Infra v. 11, 12.

[3.] But what is, *after the same example of unbelief?* As if one should say, why did they of old not see the land? They had received an earnest of the power of God; [and] when they ought to have believed, [then] from yielding too much to fear, and entertaining no great ideas concerning God, and being faint-hearted, they perished. Yea and somewhat else also may be said, as, that after they had accomplished the most part of the journey, when they were arrived at the very doors, at the haven itself, were they sunk into the sea. This I fear (he saith) in regard to you also. This is [the meaning of] *after the same example of unbelief.*

For that these also [to whom he is writing] had suffered much, he afterwards testifies, saying, *Call to mind the former days, in which after that ye had been enlightened, ye endured a great fight of afflictions.* Let no man then be faint-hearted, nor [when he is] near the end fall down ^{Ib. x. 32.}

through weariness. For there are, there are [indeed] those who at the beginning engage in the fight with the full vigour of zeal; but a little after, not being willing to add to all [they have done], they lose all. Your forefathers (he saith) are sufficient to instruct you not to be entangled in the same [evils], not to suffer the same things which they suffered. This is [the meaning of], *After the same example of unbelief.* Let us not faint, he means (which he says also near the end [of the Epistle]. *Lift up the hands which hang down, and the feeble knees): lest any man,* saith he, *fall after the same example.* For this is to fall indeed.

Then, lest when thou hearest, *lest any man fall after the same example,* thou shouldest conceive of the same death which they also underwent, see what he saith: *For the Word of God is living and powerful and sharper than any two-edged sword.* For the Word falls upon the souls of these [men] more severely than any sword, causing grievous wounds; and inflicts fatal blows. And of these things he needs not to give the proof, nor to establish them by argument, seeing that the history he has is so fearful. For (he would say) what kind of war destroyed them? what sort of sword? did they not fall simply of themselves? For let us not grow careless because we have not suffered the same things. As long as *it is called To-day,* it is in our power to recover ourselves.

For lest on hearing the things that belong to the soul [alone] we should grow negligent, he adds also what concerns the body. For then is it so as a king when his officers are guilty of some great misconduct, first of all strips them (say) of their command, and after depriving them of their belt, and their rank, and their herald [b], then punishes them: so also in this case doth the sword of the Spirit work.

[4.] Next he discourseth of the Son, *with whom we have to do,* he saith. What is *with whom we have to do?* To Him (he would say) we have to render account for the things we have done? Even so. How then [must we act] that we fall not, nor be faint-hearted?

---

[b] Having a κῆρυξ was a special mark of dignity, belonging to certain offices. See Mr. Field's notes.

Well then (he would say) these things even [alone] are H**E**.iv.14. sufficient to instruct us. But we have also *a great High Priest, that is passed through the heavens,* J**ESUS** *the Son of God.* For as it was on this account that he added [it], (2) he subjoined, *For we have not an High Priest who cannot be touched with the feeling of our infirmities.* For this cause he said above, *In that He hath suffered Himself being tempted, He is able to succour them which are tempted.* See then how in this place also he does the same. And what he says is to this effect: He went (saith he) on the road which we also [are going] now, or rather even a more rugged one. For He had experience of all human [sufferings].

He had said above *There is no creature that is not manifest in His sight,* intimating His Godhead; then since he had begun to speak of [His] flesh [His Human nature], he again discourses more condescendingly, saying, (ver. 14) *Having then a Great High Priest, that is passed through the heavens:* and shews that His care is greater and that He protects them as if [they were] His own, and wills not that they should fall away. For Moses indeed (he saith) did not enter into the rest, while He [Christ] did enter in. And how it is that he has nowhere stated this itself is strange; [it was] lest they might [herein] seem to find an excuse; he however implied it and [at the same time] that he might not appear to bring an accusation against that man[1], he did not say it openly. For if, when none of these [1 i.e. Moses things had been said, they yet brought forward these [charges], saying, This man hath spoken against Moses See Acts and against the law; much more, if he had said, It is not xxi. 21, 28. Palestine but Heaven[c], would they have said stronger things than these.

[5.] But he attributes not all to the Priest, but requires also what is [to come] from us, I mean our confession. For *having,* he saith, *a great High Priest, who is passed through the heavens,* J**ESUS** *the Son of God, let us hold fast our profession* [or *confession*[2]]. What sort of confession [2 ὁμολο- does he mean? That there is a Resurrection, that there γία used of the Creed.

[c] There are two points of superiority over Moses implied in the words *that is passed into the Heavens.* i. that Christ entered into the Rest which He promised His people, while Moses did not. ii. That that Rest is Heaven, not the earthly Canaan.

is a recompensing: that there are good things innumerable; that Christ is GOD, that the Faith is right. These things let us confess, these things let us hold fast. For that they are true, is manifest from the fact, that the High Priest is within. We have not failed of [our hopes], let us confess; although the realities are not present, yet let us confess: if already they were present they were but a lie. So that this also is true, that [our good things] are deferred. For our High Priest also is Great.

ver. 15. *For we have not an High Priest, who cannot be touched with the feeling of our infirmities.* He is not (he means) ignorant of what concerns us, as many of the High Priests, who know not those in tribulations, nay nor even that there is any tribulation at all. For in the case of men it is impossible that he should know the affliction of the afflicted who has not had experience, and gone through the actual sensations. Our High Priest endured all things. For for this cause He endured first and then ascended, that He might be able to sympathize with us.

But [one] that was *in all points tempted like as we are,* (lit. *after the likeness* [*of our temptation*]) *without sin.* Observe how both above he has used the word "in like manner[1]" and here "after the likeness." That is, He was persecuted, was spit upon, was accused, was mocked at, was falsely informed against, was driven out, at last was crucified.

After our likeness, without sin. In these words another thing also is intimated, that it is possible even for one who is in afflictions to go through them without sin. So that also when he says *in the likeness of flesh,* he means not that He took on Him [merely] *the likeness of flesh,* but *flesh.* Why then did he say *in the likeness?* Because he was speaking about *sinful flesh*[d]: for [His flesh He assumed] was *like* our flesh, since in nature it was the same with us, but in sin no longer the same.

[6.] ver. 16. *Let us come then boldly* [*with confidence*] *unto the throne of His grace, that we may obtain mercy, and find grace to help in time of need.*

What *throne of grace* is he speaking of? that royal throne

---

[1] παραπλησίως supra ii. 14.

Rom. viii. 3.

[d] The words of Rom. viii. 3. to which S. Chrys. alludes, are *God sending His own Son in the likeness of sinful flesh &c.*

concerning which it is said, *The* LORD *said unto my Lord,* HE.iv.16.
Sit Thou on My right hand. Ps. cx. 1.

What is *let us come with confidence?* [It is] that *we have an High Priest* Who is without sin, that contends with and subdues the world. For, saith He, *Be of good cheer, I have* S. John *overcome the world.* For, to suffer all things, and yet to xvi. 33. be pure from sins is this, [viz. to overcome the world]. Although we (he means) are under sin, yet is He one who cannot sin.

How is it that we should *approach with confidence?* Because *now* it is a throne of Grace, not a throne of Judgement. For this cause [he says] *with confidence, that we may obtain mercy,* and such [mercy] as we are seeking. For the affair is [one of] munificence, a royal largess.

And may find grace for help in time of need [*for help in due season*]. He well said, *for help in due season.* If thou approach now (he means) thou wilt receive both grace and mercy, for thou approachest *in due season;* but if thou approach *then*[e], no longer [wilt thou receive it]. For *then* thy approach is unseasonable, for it is not *then a throne of Grace.* Till that time He sitteth granting pardon, but when the end [is come], then He riseth up to judgment. For saith one, *Arise, O God, judge Thou the earth.* (*Let us come with* Ps. *confidence,* or he says again that [which he had said before], lxxxii. 8. having no *evil conscience,* that is, not being in doubt, for such an one cannot *come with confidence.*) On this account it is said, *I have heard thee in an accepted time and in a* 2 Cor. vi. *day of salvation have I succoured thee.* Since even *now* for 2. those to find repentance who sin after baptism is of grace.

But lest when thou hearest of an High Priest, thou shouldst think that He standeth, he forthwith leads [thee] to the throne[f]. But a Priest doth not sit but stands. Seest thou that [for Him] to be made High Priest, is not of nature[g], but of grace and condescension, and humiliation?

---

[e] τότε, "at the day of Judgment" opposed to, "now," "in this life;" as ἐκεῖ, "there," "yonder," is the usual expression for the future state, opposed to ἐνταῦθα, "here," "in this world."

[f] The *throne of grace,* as he has said, is that of Christ, on which He sits at the right hand of the Father.

[g] The Arians maintained that our Lord was Priest in His Divine Nature antecedent to the Incarnation. See the Oxford translation of S. Athanasius against Arianism p. 292. note m. [add p. 267 note l. cf. also S. Cyril, Book 3 against Nestorius].

Hom. 7. This is it seasonable for us also now to say, *Let us draw near* asking *with confidence:* let us only bring Faith [as our offering] and He gives all things. Now is the time of the largess; let no man despair of himself. Then [will be] the time of despairing, when the bride-chamber is shut, when the King is come in to see the guests, when they who shall be accounted worthy thereof, shall have received as their portion the Patriarch's bosom: but now it is not as yet so. For still are the spectators assembled, still is the contest going on, still is the prize in suspense.

(3) [7.] Let us then labour in earnest. For even Paul saith,
1 Cor. ix. *I so run not as uncertainly.* There is need of running, and
26. of running vehemently. He that runneth [a race] seeth none of those that meet him; whether he be passing through meadows, or through dry and dusty places : he that runneth looketh not at the spectators, but at the prize. Whether they be rich or whether they be poor, whether one mock at him, or praise him, whether one insult, or cast stones at him, or plunder his house, whether he see children, or wife, or any thing whatever. He is occupied in one thing alone, in running, in gaining the prize. He that runneth, in no case standeth still, since even if he slacken a little, he has lost the whole. He that runneth, not only diminisheth nothing [of his exertions] before the end, but even then most especially straineth his speed.

This have I said for those who say; In our younger days
[1] ἠσκήσα- we took pains to acquire holiness[1], in our younger days
μεν we fasted, *now* we are grown old. *Now* most of all would it behove you to make your carefulness more intense. Do not be counting up to me the things which thou hast formerly done well : be now most of all youthful and vigorous. For he that runneth this bodily race, when grey hairs have overtaken him, probably is not able to run as he did before : for the exertion depends entirely on the body; but thou— wherefore dost thou lessen thy speed? For in this race there is need of a soul, a soul thoroughly awakened : and the soul is strengthened in old age; then it is in its full vigour, then is it in its pride.

For just as the body, so long as it is oppressed by fevers and by one sickness after another, even if it be strong, is grievously afflicted, but when it is freed from this attack, it recovers its proper force, so also the soul in youth is feverish, and is chiefly possessed by the love of glory, and of luxurious living, and of sensual lusts, and of many other imaginations; but old age, when it comes on, drives away all these passions, some through satiety, some through philosophy. For old age relaxes the powers of the body, and does not permit the soul to make use thereof, even if it wish, but repressing them as enemies of various kinds, it sets her in a position free from troubles and produces a great calm, and brings in a greater fear.

For if none else does, yet they who are grown old know, that they are drawing to their end, and that they are most certainly standing near to death. When therefore the desires of this life are gradually withdrawing, and the expectation of the judgment-seat is coming on in their stead, softening the stubbornness of the soul, does it not become more disposed to give attention, if one be willing?

[8.] What [is to be said] then (you allege) when we see old men more intractable than young ones? Thou tellest me of an excess of wickedness. For in the case of madmen too, we see them going over precipices, when no man pushes them. When then an old man too is disordered by the [diseases] of the young, this is an excess of wickedness; besides not even in youth would such an one have an excuse: since he is not able to say, *Remember not the sins of my youth, and my ignorances.* For he who in old age remains the same, shews that in youth too he was such [as he was] not from ignorance, nor from inexperience, nor from the time of life, but from unwillingness to exert himself. For that man may say, *Remember not the sins of my youth, and mine ignorances,* who does such things as become an old man, who changes in his old age. But if even in age he continue the same unseemly courses, how can such an one be worthy of the name of an old man, who has no reverence even for [his own] age? For he who says, *Remember not the sins of my youth, nor my ignorances,* utters this, as being one that is doing right in his old age. Do not thou then, by the deeds of thine age, deprive thyself also of pardon for the sins of thy youth.

HOM. 7. For how can that which is done be other than unreasonable, and beyond pardon? An old man sits in taverns. An old man hurries to horse-races—an old man goes up into theatres, running with the crowd like little children. In truth it is a shame and a mockery, to be adorned outside with grey hairs, but within to have the mind of a child.

And indeed if a young man insult [him], he immediately puts forward his grey hairs. Do thou thyself be the first to reverence them; if however thou dost not reverence thy own grey hairs, and that when thou art an old man, how canst thou demand of the young man to reverence them? Thou dost not reverence the grey hairs, but puttest them to shame. God hath honoured thee with whiteness of hairs: He hath given thee high precedence. Why dost thou betray [thine] honours? how shall the young man reverence thee, when thou art more wanton than he? For the hoary head is then venerable, when it acts worthily of the grey head; but when it plays a youthful part, it will be more contemptible than the young. How then will you old men be able to give these exhortations to the young man when you are intoxicated by your disorderliness?

[9.] I say not these things as accusing the old, but [rather] the young. For in my judgment they who act thus even if they have come to their hundredth year, are still young; just as the young if they be but children, yet if they are sober-minded are better than the old. And this doctrine is not my own, but Scripture also recognizes the distinction. *For* (it saith) *honourable age is not that which standeth in length of time, and an unspotted life is old age.*

<small>Wisd. iv. 8, 9.</small>

(4) For we honour grey hairs, not because we esteem the white before the black, but because they are an indication of a virtuous life; and when we see them we conjecture therefrom the inward hoariness. But if men continue to do what is inconsistent with the hoary head, they will for this become the more contemptible. Since we also honour the Emperor, and the purple and the diadem, inasmuch as they are symbols of his office. But if we should see him, with his purple, spitted on, trodden under foot by his guards, seized by the throat, cast into prison, torn to pieces, shall we then

reverence the purple or the diadem, and not rather weep He.iv.16.
over the stateliness itself? Claim not then to be honoured
for thy hoary head, when thou thyself wrongest it. For
it ought indeed itself to receive satisfaction from thee, in
that thou bringest disgrace on a condition so noble and so
honourable.

We say not these things against all [old persons], nor is
our discourse against old age simply (I am not so mad as
that) but against a youthful spirit that brings dishonour on
old age. Nor is it concerning those who are grown old
that we say these things in sorrow, but concerning those
who disgrace the hoary head.

For the old man is an emperor, if you will, and more royal
than he who wears the purple, if he master his passions,
and keep them under subjection, in the rank of guards.
But if he be dragged about and made to descend from his
throne, and become a slave to the love of money, and to
vain-glory, and beautifying his person, and luxuriousness,
and drunkenness, anger, and sensual pleasures, and has his
hair dressed out with oil, and exposes his age insulted by
his way of life, of what punishment would not such an one
be worthy?

[10.] But may ye not be such, O young men! for not
even for you is there the excuse for sinning. Why so? you
will ask. Because it is possible to be old in youth: just
as there are youths in old age, so also the reverse. For as
in the one case the hair by being white saves no man, so
in the other by being black it is no impediment. For if it
is disgraceful for the old man to do these things of which I
have spoken, much more than for the young man, yet still
the young man is not freed from accusation. For a young
man can have an excuse only, in case he is called to the
management of affairs, when he is still inexperienced, when
he needs time and practice; but when it is necessary to
display temperance and courage, then no longer is there excuse for him; nor yet when it is needful to keep his property.

For it sometimes happens that the young man is blamed
more than the old. For the one needs much care and
nursing, seeing that old age makes him altogether feeble:

but this young man who is able, if he have the will, to provide for himself, what sort of excuse should he meet with, when he plunders more than the old, when he remembers injuries, when he is contemptuous, when he does not stand forward to protect others more than the old man, when he utters many things unseasonably, when he acts with insolence, when he reviles, when he is drunken?

And if in the [matter of] chastity he think that he cannot be impleaded[h], consider that here also he has many helps, if he will. For although desire trouble him more violently than it doth the old, yet nevertheless there are many things which he will be able to do more than an old man, and so charm that wild beast. What are these things? labours, readings, watchings through the night, fastings.

[11.] What then are these things to us (saith one) who are not leading monastic lives? Sayest thou this to me? say it to Paul, when he saith, *Watching in all perseverance and supplication,* when he saith, *Make not provision for the flesh, to fulfil the lusts thereof.* For surely he wrote not these things to solitaries only, but to all that are in cities. For ought the man who lives in the world to have any advantage over the solitary, save only the living with a wife? In this point he has allowance, but in others none at all, but it is his duty to do all things equally with the solitary.

Moreover the Beatitudes [pronounced] by Christ, were not addressed to solitaries only: since in that case the whole world would have perished, and we should be accusing God of cruelty. And if these beatitudes were pronounced to solitaries only, and it be not possible for the secular person to succeed in [attaining] them, while at the same time He Himself permitted marriage, the conclusion is that He has Himself destroyed all men. For if it be not possible, with marriage, to perform the duties of solitaries, all things have perished and are destroyed, and the [functions] of virtue are shut up into a narrow [compass].

And, how can marriage be honourable, which so greatly impedes us? What then? It is possible, yea very possible, even if we have wives to pursue after virtue, supposing we

---

[h] that is, if he have fallen into sin in this respect.

have the will. How? If having *wives*, we *be as though* He.iv.16. *we had none,* if we rejoice not over our *possessions,* if we 1 Cor. vii. 29, 31. *use the world as not abusing [using] it.*

And if any persons have been hindered by their married state, let them know that it is not marriage which is the hindrance, but their will which made an ill use of marriage. Since it is not wine which causes drunkenness, but the evil will, and the using wine beyond due measure. Use the married state with moderation, and thou shalt be first in the kingdom, and shalt enjoy all good things, which may we all attain by the grace and mercy of our Lord Jesus Christ with Whom to the Father and also to the Holy Ghost be glory, might, honour, now and for ever and world without end. Amen.

HOMILY VIII.

Heb. v. 1—3.

For every high priest taken from among men, is ordained for men in things pertaining to God, that he may offer both gifts and sacrifices for sins: who can have compassion on[1] the ignorant and on them that are out of the way, for that he himself also is compassed with infirmity; and by reason hereof he ought, as for the people so also for himself to offer for sins.

[1] μετριοπαθεῖν

The blessed Paul wishes to shew in the next place that this covenant is far better than the old. This then he does by first laying down as a foundation considerations far remote. For inasmuch as there was nothing bodily or that made a shew[2], no temple for instance, nor Holy of Holies, nor Priest with so great furniture, no legal observances, but all things more lofty and more perfect, and there was nothing of what is bodily things, but the whole was in things spiritual, and things spiritual did not attract the weak, as do things bodily; [for this cause] he opens this whole discussion.

[2] φανταστικὸν

And observe his wisdom: he makes his beginning from the priest first, and continually calls Him an High Priest, and from this first shews the difference [of the two Dispensations]. On this account he first of all defines what a Priest is, and shews if He has any things proper to a Priest, and if there are any signs of priest-hood. It was however an objection in his way that He [Christ] was not even of noble birth, nor was He of the sacerdotal tribe, nor a priest on earth. How then was He a Priest? some one may say.

And just as in the Epistle to the Romans, having taken

up an argument of which they were not easily persuaded, that Faith effects that which the labour of the Law had not strength for, nor the sweat and toil of [a man's] course of life, he betook himself to the Patriarch and referred the whole [question] to that time: so now in this place also he opens out the other path of the Priesthood, shewing its superiority from the things which happened before. And just as, in [the matter of] punishment, he brings before them not Hell alone, but also what happened in the case of their fathers [1], so now here also, he first establishes this position from things present. For it were right indeed that earthly things should be proved from heavenly, but when the hearers are weak, the opposite course is taken.

HEB. v. 4.

[1] sup. iii. 7 &c.

[2.] Up to a certain point he lays down first the things which are common [to Christ and their High Priests], and then shews that He is superior. For comparative [2] excellence arises thus, when in some respects there is community, in others superiority; if not, it is no longer comparative.

[2] ἡ κατὰ σύγκρισιν

For every High Priest taken from among men, this is common to Christ, *is ordained for men in things pertaining to God*, and this also, *that he may offer both gifts and sacrifices for the people*, and this too, [yet] not entirely: what follows however is no longer so: *who can have compassion on the ignorant, and on them that are out of the way*, from this point forward is the superiority, *inasmuch as himself also is encompassed with infirmity; and on account of this* [infirmity] *he ought as for the people, so also for himself, to offer for sins.*

Then also [there are] other points: He is made [Priest] (he says) by Another and does not of Himself intrude into [the office]. This too is common (ver. 4) *And no man taketh this honour to himself, but on being called of God as was Aaron.*

Here again he deals gently with [3] them in another point, [saying] that He was sent from God: which Christ was wont to say throughout in discoursing with the Jews. *He that sent Me is greater than I*, and, *I came not of Myself.* He appears to me in these words also to hint at the priests of the Jews, as being no longer priests, in that they

[3] θεραπεύ-ει

S. John xii. 49; xiv. 28; viii. 42.

were intruders and corrupted the law of the priesthood; (ver. 5) *So Christ also glorified not Himself to be made an High Priest.*

On what occasion then was He appointed (saith one)? for Aaron's appointment was many times shewn as in the [matter of the] Rod, and when the fire came down and destroyed those who wished to intrude into the priesthood. But in this instance, on the contrary, they [the Jewish Priests] not only suffered nothing, but even are in high esteem. Whence then [is His appointment shewn]? He shews it from the prophecy. He has nothing [to allege] that is cognizable by sense, nothing visible. For this cause he affirms it from prophecy, from things future; *But He that said unto Him Thou art My Son, to-day have I begotten Thee.* What has this [appointment] to do with [His being] the Son? Yea (saith he) it is a preparation for His being appointed by God.

(ver. 6) *As He saith also in another place, Thou art a Priest for ever after the order of Melchisedech.* Unto whom now was this spoken? Who is *after the order of Melchisedech?* No other [than He]. For they all were under the Law, they all kept sabbaths, they all were circumcised; one could not point out any other [than Him].

[3.] ver. 7, 8. *Who in the days of His flesh, when He had offered up prayers and supplications with strong crying and tears, to Him that was able to save Him from death, and was heard in that He feared; though He were a Son, yet learned He obedience by the things which He suffered.* Seest thou that [he doth] nothing else than set forth His anxious care [for us] and the exceeding greatness of His love? For what means the [expression] *with strong crying?* The Gospel no where saith this, nor that He wept when He prayed, nor yet that He uttered any cry. Seest thou that it was a condescension? For it was not in the Apostle [merely] to say that He prayed, but also *with strong crying.*

And having been heard (saith he) *in that He feared; although He were a Son, He learned obedience from the things which He suffered.* (ver. 9, 10) *And being made perfect He became the Author of eternal salvation to all them that obey Him: called of God a High Priest after the order of Melchisedech.* HEB. V. 8.

Be it that [He entreated] with *crying,* why also *strong [crying] and tears? Having offered* (he saith) *and having been heard in that He feared.* What sayest thou? let the Heretics [a] be ashamed. The SON of God *was heard in that He feared.* And what more could any man say concerning the prophets? And what sort of sequence is it to say, *He was heard in that He feared, though He were* SON, *yet learned He obedience from the things which He suffered?* Would any man say these things concerning God? why, who was ever so mad? and who, even if he were beside himself, would have uttered these things? *Having been heard* (he says) *in that He feared, He learned obedience from the things which He suffered.* What obedience? He that before this had been obedient, as a Son to His Father, even unto death, how did He afterwards learn [obedience]? Seest thou that this is spoken concerning the Incarnation? (2)

Tell me now, did He pray the Father that He might be saved from death? and was it for this cause that He was *exceeding sorrowful, and said, If it be possible, let this cup pass from Me?* yet no where prayed the Father concerning His resurrection, but on the contrary Himself openly declares, *Destroy this temple and within three days I will raise it up.* And, *I have power to lay down My life, and I have power to take it again. No man taketh it from Me, I lay it down of Myself.* What then is it; for what purpose did He pray? (And again He said, *Behold we go up to Jerusalem, and the Son of Man shall be betrayed unto the chief priests and scribes, and they shall condemn Him to death. And they shall deliver Him to the Gentiles, to mock, and to scourge, and to crucify Him: and the third day He shall rise again,* and said not, " My Father shall raise Me up again"). How then was it that He prayed concerning this? But further, for whom did He pray? For those who had believed on Him. S. Matt. xxvi. 38, 39. S. John ii. 19. Ib. x. 18. S. Matt. xx. 18, 19.

And what he means is to this effect, 'He is readily listened to.' For inasmuch as they had not yet the right

---

[a] Heretics who denied the reality of our Lord's Human Nature.

opinion concerning Him, he said that He was heard. Just as He Himself also when consoling His disciples, said, *If ye loved Me, ye would rejoice, because I go to My Father,* and *My Father is greater than I.* But how did He not glorify Himself He who made Himself of no reputation, He who gave Himself up? For, it is said, *He gave Himself up for our sins.* And again, *Who gave Himself a ransom for us all.* What is it then? Thou seest that it is on account of the flesh that He speaks lowly things concerning Himself: So in this place also, *Although He were Son, He was heard in that He feared,* saith [the Apostle]. He wishes to shew, that the success was of Himself, rather than of God's favour. So great (saith he) was His reverence, that even on account thereof God had respect unto Him.

He learned, he saith, *to obey* GOD. Here again he shews how great is the gain of sufferings. *And having been made perfect,* he saith, *He became the Author of salvation to them that obey Him.* But if He, being the SON, gained obedience from His sufferings, much more shall we. Dost thou see how many things he says in his discourse about obedience, that they might be persuaded to it? For it seems to me that they would not be restrained. *From the things,* saith he, *which He suffered He* continually *learned* to obey GOD. And being *made perfect* through His sufferings. This then is perfection, and by this means must we arrive at perfection. For not only was He Himself saved [thereby], but this became to others also an abundant supply of salvation. For *being made perfect He became Author of salvation to them that obey Him.*

[4.] *Being called,* saith he, *of* GOD *High Priest after the order of Melchisedech:* (ver. 11) *Of whom we have many things to say and hard to be uttered* [or explained]. When he was about to proceed to speak of the difference of the Priesthood, he first reproves them, pointing out both that this his so great condescension was *milk,* and that it was because they were children that he dwelt longer on the lowly subject, that [namely] which has relation to the flesh, and speaks [about Him] as about any righteous man. And see, he neither kept silence as to the doctrine altogether, nor did he utter it. For the one [he did] that he might raise up their thoughts, and persuade them to be perfect, HE. v. 11. and not to allow themselves to be deprived of the great doctrines; the other that he might not overwhelm their minds.

Of whom, he saith, *we have many things to say and hard to be explained, seeing ye are dull of hearing.* Because they do not hear, on this account it is that the doctrine is *hard to be explained.* For when a person has to discourse with men who do not go along with him nor apprehend the things that are spoken, he cannot well explain the subject to them.

But perhaps some one of you that stand here, is puzzled, and thinks it a hard case, that owing to the Hebrews, he himself is hindered from hearing the more perfect doctrines. Nay rather, I think that perhaps here also, with the exception of a few, there are many such [as they], so that this may be said concerning yourselves also: but for the sake of those few I will speak.

Did he then keep entire silence, or did he resume the subject again in what follows; and do the same as in the Epistle to the Romans? For there too, when he had first stopped the mouths of the gainsayers, and said, *Nay but, O* Rom. ix. *man, who art thou that repliest against God?* he then sub- 20. joined the solution. And for my own part I think that he was not even altogether silent, and yet did not speak it out, in order to lead the hearers to a longing [for the knowledge]. For having mentioned [the subject], and said that certain great things were stored up in the doctrine, see how he frames his reproof in combination with panegyric.

For this is ever a part of Paul's wisdom, to mix painful things with kind ones. Which he also does in the Epistle to the Galatians, saying, *Ye did run well; who did hinder* Gal. v. 7. *you?* And, *Have ye suffered so many things in vain? if* Ib. iii. 4. *it be yet in vain,* and, *I have confidence in you in the Lord.* Ib. v. 10. Which he says also to these [Hebrews], *But we are per-* Infra vi. *suaded better things of you, and things that accompany* 9. *salvation.* For these two things he effects, he does not overstrain them, nor suffer them to fall back; for if the examples of others are sufficient to raise up the hearer, and to lead him to emulation; when a man has the example [drawn] from his own conduct and is bidden to emulate himseif, the possibility [of his doing it] is already therein implied.

He therefore shews this also, and does not suffer them to fall back as men utterly condemned, nor as being alway evil, but [says] that they were once even good; (ver. 12) for *when for the time ye ought to be teachers,* saith he. Here he shews that they had been believers a long while ago, and he shews also that they ought to instruct others.

[5.] At all events observe him continually travailing to introduce the discourse concerning the High Priest, and still putting it off. For hear how he began: *Having a great High Priest who hath passed through the heavens;* and omitting to say in what manner He was great, he says again, *For every High Priest taken from among men, is appointed for men in things pertaining to God.* And again, *So Christ also glorified not Himself to be made an High Priest.* And again after saying, *Thou art a Priest for ever after the order of Melchisedec,* he again puts off [the subject], saying, *Who in the days of His Flesh offered prayers and supplications.* When therefore he had been so many times repulsed, he says, as though he were excusing himself, The blame is with you. Alas! how great a difference! When they ought to be teaching others, they are not even simply learners, but the last of learners. ver. 12. *For when for the time ye ought to be teachers, ye have need again that some one*[b] *teach you the very first elements*[1] *of the oracles of God.* Here he means the Human Nature [of Christ]. For as in external literature it is necessary to learn the elements first, so also here they were instructed first concerning the human nature [of Christ].

Thou seest what is the cause of his uttering lowly things. So Paul did to the Athenians also, discoursing and saying, *The times then of ignorance God winked at: but now commandeth all men every where to repent, because He hath appointed a day in the which He will judge the world in righteousness by that Man whom He hath ordained, whereof*

---

[b] τινα. The common editions have τίνα, "that one teach you which be &c." as is read in the received version of the Epistle, where Lachman adopts the reading τινα.

He hath given assurance unto all men, in that He hath raised Him from the dead. He.v.12. For this cause, if he says any thing lofty, he expresses it briefly, while the lowly statements are scattered about in many places through the whole Epistle. And in this very way too His loftiness is indicated; since the extreme lowliness [of what is said] forbids the suspicion that these things relate to His Divine Nature. So in this place also the safe ground was kept[c].

But what produces this dulness? This he intimates especially in the Epistle to the Corinthians, saying, *For whereas there is among you envy and strife and divisions, are ye not carnal?* 1 Cor. iii. 3. But observe, I beseech you, his great wisdom, how on each occasion he addresses himself in a way corresponding to the distempers before him. For there [in the case of the Corinthians] the weakness arose chiefly from ignorance, or rather from sinful acts; but here [in the case of the Hebrews] not from sins only, but also from their continual afflictions. Wherefore he also uses expressions calculated to shew the difference, not saying, *ye are become carnal,* but *dull:* in that case *carnal,* but in this the pain is greater. For they [the Corinthians] indeed were not able to endure [his reproof], inasmuch as they were carnal: but these were able. For in saying, *Seeing ye are become dull of hearing,* he shews plainly that formerly they were sound in health, and were strong, fervent in zeal, which he also afterwards testifies respecting them. supra ver. 11.

[6.] *And are become such as have need of milk, not of strong meat.* On every occasion he calls the lowly doctrine *milk,* both in this place and in the other. *When,* saith he, *for* [i. e. *because of*] *the time ye ought to be teachers:* that very thing because of which especially ye are become faint and supine, [I mean] *because of the time,* because of that especially ye ought to be strong. Now he calls it *milk,* on account of its being suited to the more simple. But it is injurious to those who are more perfect, and the dwelling on these [lowly] things is hurtful to them. So that it were not right that practices pertaining to the Law should be introduced[d] now or the comparison made from these [points],

[c] That is, he took care to provide against being understood to refer to His Divine Nature, when he said lowly things concerning Christ.
[d] The allowing the observances of the law, as well as the dwelling thus

_{Hom. 8.} that He was a High Priest, and offered sacrifice, and needed crying and supplication. Wherefore see how these things are unhealthful[e] to *us;* but them at that time they nourished, being in no respect unhealthful to them.

So then it seems the oracles of God are true nourishment. *For I will give unto them,* he saith, *not a famine of bread, nor a thirst of water, but a famine of hearing the word of the Lord.*

_{Amos viii. 11.}

_{1 Cor. iii. 2.} *I gave you milk to drink, and not meat;* He did not say, I fed you, intimating that such [nourishment] as this is not food, but that the case is like that of little children who cannot be fed with bread. For such have not drink given them, but their food is to them instead of drink.

Moreover he did not say, "ye have need," but *ye are become such as have need of milk and not of strong meat.* That is, ye willed [it]; ye have reduced yourselves to this state, this need.

ver. 13. *For every one that partaketh of milk is unskilled in the word of righteousness for he is a babe.* What is *the Word* [doctrine] *of righteousness?* He seems to me here to hint at conduct also. That which Christ also said, *Except your righteousness shall exceed the righteousness of the Scribes and Pharisees,* this he says likewise, *unskilled in the word of righteousness,* that is, he that is unskilled in the philosophy that is above, is unable to embrace a life perfect and exact[1]. Or else by *righteousness* he here means Christ, and the high doctrine concerning Him.

_{S. Matt. v. 20.}

_{1 ἄκρον καὶ ἠκριβω-μένον}

That they then were *become dull,* he said; but from what cause [they were so], he did not add, leaving it to themselves to know it and not being willing to make his discourse hard to bear. In the case of the Galatians on the contrary he both *marvelled* and *stood in doubt,* which tends much more to encourage, as it is the language of one who would never have expected that this should happen. For this is [what] the doubting [implies].

_{Gal. i. 6; iv. 20.}

Thou seest that there is another infancy. Thou seest that there is another full age[2]. Let us become of *full age*

_{2 τελειό-της}

---

[e] on the Human characteristics of our Lord, were suited for the beginners, but would be injurious to us.

[e] προσίσταται. Said of that which cannot be digested or causes nausea.

in this sense: It is in the power even of those who are children, and young persons, to arrive at that *full age:* For it is not of nature but of virtue.

[7.] ver. 14. *But strong meat belongeth to them that are of full age* [perfect], *even them who by reason of use have their senses exercised to discern both good and evil.* Those persons had not *their senses exercised,* nor did they *know good and evil.* He is not speaking now concerning life [and conduct], when he says *to discern good and evil,* for this is possible and easy for every man to know, but concerning doctrines that are wholesome and sublime, and those that are corrupted and low. The babe knows not how to distinguish the bad and the good food. Oftentimes at least it puts even dirt into its mouth, and takes what is hurtful; and it does all things without discernment; but not [so] that which is *of full age.* Such [babes] are they who listen to all things without distinction, and give up their ears indiscriminately: which seems to me to imply blame on these [Hebrews] also, as being lightly *carried about,* and now giving themselves to these, now to those. Which he also hinted at near the end [of the Epistle], saying, *Be not carried aside by divers and strange doctrines.* This is the meaning of *to discern good and evil.* For the *mouth tasteth food, but the soul trieth words.*

He. v. 14.

Infra xiii. 9. Job xxxiv. 3.

[8.] Let us therefore ourselves also learn this lesson. Do not thou when thou hearest that a man is not a Heathen nor a Jew, straightway believe him to be a Christian; but examine also into all the other points; for even Manichæans, and all the heresies, have put on this mask, in order thus to deceive the more simple. But if we *have the senses* of the soul *exercised to discern both good and evil,* we are able to discern such [teachers].

(4)

But how do our *senses* become *exercised?* By continual hearing; by experience of the Scriptures. For when we set forth the error of those [Heretics], and thou hearest to-day and to-morrow; and ascertainest by testing that it is not right, thou hast learnt the whole, thou hast known the whole: and even if thou shouldest not comprehend to-day, thou wilt comprehend to-morrow.

HOM. 8. *That have,* saith he, their *senses exercised.* Thou seest that it is needful to exercise our hearing by divine studies, so as not to be addressed in a strange language? *Exercised,* saith he, *for discerning,* that is, to be skilled.

One man says, that there is no Resurrection; and another looks for none of the things to come; another says there is a different God; another that He has His beginning from Mary. And see at once how they have all fallen away from want of moderation [1], some in the way of excess, others in that of defect. As for instance, the first Heresy of all was that of Marcion, this introduced besides [the true] a different God, which has no existence. See the excess. After this was the [heresy] of Sabellius, saying that the Son and the Spirit and the Father are One [f]. Next that of Marcellus and Photinus, which also taught the same things. Moreover that of Paul of Samosata, saying that He had His beginning from Mary. Afterwards that of the Manichæans; for this is the most modern of all. After these the heresy of Arius. And there are others too.

But on this account have we had the Faith handed down to us, that we might not be compelled to engage with innumerable heresies, and to be troubled [therewith], but whatever any man might have endeavoured either to add to or take from it, that we might hold to be spurious. For just as those who give the standards [measures] do not oblige [people] to busy themselves about measures innumerable, but bid them keep to that which has been given them; so also in the case of doctrines.

[9.] But no man is willing to give attention to the Scriptures. For if we did give attention, not only should we not be ourselves entangled by deceit, but we should also set others free who are deceived, and should draw them out of dangers. For the strong soldier is not only able to help himself, but also to protect his comrade, and to free him from the malice of the enemy. But as it is, some do not even know that there are any Scriptures. Yet the Holy Spirit indeed made so many wise provisions in order that they might be safely kept.

And look at it from the first, that ye may learn the un-

[1] ἐξ ἀμετρίας cf. S. Irenaeus iv. 33. 2. p. 405 O.T.

[f] ἕν. The common texts add πρόσωπον, "one person."

speakable love of GOD towards man. He inspired the blessed Moses; He engraved the tables, He detained him on the mount forty days; and again as many [more] to give the Law. And after this He sent prophets who suffered woes innumerable. War came on; they slew them all, they cut them to pieces, the [sacred] books were burned. Again, He inspired another admirable man to publish them, Ezra I mean, and caused them to be put together from the remains. And after this He arranged that they should be translated by the seventy. They did translate them. Christ came, He acknowledges them; the Apostles disperse them among men. Christ wrought signs and wonders. HE. v. 14.

What then after so great painstaking? The Apostles also wrote, even as Paul likewise said, *they were written for our admonition, upon whom the ends of the world are come.* And again Christ said, *Ye do err not knowing the Scriptures:* And again Paul said, *That through patience and comfort of the Scriptures we may have hope.* And again, *All Scripture is given by inspiration of God, and is profitable.* And *let the word of Christ dwell in you richly.* And the prophet, *he shall meditate in His Law day and night,* and again in another place, *Let all thy communication be in the law of the Most High.* And again, *How sweet are Thy words unto my throat.* (He said not to my hearing, but to my *throat*) *more than honey and the honeycomb to my mouth.* And Moses saith, *Thou shalt meditate in them continually, when thou risest up, when thou sittest, when thou liest down. Be in them,* saith he. And innumerable things one might say concerning them. But notwithstanding, after so many things there are some who do not even know that there are Scriptures at all. For this cause, believe me, nothing sound, nothing profitable comes from us. 1 Cor. x. 11.

S. Matt. xxii. 29. Rom. xv. 4.

2 Tim. iii. 16. Col. iii. Ps. i. 2. Ecclus. ix. 15. Ps. cxix. 103.

Deut. vi. 7.

1 Tim. iv. 15.

[10.] Yet, if any one wished to learn military affairs, of necessity he must learn the laws affecting military affairs. And if any one was disposed to acquire the knowledge of steering or of carpentering, or any thing else, of necessity he must learn the [principles] of the art. But in this case they will not do anything of the kind, and that, notwithstanding this is a science which needs much wakeful attention. For that it too is an art which needs teaching, hear the prophet saying, *Come, ye children, hearken unto me, I will teach you the fear of the Lord.* It follows therefore certainly that the fear of God needs teaching. Then he saith, *What is man is he that would have life?* he means the life yonder; and again, *Keep thy tongue from evil and thy lips that they speak no guile; turn aside from evil and do good, seek peace and pursue it.*

<small>Hom. 8.
Ps. xxxiv. 11.

Ib. 12.
Ib.13,14.</small>

Do you know who it is that said these things, a prophet or a writer of history, or an apostle, or an evangelist? For my own part I do not think you do, except a few. Yea and these themselves again, if we bring forward a testimony from some other place, will be in the same case as the rest of you. For see, I repeat the same statement expressed in other words. *Wash ye, become clean, put away your wickednesses from your souls before Mine eyes, learn to do well, seek out judgment. Keep thy tongue from evil, and do good: learn to do well.* Thou seest that virtue needs to be taught? For this one saith, *I will teach you the fear of the Lord,* and the other *Learn to do well.*

<small>Is. i. 16, 17.</small>

Now then do you know where these words are in [the Scripture]? For myself I do not think you do, except a few. And yet every week these things are read to you twice or even three times: and the reader when he goes up [to the desk] first says whose the book is, [the book] of such a prophet, and then says what he says, so that it shall be more intelligible to you and you may not only know the contents of the Book, but also the occasion of what is written, and who it was that spake these things. But all in vain; all to no purpose. For your interest is wholly on things of this life, and of things spiritual no account is made.

For this cause not even do those [worldly] matters turn out according to your wishes, but there also many difficulties [befal you]. For Christ saith, *Seek the Kingdom of God, and all these things shall be added unto you.* These things He said, shall also be given in the way of addition: but we have inverted the order and seek the earth and the good things which are in the earth, as if those other [heavenly] things were to be given us in addition. For this cause we have neither the one nor the other. Let us then

<small>S. Matt. vi. 33.</small>

at last wake up and become coveters of the things which shall be hereafter; for so these also will follow. For it is not possible that he who seeks the things that relate to God, should not also attain human [blessings]. It is the declaration of the Truth itself which says this. Let us not then act otherwise, but let us hold fast to the counsel of Christ, lest we fail of all. But God is able to give you compunction and to make you better, in Christ Jesus our Lord, with whom to the Father and also to the Holy Ghost be glory, power, honour, now and for ever and world without end. Amen.

He. v. 14.

HOMILY IX.

Heb. vi. 1—3.

Wherefore leaving the principles of the Doctrine of Christ[a], let us go on unto perfection, not laying again the foundation of repentance from dead works, and of faith towards God; of the doctrine of baptisms, and of laying on of hands; and of resurrection of the dead, and of eternal judgment. And this we will do, if God permit.

You have heard how much Paul found fault with the Hebrews for wishing to be always learning about the same things. And this he did with good reason: *For when for the time ye ought to be teachers, ye have need again that some one teach you the elements of the first principles[1] of the oracles of God.*

<small>supra v. 12.</small>

<small>[1] τὰ στοιχεῖα τῆς ἀρχῆς</small>

I am afraid that this might very appropriately be said to you also, that *when for the time ye ought to be teachers*, ye do not even maintain the rank of learners, but ever hearing the same things, and on the same subjects, you are in the same condition as if you heard no one. And if any man should question you, no one will be able to answer, except a very few who may soon be counted.

But this is no trifling loss. For oftentimes when the teacher wishes to go on further, and to touch on higher and more mysterious doctrines, the want of attention in those who are to be taught does not permit him [to do so].

For just as in the case of a grammar-master, if a boy is continually being taught the first elements without retain-

---

[a] τὸν λόγον τῆς ἀρχῆς τοῦ Χριστοῦ. Literally "the discourse of the beginning of Christ;" but presently S. Chrys. substitutes for this, ἡ ἀρχὴ τοῦ λόγου, "the beginning of the doctrine," as the words are translated in our Version.

ing them, it will be necessary for him to be continually dinning them into the boy, and he will not leave off teaching, until the other has been able to learn them accurately, for it is great folly to lead him on to other things, without having put well into him what comes first; so too in the Church, if while we constantly say the same things you learn never the more, we shall not ever cease saying the same things. He.vi.1-3.

For if our preaching were a matter of display and ambition, it would have been right for us to pass quickly from one subject to another and to be continually digressing, as having no thought for you yourselves, but only for your applauses. But since it is not to this that we have devoted our zeal, but our labours are all for your profit, we shall not cease discoursing to you on the same subjects, till you succeed in learning them. For I might have said much about the Gentile superstition, and about the Manichæans, and about the Marcionists, and by the grace of God have given them heavy blows, but this sort of discourse is out of season. Since to persons who do not as yet know accurately what concerns their own selves, to persons who have not yet learned that to be covetous is evil, who would utter such discourses as those, and lead them on to other subjects before the time?

We then for our part shall not cease to say the same things, whether ye be persuaded or not. We fear however, that by continually saying the same things, if ye hearken not, we may make the condemnation heavier for them that are disobedient.

I must not however say this in regard to you all; for I know many who are benefited by their coming into this place, who might with justice complain loudly against those others, as insidiously injuring them[1] through their ignorance and inattention. However not even thus will they be injured. For hearing the same things continually is useful even to those who know them, since by often hearing what we know, we are more deeply affected. We know, for instance, that Humility is an excellent thing, and that Christ often discoursed about it; but when we also listen to His very words and the reflections made upon

[1] ἐνεδρευόντων αὐτοὺς

them, we are yet more affected, even if we hear them ten thousand times.

[2.] It is not out of place then for us also to say now to you, *Wherefore leaving the beginning of the doctrine of Christ, let us go on unto perfection.*

What is *the beginning of the doctrine*[1]? He goes on to state it himself saying, *not laying again* (these are his words) *a foundation of repentance from dead works, and faith toward God, of the doctrine of baptisms and of laying on of hands, of the resurrection of the dead, and of eternal judgment.*

[1] ἡ ἀρχὴ τοῦ λόγου

But if this be *the Beginning*, what else is our doctrine save to repent *from dead works*, and through the Spirit to receive *the faith*[b] in *the resurrection of the dead, and eternal judgment?* But what is *the Beginning?* The Beginning, he says, is nothing else than this, when there is not also a strict life. For just as for one who is entering on the study of grammar, it is necessary to be instructed in the Elements[2] first, so is it for the Christian also to know these things accurately, and to have no doubt concerning them. And should he again have need of teaching, he does not as yet possess the foundation. For one who is firmly grounded ought to be fixed and to stand steady, and not be moved out of his place. But if a person who has been catechized and baptized is going ten years afterwards to learn again about the Faith, and that we ought to *believe* in *the resurrection of the dead*, he does not yet possess the foundation, he is again seeking after the beginning of the Christian religion. For that the Faith is the foundation, and the rest is the building, hear [the Apostle] himself saying; *I have laid the foundation and another buildeth thereupon. If any man build upon this foundation, gold, silver, precious stones, wood, hay, stubble.*

[2] *or the letters*

1 Cor. iii. 10.
Ib. 12.

Not laying again (saith he) *a foundation of repentance from dead works.*

(2) [3.] But what is, *let us go on unto perfection?* Let us henceforth proceed (he means) even to the very roof, that is, let us have the most excellent life. For just as in the case

---

[b] The Faith; πίστις with the Article in this place and a little below means the Creed; as we say "the Belief."

of the letters the Alphabet[1] contains the whole, and as the foundation holds together the whole building, so also does full assurance concerning the Faith maintain purity of life. And without this it is not possible to be a Christian, any more than for a building [to exist] without foundations; or for a man to become skilled in literature without the letters. Still if a person should be always going round about the letters, or if he should be [always engaged] about the foundation, not about the building, he will not yet have gained any thing. *(margin: Heb.vi.1. τὸ ἄλφα)*

Do not thou however think that the Faith is depreciated by being called elementary: for it is indeed the whole power: for when he says, *For every one that useth milk is unskilled in the word of righteousness, for he is a babe,* it is not this which he calls *milk.* But to be still doubting about these things is [a sign] of a feeble mind, and one that needs many discourses. For these are the wholesome doctrines. Since we call him *a perfect man* [i.e. *of full age*] who with the faith has a right life; but if any one has faith, but yet does evil, and is in doubts concerning [the faith] itself, and brings disgrace on the doctrine, him we shall with reason call *a babe,* in that he has gone back again to the beginning. So that if we have been even ten thousand years in the faith, and yet are not firm in it, we are babes; when we exhibit a life not suitable to it; when we are still laying a foundation. *(margin: supra v. 13.)*

[4.] But besides [their way of] life he brings another charge also against these [Hebrews], as being shaken from their position, and needing *to lay a foundation of repentance from dead works.* For when a man changes from one thing to another, giving up this, and choosing that, he ought first to condemn himself, and to depart from [what he held] in disposition and then to pass to the other. But if he intends again to lay hold on the first, how shall he touch the second?

What then is to be said of the Law (saith one)? we have condemned it, and again we go back to it. This is not a shifting about, for here also [under the Gospel] we have a law. *Do we then* (he saith) *make void the law through faith? God forbid, yea we establish the Law.* I was speak- *(margin: Rom. iii. 31.)*

ing concerning evil deeds. For he that intends to pursue virtue ought to condemn wickedness first, and then go in pursuit of it. For repentance had not the power to make[1] them clean. For this cause they were straightway baptized, that what they were unable to accomplish by themselves might be effected by the grace of Christ. Neither then is repentance sufficient for purification, but it is necessary to receive baptism. At all events, after having previously condemned the sins one had committed and given a decision against them, it was necessary to come to baptism.

But what is *the doctrine of baptisms?* The expression is used not as if there were many baptisms, but one only[c]. Why then did he express it in the plural number? because he had said, *not laying again a foundation of repentance.* For if he had again baptized them and catechised them afresh, and after having been baptized anew[2] they were being taught what things ought to be done and what ought not, they would be in the way to remain perpetually uncorrected.

And of laying on of hands. For thus did they receive the Spirit, *when Paul had laid his hands on them,* it is said.

And of the resurrection of the dead. For this is both effected in baptism, and is affirmed in the confession.

And of eternal judgment. But wherefore saith he this? Because it was likely that after having already believed they would either be shaken from [their faith], or would lead evil and slothful lives, he saith, *be wakeful.*

It is not open to them to say, If we live slothfully we will be baptized again, we will be catechized again, we will again receive the Spirit, even if now we fall from the faith, we shall be able again by being baptized, to wash away our sins, and to attain to the very same state as before. Ye are deceived (he saith) in supposing these things.

[5.] ver. 4, 5. *For it is impossible for those who have been once enlightened and have tasted of the heavenly gift, and have been made partakers of the Holy Ghost, and have tasted the good word of God, and the powers of the world to come, and have fallen away, to renew them again unto repentance,*

---

[c] That is, the Apostle repudiates the teaching of more than one baptism.

crucifying[d] *unto themselves the Son of God afresh, and putting Him to an open shame.* HEB.vi.6.

And see how touchingly[1] and positively [forbiddingly] he begins. *Impossible.* No longer (he would say) expect that which is not possible (for he said not, It is not seemly, or, It is not expedient, or, It is not lawful, but *impossible*, so as to cast [them] into despair), if ye have once been altogether enlightened. [1] ἐντρεπτικῶς

Then he adds, *and have tasted of the heavenly gift. If ye have tasted* (he says) *of the heavenly gift*, that is, of forgiveness. *And been made partakers of the Holy Ghost, and tasted the good word of God* (he is speaking here of the doctrine) *and the powers of the world to come* (what powers is he speaking of? either the working of miracles, or *the earnest of the Spirit*) *and have fallen away, to renew them again unto repentance, seeing they crucify to themselves the Son of God afresh and put Him to an open shame*. *Renew them*, he saith, *unto repentance*, that is, by repentance, for unto repentance is by repentance. (3)

2 Cor. i. 22.

What then, is repentance excluded? Not repentance, God forbid! but the renewing again by the Washing[2]. For he did not say, *impossible* to be renewed *unto repentance*, and then stop, but added how, *impossible* [by] *crucifying afresh*. [2] διὰ λουτροῦ

To *be renewed*, that is, to be made new, for to make men new is [the work] of the Washing only: for (it is said) *thy youth shall be renewed as the eagle's*. But it is [the work of] repentance, when those who have been made new, have afterwards become old through sins, to set them free from this their old age, and to make them strong[3]. To bring them to that former brightness however, is not in its power; for there the whole was Grace. Ps.ciii.5.

[3] στερροὺς καινοὺς Sav. Ben.

[6.] *Crucifying to themselves*, saith he, *the Son of God afresh, and putting Him to an open shame*. And what he means is this. Baptism is a Cross, and *our old man was crucified with* [*Him*], for we were *made conformable to the likeness of His death*, and again, *we were buried therefore with Him by baptism into death*. Wherefore, just as it is not

Rom. vi. 6.
Ib. 5. cf. Phil. iii. 10.
Rom. vi.

---

[d] S. Chrys. exposition requires this literal translation of the participle. He gives two explanations of it, "to renew them by crucifying afresh," and "seeing they crucify afresh."

possible that Christ should be crucified a second time, for this is to *put Him to an open shame* [e]. For *if death shall no more have dominion over Him*, if He rose again, by His resurrection becoming superior to death; if by death He wrestled with and overcame death, and then is crucified again, all those things become a fable and a mockery. He then that baptizeth [f] a second time, crucifies Him again.

But what is *crucifying afresh?* [It is] crucifying over again. For just as Christ died on the cross, so do we in baptism, not as to the flesh, but as to sin. Behold two deaths. He died as to the flesh; in our case the old man was buried, and the new man arose, which had been made conformable to the likeness of His death. If therefore it is necessary to be baptized [again[1]], it is necessary that this same [Christ] should again die. For baptism is nothing else than the putting to death and the rising of that person who is baptized.

And well said he, *crucifying afresh unto themselves*. For he that doth this, as having forgotten the former grace [g], and ordering his own life carelessly, acts in all respects as if there were another baptism. It behoves us therefore to take heed and to be cautious.

[7.] What is, *having tasted of the heavenly gift?* it is, "of the Remission of sins:" for this is of God alone to bestow, and the grace is a grace once for all. *What then? shall we continue in sin that grace may abound? God forbid!* But if we should be always going to be saved by grace we shall never at any time be good. For here where there is but one grace, even so we are indolent, should we then cease sinning if we knew that it is possible again to have our sins washed away? For my part I think not.

In this place he indicates that the gifts are many: and to explain it, "Ye were counted worthy (he says) of forgiveness so great, for he that was sitting in darkness, he that was at enmity, he that was at open war, that was alienated,

---

[e] The common editions add οὕτως οὐδὲ βαπτισθῆναι, "so neither [is it possible] to be baptized [a second time]." The apodosis is wanting in the older text, as it is in several other places.

[f] The later texts add ἑαυτὸν, "that baptizeth himself." S. Chrys. however is speaking of a Bishop who repeats baptism.

[g] χάρις. The word is used throughout this passage in the sense of Remission, as explained in the next clause.

that was hated of God, that was utterly lost, this man hav- HEB.vi.6.
ing been suddenly enlightened, counted worthy of the Spirit,
of the heavenly gift, of adoption as a son, of the kingdom
of heaven, of those other good things, the mysteries that
are not to be spoken of; and who does not even thus become
better, and yet when he was indeed worthy of perdition,
had obtained salvation and honour, as if he had successfully
accomplished some great things; how could he possibly be
again baptized?

On two grounds then he said that the thing was impossible, and he put the stronger last: first, because he to whom such [blessings] have been vouchsafed, and who has betrayed all that was granted to him, is not worthy to be again renewed, neither [h] is it possible that Christ should again be crucified afresh: for this is to *put Him to an open shame.*

There is not then any second Washing: there is not [indeed]. And if there is, there is also a third, and a fourth; for the former one is continually disannulled by the later, and this continually by another, and so on indefinitely.

And tasted, he says, *the good word of God;* and he does not unfold it; *and the powers of the world to come,* for to live as Angels and to have no need of earthly things, to know that this is the means of our introduction to the enjoyment of the worlds to come; this may we learn through the Spirit, and enter into those sacred recesses.

What are *the powers of the world to come?* Life eternal, angelic conversation. Of these then we have already received the earnest through our Faith from the Spirit. Tell me then, if after having been introduced into a Palace, and having had all things therein entrusted to thee, thou hadst then notwithstanding betrayed all, wouldest thou have been again entrusted with them [i]?

[8.] What then (you say)? Is there no repentance? There (4)

---

[h] The longer text in Sav. and Ben. adds, δευτέρῳ δὲ ὅτι οὐ, "and secondly because it is not &c": the shorter text has only οὐδὲ omitting "secondly." There are many other instances of a similar negligence of Style in the genuine text, as also in other works of S. Chrys.

[i] The common texts add τὰ ἐκεῖ, "the things in heaven." But S. Chrys. is speaking of present privileges here on earth.

is repentance, there is however no second baptism: but Repentance there is, and great is the force it has, in that it is able to set free from the burden of his sins, if he will, even him that hath been utterly immersed in sins, and to establish in safety him who is in danger, even though he should have come unto the very lowest depth of wickedness. And this is evident from many places. *For*, saith one, *doth not he that falleth rise again? or he that turneth away, doth not he turn back to* [*God*]*?* It is possible, if we have the will, that Christ should be formed in us again: for hear Paul saying, *My little children of whom I travail in birth again, until Christ be formed in you.* Only let us lay hold on repentance.

For behold the kindness of God to man! we ought on every ground to have been punished at the first; in that having received the natural law, and also enjoyed innumerable blessings, we have not acknowledged our Master, and have lived an unclean life. Yet He not only has not punished us, but has even made us partakers of countless blessings, just as if we had successfully accomplished some great things. Again we fell away, and not even so does He punish us, but has given us the medicine of repentance, which is sufficient to put away and blot out all our sins; provided only that we know the nature of the medicine, and in what manner we ought to apply it.

Of what nature then is the medicine of Repentance? and how is it made up? First, of the condemnation of our own sins [k]; *For* (saith he) *my iniquity have I not hid: And, I will confess against myself mine iniquity unto the Lord, and Thou forgavest the impiety of my heart.* And again, *Declare thou at the first thy sins, that thou mayest be justified.* And, *The righteous man is an accuser of himself at the first speaking.*

Secondly, of great humbleness of mind: For it is like a golden chain; if one have hold of the beginning, all will follow. Because if thou confess thy sin as one ought to confess, the soul is humbled. For conscience turning it on itself[1] causeth it to be subdued.

Other things too must we needs add to humbleness of

---

[k] The common texts add καὶ ἀπὸ ἐξαγορεύσεως, "and [of] from confession."

mind if it be such as the blessed David knew, when he said, *A broken and humbled heart God will not despise.* For that which is broken does not rise up, does not strike, but is prepared to be ill-treated and itself riseth not up. Such is Contrition of heart: though it be insulted, though it be evil entreated, it remaineth quiet, and is not eager to take vengeance. Heb. vi. 6.
Ps. li. 17.

And after humbleness of mind, there is need of intense prayers, of many tears, tears by day, and tears by night: for, saith he, *every night will I wash my bed, I will water my couch with my tears. I am weary with my groaning.* And again, *For I have eaten ashes as it were bread, and mingled my drink with weeping.* the fourth

Ib. vi. 6.

Ib. cii. 9.

And after prayer thus intense, there is need of much almsgiving: for this it is which especially gives strength to the medicine of Repentance. And just as in the case of the aids administered by physicians there are medicines into which many herbs are put, but one that is essential, so also in case of Repentance this herb is the most essential, yea, is every thing. For hear what the Divine Scripture saith, *Give alms, and all things shall be clean.* And again, *By almsgiving and acts of faithfulness*[1] *sins are purged away.* And, *Water will quench a flaming fire, and alms will do away with great sins.* the fifth

S. Luke xi. 41.
Prov. xvi. 6.
Ecclus. iii. 30.

Next not being angry with any one, not bearing malice; the forgiving all men's trespasses. For, saith one, *Man retaineth wrath against man, and yet seeketh healing from the Lord. Forgive that ye may be forgiven.* the sixth
Ib. xxviii. 3.

S. Mark xi. 25.

Also, the converting our brethren from their wandering. For, it is said [m], *Go thou, and convert thy brethren, that thy sins may be forgiven thee.* And from one's being in close relations with [1] the priests, *and if*, it is said, *a man hath committed sins it shall be forgiven him.* To stand forward in defence of those who are wronged. Not to retain anger: to bear all things meekly. the ·
seventh
the eighth
S. James v. 15.
ἔχειν
οἰκείως

[9.] Now then, before you learned that it is possible to

---

[1] καὶ πίστεσιν. [These same two words ἐλεημοσύναι καὶ πίστεις, *almsgiving and acts of faithfulness*, are used by the Septuagint to translate *mercy and truth* in Prov. iii. 3 also, as if πίστεις were the distinct *acts of faithfulness* which go to make up *truth*, comp. *true of heart* throughout the psalms.]

[m] This seems to be an expression of the doctrine of S. James v. 19, 20, partially in the language of our Lord, S. Luke xxii. 23. [cf. Acts iii. 19.]

have our sins washed away by means of repentance, were ye not in an agony of fear, because there is no second Washing, and were ye not in despair of yourselves? But now that we have learned by what means Repentance and remission is brought to a successful issue, and that we shall be able entirely to escape, if we be willing to use it aright, what consideration can we possibly obtain, if we do not even enter on the thought of our sins? since if this were done, all would be accomplished.

For as he who has entered the door, is within [the house]; so he who reckons up his own evils will also most certainly come to get them cured. But should he say, I am a sinner, without reckoning them up specifically¹, and saying, This and this sin have I committed, he will never leave off, confessing indeed continually, but never in earnest caring for amendment. For should he have laid down a beginning, all the rest will unquestionably follow too, if only in one point² he have manifested a beginning: for in every case the beginning and the preliminaries are difficult. This then let us lay as a foundation, and all will be smooth and easy.

Let us begin therefore, I entreat you, one with making his prayers intense: another with continual weeping: another with downcast³ countenance. For not even is this which is so small a matter, unprofitable; for *I saw* (it is said) *that he was grieved and went downcast, and I healed his ways.*

But let us all humble our own souls by almsgiving and forgiving our neighbours their trespasses, by not remembering injuries, nor avenging ourselves. If we continually reflect on the things we have done amiss, no external circumstances will have power to make us elated: neither riches, nor power, nor authority, nor honour; nay, even should we be seated in the imperial chariot itself, we shall sigh bitterly: Since even the blessed David was a King, and yet he said, *Every night I will wash my bed,* [&c]: and he was not at all hurt by the purple robe and the diadem: he was not puffed up; for he knew himself to be a man, and inasmuch as his heart had been made contrite, he went mourning.

[10.] For what are all things human? ashes and dust, HEB.vi.6. and as it were spray before the wind; a smoke and a shadow, and a leaf driven here and there; and a flower; a dream, and a tale, and a fable, wind and air vainly puffed out and dispersing; a feather that hath no stay, a stream flowing by, or if there be aught of more nothingness than these.

For, tell me, what dost thou esteem great? what dignity thinkest thou to be great? is it that of the Consul? for the many think no dignity greater than that. Let me tell thee that he who is not Consul is not a whit inferior to him who is in so great splendour, who hath been held in so great admiration. Both one and the other are of the same dignity; each of them alike, after a little while, is no more.

When was he made [Consul]? for how long a time? tell me: for two days? Nay, this takes place even in dreams. But that is [only] a dream, you say. And what is this? for (tell me) what is by day, is it [therefore] not a dream? Why do we not rather call these things a dream? for just as dreams when the day comes on are proved to be nothing; so these things also, when the night comes on, are proved to be nothing. For night and day have received each an equal portion of time, and have equally divided the whole of duration. Therefore as in the day a person rejoices not in what happened at night, so neither in the night is it possible for him to reap the fruit of what is done in the day. Thou hast been made Consul? So was I in the night; only I was so in the night, thou in the day. And what of this? Not even so hast thou any advantage at all over me, except haply its being said, Such an one is Consul, and the pleasure that springs from the words, gives him the advantage.

I mean something of this kind, for I will express it more plainly: if I say 'Such an one is Consul,' and bestow on him the name, is it not gone as soon as it is spoken? Of such kind also are the things themselves; no sooner does the Consul appear, than he is no more. But let us suppose [that he is Consul] for a year, or two years, or three or four years. Where are they who were ten times Consul? Nowhere.

Hom. 9. But it is not so with Paul. For he was even living continually: he did not live one day, nor two, nor ten, and twenty; nor thirty [days]; nor ten and twenty, nor yet thirty years—and die. Even the four hundredth year is now past, and still even yet is he illustrious, yea much more illustrious than when he was alive. And besides these things indeed [are] on earth, but the glory of the saints in heaven what discourse could represent?

Wherefore I entreat you, let us seek this glory; let us pursue after it, that we may attain it. For this is the true glory. Let us henceforth separate ourselves from the things of this life, that we may find grace and mercy in Christ Jesus our Lord: with whom to the Father, together with the Holy Ghost, be glory, power, honour and worship, now and for ever, and world without end. Amen.

HOMILY X.

Heb. vi. 7, 8.

For the Earth which drinketh in the rain that cometh oft upon it, and bringeth forth herbs meet for them by whom it is dressed, receiveth blessing from God. But if it bear[a] *thorns and briars it is rejected, and nigh unto cursing, whose end is to be burned.*

Let us listen to the oracles of God with fear, with fear and much trembling. For (it is said) *Serve the Lord with* Ps. ii. 11. *fear, and rejoice unto Him with trembling.* But if even our joy and our exultation ought to be *with trembling*, of what punishment are we not worthy, if we listen not with terror to what is said, when the things spoken are themselves fearful, such as those now [uttered]?

For having said that *it is impossible for those who have fallen away* to be baptized a second time, and to receive the remission which is [given] through the Washing, and having pointed out the awefulness of the case, he goes on to say, *for land which has drunk in the rain that cometh often upon it, and bringeth forth herbs meet for them by whom also it is cultivated, partaketh of blessing from God. But if it bear thorns and thistles, it is rejected*[1], *and near to a curse; whose end is for burning.*

[1] ἀδόκιμος reprobate

Let us then fear, my beloved! This threat is not Paul's, these are not the words of man: they are the words of the Holy Ghost, of Christ that speaketh in him. Is there

---

[a] The received version is necessarily altered here: S. Chrysostom's commentary will be more readily understood if it is kept in mind that the exact translation would be as below: "The "land which hath drunk in &c partak-"eth of blessing &c. But if it bear "thorns and thistles, it is reprobate, "and nigh unto a curse, whose end "is for burning."

then any one that is clear from these thorns? And even if we were clear, not even so ought we to be confident, but to fear and tremble lest at any time thorns should spring up in us. But when we are wholly and throughout *thorns and thistles,* whence is it (tell me) that we are confident? and are becoming supine? what is it which makes us inert? If *he that thinketh he standeth* ought to fear *lest he fall;* for (he saith) *Let him that thinketh he standeth, take heed lest he fall;* he that hath fallen, how anxious ought he to be that he may rise up again! If Paul fears, *lest that by any means, when he had preached to others, himself should be a castaway*; and he who had been so approved is afraid lest he should become disapproved[b]: what pardon shall we have who are already disapproved, if we have no fears, but fulfil our Christianity as a custom, and to clear off a duty. Let us then fear, beloved: *For the wrath of God is revealed from heaven.* Let us fear, for it *is revealed* not *against impiety* only but *against all unrighteousness.* What is *against all unrighteousness?* [against all] both small and great.

[2.] In this passage he intimates the loving-kindness of God towards man: and the teaching [of the Gospel] he calls *rain:* and what he said above, *when for the time ye ought to be teachers,* this he says here also. Indeed in many places the Scripture calls the teaching *rain.* For (it says) *I will command the clouds that they rain no rain upon it,* speaking of *the vineyard.* The same which in another place it calls *a famine of bread, and a thirst of water.* And again, *The river of God is full of waters.*

For land, saith he, *which hath drunk in the rain that cometh often upon it.* Here he shews clearly that they had received and had drunk in the word, yea and had often enjoyed this, and yet not even so had they profited. For if (he means) thou hadst not been tilled, if thou hadst enjoyed no rains, the evil would not have been so great. For (it is said) *If I had not come and spoken unto them they had*

---

[b] ἀδόκιμος. In the original it is one and the same word which in the text, Heb. vi. 8, is translated *rejected,* in 1 Cor. ix. 27, *a castaway;* it is in this clause opposed to δόκιμος, *approved, accepted.* It means rejected after testing, as in case of metals: which may take place, as S. Chrys. implies in this passage, either here or hereafter; either for a time or for eternity.

not had sin. But if thou hast often drank and received HEB.vi.8. [nourishment], wherefore hast thou brought forth other things instead of fruits? For (it is said) *I waited that it* Is. v. 2. *should bring forth grapes, and it brought forth thorns.*

Thou seest that everywhere the Scripture calleth sins *thorns.* For David also saith, *I was turned into mourning* Ps. xxxii. *when a thorn was fixed in me.* For it does not simply 4. (so LXX) come on us, but is fixed in; and even if but a little of it remain in, even if we take it not out entirely, that little portion of itself in like manner causes pain, just as in the case of a thorn. And why do I say, 'that little of itself?' even after it has been taken out, it leaves therein for a long time the pain of the wound. And much care and treatment is necessary, that we may be perfectly freed from it. For it is not enough merely to take away the sin, it is necessary also to treat the wounded place.

I fear however that the things said [here] apply to us more than to others. *For,* he saith, *land which hath drunk in the rain that cometh often upon it.* We are ever drinking, ever hearing, but *when the sun is risen* we straightway lose S. Matt. our moisture, and for this cause we bring forth thorns. xiii. 6. What then are the thorns? Let us hear Christ saying, that *the care of this world, and the deceitfulness of riches, choke* Ib. 22. *the word, and it becometh unfruitful.*

[3.] *For land which hath drunk in the rain that cometh oft upon it,* he saith, *and bringeth forth meet herbs.* Because (2) nothing is so meet as purity of life, nothing so suitable as the most excellent life, nothing so meet as virtue.

And bringeth forth (saith he) *herbs meet for them by whom it is cultivated, partakes of blessing from God.* Here he says that God is the cause of all things, giving the heathen a quiet blow, who ascribed the production of fruits to the power of the earth. For (saith he) it is not the hands of the husbandman which stir up the earth to bear fruits, but the command which comes from God. For this cause he says, *partakes of blessing from God.*

And see how in speaking of the thorns, he said not, "bringing forth [1] thorns," nor did he use this word expres- [1] τίκτουσα sive of what is good and useful; but what said he? *bearing* [2] [2] ἐκφέ- [literally *putting out*] *thorns,* as if one should say, 'forcing ρουσα out,' 'throwing out.'

HOM. 10.   *Rejected* (he saith) *and nigh unto a curse.* Oh! how great consolation is there in this word! For he said *nigh unto a curse,* not "a curse." Now he that hath not yet fallen into a curse, but is come to be near [thereto], may also come to be far off [therefrom].

And not by this word only did he encourage them, but also by what follows. For he did not say *rejected and nigh unto a curse,* "which shall be burned," but what then? *Of which the end is for burning,* if he continue [such] (he means) unto the end. So that, if we cut out and burn the thorns, we shall be able to enjoy those good things innumerable and to become approved, and to partake of blessing.

[¹ τρίβολον, *a burr*]   And with good reason did he call sin *a thistle*¹, saying *that which beareth thorns and thistles;* for on whatever side you lay hold on it, it wounds and stings [you], and it is unpleasant even to look at.

[4.] Having therefore sufficiently rebuked them, and alarmed and wounded them, he in turn soothes them, so as not to cast them down too much, and make them supine. For he that strikes one that is *dull,* makes him more dull. So then he neither flatters them throughout, lest he should make them supine, nor does he wound them throughout, but having inserted a little which was calculated to wound them, he applies much that is of a soothing and healing nature in what follows.

For what saith he? We say not these things, as having already condemned you, nor as thinking you to be full of thorns, but in the fear that this should come to pass. For it is better to terrify you by words, that ye may not suffer by the realities. And this is specially a sign of Paul's wisdom.

Moreover he did not say, We think, or, we conjecture, or, we expect, or, we hope, but what? (ver. 9) *But beloved, we are persuaded better things of you, and things that accompany salvation, though we thus speak.* Which Gal. v. 10.   word he also used in writing to the Galatians: *But I am persuaded of you in the Lord, that ye will be none otherwise minded.* For in that instance, inasmuch as they were greatly to be condemned and he could not praise them from things present, he does it from things future (*that ye will be none otherwise minded,* he says): he said not, ye *are,* but *ye will be none otherwise minded.* But in this place he encourages them from things present. *We are persuaded better things of you, beloved, and things that belong to salvation, though we thus speak.* And since he was not able to say so much [as he would] from things present, he confirms his consolation from things past; and says,

ver. 10. *For God is not unrighteous to forget your work, and* ^c *the love, which ye have shewed towards His name, in that ye have ministered unto the saints and do minister.* O how did he here recover their spirit, and give them fresh strength, by reminding them of former things, and bringing them to the necessity of not anticipating that God had forgotten [them]. (For he cannot but sin who is not fully assured concerning his hope, and says that God is unrighteous. Accordingly he obliged them by all means to look forward to those future things. For a man who has become desponding owing to the present state of things, and has given up exerting himself, may be restored by [the prospect of] things future.) As he himself also said in writing to the Galatians, *Ye did run well:* And again *Have ye suffered so many things in vain? if it be yet in vain.*

He.vi.10.

Gal. v. 7.
Ib. iii. 4.

And as in this place he puts the commendation together with the reproof, saying, *When for the time ye ought to be teachers,* so also there, *I marvel that ye are so soon removed.* The commendation [is mingled] with reproof. For it is respecting great things that we marvel, when they fail. Thou seest that praise is concealed under the accusation and the blame.

supra v. 12.
Gal. i. 6.

Nor does he say this concerning himself only, but also concerning all. For he said not, I am persuaded, but *we are persuaded better things of you,* even good things (he means). He says this either in regard to matters of conduct, or to the recompense.

In the next place, having said above, that it is *rejected and nigh unto a curse,* and that it *shall be for burning,* he says, we do not by any means say this of you. *For God is not unrighteous to forget your work, and your love.*

^c Sav. and Ben. here, and in other places where the text is cited, insert τοῦ κόπου *the labour* of love &c. These words are probably not part of the sacred text. They are not referred to by S. Chrysostom.

[5.] With what object then did we say these things? (ver. 11, 12) *But we desire that each of you shew the same zeal for the full assurance of hope unto the end, that ye be not slothful, but followers of them who through faith and patience inherit the promises.*

(3) *We desire,* he says, and we do not therefore merely labour for, or even so far as words go, wish this. But what? *We desire* that ye should hold fast to virtue, not as condemning your former conduct (he means), but fearing for the future. And again he did not say, 'not as condemning your former conduct, but your present; for ye have fainted, ye are become too indolent;' but see how gently he indicated it, and yet at the same time did not wound them.

For what saith he? *But we desire that each of you shew forth the same zeal unto the end.* For this is the admirable part of Paul's wisdom, that he does not expressly say that they *had* given in, that they *had* become negligent. For when he says, *We desire that each of you*—it is as if one should say, I wish thee to be always in earnest; and such as thou wert before such to be now also, and for the time to come. For this made his reproof more gentle and easy to be received.

And he did not say, "I will that," which would have been expressive of the authority of a teacher, but what is expressive of the affection of a father, and what is more than "willing," *we desire.* All but saying, Pardon us, even if we say what is somewhat distasteful.

We desire that each of you shew forth the same zeal, for the full assurance of your hope unto the end. Hope (he means) carries us through: it recovers us again. Be not wearied out, do not despair, lest your hope should be in vain. For he that worketh that which is good hopeth also that which is good, and never at any time despairs of himself.

That ye may not become dull[d]. Still[1] *that ye may not become;* and yet he said above, *seeing ye are become dull*[d] *of hearing.* Observe however how he limited the dullness

[1] ἀκμὴν supra v. 11.

[d] νωθροί. The same word is translated *slothful* and *dull* in these two passages. It means "sluggish," "stupid" "without quickness in perception or energy in action."

to the hearing. And in this place he insinuates the very H*e*.vi.12. same thing; instead of "that ye may not continue in it," he says [this]. But again he leads it on into that future time for which as yet they had no account to render; saying in effect "that ye may not become too slothful:" since for that which is not yet come we could not be subject to account. For he who in regard to the present time is exhorted to be in earnest, as being remiss, will perhaps become even more slothful, but he who is exhorted with reference to the future, not so.

We desire (saith he) *that each of you.* Great is his affection for them: he cares equally for great and small; moreover he knows all, and overlooks no one, but displays the same tender care for each, and equal value for all: from which cause also he the rather persuaded them to receive what was distasteful in his words.

That ye be not slothful, he saith. For just as inactivity is hurtful to the body, so also inactivity as to what is good renders the soul more supine and feeble.

[6.] *But followers* (he saith) *of them, who through faith and patience inherit the promises.* And who they are, he says afterwards. He said therefore, "Imitate your own former well-doings." Then, lest they should say, What [well-doing]? he leads them back to the Patriarch: bringing before them examples of well-doing indeed from their own history[1], but of the thought of being forsaken, from [1] οἴκοθεν the Patriarch; that they might not suppose that they were disregarded and forsaken as being of no account, but might know that this is [the portion] of the very noblest men to make the journey of life through temptations; and that God has thus dealt with great and admirable men.

Now we ought (he says) to bear all things with patience: for this also is believing: whereas if He say that He gives and thou immediately receivest, how hast thou also believed? since in that case this no longer [comes] of thy faith, but of Me, He says, who have given [what I promise at once]. But if on the other hand I say that I give, and give after an hundred years, and thou hast not despaired; then hast thou accounted Me worthy to be believed, then thou hast the right opinion concerning Me. Thou seest that oftentimes unbelief arises not from want of hope only, but also from faintheartedness, and want of patience, not from condemning him who made the promise.

For God (he saith) *is not unrighteous to forget your love* and the zeal *which ye have shewed toward His Name, in that ye have ministered unto the saints, and yet do minister.* He testifies great things of them, not deeds only, but deeds done with alacrity, which he says also in another place, *and not only so, but they gave themselves also to the Lord and to us.*

Which (he saith) *ye have shewed toward His Name, in that ye have ministered to the saints, and yet do minister.* See how again he soothes them, by adding *and yet do minister.* Still even at this time (he says) ye are ministering, and he raises them up by shewing that they had done [what they did] not to them [the saints], but to God. *Which ye have shewed* (saith he); and he said not "unto the saints," but *towards God,* for this is *toward His Name.* It is for His Name's sake (he means) that ye have done all. He therefore who willingly takes from you the fruit of[2] so great zeal and love, will not at any time despise you nor forget you.

(4) [7.] Hearing these things, let us, I beseech you, *minister to the saints.* For every believer is a saint in that he is a believer. Though he be a person living in the world, he is a saint. *For* (he saith) *the unbelieving husband hath been sanctified by the wife, and the unbelieving wife by the husband.* See how the faith makes the saintship. If then we see even a secular person in misfortune, let us stretch out a hand [to him]. Let us not be good to those only who dwell in the mountains; they are indeed saints both in life and in faith; these others however are saints by their faith, and many of them also in life. Let us not, if we see a monk [cast] into prison, in that case go in; but if it be a secular person, refuse to go in. This last is also a saint and a brother.

What then (you say) if he be unclean and polluted [are we to help him]? Listen to Christ saying, *Judge not that ye be not judged.* Do thou act for God's sake. Nay what am I saying? Even if we see a heathen in misfortune, we ought to shew kindness to him, and to every man without exception who is in misfortunes, and much more to a believer who is in the world. Listen to Paul, saying, *Do good unto all men, but especially to those who are of the household of faith.* ^{He.vi.12.} ^{Gal. vi. 10.}

But I know not whence this [notion] has been introduced, or whence this custom hath prevailed. For he that only seeks after the solitaries, and is willing to do good to them alone, and with regard to the others on the contrary is over-curious in his enquiries, and says, 'unless he be 'worthy[e], unless he be righteous, unless he work miracles, 'I stretch out no hand:' [such an one] has taken away the greater part of charity[1], yea and in time he will in turn utterly destroy the very thing itself. And yet that is charity which [is shewn] towards sinners, towards the guilty. For this is charity, not the pitying those who have done well, but those who have done wrong.

[1] ἐλεημο-σύνη merciful-ness or almsgiv-ing

[8.] And that thou mayest understand this, listen to the Parable: *A certain man* (it saith) *went down from Jerusalem to Jericho, and fell among thieves:* and when they had beaten him, they left him by the way-side, having bruised him exceedingly. A certain Levite came, and when he saw him, he passed by; A priest came, and when he saw him, he hastened past; then a certain Samaritan came, and great was the care he bestowed upon him. For he *bound up his wounds,* dropped oil on them, set him upon his ass, *brought him to the inn, said to the host Take care of him* (and observe his great liberality); *and I,* says he, *will give thee whatsoever thou shalt expend.* Who then is his neighbour? *He,* it is said, *that shewed mercy on him. Go thou then also,* He saith, *and do likewise.* And consider what a parable He spake. He said not that a Jew did [so and so] to a Samaritan, but that a Samaritan displayed all that liberality. Having then heard these things, let us not have care only for *those that are of the household of faith,* and ^{S. Luke x. 30, &c.} ^{Ib. 34.} ^{Ib. 35.} ^{Ib. 37.} ^{Gal. vi. 10.}

[e] ἐὰν μὴ ᾖ ἄξιος, ἐὰν μὴ ᾖ δίκαιος. Mr. Field retains μὴ in these clauses, in accordance with the common editions, though all the MSS. omit the negative in the first clause, and the best MSS. in the second also, and it was not read by Mutianus. If it be omitted, the passage would run thus, "and says, If "he be worthy, if he be righteous [I "will help him]. Unless he work mi-"racles I stretch out no hand" &c.; which seems to give a good sense.

neglect the rest. In this way then thyself also, if thou see any man in affliction, be not curious to enquire further. His being in affliction involves a just claim on thy aid [1]. For if when thou seest an ass choking thou raisest him up, and dost not curiously enquire whose he is, much more about a man one ought not to be over-curious in enquiring whose he is. He is God's, be he heathen or be he Jew; since even if he is an unbeliever, still he needs assistance. For if indeed it had been committed to thee to enquire and to judge, thou wouldst have well said thus, but, as it is, his misfortune does not suffer thee to search out these things. For if even about men in good health it is not right to be over-curious, nor to be a busy body in other men's matters, much less about those that are in affliction.

[9.] But on another view what [shall we say]? Didst thou see him in prosperity, in high esteem, that thou shouldst say that he is a wicked and worthless person? But if thou seest him in affliction, do not say that he is wicked. For when a man is in high credit, we fairly say these things; but when he is in calamity, and needs help, it is not right to say that he is wicked. For this is cruelty, inhumanity and arrogance. Tell me what was ever more iniquitous than the Jews. But nevertheless while God punished them, and that justly, yea, very justly, yet He approved of those who compassionated them, and those who rejoiced over them He punished. For *they were not grieved,* it is said, *at the affliction of Joseph.*

And again it is said *Redeem* [*Ransom*] *those who are ready to be slain: spare not.* (He said not, enquire curiously, and learn who he is; and yet, for the most part, they who are led away to execution are wicked,) for this is in a special way a charity. For he that doeth good to a friend, doeth it not altogether for God's sake: but he that [doeth good] to one who is unknown to him, this man acts purely for God's sake. *Do not spare* thy money, even if it be necessary to spend all, yet give.

But we, when we see persons in extreme distress [2], bewailing themselves, suffering things more grievous than ten thousand deaths, and oftentimes unjustly, we [I say] are sparing of our money, and unsparing of our brethren; we are careful of lifeless things, and neglect the living soul. He.vi.12. And yet Paul says, *in meekness instruct those that oppose themselves, if peradventure God should give them repentance to the acknowledging of the truth, and they should awaken out of the snare of the devil who have been taken captive by him, at His will.* 2 Tim. ii. 25, 26. *If peradventure*, saith he; thou seest of how great long-suffering the word is full.

Let us also imitate Him, and despair of no one. For the fishermen too, when they have cast many times [suppose it], have not succeeded; but afterwards having cast again, have gained all. So we also expect that ye will all at once shew to us ripe fruit. For the husbandm too,na after he has sown, waits one day or two days, and is a long while in expectation: and all at once he sees the fruits springing up on every side. This we expect will take place in your case also by the grace and mercy of our Lord Jesus Christ, with whom to the Father and also to the Holy Ghost be glory might honour now and for ever and world without end. Amen.

HOMILY XI.

HEB. vi. 13—16.

For when God made promise to Abraham, because He could swear by no greater, He sware by Himself, saying, Surely blessing I will bless thee, and multiplying I will multiply thee. And so after he had patiently endured, he obtained the promise. For men verily swear by the greater, and an oath for confirmation is to them the end of all strife.

HAVING boldly reflected on the faults of the Hebrews, and sufficiently alarmed them, he consoles them, first, by his commendations, and secondly (which also is the stronger ground), by the [thought] that they would certainly attain the objects of their hope. Moreover he draws his consolation, not from things future, but again from the past, which indeed had more power to persuade them. For as in the case of punishment, he alarms them rather by those [viz. things future], so also in the case of the prizes [set before them], he encourages them by these [viz. by things past], shewing [herein] God's way of dealing. And that is, not to bring in what has been promised immediately, but after a long interval of time. And this He does, both to present the greatest proof of His own power, and also to lead us to Faith, that they who are living in tribulation without receiving the promises, or the rewards, may not faint under their troubles.

And omitting all [the rest], though he had many whom he might have mentioned, he brought forward Abraham both on account of the dignity of his person, and because this had occurred in a special way in his case.

Infra xi. 13.
And yet at the end of the epistle he says, that *all these, having seen the promises afar off, and having embraced*

them, received them not, that they without us should not be HE.vii.16.
made perfect. For when God made promise to Abraham, Infra xi. 39, 40.
(he saith [here]), *since He could swear by no greater, He sware by Himself, saying, Surely blessing I will bless thee, and multiplying I will multiply thee. And thus after patiently enduring, he attained the promise.* How then does he say at the end [of the Epistle] that *he received not the promises,* and here, that *having patiently endured he obtained the promise?* In what sense did he not receive? in what sense did he obtain? He is not speaking of the same things in this place and in the other, but makes his consolation twofold. God made promises to Abraham, and whereas after a long space of time He gave the things [spoken of] in this place, those others [He has] not [given] yet.

And so after he had patiently endured, he obtained the promise. Seest thou that the promise alone did not effect the whole, but the patient waiting as well? In this place he alarms them, pointing out that oftentimes a promise is hindered of its effect through faintheartedness [1]. And this [1] ὀλιγο- he had indeed shewn through [the instance of] the [Jewish] ψυχίαν people: for inasmuch as they were fainthearted, for that cause they obtained not the promise. But now he exhibits the contrary, and that in the case of Abraham. Afterwards near the end [of the Epistle] he proves something more also: [viz.] that even though they had patiently endured, they did not attain; and yet not even so are they indignant.

[2.] *For men verily swear by the greater, and an Oath for confirmation is to them an end of all strife. But God because He could swear by no greater, sware by Himself.* Well, who then is He that sware unto Abraham? Is it not the Son? No, saith one. Yea indeed most certainly it was He: however I shall not dispute [thereon]. So when He [the Son] sweareth the same oath, *Verily, verily, I say unto you,* is it not plain that it was from His not being able to swear by any greater? For as the Father sware, so also the Son sweareth by Himself, saying, *Verily, verily, I say unto you.* He here reminds them also of the oaths of Christ, which He was constantly uttering. *Verily,* S. John *verily, I say unto thee, he that believeth on Me shall never die.* xi. 26.

What is, *And an oath for confirmation is to them an end*

HOM. 11. *of all strife?* it is instead of, "by this every doubtful question is solved:" not this, or this, but every one.

God, however, ought to have been believed even without an oath: (ver. 17) *wherein* (saith he) *God being willing more abundantly to shew unto the heirs of promise the immutability of His counsel, confirmed it* [lit. mediated¹] *by an oath*. In these words he comprehends also the believers. For this cause he mentions also this *promise* which was made to us [Christians] in common [with them]. *He mediated* (saith he) *by an oath.* Here again he says that the Son was mediator between men and God.

(ver. 18) *That by two immutable things, in which it was impossible that God should lie.* What are these two? The speaking and promising; and the adding an oath to the promise. For inasmuch as among men that which is [confirmed] by an oath is thought more worthy of credit, on this account He added that also.

(2) Thou seest that He regardeth not His own dignity, but how He may persuade men; and He endures to have unworthy things said concerning Himself. That is [He did this] wishing to impart full assurance. And in the case of Abraham indeed [the Apostle] shews that the whole was of God, not of his patient enduring, inasmuch as He even endured to add an oath, since He by whom men swear, by Him also God *sware*, that is *by Himself.* They however swear [by Him] as one greater [than themselves], but He as by one not greater. And yet He did it. For it is not the same thing for man to swear by himself, and for God [to do so]. For man has no power over himself.

Thou seest then that this is said not more [with reference] to Abraham than to ourselves: *that we* (saith he) *might have strong consolation, who have fled for refuge to lay hold on the hope set before us.*

Here too again ᵃ, *having patiently endured he attained the promise.*

¹ ἐμεσί-τευσεν

² ἐπειδὴ "at the very time that"

Now he means, and he did not say "when ² He swore."

ᵃ This observation seems to be suggested by the words *the hope set before us:* i.e. this is another instance of obtaining a future blessing by patient waiting. The next clause bears on the Apostle's statement that this oath was made *that we might have consolation,* we, *now,* at this time; not Abraham, to whom the oath was originally made.

But what the oath is, he plainly shewed, by speaking of the Hɛ.vi.20. swearing by a greater. But since the race of men is hard of belief, He condescends to the same [things] with ourselves. As then for our sake He swears, although it be unworthy of Him that He should not be believed, so also did [the Apostle] make that other statement: *He learned* supra v. *from the things which He suffered,* inasmuch as men think 8. this more worthy of reliance—the going through the actual experience [of things].

What is *the hope set before us?* from these [past events] (saith he) we conjecture the future. For if these came to pass after so long a time, so certainly these others will. So that the things which happened in regard to Abraham give us confidence also concerning the things that are yet to come.

[3.] (ver. 19, 20) *Which [hope] we have as an anchor of the soul both sure and stedfast, and which entereth into that within the veil: whither the forerunner is for us entered, even* Jɛsus, *made High Priest for ever after the order of Melchisedec.* He points out, that whilst we are still in the world, and not yet departed from [this] life, we are already among the things that have been promised. For through hope we are already in heaven. He had said, "Wait; for it shall surely be." Afterwards giving them full assurance, he saith, "nay rather by hope" [&c] [b]. And he said not, "We are within," but "It hath entered within," which plainly was more true and more persuasive. For just as the anchor when it is dropped from the vessel does not allow it to be carried about, even if ten thousand winds agitate it, but being fastened and dropt makes it steady, so also does hope.

And see how exceedingly suitable an image he has discovered: For he said not, Foundation; which would not have been suitable; but, *Anchor.* For that which is on the surf, and seems not to be very firmly fixed, stands on the water as upon dry land, and is shaken and yet is not shaken. For in regard to those who are very firm, and philosophic, Christ with good reason made that statement, saying, *Whosoever* [&c.] *hath built his house on a rock.* S. Matt. But in respect of those who are giving way, and who ought vii. 24.

[b] Sav. and Ben. add ἤδη ἐτύχετε, "ye have already attained it."

to be carried through by hope, Paul hath suitably set down this. For the surge and the great storm toss the boat; but hope suffers it not to be carried hither and thither, although winds innumerable agitate it: so that, unless we had had this [hope] we should have long since been sunk in the sea. Nor is it only in things spiritual, but also in the affairs of this life, that one may find the power of hope great. For instance, in merchandise, in husbandry, in a military expedition, unless a person from the first sets this before him, he would not even touch any work. But he said not simply *Anchor*, but *sure and stedfast* [i.e.] not shaken. *Which entereth into that within the veil;* instead of "which reacheth through even to heaven."

[4.] Then after this he introduced the Faith also, that there might not only be hope, but an exceeding real and true [hope]. For after the oath he sets down another thing too, even demonstration by facts, in that *the forerunner is for us entered in, even* JESUS. But a forerunner is a forerunner of some one, as John was of Christ.

Now he did not simply say, *He is entered in,* but *where He is entered in a forerunner for us,* as though we also ought to attain to it. For there is no great interval between the forerunner and those who follow: otherwise he would not be a forerunner at all; since the forerunner and those who follow ought to be in the same road, and to arrive after [each other].

Being made an High Priest for ever after the order, he saith, *of Melchisedec.* Here is also another consolation, if our High Priest is on high, and far better than those among the Jews, not in the kind [of Priesthood] only, but also in the place, and the tabernacle, and the covenant, and the person [of the Priest]. And this also is spoken with reference to that which is according to the flesh.

[5.] It is right then that those whose High Priest He is, should be very greatly superior. And as the difference is great between Aaron and Christ, so great should that be which is between us and the Jews. For see, we have our victim[1] on high, our priest on high, our sacrifice[2] on high: let us bring such sacrifices as can be offered on that altar,

---

[1] ἱερεῖον
[2] θυσία
"the act of sacrificing."

no longer sheep and oxen, no longer blood and steamy savour. All these things have been done away; and there has been brought in in their stead *the reasonable service.* But what is *the reasonable service?* the [offerings made] through the soul; those made through the spirit *(God,* it is said, *is a Spirit, and they that worship Him must worship Him in spirit and in truth);* things which have no need of a body, no need of instruments, nor of special places, whereof each one is himself the Priest, such as, moderation, temperance, mercifulness, enduring ill-treatment, long-suffering, humbleness of mind.

<small>He.vi.20.
Rom. xii. 1.
S. John iv. 24.</small>

These sacrifices one may see in the Old [Testament] also, shadowed out beforehand from the first. *Offer to God,* it is said, *a sacrifice of righteousness; Offer a sacrifice of praise;* and, *a sacrifice of praise shall glorify Me,* and, *the sacrifice of God is a broken spirit;* and *what doth the Lord require of thee but* to hearken to Him? *Burnt-offerings and sacrifices for sin Thou hast had no pleasure in: then I said, Lo I come to do Thy will, O God!* and again, *To what purpose do ye bring the incense from Sheba? Take thou away from Me the sound of thy songs, and I will not hear the melody of thy viols.* But instead of these *I will have mercy and not sacrifice.* Thou seest with what kind of *sacrifices* God *is well pleased.* Thou seest also that already from the first the one class have given place, and these others have come in their stead.

<small>Ps. iv. 5.
Ps. l. 14.
Ib. 23.
Ps. li. 17.
Mic. vi. 8.
Ps.xl.6,7.
Jerem. vi. 20.
Amos v. 23.
Hos.vi.6.
Infra xiii. 16.</small>

These therefore let us bring, for those other indeed are [the offerings] of wealth and of persons who have [possessions], but these of virtue: those from without, these from within: those any chance person even might perform; these only a few. And as much as a man is superior to a sheep, so much is this sacrifice superior to that; for here thou offerest thy soul as a victim.

[6.] And other sacrifices also there are, which are indeed whole burnt-offerings, the bodies of the martyrs: there both soul and body [are offered]. These have a great savour of a sweet smell. Thou also art able, if thou wilt, to bring a sacrifice such as this.

For what, if thou dost not burn thy body in the fire? yet in a different fire thou canst; for instance, in that of voluntary poverty, in that of affliction. For to have it in one's power to spend one's days in luxury and expense, and yet to take up a life of toil and bitterness, and to mortify the body, is not this a whole burnt-offering? Do thou mortify thy body, and crucify it, and thou shalt thyself also receive the crown of this martyrdom. For what in the other case the sword accomplishes, that in this case let a willing mind effect. Let not the desire of wealth burn, or possess you. On the contrary let this unreasonable appetite itself be utterly consumed and quenched by the fire of the Spirit; let it be cut in pieces by the sword of the Spirit.

This is an excellent sacrifice, not needing a priest, but only himself who brings it. This is an excellent sacrifice, performed indeed below, but forthwith taken up on high. Are we not amazed that of old time fire used to come down and consume all? It is possible now also that fire may come down far more wonderful than that, and consume all the presented offerings[1]: nay rather, not consume, but bear them up to heaven. For it does not reduce them to ashes, but offers them as gifts to God.

[7.] Of such a kind were the offerings of Cornelius. For (it is said) *thy prayers and thine alms are come up for a memorial before God.* Thou seest [this] most excellent union. Then are we heard, when we ourselves also hear the poor who come to us. *He* (it is said) *that stoppeth his ears that he may not hear the poor,* his prayer God will not hearken to. *Blessed is he that considereth the poor and needy: the Lord will deliver him in the evil day.* But what day is evil except that Day, which is an evil day to sinners?

What is meant by *he that considereth?* He that understandeth what it is to be a poor man, that has become thoroughly acquainted with the affliction of the poor man. For he that has become acquainted with his affliction, will certainly and immediately have compassion on him. When thou seest a poor man, do not hasten past, but immediately reflect what thou wouldst have been, hadst thou been he. What wouldst thou not have wished that all should do for thee? *He that considereth* (saith he). Reflect that he is

[1] τὰ προκείμενα

a free-man like thyself, and shares the same noble birth He.vi.20. with thee, and possesses all things in common with thee; and yet oftentimes he is not on a level even with thy dogs. On the contrary, while they have their full, he often-times lies down to sleep in hunger, and the free-man is more dishonoured than thy slaves.

But they perform needful services for thee. What, I ask, are these? That they serve thee well? Suppose then I shew that this [poor man] too performs services in thy need, far greater than they do. For he will stand by thee in the Day of judgement, and will deliver thee from the fire. What do all thy slaves do that is like this? When Tabitha died, who raised her up? the slaves who stood around or the poor? But thou art not willing to put the free-man on an equality even with thy slaves. The frost is hard, and the poor man is cast [on the ground] in rags, well-nigh dead, with his teeth chattering, both by his looks and his dress calculated to move thee: and thou passest by, warm and full of drink; and how dost thou expect that God should deliver thee when thou art in misfortune?

And oftentimes thou sayest this too: "If it had been myself, and I had found one that had done many wrong things, I would have forgiven him; and does not God forgive?" Say not this. Him that has done *thee* no wrong, whom thou art able to deliver, him thou neglectest. How shall He forgive thee, who art sinning against Him? Is not this deserving of hell?

And how amazing! Oftentimes a body that is dead, insensible, no longer perceiving the honour [done to it], thou adornest with vestments innumerable, of varied colours and wrought with gold; whilst that which is in pain, and lamenting, and tormented, and racked, by hunger and frost, thou neglectest; and givest more to vain glory, than to the fear of God.

[8.] And would that it stopped here; but immediately accusations are brought against him who applies [for aid]? For why does he not work (you say)? and why is he to be maintained in idleness? But (tell me) is it by working that thou hast what thou hast, didst thou not receive it as an inheritance from thy fathers? And even if thou dost work, is this a reason why thou shouldest reproach another? Hearest thou not what Paul saith? For after saying, *He that worketh not, neither let him eat,* he says, *But you be ye not weary in well doing.*

(4) But what say they? He is an impostor[1]. What sayest thou, o man? callest thou him an impostor, for the sake of a single loaf or of a garment? But (you say) he will sell it immediately. And dost thou manage all thy affairs to perfection? But what? are all poor through idleness? is no one so from a shipwreck? none from lawsuits? none from being robbed? none from dangers? none from illness? none from any other difficult circumstances? If however we hear any one bewailing such evils, and crying out vehemently, and looking up naked towards heaven, and with his hair long, and clad in rags, at once we call him, The impostor! the deceiver! the swindler! Art thou not ashamed? Whom dost thou call impostor? Give nothing, and do not accuse the man.

But (you say) he has means, and yet makes himself this figure. This is a charge against thyself, not against him. He knows that he has to deal with cruel people, with wild beasts rather than with men, and that, even if he utter a pitiable story, he attracts no one's attention: And on this account he is forced to assume also a more miserable guise, that he may melt thy soul. If we see a person coming to beg in a respectable dress, This is an impostor (you say), and he comes in this way that he may be supposed to be of good birth. If we see one in the contrary guise, him too we think dishonest. What then are they to do? O the cruelty, O the inhumanity!

And why (you say) do they expose their maimed limbs? Because of thee. If we were compassionate, they would have no need of these artifices: if they persuaded us at the first application, they would not have adopted so many artifices. Who is there so wretched, as to be willing to cry out so much, as to be willing to behave in an unseemly way, as to be willing to make public lamentation, with his wife destitute of clothing, with his children, to sprinkle ashes on himself. How much worse than poverty are these things?

Hom. 11.

2 Thess. iii. 10.
Ib. 13.

[1] ἐπιθέτης

Yet on account of them not only are they not pitied, but are even accused by us. HE.vi.20.

[9.] Shall we still then be indignant, because when we pray to God, we are not listened to? Shall we then still be vexed, because when we entreat we do not persuade? Do we not tremble for fear, my beloved?

But (you say) I have often given. And art thou not always eating? and dost thou drive away thy children that are often begging of thee? O the shamelessness! Dost thou call a poor man shameless? And whilst thou art not shameless when plundering, he is shameless when begging for bread! Considerest thou not how great are the necessities of the belly? Dost not thou do all things for this? dost thou not for this neglect things spiritual? Is not heaven set before thee and the kingdom of heaven? and thou fearing the tyranny of that [appetite]endurest all things, and thinkest lightly of that [kingdom]. This *is* shamelessness.

Seest thou not old men maimed? But O what trifling! "Such an one (you say) lends out so many pieces of gold, and such an one so many, and yet begs." You repeat the stories and trifles of children; for they too are always hearing stories of this kind from their nurses. I am not persuaded of it. I do not believe this. God forbid it should be so. Does a man lend out money, and so go a begging when he has abundance? For what purpose, tell me? And what is more disgraceful than begging? It were better to die than to beg. Where does our inhumanity stop? [And if it be so] what then? Do all lend money? are all impostors? is there no one really poor? "Yea (you say) and many." Why then dost thou not assist those persons, seeing thou art so strict an enquirer into their lives? All this is an excuse and a pretence.

Give to every one that asketh of thee, and from him that would borrow of thee turn not thou away. Stretch out thy hand, let it not be closed up. We have not been constituted examiners into men's lives, since so we should have compassion on no one. Why is it that when thou callest upon God thou sayest, Remember not my sins? So then, if that person even be an exceeding great sinner, make this allowance in his case also, and do not remember his sins. S. Matt. v. 42.

Hom. 11. It is the season of kindness not of strict enquiry; of mercy not of calculation. He wishes to be maintained: if thou art willing, give [him something]; but if thou art not willing, send him away without adding questions to put him in a difficulty[1]. Why art thou wretched and miserable? why dost thou not even thyself pity him, and also turnest away those who would? For when such a one hears from thee, This [fellow] is a cheat; that a hypocrite; and the other lends out money; he neither gives to the one nor to the other; for he suspects all to be such. For you know that we easily suspect evil, but good, not [so easily].

[1] ἐπαπορήσας

S. Luke vi. 36.   [10.] Let us *be merciful*, not simply so, but *as our heavenly Father is*. He feeds even adulterers, and fornicators, and sorcerers, and what shall I say? persons having every species of wickedness. For in so large a world there must of necessity be many such as well [as others]. But nevertheless He feeds all; He clothes all. No one ever perished of hunger, unless one did so of his own choice. In this way let us be merciful. If a person be in want and in necessity, help him.

But now as it is, we are come to such a degree of unreasonableness, as to act thus not only in regard to the poor who walk up and down the alleys, but even in the case of men that live in [religious] solitude[2]. Such an one is an impostor, you say. Did I not say this at first, that if we give to all indiscriminately, we shall always be compassionate; but if we begin to make over-curious enquiries, we shall never be compassionate? What dost thou mean? is a man an impostor in order to get a loaf? If indeed he asks for talents of gold and silver, or costly clothes, or slaves, or anything else [of this sort], one might with good reason call him a swindler. But if he ask none of these things, but only food and shelter, things which are suited to a philosophic life [c], tell me, is this the part of a swindler? Cease we from this unseasonable fondness for meddling, which is Satanic, which is soul-destroying.

[2] μοναζόντων ἀνδρῶν

For indeed, if a man say that he is on the list of the Clergy, or calls himself a Priest, then busy thyself [to en-

---

[c] ἃ φιλοσοφίας ἐστί, i.e. of the ascetics or solitary life.

quire], make much ado: since in that case the communi-cating¹ without enquiry is not without danger. For the risk is about matters of importance, for thou dost not give but receivest. But if he want food, make no enquiry.

HE.vi.20.
¹ κοινωνία

Make enquiry, if thou wilt, how Abraham displayed his hospitality towards all who came to him. If he had been over-curious about those who came to him for refuge, he would not have *entertained angels*. For perhaps not thinking them to be angels, he would have thrust away them too with the rest. But inasmuch as he was used to receive all, he received even angels.

Infra xiii. 2.

What? Is it from the life of those that receive [thy bounty] that God grants thee thy reward? Nay [it is] from thine own purpose, from thy abundant liberality; from thy lovingkindness; from thy goodness. Let this be [found], and thou shalt attain all good things, which may we all attain, through the grace and mercy of our Lord Jesus Christ, with Whom to the Father and also to the Holy Ghost, be glory power honour, now and for ever and world without end. Amen.

HOMILY XII.

Heb. vii. 1—3.

For this Melchisedec, King of Salem, Priest of the most High God, who met Abraham as he was returning from the slaughter of the Kings, and blessed him: to whom also Abraham gave a tenth part of all; first being by interpretation King of Righteousness, and after that also King of Salem, which is, King of Peace, without father, without mother, without genealogy, having neither beginning of days, nor end of life, but made like unto the Son of God, abideth a Priest continually.

PAUL wishing to shew the difference between the New and Old Covenant, introduces the subject in many different places; and shoots from afar, and ringeth in the ears of [his] hearers[1], and exerciseth beforehand. For at once, even from the introduction of the Epistle, he laid down this as a foundation, saying, that *to them indeed He spake by prophets, to us by The Son*, and to them *at sundry times and in divers manners*, to us through the Son. Afterwards, having discoursed concerning the Son, who He was and what He had wrought, and given an exhortation to obey Him, lest we should suffer the same things as the Jews; and having said that He is *High Priest after the order of Melchisedec*, and having oftentimes wished to enter into [the subject of] this difference, and having used much preparatory management; and having rebuked them as weak, and again soothed and recovered them to feelings of confidence; then at last he introduces the discussion on the difference [of the two dispensations] to ears [as it were]

[1] διακωδωνίζει

supra i. 1, 2.

Ib. vi. 20.

in their full vigour. For he who is depressed in spirits would not be a ready hearer. And that you may understand this, hear the Scripture which saith, *They hearkened not to Moses for littleness of spirit* [1]. For this cause having first cleared away their despondency by many considerations, some fearful, some more gentle, he then from this point enters upon the discussion of the difference [of the dispensations].

He.vii.3.
Exod. vi. 9.
[1] ὀλίγο-ψυχίαν *faint-heartedness*

[2.] And what saith he? *For this Melchisedec, King of Salem, Priest of the Most High God.* And, what is especially worthy of admiration, he shews the difference to be great by the Type itself. For as I [before] said, he continually confirms the truth from the Type, from things past, on account of the weakness of the hearers. *For* (saith he) *this Melchisedec, King of Salem, Priest of the Most High God, who met Abraham returning from the slaughter of the Kings, and blessed him, to whom also Abraham assigned a tenth part of all.* Having concisely set down the whole narrative, he contemplated [2] it mystically.

And first from the name. *First* (saith he) *being by interpretation King of righteousness:* for Sedec means *righteousness;* and Melchi, *King:* Melchisedec, *King of righteousness.* Thou seest his exactness even in the names? But who is *King of righteousness,* save our Lord Jesus Christ? *King of righteousness. And after that also King of Salem,* from his city, *that is, King of Peace,* which again is [characteristic] of Christ. For He has made us righteous, and has *made peace* for *things in Heaven and things on earth.* What man is *King of Righteousness and of Peace?* None, save only our Lord JESUS Christ.

[2] ἐθεώ-ρησε drew out the mystical senses.

Col. i. 20.

[3.] He then adds another distinction, *Without father, without mother, without genealogy, having neither beginning of days nor end of life, but made like unto the Son of God, abideth a priest continually.* Since then there lay in his way [as an objection] the [words] *Thou art a Priest for ever, after the order of Melchisedec,* whereas he [Melchisedec] was dead, and was not *Priest for ever,* see how he explained it mystically.

'And who can say this concerning a man'? I do not assert this in fact (saith he); the meaning is, we do not know when^a [or] what father he had, nor what mother, nor when he received his beginning, nor when he came to an end. And what of this (saith one)? for does it follow, because we do not know it, that therefore he did not die, [or] had no parents? Thou sayest well: he both died and had parents. In what sense then [was he] *without father, without mother?* In what sense *having neither beginning of days nor end of life?* In what sense? [why] from its not being expressed¹. And what of this? That just as this man is so, from his genealogy not being given, so is Christ from the very nature of the reality.

(2) See here is the *without beginning.* See here is the *without end.* As in case of this man, we know not either *beginning of days*, or *end of life*, because they have not been written; so we know [them] not in the case of JESUS, not because they have not been written, but because they do not exist. For that indeed is a figure², and therefore [we say] 'because it is not written,' but this is the reality³, and therefore [we say] 'because it does not exist.' For just as in regard to the names also (for there *King of Righteousness* and *of Peace* are appellations, but here the reality of things actually existing) so these too are appellations in that case, in this the reality of things actually existing. In what sense then hath He a beginning? Thou seest that the Son is *without beginning*⁴, not in respect of His not having a cause⁵, for this is impossible: for He has a Father, otherwise how is He Son? but in respect of His *not having beginning or end of life.*

But made like unto the Son of God. Where is the likeness? That we know not of the one or of the other either the end or the beginning. Of the one because they are not written; of the other, because they do not exist. Here is the likeness. But if the likeness were to exist in all respects, there would no longer be figure and reality; but both would be figure. [Here] then just as in representations⁶ ᵇ

¹ ἐμφέ-
ρεσθαι

² τύπος
³ ἀλήθεια

⁴ ἄναρχον
⁵ αἴτιον

⁶ εἰκόνων

---

^a Mr. Field reads πότε making a double question. The other editions have ποτε " at all."

^b The comparison is not between the living object and the picture, but between representations in drawing and in painting; the word εἰκών, as our "likeness," being applicable to both. The passage is considerably altered in the common editions so as to avoid an apparent difficulty.

[by painting or drawing], there is somewhat that is like and somewhat that is unlike. By means of the lines indeed there is a likeness of features¹, but when the colours are put on, then the difference is plainly shewn, and [that] part is like and part is unlike.

[4.] ver. 4. *Now consider* (saith he) *how great this man is to whom even the Patriarch Abraham gave the tenth of the spoils²*. Up to this point he has been applying the type: henceforward he confidently shews him [Melchisedec] to be more glorious than the very realities which existed among the Jews. But if he who bears a type of Christ is so much better not merely than the priests, but even than the forefather himself of the priests, what should one say of the reality? Thou seest from what a superabundance [of proof] he shews the superiority.

Now consider (saith he) *how great this man is to whom even the Patriarch Abraham gave a tenth out of the choice portions*. Spoils [taken in battle] are called *choice portions*³. And it cannot be said that he gave them to him as having a part in the war, for on this account (he said) he met him *returning from the slaughter of the kings*, for he had staid at home (he means), and yet [Abraham] gave him the first-fruits of his labours.

ver. 5. *And verily that are of the sons of Levi who receive the office of Priesthood, have commandment to take tithes of the people according to the law, that is, of their brethren, although they are come out of the loins of Abraham.* So great (he would say) is the superiority of the priesthood, that they who from their ancestors are of the same dignity, and have the same forefather, are yet far better than the rest. At all events they *receive tithe* from them. When then one is found, who receives tithes from these very persons, are not they indeed in the rank of laymen, and he among the Priests?

And not only this; but neither was he of the same dignity with them, but of another race: so that he would not have given tithes to a stranger unless his dignity had been great. Astonishing! what has he accomplished? He has made quite clear a greater point than those relating to faith which he treated in the Epistle to the Romans. For there

HE. vii. 5.

¹ χαρακτήρων

² choice portions

³ ἀκροθίνια

HOM. 12. indeed he declares Abraham to be the first father both of our polity and also of the Jewish. But here he is exceeding bold against him, and shews that the uncircumcised person is far superior. How then did he shew that Levi paid tithes? Abraham (saith he) paid them. 'And how does this concern us?' It most particularly concerns you: for you will not be so contentious as to say that the Levites are superior to Abraham. ver. 6. *But he whose descent is not counted from them, received tithes of Abraham.*

And after that he did not simply pass on, but added, *and blessed him that had the promises.* Inasmuch as throughout, this it was that was regarded with reverence, he shews that Melchisedec was to be reverenced more than Abraham, from the common judgment of all men. (ver. 7) *And without all contradiction,* saith he, *the inferior is blessed by the superior,* i. e. in the opinion of all men it is the inferior that is blessed by the superior. So then the type of Christ is superior even to *him that had the promises.*

(ver. 8) *And here men that die receive tithes: but there he of whom it is testified that he liveth.* However lest we should say, Tell us, why goest thou so far back? he says, (ver. 9) *And as I may so say* (and he did well in [thus] softening it) *Levi also who receiveth tithes was tithed in Abraham.* How? (ver. 10) *For he was yet in his loins when Melchisedec met him,* i. e. Levi was in him, although he was not yet born. And he said not the Levites but Levi.

Hast thou seen the exceeding superiority? Hast thou seen how great is the interval between Abraham and Melchisedec, who bears the figure of our High Priest? And he shews that the superiority had been caused by authority, not necessity. For the one paid the tithe, which indicates the priest: the other gave the blessing, which indicates the superior. This superiority passes on also to the descendants.

In a marvellous and triumphant way he cast out the Jewish [system]. On this account he said, *Ye are become dull,* inasmuch as he wished to lay these foundations, that they might not start away. Such you see is the wisdom of Paul, first preparing them well, he so leads [1] them into what he wishes. For the human race is hard to persuade, and needs much attention, even more than plants. Since in that

supra v. 12.

[1] ἐμβάλλει

case there is [only] the nature of material bodies, and earth, HE.vii.10.
which yields to the hands of the husbandmen: but in this
there is will, which is liable to many alterations, and now
prefers this, now that. For it readily inclines to the side
of evil.

[5.] Wherefore we ought always to *guard* ourselves, lest (3)
at any time we should fall off to slumber. For *Lo* (saith
one) *he that keepeth Israel shall neither slumber nor sleep,* Ps. cxxi.
and *Do not suffer*[c] *thy foot to be moved.* He did not say, 4.
"be not moved" but *do not thou suffer,* &c. It depends Ib. 3.
then on ourselves to allow [this], and not on any other
person. For if we are willing to stand *stedfast and unmove-* 1 Cor.
able, we shall not be shaken. xv. 58.

What then? does nothing depend on God? All indeed
depends on God, but not so as that our free-will is impaired. 'If then it depend on God (saith one), why does
He blame us'? on this account I said, 'so as that our free-
will is not impaired.' It depends then on us, and on Him.
For we must first choose what is good; and then He [1] εἰσάγει
contributes what [comes] from Himself[1]. He does not τὰ παρ'
anticipate our wishes[d], lest our free-will should be impaired. ἑαυτοῦ,
But when we have made our choice, then great is the assist- His part
ance He contributes to us.

How is it then that Paul saith, *not of him that willeth,* Rom. ix.
if it depend on ourselves also, *nor of him that runneth, but* 16.
of God that sheweth mercy?

In the first place, he did not introduce it as his own
opinion, but inferred it from what was before him and from
what had been put forward[e] [in the discussion]. For after

[c] In Psalm cxxi. 3 (cxx. 3. Sept.) where we have "He shall not suffer" &c. the LXX. have, μὴ δῴης εἰς σάλον τὸν πόδα σου, μηδὲ νυστάξῃ (Vat.) ὁ φυλάσσων σε, "Lest thou suffer &c. and lest he that keepeth thee slumber." S. Chrys. substitutes δῷς for δῴης, making the sense, "Do not suffer &c. and let not him that keepeth thee slumber." This he applies to the Christian keeping guard over himself (his words are χρὴ πάντοτε φυλάττειν ἑαυτοὺς, μήποτε ἀπονυστάξωμεν): and so he seems to have understood ver. 4, of the Christian: that a watchman of

Israel ought not to slumber or sleep. The Alex. MS. has νυστάξει in the third verse.

[d] Βουλήσεις. Those acts of the soul whereby we desire and aim at what is good.

[e] προκειμένου... προβληθέντος. The former word is used by S. Chrys. to express the portion of Scripture on which he is treating: the latter is a received term in the dialectical method of the Greeks to express a proposition put forward to be argued from, to see what consequences follow from it, with a view of shewing it to be untrue, or

saying *It is written, I will have mercy on whom I will have mercy, and I will have compassion on whom I will have compassion,* he says, *It follows then*[1] *that it is not of him that willeth, nor of him that runneth, but of God that sheweth mercy.* Thou wilt say then unto me, why doth He yet find fault?

And secondly that other explanation may be given, that he represents all as His, whose the greater part is. For it is our's to choose [2] and to wish; but God's to accomplish, and to bring to an end. Since therefore the greater part is of Him, he says all is of Him, speaking according to the custom of men. For so we ourselves also do. I mean for instance: We see a house well built, and we say the whole is the Architect's [doing]; and yet certainly it is not all his, but the workmen's also, and the owner's, who supplies the materials, and many others', but nevertheless since he contributed the greatest share, we call the whole his. So then [it is] in this case also. Again, with respect to a number of people, where the many are, we say All are: where few, nobody. So also Paul in this place saith, *not of him that willeth, nor of him that runneth, but of God that sheweth mercy.*

And herein he establishes two great truths: one, that we should not be lifted up [f]: even shouldst thou run (he would say) even shouldst thou be very earnest, do not consider that the success in well doing [3] is thine own. For if thou obtain not the impulse [g] that is from above, all is to no purpose. Nevertheless that thou wilt attain that which thou earnestly strivest after is very evident; so long as thou runnest, so long as thou willest.

He did not then assert this, that we run in vain, but that, if we think the whole to be our own, if we do not assign the greater part to God, we run in vain. For nei-

---

Hom. 12.
Rom. ix. 15.
Ib. 16.
[1] Ἄρα οὖν
Ib. 19.

[2] or, purpose and will, προελέσθαι καὶ βουληθῆναι

[3] κατόρθωμα

---

determining the sense in which it is true. S. Chrys. means to say that this proposition was only thus argumentatively inferred by S. Paul.

[f] In the genuine text here as in some other places, there is no mention of the second point. The longer text has "one that we should not be lifted "up by what we do well: the other that "when we do anything well, we should "attribute to God the cause of our success in well-doing. Therefore" &c. Mr. Field thinks that either the thread of the discourse is broken, and the second point not mentioned or (which seems more probable) that it is contained in the words; Nevertheless &c.

[g] ῥοπὴ: "The inclining of the balance:" or, "the weight which makes it turn."

ther hath God willed that the whole should be His, lest He.vii.10. He should appear to be crowning us without cause: nor again our's, lest we should fall away to pride. For if when we have the smaller [share], we think much of ourselves, what should we do if the whole depended on us?

[6.] Indeed God hath done away many things for the purpose of cutting away our boastfulness, and still there is the ʰ high hand. With how many afflictions hath He encompassed us, so as to cut away our proud spirit! with how many wild beasts hath He encircled us! For indeed when some say, 'what means this?' 'of what use is this?' they utter these things against the will of God. He hath placed thee in the midst of so great fear, and yet not even so art thou lowly-minded; but if thou ever attain a little success, thou reachest to Heaven itself in thy pride.

For this cause [are] the very rapid changes and reverses (4) [which occur]; and yet not even so are we instructed. For this cause are there continual and untimely deaths, but our thoughts and feelings are as if we were immortal, as if we should never die. We plunder, we over-reach, as though we were never to give account. We build as if we were to continue here for ever. And not even the word of God daily sounded into our ears, nor the events themselves, instruct us. Not a day, not an hour can be mentioned, in which we may not see continual funerals going forth. But all in vain: and nothing reaches our hardness [of heart]: nor are we even able to become better by the calamities of others; or rather, we are not willing. When we ourselves only are afflicted, then we are subdued, and yet if God take off His hand, we again lift up our hand: no one has the thoughts and feelings that become a human being ⁱ, no one despises the things on earth; no one looks to Heaven. But just as swine turn their heads downwards, stooping towards their belly, wallowing in the mire; so too the great

---

ʰ Sav. and Ben. add αὑτοῦ, "His hand is high:" but the reference is to our sinning "with a high hand," as appears from what follows in the next paragraph..

ⁱ οὐδεὶς ἀνθρώπινα φρονεῖ. This is the reading also of Savile and Morell. It is supported by one MS. and the pr. m. of another: which had been corrected to οὐδ. οὐράνια φ., the reading of the Verona Edition. Mutianus has *nemo divina sapit:* and the later translator *cœlestia.* The other MSS. have ἀνθρώπινα περιφρονεῖ, ταπεινὰ φρονεῖ, ταπεινοφρονεῖ. Montfaucon conjectured τὰ ἄνω φρονεῖ.

body of mankind are defiling themselves with the most intolerable filth, without being conscious of it.

[7.] For better were it to be defiled with unclean mud than with sins; for he who is polluted with the one, washes it off in a little time, and becomes like one who had never from the first fallen into that slough: but he who has fallen into the deep pit of sin has contracted a pollution that is not cleansed by water, but needs long time, and strict penitence, and tears and lamentations, and more wailing, and hat more fervent, than ye display over your dearest friends. For this defilement attaches to us from without, wherefore we also speedily put it away; but the other is generated from within, wherefore also it is with difficulty that we wash it off, and cleanse ourselves from it.

For from the heart (saith He) *proceed evil thoughts, fornications, adulteries, thefts, false witnesses.* Wherefore also the Prophet said, *Create in me a clean heart, O God.* And another, *Wash thine heart from wickedness, O Jerusalem.* (Thou seest that it is both our [work] and God's.) And again, *Blessed are the pure in heart for they shall see God.*

Let us become clean to the utmost of our power. Let us wipe away our sins. But how it is possible to wipe them away, the prophet teaches, saying, *Wash you, make you clean, put away your wickednesses from your souls, before Mine eyes.* What is *before Mine eyes?* Because some seem to be free from wickedness, but only [seem so] to men, whilst to God they are manifest as being *whited sepulchres.* For this cause He saith, "so put them away as "I see." *Learn to do well; seek out judgment, do justice for the poor* and lowly. *Come now, and let us reason together, saith the Lord: and though your sins be as scarlet, I will make you white as snow, and if they be as crimson, I will make you white as wool.* Thou seest that we must first cleanse ourselves, and then God cleanses us. For having said first, *Wash you, make you clean,* He then added *I will make you white.*

Let no one then, [even] of those who are come to the very extreme of wickedness, despair of himself. For (He saith) even if thou hast passed into the habit, yea and almost into the nature of wickedness itself, be not afraid.

For, for this cause taking [the instance of] colours that are He.vii.10.
not superficial but almost united with the very substance
of the materials, He said that He would bring them permanently into the opposite state. For He did not simply
say that He would *wash* us, but that He would *make* us
white, as snow and as wool, in order to suggest good hopes
for us. Great then is the power of repentance, at least if
it makes us as snow, and whitens us as wool, even if sin
have first got possession and dyed our souls.

Let us labour earnestly then to become clean; He has
enjoined nothing burdensome. *Judge for the fatherless, and* Is. i. 17.
do justice for the widow. Thou seest on every side how
great account God makes of mercy, and of standing forward
in behalf of those that are wronged. These good deeds let
us pursue after, and we shall be able also, by the grace of
God, to attain to the blessings to come: which may we all
be counted worthy of, in Christ Jesus our Lord, with whom
to the Father and also to the Holy Ghost, be glory power
honour, now and for ever and world without end. Amen.

HOMILY XIII.

HEB. vii. 11—14.

¹ *by means of*

² *takes place*

³ *from*

*If therefore perfection were by¹ the Levitical priesthood; (for under it the people have received the law*ᵃ*) what further need was there that another priest should arise after the order of Melchisedec, and not be called after the order of Aaron? For the priesthood being changed, there is² of necessity a change also of the law. For He of whom these things are spoken, pertained to another tribe, of³ which no man gave attendance at the altar. For it is evident that our Lord sprang out of Judah, of which tribe Moses spake nothing concerning priests*ᵇ.

IF therefore (he saith) *perfection were by the Levitical priesthood.* Having spoken concerning Melchisedec, and pointed out how much superior he was to Abraham, and having proved that the difference was great between them, he begins from this point forward to prove the wide difference as to the covenant itself, and how the one is imperfect and the other perfect. However he does not even yet enter on the matters themselves, but first contends on the ground of the priesthood, and the tabernacle. For these things would be more easily received by the unbelieving, when the proof was derived from things already allowed, and believed.

He had shewn that Melchisedec was greatly superior both to Levi and to Abraham, being to them in the rank of the

---

ᵃ νενομοθέτηται is the reading of the best MSS. of S. Chrys. here and throughout the Homily. The common editions had νενομοθέτητο. So while the common editions of the N.T. read νενομοθέτητο, the critical editors have νενομοθέτηται.

ᵇ ἱερέων. The editions had ἱερωσύνης: So the common text of the New Test. read ἱερωσύνης, the critical editions have ἱερέων.

A new Priesthood, implies the imperfection of the former. 161

priests. [Now] he argues again from a different point. HE.vii.11.
What then is this? Why (saith he) did he not say, *after
the order of Aaron?* And observe, I pray you, the great
superiority [of his argument]. For from the very circumstance for which it were natural to exclude His priesthood, viz. that He was not *after the order of Aaron*, from that he establishes Him, and excludes the others. For this is the very thing that I say (saith he); why has He *not been made after the order of Aaron?*

And the [saying] *what further need* has much emphasis. For if the Christ had been *after the order of Melchisedec* according to the flesh, and then afterwards the law had been introduced, and all that pertained to Aaron, a person might reasonably say that the latter as being more perfect, annulled the former, seeing that it had come in after it. But if the Christ comes later, and takes a different type, as that of His priesthood, it is evident that He does this on the ground that that [Aaronic] system was imperfect. For (he would say) let us suppose for argument's sake, that all has been fulfilled, and that there is nothing imperfect in the priesthood. *What need* was there in that case that He should be called *after the order of Melchisedec and not after the order of Aaron?* Why did He set aside Aaron, and introduce a different priesthood, that [namely] of Melchisedec?

If then perfection, that is the perfection of the things themselves, of the doctrines, of life [c], *had been by the Levitical priesthood.*

And observe how he goes forward on his path. He had said that [He was] *after the order of Melchisedec*, implying that the [priesthood] *after the order of Melchisedec* is superior: for [he was][1] far superior. Afterwards he shews this from the time also, in that He was after Aaron; evidently as being better.

[1 or [it is]. S. B. have ἐκεῖ- νος in the text.]

[2.] And what is the meaning of what follows next? *for* (saith he) *under* [or *upon*] *it the people have received the Law* [or *have been legislated for*]. What is, *under it* [&c.]? regulateth itself[2] by it; through it does all things. You [2 στοιχεῖ]

[c] εἰ μὲν οὖν τελείωσις, τουτέστι τῆς τῶν πραγμάτων, τῆς τῶν δογμάτων, τοῦ βίου ἡ τελείωσις. It is not clear, as Mr. Field remarks, to what the article τῆς, τῆς are to be referred.

VOL. VII.   M

cannot say that it was given to others, *the people under it have received the law,* that is, have used it and did use it. You cannot say that it indeed was perfect, but that it did not rule and protect the people, *they have been legislated for upon it,* that is, they used it.

What need was there then of another priesthood? *For the priesthood being changed, there is of necessity a change of the law also.* But if there must be a different priest, or rather a different priesthood, there must of necessity be also a different law. This is directed against those who say, What need was there of a new Covenant? For he could indeed have alleged a testimony from prophecy also. *This is the covenant which I made with your fathers* [&c.] But for the present he contends on the ground of the priesthood. And observe, how he says this from the first. He had said, *According to the order of Melchisedec.* By this he excluded the order of Aaron. For he would not have said *After the order of Melchisedec,* if this other had been better. If therefore another priesthood has been brought in, there must needs be also [another] Covenant; for neither is it possible that there should be a priest, without a covenant and laws and ordinances, nor that having received a different priesthood He should use that former [covenant].

In the next place, as to that which was the very ground of objection: "How could He be a priest if He were not a "Levite?" having previously overthrown this by what had been said above, he does not even condescend to solve it, but introduces it in passing. I said (saith he) that the priesthood was changed, therefore also the Covenant is. And it was changed not only in its character¹, or in its ordinances, but also in its tribe. For of necessity [it must be changed] in its tribe also.. How? *For the priesthood being changed* [or *transferred*], *from tribe to tribe,* from the sacerdotal to the regal [tribe], that the same might be both sacerdotal and regal.

And observe the mystery. First it was royal, and then it is become sacerdotal: therefore it is just as in the case also of Christ: for King indeed He always was, but has become Priest from the time that He assumed the Flesh,

¹ τρόπῳ

that He offered the sacrifice. Thou seest the change, and He.vii.16. the very things which were ground of objection these he introduces, as though the natural order of things required them. *For* (saith he) *He of whom these things are spoken pertained to another tribe.* I myself also say it, I know that this tribe [of Judah] had nothing of priesthood. For there is a transferring.

[3.] Yea and I am shewing another difference also (he would say): not only from the tribe, nor yet only from the Person, nor from the character [of the Priesthood], nor from the covenant, but also from the type itself. (ver. 16) *Who was made* [*became so*], *not according to the law of a carnal commandment, but according to the power of an endless life.* He became (saith he) *a priest, not according to the law of a carnal commandment:* for that law was in many respects unlawful [1].   (2)

[1] ἄνομος

What is [the meaning of] *a carnal commandment?* Circumcise the flesh, it says; Anoint the flesh; Wash the flesh; Purify the flesh; shave the flesh; bind upon the flesh [2]; cherish the flesh; rest from work as to the flesh. And again its blessings, what are they? Long life for the flesh; milk and honey for the flesh; peace for the flesh: luxury for the flesh. From this law it was that Aaron received the priesthood: Melchisedec however not so.

[2] see Deut. vi. 8.

ver. 15. *And it is yet far more abundantly evident, if after the similitude of Melchisedec there ariseth another priest.* What is evident? the interval between the two priesthoods, the difference; how much superior He is *who was made not according to the law of a carnal commandment.* (Who [is this?] Melchisedec? Nay; but the Christ). *But according to the power of an endless [3] life. For He testifieth, Thou art a Priest for ever after the order of Melchisedec;* that is, not for a time, nor having any limit, *but according to the power of an endless life,* that is, by means of power, by means of *indestructible life.*

[3] ἀκατα-λύτου in-destructible

And yet this does not follow naturally after, *who was made not according to the law of a carnal commandment:* for what would follow naturally would be to say, "but according to that of a spiritual one." However by its being *carnal,* he implied its being temporary. Just as he says also in another place, *carnal ordinances imposed until the time of reformation.*

Hom. 13.
infra ix. 10.

According to the power of life, that is, because He lives by His own power.

[4.] He had said, that a change of law also takes place, and up to this point he has shewn it; Henceforward he enquires into the cause, that which above all things gives full assurance to men's minds, [I mean] the knowing the cause thoroughly; and it leads us more to faith [1] when we have learned the cause as well, and the principle according to which [the thing] is done.

[1] *or* conviction

ver. 18. *For there is indeed* (saith he) *a disannulling of the commandment going before, on account of the weakness and unprofitableness thereof.* Here the Heretics[d] press on. But listen thou attentively. He did not say "on account of the evil," nor, "on account of the viciousness," but *on account of the weakness and unprofitableness [thereof],* yea and in other places also he points out its weakness; as when he says *In that it was weak through the flesh.* It is not then [the law] itself which is weak, but we.

Rom. viii. 3.

ver. 19. *For the Law made nothing perfect.* What is, *made nothing perfect?* made no man perfect, being disobeyed. And besides, not even if it had been listened to, would it have made one perfect and virtuous. But as yet he does not say this here, but that it had no strength: and with good reason. For written precepts were there set down, Do this and Do not that, being enjoined only, not at the same time giving power within [2]. But *the Hope* is not of such a character.

[2] ἐντιθέν-τα

What is *a disannulling?* a casting out. A *Disannulling* is a disannulling of things which are of force. So that he intimated, that it [once] was of force, but henceforward was held of no account, seeing that it accomplished nothing. Was the Law then of no use? It was indeed of use: and of very great use: but to make men perfect it was of no use. For it is in this respect that he saith, *The law made nothing perfect.* All things were figures, all shadow; circumcision, sacrifice, sabbath. Therefore they had not power to reach through into the soul, wherefore they pass

[d] The early Heretics denied the divine character of the Mosaic dispensation.

away and gradually withdraw. *But [it was] the introduc-* He.vii.22.
tion of a better hope, by which we draw nigh unto God.

[5.] (ver. 20) *And forasmuch as not without the taking of an oath*[1]. Thou seest that the point of the oath becomes necessary for him in this place. Accordingly for this reason he previously treated much [hereon], how that God sware;·and sware for the sake of [our] fuller assurance.

[1] ὁρκωμο-σίας

But the introduction of a better hope. For that other system also had a hope, but not such as this. For their hope was, that if they were well pleasing [to God] they should possess the land, that they should suffer nothing fearful. But in this [dispensation] our hope is, that if we have pleased [God], we shall possess not earth, but heaven; or rather (which is far better) we hope to be placed near to God, to come even unto the very throne of the Father, to minister unto Him among the Angels. And see how he introduces these things by little and little. For above he says *which entereth into that within the veil,* but in this place, *by which we draw nigh unto God.*

supra vi. 19.

And forasmuch as not without the taking of an oath. What is *And forasmuch as not without the taking of an oath?* that is, there is another difference also. Besides, neither were these things merely promised (saith he). *For they indeed became priests without the taking of an oath,* (ver. 21, 22) *but He with the taking of an oath, through Him who said to Him, The Lord sware and will not repent, Thou art Priest for ever after the order of Melchisedec. By so much was Jesus made surety of a better covenant*[c]. He lays down two points of difference, that it hath not any end as the [covenant] of the Law had [f]; and this he proves from [its being] Christ who exercises [the priesthood]; for he saith *according to the power of an endless life.* And he proves it also from the oath, because [*The Lord*] *sware* &c, and from the fact; for if that other was cast out, because it was weak, this stands firm, because it is powerful. He proves it also from the priest. How? Because there is

---

[c] The common editions add here ver. 23, 24. "and they truly were many "priests, because they were not suf-"fered to continue by reason of death; "but this [man] because he continueth "ever, hath an unchangeable priest-"hood." S. Chrys. alludes to these words in what follows: but without citing them.

[f] The common texts add here "and that it is with oath-taking": this is probably to be understood: as if he had said, He lays down a second point of difference that &c.

One [only]; and there would not have been One [only], unless He had been immortal. For as there were many priests, because they were mortal, so [here is] The One, because He is immortal. *By so much was Jesus made surety of a better covenant,* inasmuch as He sware to Him that He should alway be [Priest]; which He would not have done, if He had not been Living.

[6.] (ver. 25) *Wherefore He is able also to save them to the uttermost, who come unto God by Him, seeing He ever liveth to make intercession for them.* Thou seest that he saith this in respect of that which is according to the flesh. For when He [appears] as Priest, then He also intercedes. Wherefore also when Paul says, *who also maketh intercession for us,* he insinuates the same thing; it is the High Priest that maketh intercession. For He *that raiseth the dead as He will, and quickeneth them,* and that *even as the Father* [doth], how [is it that] when there is need to save, He *maketh intercession?* He that hath *all judgment,* how is it that He *maketh intercession?* He that *sendeth His angels,* so as to *cast* some into *the furnace,* and to save others, how is it that He *maketh intercession?* Wherefore (saith he) *He is able also to save.* For this cause then He saves, because He dies not. Inasmuch as *He ever liveth,* He hath (he means) no successor: And if He have no successor, He is able to stand forward in behalf of all men. For there [under the Law] indeed, the High Priest although he were worthy of admiration, [was so] only for the time during which he was [High Priest] (as Samuel for instance, and any other such), but, after this, no longer; for they were dead. But here it is not so, but *He saves to the uttermost*[1].

What is *to the uttermost?* He hints at some mystery. Not here[2] only (saith he) but there[3] also He saves them that *come unto God by Him.* How does He save [them?] *in that He is ever living* (saith he) *to make intercession for them.* Thou seest the humiliation? Thou seest the manhood? For he saith not, that He obtained this, by making intercession once for all, but [does it] continually, and whensoever it may be needful to intercede for them.

To the uttermost. What is it? Not for a time only, but there also in the future life. 'Does He then always need to

---

Hom. 13.

Rom. viii. 34.

S. John v. 21.

Ib. 22.

S. Matt. xiii. 41, 42.

[1] εἰς τὸ παντελές
[2] in this world
[3] in the other world

'pray? and yet how can [this] be reasonable? Even men Hᴇ.vii.26. 'indeed that are righteous, have oftentimes accomplished 'all by one entreaty, and is He always praying? For what 'purpose then is He throned with [the Father]?' Thou seest that it is a condescension. The meaning is: Be not afraid, nor say, Yea, He loves us indeed, and He has confidence towards the Father, but that He should live alway is not possible. For He doth live alway.

[7.] (v. 26) *For such an High Priest also* [g] *became us, who is holy, harmless, undefiled, separate from the sinners.* Thou seest that the whole is said with reference to the manhood. (But when I say 'the manhood,' I mean [the manhood] having Godhead; not dividing [one from the other], but leaving [you] to suppose [1] what is suitable). Didst thou mark the difference of the High Priest? He has summed up what was said before, *in all points tempted like as we are yet without sin.* For (saith he) *such an High Priest also became us, who is holy, harmless. Harmless:* what is it? without wickedness: that which another [h] Prophet says: *guile was not found in His mouth,* that is, [He is] not crafty. Is. liii. 9. Could any one say this concerning God? and is one not ashamed to say that God is not crafty, nor deceitful? Concerning Him, however, viewed in respect of the Flesh it might be reasonable [to say it]. *Holy, undefiled.* This too would any one say concerning God? for has He a nature capable of defilement? *Separate from sinners.*

[1] ὑποπτεύ- ειν

---

[g] In Mr. Field's ed. καὶ is read here, and where the words are cited afterwards, in the common texts it is omitted. So critical editors consider that the sacred text is τοιοῦτος γὰρ ἡμῖν καὶ ἔπρεπεν κ. λ.

[h] As this passage is cited by Facundus Hermianensis, an African Bishop, writing about the year 547: it may be well to give his words and also the two Greek texts corresponding to them, as an evidence that the text which he had, was of the short and simple form now restored in Mr. Field's edition.

"In interpretatione quoque Epistolæ ad Hebræos, Sermone xiv, de eo quod scriptum est, *Sicut consummatio per Leviticum sacerdotium erat,* ita locutus est: Dicit alter propheta, Dolus non est inventus in ore ejus, hoc est nulla calliditas. Hoc forsitan quisquam de Deo dicat, et non erubescit dicens, quia Deus non est callidus, neque dolosus. De eo vero qui secundum carnem est, habebit forsitan rationem. (pro def. trium capp. lib. xi. c. 5 p. 488. ed. Sirm.) [Gall. Bibl. Patr. xi. 789.]

Mr. Field's text is, ὁ (ὁ om. MS. R.) λέγει ἕτερος προφήτης· δόλος οὐχ εὑρέθη ἐν τῷ στόματι αὐτοῦ (τουτέστιν, οὐχ ὕπουλος· τοῦτο ἄν τις περὶ Θεοῦ εἴποι; καὶ οὐκ αἰσχύνεται λέγων, ὅτι ὁ Θεὸς οὐκ ἔστιν ὕπουλος, οὐδὲ δολερός; περὶ μέντοι τοῦ κατὰ σάρκα ἔχοι ἂν λόγον.

The text of Savile and the Benedictines οὐχ ὕπουλος· καὶ ὅτι τοιοῦτος, ἄκουε τοῦ προφήτου λέγοντος· οὐδὲ εὑρέθη δόλος ἐν τῷ στόματι αὐτοῦ, τοῦτο οὖν ἄν τις περὶ Θεοῦ εἴποι; ὁ δὲ οὐκ αἰσχύνεται λέγων, ὅτι ὁ Θεὸς οὐκ ἔστιν ὕπουλος, οὐδὲ δολερός; περὶ μὲν οὖν τοῦ κατὰ σάρκα ἔχοι ἂν λόγον.

HOM. 13. [8.] Does then this alone shew the difference, or does the very sacrifice itself as well? How? (ver. 27) *He hath no need* (saith he) *daily, as the High Priest*[1], *to offer up sacrifices for his sins, for this He did once for all, when He offered Himself.* This, what? Here he proceeds to sound as it were a prelude, concerning the exceeding greatness of the spiritual sacrifice and the interval [between them]. He has mentioned the point of the priest; he has mentioned that of the faith; he has mentioned that of the Covenant; not entirely indeed, still he has mentioned it. In this place he proceeds to prelude also concerning the sacrifice itself.

Do not then, because thou hast heard that He is a Priest, suppose that He is alway executing the priest's office. For He executed it once for all, and thenceforward *sat down.* That thou mayest not suppose that He is standing on high, and is a minister, he points out that the matter is [part] of a dispensation [or economy]. For just as He became a servant, in the same manner also [He became] a Priest and a Minister. But as after becoming a servant, He did not continue a servant, so also, having become a Minister He did not continue a Minister. For it belongs not to a minister to sit, but to stand.

infra x. 12.

This then he hints at here, and also the greatness of the sacrifice, if being [but] one, and having been offered up once only, it effected that which all [the rest] were unable to do. But he does not yet [treat] of these points.

ib. viii. 3. *For this He did,* saith he. *This;* what? *For* (he saith) *it is of necessity that this* [*Man*] *have somewhat also to offer.* Not [to offer] for Himself; for how did He offer for Himself? but for the people. What sayest thou? And is He able to do this? Yea (saith he). *For the Law maketh men high priests, which have infirmity.* And doth He not need to offer for Himself? No, saith he. For, that you may not suppose that the [words, *this*] *He did once for all,* are said respecting Himself, as well [as others], hear what he says: *For the law maketh men high priests, which have infirmity.* On this account they both offer continually, and for themselves. He however who is mighty, He that hath

---

[1] This is the reading adopted by Mr. Field. The common texts give the passage as it stands in the Text of the Epistle. Indeed what is omitted must plainly be intended to be supplied.

no sin, for what cause should He offer for Himself, or often- He.vii.28.
times for the others?

*But the word of the oath-taking which was since the Law
[maketh] the Son who has been consecrated [perfected] for
evermore. Perfected:* what is that? Paul does not set down
the expressions of contrast that are required in strictness[1]; [1] τὰς ἀντιδιαστολὰς κυρίας
for after saying *having Infirmity,* he did not say *the Son
who is mighty,* but *perfected:* i.e. mighty, as one might
say. Thou seest that the name Son is used in contradistinction to that of servant. And by *infirmity* he means either
sin or death.

What is, *for evermore?* Not now only without sin but
always. If then He is perfect, if He never sins at any
time, if He lives always, for what purpose shall He offer
many sacrifices for us? But for the present he does not
insist strongly on this point: but what he does strongly
insist upon is, His not offering on His own behalf.

[9.] Seeing then that we have such an High Priest, let
us imitate Him; let us walk in His footsteps. There is
no other sacrifice: one alone has cleansed us, and after this,
fire and hell. For indeed it is on this account that he repeats it over and over, saying, "one Priest," "one Sacrifice,"
lest any man supposing that there are many [sacrifices]
should sin without fear. Let us then, as many as have
been counted worthy of The Seal[2], as many as have enjoyed [2] *i.e.* Baptism
The Sacrifice, as many as have been partakers of the Immortal Table, [let us, I say] continue to guard our noble
birth and our dignity: for our falling away is not without
danger.

And as many as have not yet had these [privileges]
vouchsafed, let not these either be confident on that account. For when a person goes on in sin, with the view of
receiving holy baptism at the last gasp, perhaps (as often
happens) he will not obtain it. And, believe me, it is not
to terrify you that I say what I am going to say. I have
myself known many persons, to whom this has happened,
who in expectation indeed of the enlightening[3] sinned [3] Baptism
much, and on the day of their death went away empty.
For God gave us baptism for this cause, that He might do
away our sins, not that He might increase our sins. Where-

170   *Delaying Baptism; to live in sin, and yet be saved.*

Hom. 13. as if any man have employed it as a security for sinning more, it becomes a cause of negligence. For if there had been no Washing, they would have lived more warily, as not having [the means of] forgiveness. Thou seest that Rom. iii. 8. it is ourselves who cause it to be said [that we say] *Let us do evil, that good may come.*

Wherefore, I exhort you, ye also who are uninitiated, be sober. Let no man follow after virtue as an hireling, no [1] ἀγνώμων man as an ungenerous and ungrateful[1] person, no man as though it were a heavy and a burdensome thing. Let us pursue after it then with ready mind, and with joy. For if there were no reward laid up, ought we not to be good? But however, at least with a reward, let us become good. And how is this anything else than a disgrace and a very great condemnation? Unless thou give me a reward (saith one), I do not become chaste. Then am I bold to say somewhat: never wilt thou be chaste, no not even when thou livest chastely, if thou dost it for a reward. Thou esteemest not virtue at all, if thou art not enamoured of it. But on account of our great weakness, God was willing that for a time it should be practised even for reward, yet not even so do we pursue it.

Let us however suppose, if you will, that a man dies, after having done innumerable evil things, having also had baptism vouchsafed him (which however I think does not readily happen), tell me, how will he depart thither? Not indeed called to account for the deeds he had done, but [2] ἀπαρ- yet without confidence[2]; as is reasonable. For when after ρησίαστος living a hundred years, he has no good work to shew[j], but only that he had not sinned, or rather not even this, but [3] i.e. that he was saved by grace[3] only, and when he sees others mercy crowned, in splendor, and highly approved: even if he fall not into hell, tell me, will he endure his despondency?

[10.] But to make the matter clear by an example, Suppose there are two soldiers, and that one of them steals, injures, overreaches, and that the other does none of these things, but acts the part of a brave man, does well in important things, sets up trophies in war, has his right hand

---

[j] [S. Cyril Alex. speaks too of those who put off Baptism till they are old and receive forgiveness through it but have nought to bring to their Master. Glaph. 273 b c.]

stained with blood; then when the time arrives, suppose that (from the same rank in which the thief also was) he is at once conducted to the imperial throne and the purple; but suppose that the other remains there where he was, and merely of the royal mercy does not pay the penalty of his deeds, let him however be in the last place, and let him be stationed under him who is [now] a King. Tell me, will he be able to endure his despair when he sees him who was [ranked] with himself ascended even to the very highest point of dignities, and made thus glorious, and master of the world, while he himself still remains below, and has not even been freed from punishment with honour, but through the grace and mercifulness of the King? For even should the King forgive him, and release him from the charges against him, still will he live in shame; For surely not even will others admire him: since in such instances of forgiveness, we admire not those who receive the gifts, but those who bestow them. And in such proportion as the gifts are greater, the more are they ashamed who receive them, when what they have done amiss is great. H<small>E</small>.vii.28.

With what eyes then will such an one be able to look on those who are in the King's courts, when they exhibit their sweatings out of number and their wounds, whilst he has nothing to shew, but has his being saved itself of the mere lovingkindness of God? For just as if one were to beg off a murderer, a thief, an adulterer, when he was going to be led away for execution, and were to command him to stay at the porch of the King's palace, he will not afterwards be able to look any man in the face, although he has been set free from punishment: so too without question is this man's case.

For do not, I beseech you, suppose that because it is called a palace [1], therefore all are to attain the same things. For if here in Kings' courts there is the Prefect, and all who are about the King, and also those who are in very inferior stations, and occupy the place of what are called Decani [k] (though the interval be so great between the Prefect and the

[1] βασιλεία *but* Sav. βασιλεία, a kingdom.

[k] "The Δεκανοὶ at Constantinople were lictors, and had the charge of burying the dead: they are otherwise called *funerum elatores, lecticarii, vespillones, libitinarii,* κοπιᾶται. Corippus lib. iii. says

Jamque ordine certo
Turba decanorum, cursorum, in rebus agentum,
Cumque palatinis stans candida turba tribunis." Suicer, Thes. Eccles. cited by Mr. Field.

Decanus) much more shall this be so in the royal court above.

And this I say not of myself. For Paul layeth down another difference greater even than these. For (saith he) as many differences as there are [in passing] from the sun to the moon and the stars, and the very smallest star, so many also [will be the differences] of those in the kingdom of Heaven]. And that the difference between the sun and the smallest star is far greater than that between the Decanus (as he is called) and the Prefect, is evident to all. For while the sun shines upon all the world at once, and makes it bright, and puts out of sight the moon and the stars, the other perhaps does not even appear, not even in the dark. For there are many stars which we do not see. When then we see others become suns, and ourselves have the rank of the very smallest stars, which are not even visible, what comfort shall we have?

Let us not, I beseech you, let us not be so slothful, let us not be so inert, let us not barter away the salvation of God on an easy life, but let us make merchandise of it, and increase it. For even if a person be only a Catechumen, still he knows Christ, still he is acquainted with the Faith, still he is a hearer of the divine oracles, still he is not far from the knowledge. He knows the will of his Lord. Wherefore then does he procrastinate? wherefore does he delay and postpone? Nothing is better than a good life whether here or there, whether in case of the Enlightened or of the Catechumens.

[11.] For tell me what burdensome command have we enjoined you? Have a wife (saith He) and be chaste. Is this difficult? How? when many, not Christians only but Heathens also, live chastely without a wife. That which the heathen goes beyond[1] for vain glory's sake, thou dost not even keep for the fear of God.

[1] ὑπερβαί-νει

Give (saith He) to the poor out of what thou hast. Is this burdensome? But in this case also heathen condemn us, who for vain-glory only have emptied out their whole possessions.

Use not filthy language. Is this difficult? For if it had not been enjoined, ought we not to have done right in this respect, to avoid appearing degraded? For that the contrary conduct is against the grain, I mean the using filthy language, is manifest from the fact that the soul is ashamed and blushes if it have been led to say any thing of that kind, and it will not even utter such things, unless by chance a man be drunk. For when sitting in a public place, even if thou doest it at home why dost thou not do it there? Because of those that are present. Why dost thou not readily do the same thing before thy wife? That thou mayest not insult her. So then thou abstainest from doing it, lest thou shouldest insult thy wife; and dost thou not blush at insulting God? For He is every where present, and heareth all things. He.vii.28.

Be not drunken, saith He. For this very thing of itself, is it not a chastisement? He did not say, Put thy body on the rack, but what? Do not make it so wild[1] as to take away the authority of the mind: on the contrary *make not provision for the lusts thereof*. ¹ἐκτραχη-λίσῃς Rom. xiii. 14.

Do not (saith He) seize by violence what is not thine own; do not over-reach; perjure not thyself. What labours do these things require! what sweatings!

Speak evil of no man (saith He) nor accuse [any] falsely. What toil is there here? Nay rather the contrary is a labour. For when thou hast spoken ill of another, immediately thou art in danger, in suspicion, [saying] Did he of whom I spake, hear? whether he be great or small. For should he be a great man immediately thou wilt be indeed in danger; but if small, he will requite thee with as much, or rather with what is far more grievous; for he will say evil of thee in a much greater degree. It is nothing difficult, nothing burdensome which we have enjoined on us, if we have the will. And if we have not the will, even the easiest things will appear burdensome to us. What is more easy than eating? but from great effeminacy many persons make a difficulty even of this, and I hear many say, that it is weariness even to eat. None of these things is wearisome if thou hast but the will. For every thing depends on the willing, after the grace from above. Let us then be willing to do things that are good, that we may attain also to the good things which are eternal, in Christ Jesus our Lord, whom to the Father and also to the Holy Ghost be glory, might honour now and for ever, and world without end. Amen.

HOMILY XIV.

Heb. viii. 1, 2.

Now of the things which we have spoken this is the sum. We have such an High Priest; who is set down at the right hand of the throne of the majesty in the heavens: a minister of the sanctuary and of the true tabernacle which the Lord pitched, and not man.

Paul mixes the lowly things with the lofty, ever imitating his own Master, so that what is lowly becomes the path to what is lofty, and through the former we are led by the hand to the other, and when we are amid the great things we learn that these [lowly ones] were a condescension. This accordingly he does here also. After declaring that *He offered up Himself,* and shewing Him to be a *High Priest,* what does he say? *But as the sum of what has been spoken, we have such an High Priest, who is set down on the right hand of the throne of the majesty.* And yet this is not [the act] of a Priest, but of Him to whom the other ought to be Priest.

A minister of the sanctuary, not simply a minister but *a minister of the sanctuary. And of the true Tabernacle, which the Lord pitched and not man.* Thou seest the condescension. Did he not a little before make a wide separation[1], saying: *Are they not all ministering spirits?* and for this cause (he saith) it is not said to them, *Sit thou on my right hand,* on the view that He that sitteth is not a minister. How is it then that he here says, *a minister,* and *a minister of the Sanctuary?* for he means here the Tabernacle.

See how he raised up the minds of those Jews who believed. For as it was likely that they would be imagining, that we have no such tabernacle [as they had], see here

[1] See Hom. iii. supra i. 14. Ib. 15.

(saith he) is our Priest, Great, yea, much greater than that HE.viii.3. other, and who has offered a more admirable sacrifice. But [they might say] is not all this mere talk? is it not a boast, and merely said to win over our minds? on this account he established it first from the oath, and afterwards also from *the tabernacle*. For this difference too was manifest: but the Apostle thinks of another also besides, *which* (saith he) *the Lord pitched* [or *made firm*] *and not man*. Where are they who say that the heaven whirls round [a]? where are they who declare that it is spherical? for both of these notions are overthrown here.

But (saith he) *for the sum of what has been spoken*. By *the sum* is always meant what is most important. Again he brings down his discourse; having said what is lofty, henceforward he speaks fearlessly.

[2.] In the next place that thou mayest understand that he used the word *minister* of the manhood, observe how he again gives a further intimation of it: *For* (saith he) *every high priest is ordained to offer both gifts and sacrifices, wherefore it is necessary that this one also have somewhat to offer*.

Do not now, because thou hearest that He sitteth, suppose that His being called High Priest is mere idle talk [1]. [1] ὕθλον For the former, viz. His sitting, belongs to the dignity of the Godhead [2], but this other to His great loving-kindness [2] τῆς ἀξίας τοῦ Θεοῦ toward man, and His tender care for us. On this account he repeatedly urges [3] this very thing, and particularly dwells [3] λιπαίνει upon it: for he feared lest that other [truth] should overthrow it [b]. On this account he again brings down his discourse to this subject: since some were enquiring for what purpose He died. He was a Priest. But there is no Priest without a sacrifice. It is necessary then that He also should have a sacrifice.

And in another way; Having said that He is on high, he affirms and proves that He is a Priest from every consideration, from Melchisedec, from the oath, from offering

---

[a] δινεῖσθαι. The common editions read κινεῖσθαι. Savile observes that it was the opinion of S. Chrys. that the heaven was stationary, and that the Sun Moon and Stars moved through it.

[b] That is, lest the belief of His Godhead should undermine our belief in His true Manhood.

sacrifice. From this last point he next frames another necessary syllogism. *For if* (saith he) *He had been on earth, He would not be a Priest, seeing that there are priests who offer the gifts according to the Law.* If then He is a Priest (as He really is), we must seek some other place for Him. For if He had been indeed *on earth, He would not have been a priest.* For how [could He be]? He offered no sacrifice, He ministered not in the Priest's office. And with good reason, for there were the priests. Moreover he shews, that it was not even possible that [He] should be a priest upon earth. For how [could He be]? There was no rising up against [the appointed Priests], he means.

[3.] At this point it is necessary to apply our minds attentively, and to consider the Apostolic wisdom. For again he points out the difference of the Priesthood. *Who* (he saith) *serve the example^c and shadow of the heavenly things.*

What are the heavenly things he is here speaking of? The spiritual things. For although they are performed on earth, yet are they nevertheless worthy of the Heavens. For when our Lord Jesus Christ lies slain [1] [as a sacrifice], when the Spirit is with us [2], when He who sitteth on the right hand of the Father is here [3], when sons are made by the Washing, when they are fellow-citizens of those in Heaven, when we have a country, and a city [a home], and citizenship there, when we are strangers as to things here, how can all these be other than *heavenly things?* But what! Are not our Hymns heavenly? Is it not [the fact] that the very things which the divine choirs of unbodied powers sing on high, these we also who are below utter in concert with them? Is not the altar also heavenly? How? It hath nothing carnal, all the things which are placed there^d become spiritual. The sacrifice does not disperse into ashes, or into smoke, or into steamy savour, it makes [the elements] that are placed there bright and splendid. How again can the rites which we celebrate be other than heavenly? For when He says, *Whosoever sins ye retain they are retained,*

---

[1] ἐσφαγ-μένος, see Rev. v. 6, 9, 12. xiii. 8.
[2] παραγί-νηται
[3] ἐνταῦθα ᾖ

S. John xx. 23.

^c ὑποδείγματι . . . . . . λατρεύουσι. i.e. "do service to and minister in that system which is a sample and "shadow."
^d τὰ προκείμενα. The Sacred Elements there set before God.

whosoever sins ye remit, they are remitted: when they have the keys of heaven, how can all be other than heavenly? _{He.viii.6.}

Who (saith he) *serve the sample and shadow of heavenly things, as Moses was warned, when he was about to finish the tabernacle, for see, saith He, thou shalt make all things according to the pattern shewed to thee in the mount.* Inasmuch as our hearing is less ready of apprehension than our sight (for the things which we hear we do not in such wise lay up in our soul, as those which we see with our very eyes), He shewed him all. Either then it is this that he means by *the sample and shadow*, or else he [speaks] of the Temple. For, he went on to say, *See* (His words are), *thou shalt make all things according to the pattern*[1] *shewed to thee in the mount.* Was it then only what concerned the furniture of the temple that he saw, or was it also what related to the sacrifices, and all the rest? Nay, one would not be wrong in saying even this; for The Church is heavenly, and is nothing else than Heaven.

[1] τύπον

[4.] (ver. 6) *But now hath He obtained a more excellent ministry*[2], *by how much also He is Mediator of a better covenant.* Thou seest (he means) how much better is the one ministration than the other, if one be a sample and figure, and the other truth [and reality]. But this did not at all profit the hearers, nor cheer them. On this account then he says what especially cheered them: *Which has been established upon better promises.* Having raised them up by speaking of the place, and the priest, and the sacrifice, he next lays down also the wide difference of the covenants, having indeed before also said that [the first] was *weak and unprofitable.*

[2] λειτουργίας *service as Priest*

And observe what safeguards he sets down, when intending to find fault with it. For in that other place after saying, *according to the power of an endless life*, he then said that *there is a disannulling of the commandment going before;* and then after that, he set forth somewhat great, saying, *by which we draw nigh unto God.* And in this place, after leading us up into Heaven, and shewing that instead of the temple, we have Heaven, and that those things were figures of ours, and having by these means exalted the

see supra vii. 18.

supra vii. 16. ib. 18.

ib. 19.

Hom. 14. Ministration [of the New Covenant], he then proceeds naturally to exalt the priesthood.

But (as I said) he sets down that which especially cheers them, in the words, *Which has been established upon better promises.* Whence does this appear? Inasmuch as the one was cast out, and the other introduced in its place: for the reason why it is of force is that it is better. For just as he says, *If perfection were by* it, *what further need were there, that a different priest should arise, after the order of Melchisedec?* so also in this place he used the same syllogism saying (ver. 7) *For if that first covenant had been faultless, there should have been no place sought for the second;* [*faultless*], that is, if it made men *faultless.* For it is because he is speaking of this that he did not say, *But finding fault with* it, but (ver. 8, 9) *But finding fault with them, He saith, Behold, the days come, saith the Lord, when I will make a new covenant with the house of Israel and with the house of Judah: not according to the covena it that I made with their fathers in the day when I took them by the hand to lead them out of the land of Egypt: because they continued not in My covenant, and I regarded them not, saith the Lord.*

supra vii. 11.

Yea verily. And whence does it appear that [the first Covenant] came to an end? He shewed it indeed also from the Priest, but now he shews more clearly by express words that it has been cast out.

But how is it *upon better promises?* For in what way, tell me, can earth and heaven be equal? But do thou consider^e, how he speaks of promises there [in that other covenant] also, that thou mayest not bring this charge against it. For in that former place also, he says *a better hope, by which we draw nigh unto God,* indicating that there was a Hope *there* also; and in this place *better promises,* intimating that *there* also He had made promises.

ib. 19.

But inasmuch as they were for ever making objections, he says, *Behold! the days come, saith the Lord, when I will establish a new covenant with the house of Israel and with the house of Judah.* He is not speaking of any old

---

^e θεώρει used of contemplating and discerning the mystical sense of the Old Testament.

Covenant: for, that they might not have [occasion] to HE.viii.10. assert this, he determined the time also. Thus he did not say simply, *according to the covenant which I made with their fathers,* lest thou shouldest say [it was] the one made with Abraham, or that with Noah: but he declares what [covenant it was], *not according to the covenant which I made with their fathers* in the Exodus. Wherefore he added also, *in the day that I took them by the hand, to lead them forth out of the land of Egypt; because they continued not in My covenant, and I regarded them not, saith the Lord.* Thou seest that the evils begin first from ourselves (*they themselves first,* saith he, *continued not in* [the *covenant*]) and the negligence is from ourselves, but the good things from Him; I mean the [acts] of loving-kindness. He here introduces, as it were, an apology shewing the cause why He forsakes them.

[5.] (ver. 10) *For this,* saith he, *is the covenant which I will make with the house of Israel after those days, saith the Lord; I will put*[1] *My laws into their heart, and on their minds will*[1 give] *I write them, and I will be to them a God, and they shall be to Me a people.* Thus it is concerning the New [covenant] that He says this, because His words are, *not according to the covenant which I covenanted.*

But what other difference is there beside this[f]? Now if any person should say that the difference is not in this respect, but in respect to its being put into their hearts; [saying that] He makes no mention of any difference of ordinances, but points out the mode of its being given: for no longer (he saith) shall the covenant be in writings, but in hearts; let the Jew in that case shew that this was ever carried into effect. However he would not find it [possible to do so]; for it was made a second time in writings after the return from Babylon. But I, on the other hand, shew that the Apostles received nothing in writing, but received [it] in their hearts through the Holy Ghost. And for this

[f] That is, besides the covenant being in itself a new one, different from the Mosaic, there is also, he says, the difference in the mode of giving it, the one being written, the other put into the heart. The Jew is supposed to allege that this second is the only difference, and that the promise in the Prophecy is that the Mosaic law shall be given into the heart, and that this was fulfilled by the reformation of the people: as for instance after the Captivity.

cause also Christ said, *When He cometh, He will bring all things to your remembrance, and He shall teach you.*

Hom. 14. S. John xiv. 26.

[6.] (ver. 11, 12) *And they shall not teach* (saith he) *every man his countryman*[g], *and every man his brother, saying, Know the Lord: for they shall all know Me from the least of them even to the greatest of them. For I will be merciful to their unrighteousnesses, and their iniquities and their sins I will remember no more.* Here is also another sign. *From the least even to the greatest of them* (he says) *they shall know Me, and they shall not say, Know the Lord.* At what time hath this been fulfilled save at the present? For our [religion][1] is manifest: but theirs [i. e. the Jews'] was not manifest, but had been shut up in a corner.

[1] τὸ ἡμέ- τερον

[A covenant] is then said to be *new*, when it is a different one and shews that it has some advantage over the old. 'Nay surely, says one [h], it is new also in this case when part 'of it has been taken away, and part not. For instance, 'when an old house is ready to fall down, if a person leaving 'the whole, has patched up the foundation, straightway we 'say, he has made it new, when he has taken some parts 'away, and brought others into their place. For even the 'heaven also is thus called *new*[2], when it is no longer *of* 'brass, but gives rain[i]; when it is not unfruitful; not, when

[2] see Is. lxv. 17. Deut. xxviii. 23.

[g] πολίτην. The common editions have πλησίον, as has the common text of the New Testament, but there also Scholz, Lachmann, Tischendorf read πολίτην, which is the word used in Jeremiah, according to the Vatican MS. It is used by the LXX. to translate the Hebrew for "neighbour."

[h] Ἰδοὺ, φησὶ, καὶ αὕτη καινὴ τυγχάνει. This is the argument of an objector, who alleges that the promise of a New Covenant was fulfilled by the modification and renewed efficacy of the Mosaic system, such as occurred after the Captivity: He alleges two senses in which the word "New" might be applied without implying the substitution of another system in place of the old, (i) as a repaired house is said to be new, and (ii) according to his interpretation, as the Heavens are new, when after long drought they again give rain. S. Chrys. replies. i. That after the Captivity the Covenant was still, as of old, unfruitful. ii. That this interpretation of the "new heaven" is incorrect. iii. That the Prophecy distinctly foretells a substitution. The common editions have changed the character of the passage by substituting ἄλλως δὲ καινὴ for καινὴ two lines above, and καινὴ δὲ καὶ αὕτη τ. for Ἰδοὺ ..... καινὴ τ. in this place : by omitting φησὶ at the end of the objection; and substituting ἵνα δείξῃ for ἐὰν οὖν δείξω.

[i] The Verona edition, one Catena, the MSS. which Mr. Field usually follows, and the Latin Versions of Mutianus and the later translator, all give the text which is here translated : ὅταν μηκέτι χαλκοῦς ᾖ, ἀλλ' ὑετὸν διδῷ ὅταν μὴ ἄκαρπος, οὐχ ὅταν μεταβληθῇ, οὐχ ὅταν τὰ μὲν αὐτοῦ ἐξαιρεθῇ, τὰ δὲ μένῃ. Mr. Field says that he has *nolens volens* admitted into the text the "amended" readings of the common editions, ὅταν μηκέτι χ. ᾖ, ἀ. ὑ. διδῷ, καὶ ἡ γῆ ὁμοίως καινὴ, ὅταν μὴ ἀ. ᾖ, οὐχ ὅταν μεταβληθῇ, καὶ οἶκος οὕτω καινὸς ὅταν τὰ μὲν κ. λ.

'it has been changed; not, when portions of it have been HE.viii.12.
'taken away, and portions remain. And in this sense, says
'he¹, he hath well termed it *a New Covenant*.' ¹ ὥστε, φησί.
    If then I shew that that covenant had become *Old* in this Sav. &c.
respect, that it yielded no fruit? And that thou mayest om.φησί
know this exactly, read what Haggai says, what Zachariah,
what the Messenger ² [says], when the return from the ²ὁ Ἄγγε-
Captivity had not yet fully taken place; and what charges λος Mal-
Esdras brings. How then did [the people] receive him ᵏ? achi
And how did no man enquire of the Lord, inasmuch as they ³ See Mal.
[the priests] themselves also transgressed, and knew it not i. 6. and
even themselves ³? Dost thou see how thy [interpretation] ⁴βεβί-
is broken down ⁴, whilst I maintain my own: that this [cove- ασται
nant] must be called *New* in the proper sense of the word? τὸ σόν;
                                                             *or how
And besides, I do not concede that the words *the heaven* Is. lxv.
shall be new were spoken concerning this. For why, when 17.
saying in Deuteronomy *the heaven shall be of brass*, did he
not set down this in the contrasted passage ⁵, " but if ye ⁵ ἐν τῇ δι-
" hearken, it shall be new."   αστολῇ
                                                          see Deut.
    And further He says that He will give *another Covenant*, xxviii.
on this account *because they did not continue in the first.* 12.

" when it is no longer of brass, but which had been previously suspended.
" gives rain: [and the earth in like On the other hand the introduction
" manner is new,] when it is no longer of "the new earth" by the interpolator
" unfruitful, not when it has been is out of place: inasmuch as unfruitful
" changed: [and in this sense the ground would represent the people not
" house is new], when portions of it the Law; neither does S. Chrys. in
" have been" &c. There does not how- the refutation which follows refer at
ever appear to be any need for this: on all to this point of "new earth." The
the contrary, while the old text is introduction of the "house" is simply
simple and intelligible, the additions needless repetition.
bring in matters which are out of place. ᵏ πῶς οὖν ἔλαβεν αὐτόν; The Catena
[The other Catena however, that of has πῶς συνέλαβον αὐτόν; which Muti-
Niketas, Archbishop of Heraklea, one anus read, translating it, "Quomodo
of Mr. Field's valuable authorities, has corripuerunt eum?" Mr. Field thinks
the bracketed bits.] that neither reading gives a suit-
    The words ὅταν μὴ ἄκαρπος apply able meaning. If the reading adopted
naturally to the heaven, when it does not by Mr. F. and followed in the transla-
supply the moisture necessary for pro- tion be the true one, it must be sup-
ducing fruit. This argument from the posed that S. Chrys. had in mind the
"new heaven" is alleged by the objector condition in which Ezra, or perhaps
as distinct from that of the " new Nehemiah, found the Jews. The words
house:" it is an instance, he would say, τί δὲ Ἔσδρας ἐγκαλεῖ; seem more ap-
of the word "new" being applied, when propriate to Nehemiah than to Ezra:
there was neither change nor substitu- and the reception of Nehemiah on his
tion, as S. Chrys. interprets the pro- second visit to Jerusalem may have
phecy; nor even partial alteration as in been the circumstance of which the
the analogy of the "new house;" but orator was thinking.
only a renewal of fertilizing action

182 *The Old Covenant gave place as being inefficient.*

Hom. 14.
Rom. viii. 3.
Acts xv. 10.

This I shew by what he says *(For what the law could not do in that it was weak through the flesh;* And again, *Why tempt ye God, to put a yoke upon the neck of the disciples, which neither our fathers nor we were able to bear?)* But *they did not continue therein,* he says.

In this place he shews that God counts us worthy of greater and of spiritual [privileges]: for it is said *their sound went out into all the earth, and their words unto the ends of the world.* That is [the meaning of] *they shall not say each man to his neighbour Know the Lord.* And again, *the earth shall be filled with the knowledge of the Lord as much water*[1] *to cover the seas.*

Ps. xix. 5. Rom. x. 18.

Hab. ii. 14.

[7.] *In calling it a new [covenant]* (he says), *He hath made the first old: but that which decayeth and waxeth old is ready to vanish away.* See what was hidden [in that word]; how he hath laid open the very mind of the prophet! He honoured the law, and was not willing to call it *old* in express terms: but nevertheless this he did call it. For if the former had been new, he would not have called this which came afterwards *new* also. So that by granting something more full and different, he implies that *it was waxen old.* Therefore it is done away and is perishing, and no longer exists.

Having taken from the prophet his boldness of speech, he attacks it with more suitableness[m], pointing out that our [dispensation] is now flourishing. That is, he shewed that the other was old: then taking up the word *old,* and adding of himself another [circumstance], the [characteristic] of old age, he took up what was omitted by the other, and says *ready to vanish away.*

You see then that the New has not simply caused the old to cease, but only as it had become aged, as it was not [any longer] useful. For on this account he said, *for the weakness and unprofitableness thereof,* and, *the law made nothing perfect;* and that *if that first had been faultless, then should no place have been sought for the second.* And *faultless;* that is, useful; not as though it [the old Cove-

supra vii. 18.
ib. 19.
supra ver. 7.

---

[1] πολὺ ὕδωρ, is the reading of the Alex. MS. of the LXX: but κατακαλύψαι θαλάσσας is substituted by S. Chrys. for κατακαλύψει αὐτούς of the LXX.

[m] μᾶλλον αὐτοῦ καθάπτεται συμφερόντως.

nant] was obnoxious to any charges, but as not being sufficient. He used a familiar form of speech. As if one should say, the house is not faultless, that is, it has some defect, it is decayed: the garment is not faultless, that is, it is now coming to pieces. He does not therefore here speak of it as evil, but only as having some fault and deficiency.

[8.] Thus then we also are new, or rather we were made new, but now are become old, and for this cause we are *near to vanishing away*, and to destruction. Let us rub off[n] this old age. It is indeed no longer possible to do it by the Washing [of baptism], but by repentance it is possible here [in this life][1]. If there be in us anything old, let us cast it off. If [there be] any *wrinkle*, if any stain, if any *spot*, let us wash it away and become fair: that *the King may desire our beauty*.

It is possible for those even who have fallen into the extremest deformity[o] to recover that beauty of which David says that the King shall desire thy beauty. *Hearken, O daughter and consider; and forget thy people and thy father's*

---

[n] ἀποξύσωμεν: alluding to the Poetic phrase ξῦσαι ἀπὸ γῆρας ὀλοιόν.

[o] [There was one who sold his patrimony,
    A dear-bought dower
That had come down from high
    In a golden shower,
It was a loss that gold could never mend,
    The heart-blood of a Friend,
From out the world's dark den he came aside,
    A monster for the sun to see,
All hideous soiled with foulest leprosy,
And he sat down upon the grass and cried,

Is there no fountain that can wash again?
   .   .   .   .

There is a fount where holy men do say
    He that doth look for aye
He shall become like that he doth behold,
    Borrowing a light more pure than gold.
There is a glass whereon he that doth bend
    Shall see pourtrayed the Heaven,
Till he forget what earth hath best to lend
In the sweet hope that he may be forgiven.

    The Rev. Isaac Williams, Thoughts in Past years,
      The Penitent. p. 151 ed. 2. 1842.]

Margin references: 2 E. viii. 13. [1] ἐνταῦθα. Eph. v. 27. Ps. xlv. 11. ib. 10, 11.

house: *and the King shall greatly desire thy beauty.* And yet forgetting doth not produce beauty. Yea verily: [it produces] the beauty of the soul. What sort of forgetting? The forgetting sins. For he is speaking in reference to the Church from among the Gentiles, exhorting her not to remember the things of her fathers, that is [of] those that sacrificed to idols; for from such was it gathered.

And he said not, 'Go not after them,' but what is more, Do not admit them into thy mind; which he says also in another place, *I will not make mention of their names through my lips.* And again, *That my mouth may not talk of the deeds of men.* As yet is this no great virtue; nay, rather, it is indeed great, but not such as this [which is here spoken of]. For what saith he in that place? He says not; 'Talk 'not of the things of men, neither shalt thou speak of the 'things of thy fathers;' but, Do not even recall them in thought, nor admit them into thy mind. Thou seest to how great a distance he would have us removed from wickedness. For he that remembers not [a matter] will not think of it, and he that does not think, will not speak of it: and he that does not speak of it, will not do it. Seest thou from how many paths he hath as it were walled us off! by what great intervals he hath removed us far away! even to a very great [distance].

[9.] Let us then also *hearken and forget* our own evils. I do not say the things which we have done amiss, for (He saith) *Remember thou first, and I will not remember.* I mean for instance, Let us no longer remember rapacity, but even restore the former [plunder]. This is to forget wickedness, and to cast out the very thought of rapacity, and never at any time to admit it, to wipe away even the things which have been already done amiss.

But by what means shall we attain to a forgetting of wickedness? By remembering good things, by remembering God. If we are continually remembering God, we cannot remember those other things also. For (saith he) *If I remembered Thee upon my bed, if I thought upon Thee in the morning dawn.* We ought then to have GOD always in remembrance, but at that time especially, when thought is undisturbed, when by means of that remembrance [a man] is able to condemn himself, when he can retain [things] in memory. For in the day-time indeed, if we do call these things to mind, other cares and troubles entering in after, drive the thought out again: but in the night it is possible to remember continually, when the soul is calm and at rest; when it is in the haven, and under a serene sky. *The things which you say in your hearts be ye grieved for on your beds*, saith he. ^{He.viii.13.} ^{Ps. iv. 4 LXX.}

For it were indeed right to retain this recollection through the day also. But inasmuch as you are always full of cares, and distracted amidst the things of this life, at least at that time remember God on your bed; at the morning dawn meditate upon Him.

If at the morning dawn we meditate on these things, we shall go forth to our business with much security. If we have first made God propitious by prayer and supplication[1], going forth thus we shall have no man our enemy. Or if thou shouldest, thou wilt laugh him to scorn, having God propitious to thee. There is war in the public places; the affairs of every day are a fight, they are a tempest and a storm. We have therefore need of arms: and prayer is a great weapon. We have need of favourable winds; we should be acquainted with every thing, so as to go through the length of the day without shipwrecks and without wounds. For every single day the rocks are many, and oftentimes our boat strikes against them and is sunk. For this cause have we most especially need of prayer morning and evening.

[1] ἐντεύξει

[10.] Many of you have many times been spectators of the Olympic games: and not only have been spectators, but have been zealous partizans and admirers of the combatants, one of this [combatant], one of that. You know then that both during the days of the contests, and during those nights, all night long the herald[2] thinks of nothing else, has no other anxiety, than that the combatant should not disgrace himself when he goes forth. For those who sit by the trumpeter admonish him not even to speak to any one, that he may not spend his breath and get himself laughed at. If therefore he who is about to engage in a contest before men, uses so great forethought, much more

[2] κῆρυξ

will it befit us to be continually thoughtful, and anxious, since our whole life is a contest. Let every night then be a night of devotion[p], and let us be careful that when we go out in the day we do not make ourselves ridiculous. And would that it were only making ourselves ridiculous. But now the Judge of the contest is seated on the right hand of the Father, hearkening diligently that we utter not any false note, any thing out of tune. For He is not the Judge of actions only, but of words also. Let us watch through the night [1], beloved; we also have those that are eager for our success, if we will. Near each one of us Angels are sitting; and yet we snore through the whole night. And would that it were only this. But many do even many licentious things, some going to the very common brothels[2], and others making their own houses places of whoredom by taking courtesans thither. Yes most certainly. For is it not so? It is in a pretty way that they are anxious about their contest. Others are drunken and speak amiss [3]; others make an uproar. Others keep vigil through the night in an evil way, and worse than those who sleep, by arranging schemes of deceit; others by calculating usurious interest; others by bruising themselves with cares, and doing anything rather than what is suited to the contest [in which they are engaged]. Wherefore, I exhort you, let us lay aside all [other] things, and look to one only, how we may obtain the prize, [how we may] be crowned with the Chaplet; let us do all by which we shall be able to attain to the promised blessings. Which may we all attain in Christ Jesus our Lord, with Whom to the Father and also to the Holy Ghost be glory, might honour now and for ever and world without end. Amen.

[1] παννυ-χίσωμεν

[2] χαμαι-τυπεία

[3] παρα-φθέγγον-ται

[p] παννυχὶs. The term applied by Christians to whole nights spent in Psalmody and Prayer; "vigils."

HOMILY XV.

HEB. ix. 1—5.

Then verily the first [covenant] had also ordinances of divine service, and a[1] *worldly Sanctuary. For there was a tabernacle made the first, wherein was the Candlestick, and the Table, and the Shew-bread, which is called the Sanctuary. And after the second veil, the tabernacle which is called the Holiest of all; which had the golden censer and the Ark of the Covenant overlaid round about with gold: wherein was the golden pot that had*[2] *manna, and Aaron's rod that budded, and the tables of the covenant: and over it the Cherubims of glory, shadowing the Mercy-seat: of which we cannot now speak particularly.*

[1] *the*
[2] *held the*

HE has shewn from the Priest, from the Priesthood, from the Covenant, that that [dispensation] was to have an end. From this point he shews it from the fashion of the tabernacle itself. How? This, he says, [was] the *Holy*[3] and the *Holy of Holies*[4]. The holy place then is a symbol of the former period (for there all things are done by means of sacrifices); but the Holy of Holies of this that is now present.

[3] [ἅγια, *the sanctuary*]
[4] [ἅγια τῶν ἁγίων, *the holiest of all*]
[5] [cf. S. Cyr. Quod Unus Christus t. v. i. 761 c d]

And by the Holy of Holies he means Heaven; and by the veil, Heaven, and also the Flesh[5]; *which entereth* [a] *into that within the veil; that is to say, through the veil of His flesh.*

supra vi. 19.
infra x. 20.

It were however well to take up this passage from the

---

[a] This passage is translated as if there was a point between τὴν σάρκα and εἰσερχομένην: and as if in the next clause τουτέστι was a part of the citation, being put by S. Chrys. before the words διὰ τοῦ καταπετάσματος, instead of after them, as in Heb. x. 20. S. Chrys. says that "the veil" represents both Heaven and "the Flesh" of our Lord; and cites the two places where it is so interpreted by the Apostle, vi. 19, x. 20. See below [4.] p. 191.

very beginning, and so to speak of it. What then does he say? *Then verily the first also* (the first what? [*The first*] *Covenant) had ordinances of Divine service.*

What are *ordinances?* symbols or rites. Had then [b], as (he means) it has not now. He indicates that it had already given place to the other, for (he says) it *had* at that time; so that now although it is standing, it is not.

And the worldly Sanctuary. He calls it *worldly*, inasmuch as it was permitted to all to tread it, and in the same house the place was manifest where the priests stood, [as also] where the Jews, the Proselytes, the Grecians, the Nazarites [stood]. Since therefore even Gentiles were permitted to tread it, he calls it *worldly*. For surely the Jews were not *the world*.

For (saith he) *there was a tabernacle made; the first, which is called holy, wherein was the Candlestick, and the Table, and the Shew-bread.* These things are symbols of the world.

And after the second veil (There was then not one veil [only], but there was a veil without also) *the tabernacle, which is called holy of holies.* Observe how everywhere he calls it a tabernacle in regard of [God's] dwelling there as in a tent [1].

[1] παρὰ τὸ σκηνοῦν ἐκεῖ

Which had (saith he) *a golden Censer, and the ark of the Covenant overlaid round about with gold: wherein was the golden pot that held the manna, and Aaron's rod that budded, and the tables of the covenant.* All these things were venerable and conspicuous memorials of the Jewish ingratitude; *and the tables of the covenant* (for they brake them) *And the manna* (for they murmured. And for this cause handing on the memory thereof to their posterity, He commanded it to be laid up in a golden pot). *And Aaron's rod that budded.*

And over it, the Cherubim of glory. What is, *the Cherubim of glory?* He either means 'the glorious,' or those which are under God [2], *shadowing the mercy-seat.*

[2] τὰ ὑποκάτω τοῦ Θεοῦ

[b] τότε. Mr. Field seems to think that the Expositor read τότε in the sacred text: though, as he observes, he presently has τό τε. Perhaps the difficulty is avoided by supposing that the word εἶχε, *had*, with which the clause begins was emphasised in delivery, the explanation of the word "ordinances" being parenthetical: and the τότε being implied in the past tense εἶχε.

But in another point of view also he extols these things Heb.ix.7. in his discourse, in order to shew that those which come after them are greater. *Of which* (he saith) *we cannot now speak particularly.* In these words he hints that these was not merely what was seen, but that they were also a sort of figures with hidden meaning[1]. *Of which* (he saith) *we cannot now speak particularly,* perhaps because they needed a long discourse.

[1] αἰνίγματα

[2.] ver. 6. *Now when these things had been thus ordained, the priests go in always into the first tabernacle accomplishing the services [of God].* That is, these things indeed were [there], but the Jews had no enjoyment of them: they saw them not. So that they were no more theirs than [ours] for whom the foreshewing as by prophecy was made [c].

(ver. 7) *But into the second the High Priest alone once*[2] *in the year, not without blood, which he offers for himself, and for the ignorances of the people.* Thou seest that the types have been already first laid down as a foundation? for, lest they should say, 'how is there [but] one sacrifice?' he shews that this was so from the beginning, since at least the more holy and the awful [sacrifice] was [but] one. And how is it that [our] High Priest offered once for all? Thus were they wont [to do] from the beginning, for then also (he saith) *the High Priest* offered *once for all.*

[2] ἅπαξ, once for all

And well said he, *not without blood.* (Not indeed without blood, yet not this blood, for the matter they were engaged in was not so great.) He signifies that there shall be a sacrifice, not consumed by fire, but rather distinguished by blood. For inasmuch as he called the Cross a sacrifice, though it had neither fire, nor logs, nor was offered many times, but had been offered in blood once for all; he shews that the ancient sacrifice also was of this kind, was offered *once for all* in blood.

Which he offers for himself; again, *for himself; and for the ignorances of the people.* He said not "sins;" but *ignorances,* that they might not be high-minded. For even if thou hast not sinned intentionally, yet unintentionally thou hast committed sins of ignorance[3], and from this no man is pure.

[3] ἡγνόησας

[c] ἢ οἷς προεφητεύετο, or, "for whom they were foreshewn" &c.: for this the common editions have προετυποῦτο, "the foreshadowing as in a type."

HOM. 15.   And on every occasion [he adds] the *for himself*, signifying that Christ is much greater. For if He be far separated from our sins, how did He *offer for Himself?* Why then saidst thou these things (saith one)? Because this is [a mark] of One that is superior.

[1] θεωρία
[2] θεωρεῖ

[3.] Thus far there is no mystical interpretation[1]. But from this point he contemplates it spiritually[2] and says, (ver. 8) *The Holy Ghost this signifying, that the way into the Holiest of all was not yet made manifest, while as the first tabernacle was yet standing.* For this cause (saith he) have these things been thus *ordained*, that we might learn that *the Holy of Holies,* that is, Heaven, is as yet inaccessible. Let us not then think (saith he) that because we do not enter them, they have no existence: inasmuch as neither did we enter the Most Holy [place].

[3] καθέστηκε
(2)
[4] ἐνεστηκότα, or *close at hand*

ver. 9. *The which* (saith he) *was established*[3] *as a figure for the time present*[4]. What does he mean by *the time present?* That before the coming of Christ: For after the coming of Christ, it is no longer a time present: For how [could it be], having arrived, and being ended?

There is too something else which he indicates, when he says this, *which* [*as*] *a figure for the time present,* that is, became the Type.

[5] καθ' ὅν [καιρὸν]

During which[5] *are offered both gifts and sacrifices, that are not able to make him that doth the service perfect, as pertaining to the conscience.* Thou seest now what is [the

supra vii. 19.
ib. viii. 7.
[6] ἤφιεσαν or *forgive*

meaning of] *The Law made nothing perfect,* and *If that first* [*covenant*] *had been faultless.* How? *As pertaining to the conscience.* For the sacrifices did not put away[6] the defilement which [came] from the soul, but still were concerned

ib. vii.
16.
[7] ἀφιέναι

with the body: *after the law of a carnal commandment.* For certainly they could not put away[7] adultery, nor murder, nor sacrilege. Seest thou? Thou hast eaten this, Thou hast not eaten that, which are matters of indifference. [*Which stood*] *only in meats and drinks, and divers washings.* "Thou hast drunk this," saith he: and yet nothing had been ordained concerning drink, but he said this, treating them as trifles[d].

[d] ἐξευτελίζων. As if they were so immaterial, that he did not think it worth while to be accurate, and mentioned "drinks," about which there were no precepts. S. Chrys. had perhaps overlooked the law of the Nazarites, Numb. vi. 3.

ver. 10. *And [in] divers washings, and carnal ordinances imposed till the time of reformation* [1]*. For this is the righteousness of the flesh.* In this place he casts down the sacrifices, shewing that they had no efficacy, and that they existed *till the time of reformation,* that is, they waited for the time that reformeth all things.

He.ix.11.
[1] διορθώ-σεως setting right

[4.] ver. 11. *But Christ being come an High Priest of the good things that are come to pass*[c] *by the greater and more perfect tabernacle not made with hands.* Here he means the flesh. And well did he say, *greater and more perfect,* since God The Word and all the power of The Spirit dwells therein; *For God giveth not the Spirit by measure [unto Him].* And *more perfect,* as being both unblameable, and accomplishing greater things.

S. John iii. 34.

That is, not of this creation. See in what sense [he said] *greater.* For it would not have been *of the Spirit,* if man had constructed it. Nor yet [part] *of this creation,* that is, not of these created things but of a spiritual [creation]; [derived] of [2] the Holy Ghost.

S. Matt. i. 20.

[2] ἐκ

Thou seest how he calls heaven and the Body [f] both tabernacle and veil; *By the greater and more perfect tabernacle, through the veil, that is, His flesh.* And again, *into that within the veil.* And again, *entering into*[g] *the Holy of Holies, to appear before the face of God.* For what cause then doth he this? According as one thing or a different one is signified. I mean for instance, the Heaven is a veil, for it walls off the Holy place; the flesh is a veil, [as] concealing the Godhead[h]; and likewise a tabernacle, [as] holding the Godhead. Again, Heaven [is] a tabernacle: for the Priest is there within.

infra x. 20.
supra vi. 19.
infra ver. 24.

[c] γενομένων: Here and afterwards μελλόντων has been substituted in the modern editions of S. Chrys. γενομένων is considered by Lachmann to be the true reading in the Epistle.

[f] A slight alteration of Mr. Field's text seems needed here. The text of the Homily which he gives in accordance with all the authorities is: ὁρᾷς πῶς καὶ σκηνὴν καὶ καταπέτασμα καὶ οὐρανὸν τὸ σῶμα καλεῖ. But there is no appearance that the Apostle called Christ's body heaven, nor do any of the texts cited shew it. If however we introduce καὶ before τὸ σῶμα, or substitute it for τὸ, we have a good sense, in accordance with the four texts cited by S. Chrys. and the explanations which he afterwards gives.

[g] εἰσερχομένην: probably used by S. Chrys. as if τὴν σάρκα had preceded.

[h] The pointing has been changed in this place. In Mr. Field's edition the passage stands thus: καταπέτασμα ὁ οὐρανός· ὥσπερ γὰρ ἀποτειχίζει τὰ ἅγια καταπέτασμα, ἡ σὰρξ κρύπτουσα τὴν θεότητα. The translation is made as if the pointing was τὰ ἅγια· καταπέτασμα ἡ σὰρξ, κρύπτουσα τὴν θ. otherwise we must supply ἡ σὰρξ before ὥσπερ.

Hom. 15. [5.] *But Christ* (he saith) *being come an High Priest:* he did not say, *being*, but *being come*, that is, having come for this very purpose, not having been successor to another. He did not come first and then become [High Priest], but came and became at the same time [1]. And he did not say *being come an High Priest* of things which are sacrificed, but *of the good things that are come to pass*, as if his discourse had not power to put the whole before us.

[1] ἀλλ' ἅμα ἦλθε or, but [became so] as soon as He came

Neither by the blood, saith he, *of goats and calves* (All things are changed) *but by His own Blood* (saith he) *He entered in once for all*[2] *into the Holy place.* See thus he called Heaven. *Once for all* (saith he) *He entered into the Holy place, having found eternal redemption.* And this [expression] *having found*, was [expressive] of things very difficult, and that are beyond expectation, how by one entering in, He *found everlasting redemption.*

[2] ἐφάπαξ

[5.] Next [comes] that which is calculated to persuade. *For if the blood of bulls and of goats, and the ashes of an heifer sprinkling the unclean, sanctifieth to the purifying of the flesh; how much more shall the Blood of Christ, Who through the Holy*[3] *Spirit offered Himself without spot to God, purge your conscience from dead works, to serve the living God.*

[3] ἁγίου so also Sav. and Ben.

For (saith he) if *the blood of bulls* is able to purify the flesh, much rather shall the Blood of Christ wipe away the defilement of the soul. For that thou mayest not suppose when thou hearest [the word] *sanctifieth*, that it is some great thing, he marks out[4] and shews the difference between each of these purifyings, and how the one of them is high and the other low. And says it is [so] with good reason, since that is *the blood of bulls*, and this *the Blood of Christ.*

[4] ἐπισημαίνεται

Nor was he content with the name, but he sets down also the manner of the offering. *Who* (saith he) *through the Holy*[1] *Spirit offered Himself without spot to God*, that is, the victim was without blemish, pure from sins. For this is [the meaning of] *through the Holy Spirit*, not by means of fire, nor of any other things.

Shall purify your conscience (saith he) *from dead works.* And well said he *from dead works;* if any man had touched

---

[1] Here and again below the Catena and Mutianus read "eternal," and so one MS. *a priori manu.*

a dead body, he was polluted; and here, if any man touch a He.ix.14. *dead work*, he is defiled through his conscience. *To serve* (he saith) *the Living and true God.* Here he declares that it is not [possible] while one has *dead works to serve the Living and true God,* for they are both dead and false; and with good reason [he does this].

[6.] Let no man then enter in here with *dead works.* (3) For if it was not fit that one should enter in who had touched a dead body, much more one that hath *dead works:* for this is the most grievous pollution. And *dead works* are, all which have not life, which breathe forth an ill odour. For just as a dead body is useful to none of the senses, but is even annoying to those who come near it, so sin also at once strikes our thinking faculties[1], and does not allow the ¹ τὸ λογι- mind itself to be quiet, but disturbs and troubles it. στικόν

And it is said too that a plague at its very commencement thoroughly corrupts[2] the living bodies; of such a ² τικτό- nature also is sin. It differs in nothing from a plague, not μενος [indeed] corrupting the air first, and then the living bodies, διαφθείρει but darting at once into the soul. Seest thou not how persons affected with the plague, are swollen and inflamed: how they writhe about, how they are full of an ill scent, how disfigured are their countenances: how wholly unclean they are? Such are they also that are sinning, though they see it not. For, tell me, is not he who is possessed by the desire of riches or carnal lust, worse than any one that is in a fever? Is he not more unclean than all these, when he does and submits to all shameless things?

[7.] For what is more degraded than a man who is in love with money? So many things as women that are harlots or on the stage refuse not to do, neither does he [refuse]. Nay it is even probable that they would refuse [to do] a thing, rather than he. He even submits to do things suited only to slaves, flattering those whom he ought not; again he is overbearing where he ought not to be, being inconsistent in every respect. He will sit by them, flattering wicked people, and oftentimes depraved old men, that are of much poorer and meaner condition than himself; and will be insolent and overbearing to others that are good and in all respects virtuous. Thou seest in both respects his unseemly conduct, his shamelessness: he is both humble beyond measure, and boastfully arrogant.

Harlots however stand in front of their house, and the charge against them is that they sell their body for money: yet, one may say, poverty and hunger compel them (although at the most not even is this a sufficient excuse: for they might gain a livelihood by work). But the covetous man stands, not before his house, but before the city, making over to the devil not his body but his soul; so that he [the devil] is in his company, and goes in unto him, as in very deed to an harlot: and having satisfied all his lust, departs; and all the city sees it, not two or three persons only.

And this again is the peculiarity of harlots, that they are his who gives the gold. Even if he be a slave or a gladiator[k], or any person whatever, yet if he offers their hire, they receive him. But the free, even should they be more noble than all, they do not accept without the money. This same do these men also do. They turn away right thoughts when they bring no money: but they cherish such as are abominable, and truly like those that fight with wild beasts[1], for the sake of the gold, and cohabit with them in an unseemly way and destroy the beauty of the soul. For as those women are naturally of odious appearance[2] and black, and awkward and gross, formless and ill-shaped, and in all respects disgusting, such do the souls of these men become, not able even to conceal their deformity by their paintings[3]. For when the ill look[1] is extreme, whatever things they may devise, they cannot succeed in their feigning.

For that it is shamelessness which constitutes harlots, hear the prophet saying, *Thou wert shameless towards all; thou hadst a harlot's countenance.* This may be said to

[1] θηριομάχοις
[2] φύσει εἰδεχθεῖς
[3] ἐπιτρίμμασι what they rub on.
Jer. iii. 3.

---

[k] μονομάχος. The reading of the common editions is κἂν ἐλεύθερος, κἂν μόναχος. The word μόναχος had been at a very early period written by some copyists for μονομάχος (Mutianus has *monachus*), and the interpolator misapprehending the drift of the passage had inserted κἂν ἐλεύθερος. Mr. Field many years ago in earlier volumes of his edition, suggested the true reading here, as also the word θηριομάχοις (*bestialibus* Mut.) just below, for which θεομάχοις had been substituted in the Common texts. Both conjectures are now confirmed by MS. authority. The gladiators, especially the *bestiarii*, who fought with wild beasts, were regarded as a most degraded class.

[1] δυσειδία. Mut. and one MS. have δυσωδία, "ill savour."

the covetous also: *Thou wert shameless towards all*, not He.ix.14.
towards these or those, but *towards all*. How? Such an
one has no respect either for father, or son, or wife, or
friend, or brother, or benefactor, absolutely not for any
person whatever. And why do I say friend, or brother, or
father? He has no respect for God Himself, but thinks
that all [we believe] is a fable; and he laughs: intoxicated
by his excessive lust, and not even admitting into his ears
any of the things which might profit him.

But O! their absurdity! and then what things they say!
"Woe to thee O Mammon, and to him that has thee not."
At this I am torn to pieces with indignation: for woe be
to those who say these things, even though they say them
in jest. For tell me, has not God uttered such a threat as
this, saying, *Ye cannot serve two masters?* And dost thou S. Matt.
set at nought[1] the threat? Does not Paul say that it is vi. 24.
Idolatry, and does he not call *the covetous man an Idolater?* Eph. v.
^{1} ἐκλύεις

[8.] And thou standest laughing, raising a laugh after 5.
the manner of women of the world, those [I mean] that (4)
are on the stage. This has overthrown, this has cast
down every thing. Our Christianity[2] is turned into laugh- ^{2} τὰ ἡμέ-
ing, and politeness[3] and facetiousness; there is nothing τερα
steady, nothing grave. I say not these things to men of ^{3} πολιτισ-
the world only; but I know those whom I am hinting at. μὸς
For the Church has been filled with laughter. If such an
one says a witty thing, laughter immediately arises in those
who are sitting [here]: and the strange thing is that many
do not leave off laughing even during the very time of the
prayer. Everywhere the Devil leads the dance[4], he has ^{4} χορεύει
entered into all, is master of all. Christ is dishonoured,
is thrust aside; the Church is made no account of. Do ye
not hear Paul when he saith, *Let filthiness and foolish* Ib. 4.
talking and jesting, be taken away from you? He places
jesting along with *filthiness*, and dost thou laugh? What
is *foolish talking?* that in which there is nothing profitable.
And dost thou laugh at all and relax thy countenance,
thou that art devoted to a solitary life? thou that art
crucified? thou that art a mourner? tell me, dost thou
laugh? Where dost thou hear of Christ-doing this? Nowhere: but that He was sad indeed oftentimes. For even

when He looked on Jerusalem, He wept; and when He thought on the Traitor He was troubled; and when He was about to raise Lazurus, He wept; and dost thou laugh? If he who grieves not over the sins of others deserves to be accused, of what consideration will he be worthy, who is without any feeling of sorrow for his own sins, yea laughs at them? This is the season of grief and tribulation, of bruising and bringing under [the body], of conflicts and sweatings, and dost thou laugh? Dost not thou see how Sarah was rebuked? dost thou not hear Christ saying, *Woe to them that laugh, for they shall weep?* Thou chantest these things every day, for, tell me, what dost thou say? 'I have laughed?' By no means; but what? *I laboured in my groaning.*

But perchance there are some persons so dissolute and silly as even during this very rebuke to laugh, because forsooth we thus discourse about laughter. For indeed such is their misguided folly, such their madness, that it is not even sensible of the rebuke.

The Priest of God is standing, offering up the prayer of all: and art thou laughing, having no fears? And while he is offering up the prayers in trembling for thee, thou art despising all. Hearest thou not the Scripture saying, *Woe, ye despisers!* dost thou not shudder? art thou not subdued? Even when thou enterest a royal palace, thou orderest thyself in dress, and look, and gait, and all other respects: and here where there is the true Palace of the King indeed, and things like those of heaven, dost thou laugh? . Thou indeed, I know, seest [them] not, but hear thou that there are angels present every where, and in the house of God especially they stand by the King, and all is filled by those incorporeal Powers.

This my discourse is addressed to women also, who in the presence of their husbands indeed do not dare readily to do this, and even if they do it, it is not at all times, but during a season of relaxation, but here they do it always. Tell me, O woman, dost thou cover thine head and laugh, when thou art sitting in the Church? Didst thou come in here to make confession of thy sins, to fall down before God, to entreat and to supplicate for the transgressions thou hast wretchedly committed, and dost thou do this with laughter? How then wilt thou be able to propitiate Him?

[9.] But (saith one) what harm is there in laughter? There is no harm in laughter; the harm is when it is beyond measure, and out of season. Laughter has been implanted in us, that when we see our friends after a long time, we may laugh; that when we see any persons downcast and fearful, we may relieve them by our smile; not that we should burst out violently¹ and be always laughing. Laughter has been implanted in our soul, that the soul may sometimes be refreshed, not that it may be quite relaxed. For carnal desire also is implanted in us, and yet it is not by any means necessary that because it is implanted in us, therefore we should use it, or use it immoderately: nay rather we hold it in subjection, and say not, Because it is implanted in us, let us use it.

Serve God with tears, that thou mayest be able to wash away the sins which thou hast committed. I know that many persons make a mock at us², saying, 'Tears directly.' For this very cause it is a time for tears. I know also that they are disgusted, who say, *Let us eat and drink, for to-morrow we die. Vanity of vanities, all is vanity.* It is not I that say it, but he who had had the experience of all things saith thus: *I builded for me houses, I planted vineyards, I made me pools of water, [I had] men servants and women servants.* And what is it that he saith after all this? *Vanity of vanities, all is vanity.*

Let us mourn therefore, beloved, let us mourn in order that we may laugh indeed, that we may rejoice indeed in the time of unmixed joy. For with this joy here grief is altogether mingled: and never is it possible to find it pure. But that other is simple and undeceiving joy: it has not in it anything treacherous, nor any admixture. In that joy let us delight ourselves; that let us pursue after. And it is not possible to obtain this in any other way, than by choosing here not what is pleasant, but what is profitable, and by voluntarily afflicting ourselves a little, and bearing all things with thanksgiving. For thus we shall be able to attain also to the Kingdom of Heaven, of which may we all be counted worthy, in Christ Jesus our Lord, with whom to the Father together with the Holy Ghost be glory now and for ever and world without end. Amen.

Marginal references: He.ix.14. ¹ ἀνακαγχάζωμεν ² διαμωκῶνται 1 Cor. xv. 32. Eccl. i. 2. Ib. ii. 4. ib. 6, 7. ib x.ii. 8.

HOMILY XVI.

Heb. ix. 15—18.

And for this cause He is the Mediator of the New Testament, that by means of death for the redemption of the transgressions that were under the first Testament, they which are called might receive the promise of an eternal inheritance. For where a testament is, there must also of necessity be the death of the testator[1]. *For a testament is of force when men are dead*[2], *since it hath no force at all whilst the testator liveth. Whereupon*[3] *neither was that first [testament] dedicated*[4] *without blood.*

[1] of him that made it
[2] in the case of the dead
[3] whence
[4] inaugurated

It was probable that many of those who were more weak in disposition would distrust the promises of Christ for this reason especially, because He had died. Paul accordingly out of a superabundance [of proofs] introduced this illustration[5], deriving it from common custom. Of what kind is it? 'Nay rather (he says) on this very account we ought to be of good courage.' On what account? Because testaments are established and obtain their force when those who have made them are not living, but dead. *And for this cause*, saith he, *is He the Mediator of the New Testament.* A Testament is made towards the last day, [the day] of death.

[5] ὑπόδειγμα

And a testament is of this character: It has some that are heirs, and some that are disinherited. So in this case also: *I will that where I am*, saith Christ, *these also may be.* And again of those who are disinherited, hear Him saying, *I pray not for all, but for them that believe on Me through their word.* Again, a testament has some things belonging to him who makes the disposition, and some to those who receive; so that they have some things to receive, and some

S. John xvii. 24.

ib. 20.

to do. So also in this case. For after having made promises innumerable, He demands also what is [to come] from them, saying, *a new commandment I give unto you.* Again, a testament ought to have witnesses. Hear Him again saying, *I am one that bear witness of Myself, and He that sent Me beareth witness of Me.* And again, *He shall testify of Me,* speaking of the Comforter. The twelve Apostles too He sent, saying, *Bear ye witness before God*[a]*.*

He.ix.15.

S. John xiii. 34.

Ib. viii. 18.

Ib. xv. 26.

[2.] *And for this cause* (saith he) *He is the Mediator of the New Testament.* What is a *Mediator?* A mediator is not owner of the thing, in respect whereof he is mediator, but the thing belongs to one person, and the mediator is another: as for instance, the mediator in regard to a marriage is not the person who contracts matrimony, but he who aids him who is about to take a wife. So then it is in this instance also. The Son became Mediator between the Father and us. The Father willed not to leave us this inheritance, but was wroth against us, and was displeased [with us] as being estranged [from Him]; He accordingly became Mediator between us and Him, and gained Him over.

And what then? How did He become Mediator? He brought words from [Him] and brought [them to us], conveying over[1] what came from the Father to us, and adding His own death thereto. We had offended: we ought to have died: He died for us and made us worthy of the Testament. In this way is the Testament secure, in that henceforward it is made unto those that are not unworthy. At the beginning indeed, He made His dispositions as a father for sons; but after we had become unworthy, there was no longer place for a testament, but there was need of punishment.

[1 διαπορθ-μεύων, see above p. 40 note g.]

Why then (he would say) art thou proud on account of the law? For it placed us in a condition of so great sin, that we could never have been saved, if our Lord had not died for us [b]; the law would not have had power, for it is weak.

---

[a] This is not a citation of any words of our Lord: but probably S. John xv. 27, which is substantially equivalent, was the passage intended; the words are those of 1 Tim. v. 21: thrown into the imperative form.

[b] Mr. Field points the passage thus: "we could never have been saved; if our

[3.] And he established this no longer from common custom only, but also from the things which had actually happened in [the case of] the old [Testament]: which especially influenced them. There was no one [it might be objected] who died there: how then could that Testament be firm? In the same way (saith he). How? For there also there was blood, just as there is blood here. And if it was not the blood of the Christ, do not be surprised; for it was a figure. *Whence,* saith he, *neither was the first* [*Testament*] *inaugurated without blood.*

What is *was inaugurated?* was confirmed, was ratified. The word *whence*[1] means "for this cause." It was needful that the symbol of the Testament should be [the symbol] also of death.

(2) For otherwise (tell me) for what object is the book of the testament sprinkled? (ver. 19, 20) *For when Moses had spoken to all the people every precept according to the law, he took the blood of calves, with water, and scarlet wool, and hyssop, and sprinkled both the book itself and all the people, saying, This is the blood of the testament, which God hath enjoined unto you.* Tell me then for what object is the book of the testament sprinkled, and also the people, except on account of the precious blood, figured from the first?

Why *with hyssop?* It is close and retentive[2 c]. And why the *water?* It indicates also the cleansing by water. And why the *wool?* this also [was used], that the blood might be retained. In this place blood and water indicate the same thing[d], for baptism is His passion[e].

[4.] ver. 21, 22. *Yea and in like manner too he sprinkled with blood the tabernacle and all the vessels of the ministry. And according to the law, almost*[3] *all things are purged with blood, and without blood-shedding no remission takes place.* Why the *almost?* why did he qualify it? Because those [ordinances] were not a perfect purification, nor a perfect

---

[1] τὸ ὅθεν. so Hom. v. 5. p. 69 on ch. iii. 1.

[2] κρατητικόν

[3] or and we may almost say that according &c.

"Lord had not died for us, the Law would not have had power"&c. The translation follows the Bened. pointing, as giving the meaning most in accordance with S. Chrys. teaching.

[c] The common text, besides other additions, adds the explanatory words,

τοῦ αἵματος "of the blood."

[d] The common editions add ὃν, determining the meaning to be "he, [or it] shews that blood and water are the same thing."

[e] See above on ch. vi. 6.

remission, but half-complete and in a very small degree. He.ix.22.
But in this case He saith, *This is the blood[f] of the New S. Matt. xxvi. 28.
Testament, which is shed for you, for remission of sins.*
Where then is *the book?* He purified their minds. They themselves then were the books of the New Testament. But where are *the vessels of the ministry?* These are themselves. And where is *the tabernacle?* Again, it is themselves; for *I will dwell in them,* He saith, *and walk in them.* 2 Cor. vi. 16.

[5.] But they were not sprinkled with *scarlet wool,* nor yet *with hyssop.* Why was this? Because the cleansing was not bodily but spiritual, and the blood was spiritual. How? It flowed not from the bodies of irrational animals, but from the Body which had been framed by the Spirit. With this blood not Moses but Christ sprinkled us, through the word which was spoken; *This is the blood of the New Testament, for the remission of sins.* This word, instead of Hyssop, having been dipped in the blood, sprinkles all. And there indeed the body was cleansed outwardly, for the purifying was bodily; but here, inasmuch as the purifying is spiritual, it entereth into the soul, and cleanseth it, not being simply sprinkled over, but springing up like a fountain in our souls. They who have been initiated know what I am speaking of. And in their case indeed [the Priest] sprinkled just the surface; and, on the other hand, the person who was sprinkled washed it off; for surely he did not go about continually stained with blood. But in the case of the soul it is not so, but the blood is mixed up with its very substance, making it vigorous and pure, and leading it to the very unapproachable perfection of beauty.

[6.] Henceforward then he shews that His death is the cause not only of confirming [the Covenant], but also of purification. For inasmuch as death was thought to be an odious thing, and especially that of the cross, he says that it wrought a purification, and a precious purification, and under greater conditions. For this cause the sacrifices preceded, because of this blood. For this cause [were] the lambs; every thing was done for this cause.

[f] Or as the position of φησὶ after αἷμα would seem to imply was the interpretation of S. Chrys.: "This blood is that of the New Testament &c."

ver. 23. *It was therefore necessary that the Patterns*[1] (he says) *of the things in the heavens should be purified with these, but the heavenly things themselves with better sacrifices than these.*

And how are they *patterns*[2] *of things in the heavens?* And what does he mean by *the things in the heavens* at this time? Does he [mean] Heaven? Or is it possible that he means the Angels? None of these, but our [Christian rites][g]. It follows then that our [services] are in Heaven, and our [services] are heavenly, even though they be accomplished on earth; since angels also are on earth, yet they are called Heavenly. And the Cherubim appeared on earth, but yet they are heavenly. And why do I say 'appeared?' nay rather they dwell on earth, just as they did in Paradise: but this is nothing; for they are heavenly. And, *Our conversation is in Heaven*, and yet we live here.

But *the heavenly things themselves*, that is, the philosophy which exists amongst us; those who have been called yonder.

With better sacrifices than these. What is *better* is better than something [else] that is good. Therefore *the patterns also of things in the heavens* have been proved good; for not even the patterns could have been evil: else the things whereof they are patterns would also have been evil.

(3) [7.] If then we are heavenly, and have obtained such a sacrifice[h], let us fear. Let us no longer continue on the earth; for even now it is possible for him that wishes it, not to be on the earth. For to be on the earth and not to be, is the effect of moral disposition and choice. For instance; God is said to be in Heaven. Wherefore? not because He is confined by space[3], God forbid, nor as having left the earth destitute of His presence, but by His close relation to and intimacy with[4] the Angels. If then we also are near to God, we are in Heaven. For what care I about Heaven when I see the Lord of Heaven, when I

Hom. 16.
[1] ὑποδείγματα
[2] or "samples," "means of shewing."
Phil. iii. 20.
[3] τόπῳ ἀποκλειόμενος
[4] σχέσει καὶ οἰκειώσει

[g] The Greek is τὰ ἡμέτερα, including all our sacraments, services, relations, life and conversation. see Hom. xiv. [3.]
[h] θυσίας. Mr. Field adopts the reading of the later MSS. (and common Editions) οὐσίας "substance," or "possession." But the three MSS. which he usually follows and the Old translation read θυσίας, which has been followed in the translation.

myself am become a Heaven? *For,* He saith, *We will come, I and the Father, and will make our abode with him.* HE.ix.23. S. John xiv. 23.

Let us then make our own soul a Heaven. The heaven is naturally bright; for not even in a storm does it become black, for it does not itself change its appearance, but the clouds run together and cover it. Heaven has the Sun; we also have the Sun of Righteousness. I said it is possible [for us] to become a Heaven; and I see that it is possible [for us] to become even better than Heaven. How? when we have the Lord of the Sun. Heaven is throughout pure and without spot; it changes not either in a storm or in the night. Neither let us then be so influenced, either by tribulations or by *the wiles of the devil,* but let us continue spotless and pure. Heaven is high and far distant from the earth. Let us also effect this [as regards ourselves]; let us withdraw ourselves from the earth, and exalt ourselves to that height, and remove ourselves far from the earth. Heaven is higher than the rains and the storms, and is reached by none of them. This we also shall be able to do, if we will. Eph. vi. 11.

It does however appear [to be affected by changes], but it is not so affected. Neither then let us be affected [by them], even if we appear to be so. For just as in a storm, people in general know not the beauty of the heaven, but think that it is changed, while philosophic men know that it is not affected at all, so with regard to ourselves also in our afflictions; the many think that we are changed with [changing circumstances], and that our affliction has touched our very heart, but philosophers know that it has not touched us.

[8.] Let us then become heaven, let us mount up to that height, and so we shall see men nowise differing from ants. I do not speak of the poor only, nor the many, but even if there be a great general there, even if the emperor be there, we shall not distinguish the emperor, nor the private person. We shall not know what is gold, or what is silver, or what is silken or purple raiment: we shall see all things as if they were flies, if we be seated in that height above. There is no tumult *there,* no disturbance, nor clamour.

Hom. 16. And how is it possible (saith one) for him who walks on the earth, to be raised up to that height? I do not tell it thee in words, but I shew thee in fact those who have arrived at that height. Who then are they?

I mean such as Paul, who being on earth, [yet] spent their lives in heaven. But why do I say "in heaven?" They were higher than the Heaven, yea than the other heaven, and mounted up to God Himself. For, *who* (he saith) *shall separate us from the love of Christ? shall tribulation, or distress, or persecution, or famine, or nakedness, or peril, or sword?* And again, *while we look not at the things which are seen, but at the things which are not seen.* Thou seest that he did not even see the things that are here. But to shew thee that he was higher than the heavens, hear him saying himself, *For I am persuaded that neither death, nor life, nor things present, nor things to come, nor height, nor depth, nor any other creature, shall be able to separate us from the love of Christ.*

Rom. viii. 35.

2 Cor. iv. 18.

Rom. viii. 38, 39.

(4) Thou seest how thought hurrying past all things, made him higher not than this creation only, not than these heavens [only], but even [than any other also] if any other there were. Thou hast seen the elevation of his mind? Thou hast seen what the tent-maker became, because he had the will, he who had spent his whole life in the market-place?

[9.] For there is no hindrance, no not any, but that we may rise above all men, if we have the will. For if we are so successful in arts that are beyond the reach of the generality, much more in that which does not require so great labour.

For, tell me, what is more difficult than to walk along a tight rope, just as on level ground, and when walking on high to dress and undress yourself, as if you were sitting on a couch? Does not the performance seem to us to be so frightful, that we are not even willing to look at it, but are terrified and tremble at the very sight? And tell me, what is more difficult than to hold a pole upon your face, and when you have put a child up upon it, to perform innumerable feats and delight the spectators? And what is more difficult than to play at ball[1] with swords? And tell me what is harder than thoroughly to search out the

[1] σφαιρίζειν

bottom of the sea? And one might mention innumerable other arts. HE.ix.23.

But easier than all these, if we have the will, is virtue, and the going up into Heaven. For in this case it is only necessary to have the will, and all [the rest] follows. For we may not say, I am unable: this would be to accuse the Creator. For if He made us unable, and then gives us commands, it is an accusation against Himself.

[10.] How is it then (some one says) that many are not able? How is it then [tell me] that many are not willing? For, if they be willing, all men will be able. For this cause also Paul saith, *I would that all men were even as I myself*, since he knew that all were able to be as himself. 1 Cor. vii. 7. For he would not have said this, if it had been impossible. Dost thou wish to become [such]? only lay hold on the beginning.

Tell me now, in the case of any arts, when we wish to attain them, are we content with wishing, or do we also engage with the things themselves[1]? As for instance, does any man wish to become a pilot, he does not say, I wish, and content himself with that, but he also puts his hand to the work. Does he wish to become a merchant, he does not merely say, I wish, but he also takes the matter in hand. Again he wishes to travel abroad, and he does not say, I wish, but he applies himself to the very thing itself. Is it then so, that in every thing wishing alone is not sufficient, but we must needs add action also; and when thou wishest to mount up to heaven, dost thou merely say, 'I wish?'

How then is it (saith he) that thou saidst that willing is sufficient? [I meant] willing joined with deeds, the [willing] when one lays hold on the thing itself; when one has laboured [at it]. For we have God working with us, and acting with us. Only let us make our choice, only let us apply ourselves to the matter as to a [real] work, only let us be anxious about it, only let us lay it to heart, and all follows. But if we sleep on, and as we snore expect to

---

[1] ἁπτόμεθα τῶν πραγμάτων. The expression (τοῦ πράγματος ἅπτεται) is repeated in each of the three instances that follow: in the translation it is varied.

enter into heaven, how shall we be able to obtain possession of the heavenly inheritance?

Let us therefore be willing, I exhort you, let us be willing. Why do we carry on all our traffic with reference to the present life, which to-morrow we shall leave? Let us make choice then of that Virtue which will suffice us through all eternity: wherein we shall be continually, and shall enjoy the everlasting good things, which may we all attain, in Christ Jesus our Lord, with whom to the Father together with the Holy Ghost be glory power honour now and for ever and world without end. Amen.

HOMILY XVII.

Heb. ix. 24—26.

For Christ is not entered into the holy places made with hands, which are the figures[1] *of the true, but into Heaven itself, now to appear in the presence of God for us. Nor yet that He should offer Himself often, as the High Priest entereth into the Holy place every year with blood of others, for then must He often have suffered since the foundation of the world. But now, once*[2], *at the end of the world, hath He appeared to put away*[3] *sin by the sacrifice of Himself.*

[1] ἀντί-
τυπα
[2] ἅπαξ
once for all
[3] or annul

THE Jews greatly prided themselves on the temple and the tabernacle. Wherefore they said, *The temple of the Lord, The temple of the Lord, The temple of the Lord.* For neither was there anywhere else in the earth a temple constructed such as this, either for costliness, or beauty, or anything else. For God who ordained it, commanded that it should be made with great magnificence, inasmuch as they also were more drawn and allured by things material. For it had bricks of gold in the walls; and any one who wishes may learn this well in the second [book] of Kings, and in Ezekiel, and how many talents of gold were there expended.

Jer. vii. 4.

But the second [temple] was a more glorious building, on account both of its beauty, and in all other respects. Nor was it on this account alone an object of reverence, but also from its being One. For they were wont to resort thither from the uttermost parts of the earth, whether from Babylon or from Ethiopia. And Luke shews this when he says in the Acts: *There were dwelling there Parthians, and Medes, and Elamites, and the dwellers in Mesopotamia,*

Acts ii. 5, 9, 10.

in Judea and Cappadocia, in Pontus and Asia, Phrygia and Pamphylia, in Egypt and in the parts of Libya about Cyrene. They then who lived in all parts of the world assembled there, and the fame of the temple was great.

What then does Paul do? The very same which [he did] in the instance of the sacrifices, this also he does here. For just as there he set against [them] the death of Christ, so here also he sets the whole heaven against the temple.

[2.] And not by this alone did he point out the difference, but also by adding that The Priest is become more near to God: for he saith, *to appear in the presence*[1] *of God.* So that he made the subject one of awe and reverence, not only by the [consideration of] heaven, but also by [that of Christ's] entering in [there]. For not merely through symbols as here, but God Himself He sees there.

Thou seest that it is for condescension's sake that the lowly things have been said throughout? How dost thou then any longer wonder that He intercedes, there where He places Himself as a High Priest? *Nor yet, that He should offer Himself often, as the High Priest.*

For Christ is not entered into the Holy Places made with hands (he saith) *which are the figures*[2] *of the True.* (Those then are true; and these are figures[3], for the temple too has been so arranged[4], as the Heaven of Heavens.)

What sayest thou? He who is every where present, and who filleth all things, doth not He *appear*[a] [in God's presence] unless He enter into Heaven? Thou seest that all things pertain to the flesh.

To appear, he saith, *in the presence of God for us.* What is *for us?* He went up (he means) with a sacrifice which had power to propitiate the Father. Wherefore (tell me)? Was He an enemy [to us]? The angels were enemies, He was not an enemy. For that the Angels were enemies, hear thou what he saith, *He made peace as to things on earth and things in Heaven*[b]. So that He also *entered into Heaven,*

[1] τῷ προσώπῳ before the Face
[2] ἀντίτυπα
[3] τύποι
[4] κατεσκεύασται

Col. i. 20.

[a] ἐμφανίζεται. "He makes Himself visible," "apparent;" so "presents Himself" or "appears in presence:" in His Human Nature.
[b] S. Chrys. understands this passage as meaning that peace was made between things on earth and those in Heaven, between us and the Angels. See his Homily on Col. i. 20. [pp. 212 sqq. O.T.] By introducing this subject of the Father not being inimical to us, he seems to guard against any misinterpretation of what he had said, Hom. xvi. [2.]

As there is one death, so there is one Sacrifice for all. 209

now to appear in the presence of God for us. He now *appeareth*, but it is *for us*. He.ix.28.

[3.] *Nor yet that He should offer Himself often, as the High Priest entereth into the Holy place every year with blood of others.* Thou seest how many are the differences between *often* and *once*, between *the blood of others*, and *His own*[1]. Great is the interval. He is Himself then both victim and Priest and sacrifice. For if it had not been so, it would have been necessary also to offer many sacrifices, He must have been many times crucified. *Since He in that case must often have suffered since the foundation of the world.* [1] see ver. 12.

In this place he has also veiled over [c] something. *But now once in the end of the world.* Why *at the end of the world?* After the many sins. Now if indeed it had taken place at the beginning, and after that no man had believed, and He must not die a second time, all would have been useless. But inasmuch as at a later time the transgressions [of men] were many, it was with reason that He then appeared: which he expresses in another place also, *Where sin abounded, grace did much more abound. But now once at the end of the world, hath He been manifested for the putting away of sin by the sacrifice of Himself.* Rom. v. 20.

[4.] (ver. 27) *And as it is appointed*[2] *unto men once for all to die, but after that, Judgement.* He next says also why He died once [only]: because He became a ransom-price of one death. *It had been reserved* (saith he) *for men once for all to die.* This then is [the meaning of] *He died once*[3], for all at once[4]. (What then? Do we no longer die that death? We do indeed die [that death], but we do not continue in it: which is [the same thing as] not to die at all. For the tyranny of death, and death indeed, is when he who has died is never more allowed to return to life. But when after dying it is [possible] to live, and that a better life, this is not death, but sleeping.) Since then death was to have possession of all men, for this cause He died that He might deliver us.

[2] ἀπόκειται laid up (2)
[3] ἅπαξ
[4] ὑπὲρ ἁπάντων

ver. 28. *So Christ also having been once for all*[5] *offered.* [5] ἅπαξ
By whom offered? evidently by Himself. Here he not only

---

[c] The Apostle has here stated something covertly. What this is S. Chrys. proceeds to explain.

HOM. 17. says that He is Priest, but Victim also, and what is sacri-
¹ θῦμα καὶ ficed¹. On this account are [the words] *having been offered.*
ἱερεῖον *Having been once for all offered* (he says) *to bear*ᵈ [or
present] the sins of many. Why *of many*, and not " of all?"
Because not all believed. For He died for all indeed, that
² ἀντίρρο- is for His part: for that death was a counterbalance²
πος against the destruction of all men. But He did not bear
the sins of all men, because they were not willing.

And what is [the meaning of] *He bare [He presented]
the sins?* Just as in the Oblation we bring up [and present]
our sins and say, "whether we have sinned voluntarily or
"involuntarily do Thou forgiveᵉ," that is, we make mention
of them first, and then ask for their forgiveness. So also
was it done here. Where has Christ done this? Hear
S. John Himself saying, *And for their sakes I sanctify*ᶠ *Myself.* Lo!
xvii. 19. He brought up the transgressions. He took them from
men, and presented them to the Father; not that He
might determine any thing against them [mankind], but
that He might remit them [the sins].

The second time without sin shall He appear (saith he) *to
them that look for Him, unto salvation.* What is *without
sin?* it is as much as to say, He sinneth not. For neither
did He die as owing the debt of death, nor yet because
of sin. But how *shall He appear?* To punish, you say.
He did not however say this, but [what was] cheering;
*without sin shall He appear to them that look for Him, unto
salvation.* So that for the time to come they no longer
need sacrifice to save themselves, but do this by works.

[5.] (chap. x. 1) *For* (he saith) *the Law having a shadow
of the good things to come, not the very image of the things;*
i. e. not the very truth [the reality itself]. For as in
painting so long as one [only] draws the outline-marks, it
is a sort of *shadow:* but when one has added the bright
painting and laid in the colours, then it becomes *an image*

ᵈ ἀνενεγκεῖν. Lit. to bring or bear up: hence to refer to or bring before a person, to present. The word is used in the Epistle to the Hebrews for "offer" as a sacrifice. vii. 27; xiii. 15.

ᵉ [This occurs, not absolutely verbally in the "prayer of Trisagion," in S. Chrys. liturgy. See Dr. Neale's Liturgies of S. Mark &c. p. 121. Hayes 1859.]

ᶠ ἁγιάζω "devote as a Sacrifice." See S. Chrys. Homily on the words, S. John xvii. 19.

[or *exact representation*]. Something of this kind also HEB.x.9. was the Law.

For (he saith) *the Law having a shadow of the good things to come, not the very image of the things,* i. e. of the sacrifice, of the remission: *by those same sacrifices* [g] *by* [1] *which they offer continually can never make the comers thereunto perfect.* (ver. 2—9) *For in that case would they not have ceased to be offered, because that the worshippers having been once for all purged, would have had no more conscience of sins? But in them there is a remembrance again made of sins every year. For it is impossible that blood of bulls and goats should take away sins. Wherefore when He cometh into the world, He saith, Sacrifice and offering Thou wouldest not, but a body hast Thou prepared Me. In burnt-offerings and sacrifices for sin Thou hast had no pleasure. Then said I, Lo! I come, in the volume of the book it is written of Me, to do Thy will, O God. Above when He said, Sacrifice, and offering, and burnt-offerings, and [offering] for sin Thou wouldest not, nor hadst pleasure therein, which are offered according to the Law, then He said, Lo! I come to do Thy will, O God! He taketh away the first that He may establish the second.*

Thou seest again the superabundance [of his proofs]? This sacrifice (saith he) is one; whereas the others were many: for from this very fact [it follows that] they had not strength, because they were many. For, tell me, what (3) need were there of many, if one had been sufficient? so that their being many, and offered *continually,* proves that they [the worshippers] were never made clean. For just as a medicine, when it is powerful and productive of health, and able to remove the disease entirely, effects all after one application; just, I say, as, if being once applied it accomplishes the whole, it proves its own strength in being no more applied, and this is its work, to be no more applied; whereas if it is applied continually, it is evident that this is a proof of its not having strength. For it is the excellence of a medicine to be applied once, and not often. So is it in this case also.

[1] αἷς : ἃς which Ben. Sav.

[g] The common editions have κατ' ἐνιαυτὸν *year by year,* before ταῖς αὐταῖς θυσίαις: as has the old Translation of Mutian.: but it is omitted in the best MSS.

HOM. 17. Why forsooth are they continually being cured with the *same sacrifices?* For if they were set free from all their sins, the sacrifices would not have gone on being offered every day. For they had even been appointed to be continually offered in behalf of the whole people, both in the evening and in the day. So that what was done was an arraignment of sins, and not a release from sins; an arraignment of weakness, not an exhibition of strength. For because the first had no strength, another also was offered: and since this effected nothing, again another; so that it was an evidence of sins. While then their being offered was an evidence of sins, their [being offered] *continually* was an evidence of weakness. But with regard to Christ, it was
[1] ἀντίτυπα the contrary: He was *offered once for all.* The types[1] therefore contain the figure only, not the power; just as in images, the image has the figure of the man, not the power. So that the truth [reality] and the type have [somewhat] in common with one another. For the figure exists equally in both, but not the power. So too also is it in respect of Heaven and of the tabernacle, for the figure was equal: for there was the Holy place, but the power and the other things were not the same.

What is, *For the putting away of sin by the sacrifice of Himself, He hath been manifested*[h]*?* What is this *putting away?* it is making contemptible. For sin has no longer any boldness; for it is made of no effect in that when it
[2] ὀφείλουσα ἀπολαβεῖν ought to have exacted[2] punishment, it did not exact it: that is, it suffered violence: when it expected to destroy all men, then it was itself destroyed.

By the sacrifice of Himself (saith he) *He has been manifested,* that is, *He was manifested* unto God, and drew near [unto Him]. For do not [think] because the High Priest was wont to do this oftentimes in the year * * *[i]. So that

---

[h] S. Chrys. here reverts to ch.ix.26, to supply an explanation of the words εἰς ἀθέτησιν τῆς ἁμαρτίας διὰ τῆς θυσίας αὐτοῦ πεφανέρωται, which he had omitted before: ἀθέτησις is properly "annulling," "rendering invalid and of no effect," thence it is used for "despising," "treating as nothing worth."

[i] This is an imperfect sentence; the interpolator substitutes for the lacuna and the next sentence the following: "that it was done simply and not because of weakness. For if it were not done because of weakness, why was it done at all? For if there are no wounds, neither is there afterwards need of medicines for the patient." Mr. Field prefers leaving it as it stands without conjecturing what is omitted: only observing that the words "this is

henceforward this is done in vain, although it is done; for HE.ix.26.
what need is there of medicines where there are no wounds?
On this account He ordained that the offerings be *continually* made, because of their want of power, and that a remembrance of sins might be made.

[6.] What then? do not we offer every day? We offer indeed, but making a remembrance of His death, and this[1] [sacrifice] is one and not many. How is it one, and not many? Inasmuch as that[2] [Sacrifice] was once for all offered, [and] carried into the Holy of Holies. This [rite] is a figure of that [sacrifice] and this [sacrifice] of that[k]. For we always offer the same Person[3], not one sheep now and to-morrow another, but ever the same[4]: so that the sacrifice is one. Since by this reasoning, inasmuch as the offering is made in many places, there are many Christs. God forbid; but Christ is one every where, being complete here and complete there also, one Body. Just then as while offered in many places, He is one body and not many bodies; so also [is there[5]] one sacrifice. He is our High Priest, who offered the sacrifice that cleanses us. That [sacrifice] we offer now also, which was then offered, which cannot be exhausted. This is done in remembrance of what was then done. For (saith He) *do this in remembrance of Me*. It is not another sacrifice that we offer[6], as the High Priest [of old], but always the same, or rather we perform a remembrance of a Sacrifice.

[1] αὕτη
[2] ἐκείνη
[k] τοῦτο ἐκείνης τύπος ἐστί, καὶ αὕτη ἐκείνης.
[3] τὸν αὐτὸν
[4] τὸ αὐτὸ
[5] *or* [is He]
S. Luke xxii. 19.
[6] ποιοῦμεν *or* make

[7.] But inasmuch as I have mentioned this sacrifice, I (4) wish to say a little in reference to you who have been initiated; little in quantity, but possessing great force and profitableness, for what we say is not our own, but the Divine SPIRIT's. What then is it? Many partake of this sacrifice once in the whole year, others twice; others many times. Our discourse then is [addressed] to all; not to those only who are here, but to those also who are settled in the desert[7]. For they partake once in the year, and often indeed at intervals of two years.

What then? which shall we approve? those [who receive]

[7] The Eremites.

"done" refer to the Levitical sacrifices continued after the completion of that on the Cross.

once [in the year] ? those who [receive] many times? those who [receive] few times? Neither those [who receive] once, nor those [who receive] often, nor those [who receive] seldom, but those [who come] with a pure conscience, from a pure heart, with an irreproachable life. Let such [as these] draw near continually; but those who are not such, not even once. Why, you will ask? Because they receive to themselves judgement, yea and condemnation, and punishment, and vengeance. And do not thou wonder [at this]. For just as food being by its nature apt to nourish, yet if it is received by a person of ill digestion, ruins and corrupts all [the system], and becomes an occasion of disease, so surely is it also with respect to the awful mysteries. Dost thou feast at a spiritual table, a royal table, and again pollute thy mouth with mire? Dost thou anoint thyself with sweet ointment, and again fill thyself with ill savours?

Tell me, I beseech thee, when after the lapse of a year thou partakest of the Communion, dost thou think that the Forty Days[1] are sufficient for thee for the purifying of the sins of all that time? And again, when a week has passed, dost thou give thyself up to the former things? Tell me now, if when thou hast been well for forty days after a long illness, thou shouldst again give thyself up to the food which caused the sickness, hast thou not lost thy former labour too? For if things natural admit of alteration, much more those which depend on moral choice. As for instance, by nature we see, and naturally we have healthy eyes; but oftentimes from a bad habit [of body] our power of vision is injured. If then the things of nature admit of alteration, much more those of moral choice. Thou assignest forty days for the health of the soul, or perhaps not even forty, and dost thou expect to propitiate God? Tell me, art thou in sport?

These things I say, not as precluding you from the one and annual coming, but as wishing you to draw near continually.

[8.] It is to the holy that these things have been given. This the Deacon also then proclaims when he calls on the

---

[1] Lent; devoted to preparation for the Easter Communion.

holy ᵐ; even by this call searching the faults of all. For as in a flock, where many sheep are in good health, and many are full of the scab, it is needful that these last should be separated from the healthy ones; so is it also in the Church: since some sheep are healthy, and some diseased, by means of this voice he separates the one from the other, the priest [I mean] going round on all sides by means of this most awful cry, and calling and drawing on [1] the holy. For inasmuch as it is not possible that he being a [mere] man should know the things of his neighbour, (for *what man*, saith he, *knoweth the things of a man, save the spirit of man which is in him?*) this voice he utters after the whole sacrifice has been completed, that no person should come to the spiritual fountain carelessly and in a chance way. For in the case of the flock also, for nothing prevents us from again using the same example, the sickly ones we shut up within, and keep them in the dark, and give them different food, not permitting them to partake either of pure air, or of simple grass, or of the fountain without [the fold]. In this case then also this voice is instead of a bond.

He.ix.26.

[1] ἕλκων

1 Cor. ii. 11.

Thou canst not say, 'I did not know, I was not aware 'that danger attends the matter.' Nay surely Paul too especially testified this. But wilt thou say, 'I never read it?' This is not an apology, but even an accusation. Dost thou come into the Church every day and yet art ignorant of this?

However, that thou mayest not have even this excuse to offer, for this cause, with a loud voice, with an awful cry, like some herald lifting up his hand on high, standing aloft, conspicuous to all, and after that awful silence crying out aloud, he invites some, and some he forbids, not doing this with his hand, but with his tongue more distinctly than with his hand. For that voice, falling on our ears, just like a hand, thrusts away and casts out some, and introduces and presents others.

(5)

Tell me then, I beseech [you], in the Olympic games does not the herald stand, calling out with loud and uplifted voice,

---

ᵐ After the Oblation was made and before the Communion the deacon proclaimed τὰ ἅγια τοῖς ἁγίοις, "The Holy things for the holy."

saying, "Does any one accuse this man? Is he a slave? Is "he a thief? Is he one of wicked manners?" And yet, those contests for prizes are not of the soul, nor yet of good morals, but of strength and the body. If then where is [merely] exercise of bodies, much examination is made about moral character, how much rather here, where the soul is alone the combatant. Our herald then even now stands, not holding each person by the head, and drawing him forward, but holding all together by the head within; he does not set against them other accusers, but themselves against themselves. For he saith not, 'Does any one accuse this man?' but what? 'If any man accuse himself.' For when he saith, The Holy things for the holy, he means this: 'If any is not holy, let him not draw near.'

He does not simply say, "pure from sins," but, "holy." For it is not merely freedom from sins which makes a man holy, but also the presence of the Spirit, and the wealth of good works. I do not merely wish (saith he) that you should be delivered from the mire, but also that you should be fair and beautiful. For if the Babylonian King, when he made choice of the youths from the captives, chose out those who were beautiful in form, and of fair countenance: much more is it needful that we, when we stand by the royal table, should be beautiful in form, [I mean] that of the soul, having our ornaments of gold, our robe pure, our shoes royal, the face of our soul well-formed, that the golden ornament should be put around it, even the girdle of truth. Let such an one as this draw near, and let him touch the royal cups.

But if any man clothed in rags, filthy, squalid, wish to enter in to the royal table, consider how much he will suffer, the forty days not being sufficient to wash away the offences which have been committed in all the time. For if hell is not sufficient, although it be eternal (for therefore also it *is* eternal), much more [is] not this short time [sufficient]. For we have not displayed a strong repentance, but a weak.

[9.] Eunuchs especially ought to stand by the King: by eunuchs, I mean those who are fair in their mind, having no wrinkle nor spot, lofty in mind, having the eye of the soul gentle and quick-sighted, active and sharp, not sleepy nor

supine; full of much freedom, and yet far from impudence Ec.ix.26.
and overboldness, wakeful, healthful, neither very gloomy
and downcast, nor yet dissolute and soft.

This eye we have it in our own power to create, and to make it quicksighted and beautiful. For when we direct it, not to the smoke nor to the dust (for such are all human things), but to the delicate breeze, to the light air, to things supernal and high, and full of much calmness and purity, and of much delight, we shall speedily recover it, and shall invigorate it, as it luxuriates in such contemplation. Hast thou seen covetousness and great wealth? do not thou lift up thine eye thereto. The thing is mire, it is smoke, an evil vapour, darkness, and great oppressiveness, and suffocating cares. Hast thou seen a man cultivating righteousness, content with what is his own, and having abundant space for recreation, having no cares, no anxieties about things here? Fix [thine eye] there, and lift [it] up on high; and thou wilt make it far the most beautiful, and more splendid, feasting it not with the flowers of the earth, but with those of virtue, with temperance, moderation, and all the rest. For nothing so troubles the eye as an evil conscience *(Mine eye*, it is said, *was troubled by reason of* Ps. vi. 7. *anger)*; nothing so darkens it. Set it free from this injury, and thou wilt make it vigorous and strong, ever nourished with good hopes.

And God grant that we all may make both it and also the other energies of the soul, such as Christ desires, that being made worthy of the Head who is set over us, we may depart thither where He wishes. For He saith, *I will that* S. John *where I am, they also may be with Me, that they may behold* xvii. 24. *My glory*. Which may we all enjoy in Christ Jesus our Lord, with Whom to the Father and also to the Holy Ghost be glory might honour now and for ever and world without end. Amen.

HOMILY XVIII.

Heb. x. 8—13.

Above when He said, Sacrifice and offering, and burnt-offerings, and [offering] for sin, Thou wouldest not, neither hadst pleasure [therein], which are offered by[1] the Law, then said He, Lo! I come to do Thy will, O God. He taketh away the first, that He may establish the second. By the which will we are [2] sanctified, by the offering of the body of Jesus *Christ, once for all. And every priest standeth daily ministering, and offering oftentimes the same sacrifices, which can never take away sins. But this [man] after He had offered one sacrifice for sins, for ever sat down on the right hand of God, from henceforth expecting till His enemies be made His footstool[3].*

[1] according to
[2] have been
[3] a footstool for His feet

In what has gone before he had shewn that the sacrifices were unavailing for perfect purity, and that they are a figure, and greatly defective. Since then there was this objection to his argument, If they are figures, how is it that after the truth is come, they have not ceased, nor given place, but are still performed? he here accordingly labours at this very point, shewing that they are not any longer performed, even as a figure, for God does not accept them. And this again he shews not from the New [Testament], but from the prophets, bringing forward from times of old the strongest testimony, that it [the old system] comes to an end, and ceases, and that they do all in vain, *alway resisting the Holy Ghost.*

Acts vii. 51.

And he shews over and above that they ceased not now [only], but at the very coming of the Messiah, nay rather, even before His coming: and how it was that Christ did not abolish them at the last, but they were abolished first, and then He came; first they were made to cease, and then

He Himself appeared. For that they might not say, Even Heb. x. 9. without this sacrifice, and by means of those others, we could have been well pleasing unto God, He waited for these sacrifices to be convicted [of weakness], and then He came Himself; for (He saith) *sacrifice and offering Thou wouldest not.* Hereby He took all away; and having spoken generally, He says also particularly, *In burnt-offerings and [sacrifice] for sin Thou hast had no pleasure.* Now all that was besides the sacrifice was an "offering." *Then said I, Lo! I come.* Of whom was this spoken? of none other than the Christ.

In this place he does not at all blame those who offer, pointing out that it is not because of their wickednesses that He does not accept them, as He saith elsewhere, but on account of the thing itself being henceforward exposed and discovered to have no strength, nor any suitableness to the times [1]. What then has this to do with *the sacrifices* being offered *oftentimes?* Not only from their being *often-times* [offered] (he means) is it manifest that they are weak, and that they effected nothing, but also from God's not accepting them, as being unprofitable and useless. And in another place it is said, *If Thou hadst wished for sacrifice I would have given it.* Wherefore by this also he makes it plain that He does not desire it. It follows accordingly that it is not sacrifices that God wills, but the abolition of sacrifices. Wherefore they sacrifice contrary to His will.

[1] προσ-ήκοντα καιρὸν

Ps. li. 16.

What is *To do Thy will?* To give up Myself, He means: This is the will of God. *By which Will we have been sanctified.* Or he even means something still further, that it is not the sacrifices which make men clean, but the Will of God. It follows then that to offer sacrifice is not the will of God.

[2.] And why dost thou wonder that it is not the will of God now, when it was not His will even from the beginning? For *who,* saith He, *hath required this at your hands?* Isaiah i. 12.
How is it then that He Himself enjoined it? [He did it] in condescension. For just as Paul says, *I would*[2] *that all men were even as I myself,* in respect of continence, and on the other hand says, *I will*[3] *that the younger women marry, bear children;* and so sets down two wills, yet the two are

[2] θέλω 1 Cor. vii. 7.
[3] βούλο-μαι 1 Tim. v. 14.

not both his own, although he gives an injunction; but the one indeed is his own, for which cause also he sets it down without expressing any reason. While the other is not his own, though he wishes it, on which account also it is added with a reason. For having previously accused them, because *they had waxed wanton against Christ,* he then says, *I will that the younger women marry, bear children.* So in this place also it was not His leading will that the sacrifices should be offered. For, as He says, *I wish not the death of the sinner, as that he should turn unto [Me] and live:* and in another place says that He not only wished, but even desired [a] this: and yet these are contrary to each other: for intense wishing is desire. How then dost Thou *not wish?* how dost Thou in another place *desire,* which is a sign of vehement wishing? So is it in this case also.

By the which will we have been sanctified, saith he. How sanctified? *through the offering of the Body of* JESUS *Christ once for all.*

[3.] *And every priest standeth daily ministering and offering oftentimes the same sacrifices.* (To stand therefore is a sign of ministering; accordingly to sit, is a sign of being ministered unto.) *But this [man] having offered one sacrifice for sins, for ever sat down on the right hand of God, from henceforth expecting till His enemies be made a footstool for His feet.* (ver 14, 15) *For by one offering He hath perfected for ever them that are sanctified. And the Holy Ghost also beareth witness to us.* He had said that those [sacrifices] are not offered, he reasoned from what is written, [and] from what is not written [b]; moreover also he put forward the prophetic word which says, *sacrifice and offering Thou wouldest not.* He had said that He had forgiven their sins. Again this also he proves from the testimony of Scripture, for *the Holy Ghost* (saith he) *witnesseth to us: for after that He had said,* (ver. 16—18) *This is the covenant, which I will make with them, after those days, saith the Lord: I will put My laws into their hearts, and on their minds will I write them, and their sins and their*

---

[a] S. Chrys. seems to refer to some place where it is said that God desired (ἐπεθύμησε) the death of the wicked. It does not appear what passage he had in view.

[b] That is from other arguments than the words of the Old Testament.

iniquities will I remember no more. But where remission (He. x. 13.) *of these is there is no more offering for sin.* So then He forgave their sins, when He gave the Covenant, and He gave the Covenant by sacrifice. If therefore He forgave the sins through the one sacrifice, there is no longer need of a second.

He sat on the right hand of God, henceforth expecting. For what purpose is the delay? *that His enemies be put under His feet. For by one offering He hath perfected for ever them that are sanctified.* But perhaps some one might say; Wherefore did He not at once put [them under His feet]? For the sake of the faithful who should afterwards be brought forth and born. Whence then [does it appear] that they shall be put under? By the saying *He sat down.* He called to mind again that testimony which saith, *until* (see above i. 13.) *I put His enemies under His feet.* But His enemies are the Jews. Then inasmuch as he had said, *Till His enemies be put under His feet,* and they [to whom he wrote] were vehemently urgent, for this cause he introduces all that follows after this; all his discourse concerning faith. But who are the enemies? All unbelievers: the dæmons. And intimating the greatness of their subjection, he said not "are subjected," but *are put under His feet.*

[4.] Let us not therefore be [of the number of] His enemies. For not they alone are enemies, the unbelievers and Jews, but those also who are full of unclean living. *For the carnal mind is enmity against God: for it is not* (Rom. viii. 7.) *subject to the law of God, for neither can it be.* What then (you say)? this is not a ground of blame. Nay rather, it is very decidedly a ground of blame. For the wicked man as long as he is wicked, cannot be subject [to God's law]; he can however change and become good.

Let us then cast out carnal tempers. But what things (2) are carnal? Whatever make the body flourish and do well, and injure the soul: as for instance, wealth, luxury, glory (all these things are of the flesh), carnal love. Let us not then be desirous of the larger share [of goods], but ever follow after poverty: for this is itself a great good.

But (you say) it makes one low and of little account.

[True:] for we have need of this, for it contributes much to our benefit. *Poverty* (it is said) *humbles a man.* And again Christ [saith], *Blessed are the poor in spirit.* Dost thou then grieve on this account, that thou art upon a path which leads to virtue? Dost thou not know that this gives us great confidence?

But, saith one, *the wisdom of the poor man is despised.* And again another saith, *Give me neither riches nor poverty,* and, *Deliver me from the furnace of poverty* [c]. And again, if riches and poverty are from the Lord, how can either poverty or riches be an evil? For what end then were these things said? They were said under [1] the Old [Covenant], where there was much account made of wealth, where there was great contempt of poverty, where the one was a curse and the other a blessing. But now it is no longer so.

But dost thou wish to hear the praises of poverty? Christ sought after it, and saith, *But the Son of Man hath not where to lay His head.* And again He said to His disciples, *Provide* [2] *neither gold, nor silver, nor two coats.* And Paul in writing said, *As having nothing and yet possessing all things.* And Peter said to him who was lame from his birth, *Silver and gold have I none.* Yea and under the Old [Covenant] itself, where wealth was held in admiration, who were the admired persons? Was not Elijah, who had nothing save the sheep-skin? Was not Elisha? Was not John?

Let no man then be humiliated on account of his poverty: It is not poverty which humiliates, but wealth, which compels us to have need of many, and forces us to be under obligations to many.

And what could be poorer than Jacob (tell me), who said, *If the Lord give me bread to eat, and raiment to put on?* Were Elijah and John then wanting in boldness [3]? Did not the one reprove Ahab, and the other Herod? The latter said, *It is not lawful for thee to have thy brother Philip's wife.* And Elias said to Ahab with boldness, *It is not I that trouble Israel, but thou and thy father's house.* Thou seest that this most especially produces boldness, poverty [I mean]? For while the rich man is a slave, being subject

[c] The words of the LXX are "He took me out of the furnace of poverty."

to loss, and affording [opportunity] to every one who will, Hɛ. x. 13.
to do him hurt, he who has nothing, fears not confiscation,
nor fine. So, if poverty had made men wanting in boldness
Christ would not have sent His disciples with poverty to
a work that required great boldness. For the poor man is
very strong, and has nothing wherefrom he may be wronged
or evil entreated. But the rich man is assailable on every
side: just in the same way as one would easily catch a man
who was dragging many long ropes after him, whereas a
man naked one could not readily lay hold on. So here also
it falls out in the case of the rich man: slaves, gold, lands,
affairs innumerable, innumerable cares, difficult circumstances, necessities, make him an easy prey to all.

[5.] Let no man then henceforth esteem poverty a cause (3)
of disgrace. For if virtue be there, all the wealth of the
world is, no not clay, nor even a mote in comparison of it.
This then let us follow after, if we would enter into the
kingdom of heaven. For, He saith, *Sell that thou hast, and* S. Matt.
give to the poor, and thou shalt have treasure in Heaven. xix. 21.
And again, *It is hard for a rich man to enter into the King-* Ib. 23.
dom of Heaven. Dost thou see that even if we have it not,
we ought to draw it to us? So great a good is Poverty.
For it guides us by the hand, as it were, on the path which
leads to Heaven, it is an anointing for the combat, a kind
of exercise great and admirable, a tranquil haven.

But (you say) I have need of many [things], and am unwilling to receive a favour from any. Nevertheless, even
in this respect the rich man is inferior to thee; for thou
perhaps askest the favour for thy support, but he shame-
lessly [asks] for ten thousand things for covetousness' sake.
So that it is the rich that are in need of many [persons],
yea oftentimes those who are unworthy of them. For instance, they often stand in need of those who are in the
rank of soldiers, or of slaves: but the poor man has no need
even of the Emperor himself, and if he should need him,
he is regarded with admiration because he has placed himself in this [condition], when he might have been rich.

Let no man then accuse poverty as being the cause of
innumerable evils, nor let him contradict Christ, who asserted it to be the perfection of virtue, saying, *If thou wilt* Ib. 21.

HOM. 18. *be perfect* [&c]. For this He both uttered in His words, and shewed by His acts, and taught by His disciples. Let us therefore follow after poverty, it is the greatest good to the sober-minded.

Perhaps some of those who hear me, avoid it as a thing of ill omen. I can readily believe it[1]. For widely spread is this disease among the generality of men, and so excessive is the tyranny of wealth, that they do not endure the renunciation of it, even as far as words, but even abominate it. Far be this from the Christian's soul: for nothing is richer than he who chooses poverty of his own accord, and with forwardness of mind.

[1] οὐκ ἀπιστῶ

[6.] How? I will tell you, and if you please I will prove that he who embraces poverty of his own accord is richer even than the king himself. For he indeed needs many [things], and is in anxiety, and is fearful lest the supplies requisite for the maintenance of his army should fail him; but the other has everything in abundance, and is fearful about nothing, and if he be fearful, it is not about so great matters. Who then, tell me, is the rich man? he who is daily making demands, and earnestly labouring to gather much together, and is fearful lest at any time he should fall short, or he who gathers nothing together, and is in great abundance and hath need of no one? For it is virtue and the fear of God, and not wealth which gives confidence. For they even reduce one to slavery. For it is said, *Gifts and presents blind the eyes of the wise, and like a muzzle on the mouth turn away reproofs.*

Ecclus. xx. 29.

Consider how that poor man Peter chastised the rich Ananias. Was not the one rich and the other poor? But behold the one speaking with authority and saying, *Tell me whether ye sold the land for so much,* and the other saying with submission, *Yea, for so much.* And who (you say) will grant to me to be as Peter? It is open to thee to be as Peter if thou wilt; cast away what thou hast. *Disperse, give to the poor,* follow Christ, and thou shalt be such as he. How? he (you say) wrought miracles. Is it this then, tell me, which made Peter an object of admiration, or the boldness which arose from his manner of life? Dost thou not hear Christ saying, *Rejoice not because the devils are subject*

Acts v. 8.

Ps. cxii. 9.

S. Luke x. 20.

unto you; If thou wilt be perfect [&c]. Hear what Peter saith: *Silver and gold have I none, but what I have give I thee.* If any man have silver and gold, he hath not those other gifts.

HE. x.13.
Actsiii. 6.

Why is it then, you say, that many have neither the one nor the other? Because they are not voluntarily poor: since they who are voluntarily poor have all things that are good. For although they do not raise up the dead nor the lame, yet, what is greater than all; they have confidence towards God. They will hear in that day that blessed voice, *Come ye blessed of My Father,* (what can be better than this?) *inherit the kingdom prepared for you from the foundation of the world: for I was an hungred and ye gave Me meat: I was thirsty and ye gave Me drink: I was a stranger and ye took Me in: I was naked and ye clothed Me: I was sick and in prison and ye visited Me. Inherit the kingdom prepared for you from the foundation of the world.* Let us then flee from covetousness, that we may attain to the kingdom [of Heaven]. Let us feed the poor, that we may feed Christ: that we may be made fellow-heirs with Him in Christ Jesus our Lord, with Whom to the Father and also to the Holy Ghost, be glory power honour, now and for ever and world without end. Amen.

S. Matt. xxv. 34—36.

HOMILY XIX.

HEB. x. 19—23.

Having therefore, brethren, boldness to enter into the holiest by the blood of JESUS, *by a new and living way which He hath consecrated*[1] *for us, through the Veil, that is to say, His flesh, and having an High Priest*[2] *over the house of God, let us draw near with a true heart, in full assurance of faith, having our hearts sprinkled from an evil conscience, and our bodies washed with pure water, let us hold fast the profession*[3] *of our hope without wavering.*

[1] new made or inaugurated
[2] a great Priest
[3] confession

(1) [1.] HAVING *therefore, brethren, boldness to enter into the holiest by the blood of Jesus, by a new and living way which He hath consecrated for us.* Having shewn the interval [between them] as to the High Priest, and the sacrifices, and the tabernacle, and the Covenant, and the promise, and that the interval is great, seeing that those are temporal, but these eternal, those *near to vanishing away,* these permanent, those powerless, these perfect, those figures, these reality, for (saith he) *not according to the law of a carnal commandment, but according to the power of an endless life.* And *Thou art a Priest for ever.* Behold the continuance of the Priest. And concerning the Covenant, That (saith he) is old (for *that which decayeth and waxeth old is ready to vanish away*) but this is new; and has remission of sins, while that [other has] nothing of the kind: for (saith he) *the Law made nothing perfect.* And again, *sacrifice and offering Thou wouldest not.* That [tabernacle] is made with hands, while this is *not made with hands:* that *has the blood of goats,* this of the LORD; that has the Priest standing, this *sitting.* Since therefore all those are inferior

supra vii. 16.
ib. v. 6.
ib. viii. 13.
ib. vii. 19.
ib. x. 5.
ib. ix. 11.
ib. 12.

and these greater, for this cause he saith, *Having therefore,* He. x. 22. *brethren, boldness.*

[2.] *Boldness:* from whence? Just as sins (he means) produce shame, so the having all things forgiven us, and being made fellow-heirs, and enjoying so great Love, [produces] boldness [and confidence].

For the entrance into the holiest. What does he mean here by *entrance?* Heaven, and the access to the spiritual things.

Which He hath inaugurated, that is, which He prepared, and which He began; for the beginning of using is thenceforth called the inaugurating; which He prepared (he means) and by which He Himself passed.

A new and living way. Here he expresses *the full assurance of hope. A new* [*way*] he saith. He is anxious to shew that we have all things greater; since now the gates of Heaven have been opened, which was not done even in the case of Abraham. *A new and living way.* For the first way was [a way] of death, leading to Hades, but this [is a way] of life. And yet he did not say, "of life," but called it *living,* (the ordinances that is,) that which abideth [a].

Through the veil (he saith) [even] *His flesh.* For this flesh first cut that way, by this He inaugurated it, in that He walked [along it]. And with good reason did he call the flesh *a veil* [b]. For when it was lifted up on high, then the things in heaven appeared.

Let us draw near (he saith) *with a true heart.* To what should we *draw near?* To the holy things, to the faith, to the spiritual service. *With a true heart, in full assurance of faith;* [*of faith*], inasmuch as nothing is seen; neither the priest henceforward, nor the sacrifice, nor the altar. And yet neither was that priest visible, but himself stood within, and they all without, [even] all the people. But here not only has this taken place, that the priest has entered into the holy place, but that we also enter in. On

---

[a] ἀλλὰ ζῶσαν αὐτὴν ἐκάλεσε· τουτέστι, τὰ προστάγματα, τὴν μένουσαν. This is the reading of all the best MSS, the Catena, and ancient Translation. The later editions omit τουτέστι, τὰ προστάγματα and add οὕτω δηλῶν. Mr. Field thinks the passage may be corrupt; the parenthetic words seem added to explain that it is the Christian *ordinances,* which he understands by the *way that abideth.*

[b] [See above p. 187 and S. Cyril Alex. Quod Unus Christus 761 C D]

Hom. 19. this account he says, *in full assurance of faith*. For it is possible absolutely to believe while doubting, as there are even now many who say, that of some there is a resurrection and of others not. But this is not faith. *In full assurance of faith* (he says); for we ought to be so persuaded as [we are] concerning things that we see: nay, even much more, for *here* it is possible to be deceived in the things that are seen, but there not: *here* we trust to the senses, there to the Spirit.

Having our hearts sprinkled from an evil conscience. He points out that not faith only, but a virtuous life also is required, and the not being conscious to ourselves of any evil. Since those who are not thus disposed the holy [places] do not receive *with full assurance;* For they are holy, and the holy of holies; and where no profane person enters. Those others were sprinkled as to the body, we as to the conscience, so that we may even now be sprinkled over; [that is], with virtue itself. *And having our body washed with pure water.* Here he speaks of the Washing, which no longer cleanses the bodies but the soul.

For He is faithful that promised. That *promised* what? That we are to depart thither and enter into the kingdom. Be then in nothing over-curious, nor demand reasonings. Our [religion[1]] needs faith.

[1] τὰ ἡμέτερα

[3.] (ver. 24, 25) *And* (he saith) *let us consider one another to provoke unto love and to good works. Not forsaking the assembling of ourselves together, as the manner of some is, but exhorting[2] one another and so much the more as ye see the day approaching.* And again in other places, *The Lord is at hand; be careful for nothing. For now is our salvation nearer: Henceforth the time is short.*

[2] or encouraging

Phil. iv. 5, 6.
Rom. xiii. 11.
1 Cor. vii. 29.

What is, *not forsaking the assembling of ourselves together?* He knew that much strength arises from assembling and gathering together. *For where two or three* (it is said) *are gathered together in My name, there am I in the midst of them;* And again, *That they may be One, as we also are;* And, *They had all one heart and* [one] *soul.* And not this only, but also because love is increased by the gathering [of ourselves] together; and love being increased, of necessity the things of God must follow also. *And earnest*

S. Matt. xviii. 20.
S. John xvii. 11.
Acts iv. 32.
ib. xii. 5.

prayer (it is said) was *made by* the people. *As the manner of some is.* Here he not only exhorted, but also blamed [them].

He. x. 24.
[1] εἰς παροξυσμὸν
to the sharpening or exciting of
Prov. xxvii.17.

And let us consider one another, he says, *to provoke unto*[1] *love and to good works.* He knew that this also arises from *gathering together.* For as *iron sharpeneth iron,* so also association increases love. For if a stone rubbed against a stone sends forth fire, how much more soul mingled with soul! But not unto emulation (saith he) but *unto the sharpening of love.* What is *unto the sharpening of love?* unto the loving and being loved in a greater degree. *And of good works;* that so they might acquire zeal. For if acting has greater force for instruction than speaking, ye also have in your number many teachers, who effect this by their deeds.

What is *let us draw near with a true heart?* that is, without hypocrisy; for *woe be to a fearful heart, and faint hands:* let there be (he means) no falsehood among us; let us not say one thing and think another; for this is falsehood; neither let us be fainthearted, for this is not [a mark] of a *true heart.* The being weak-spirited arises from not believing. But how shall this be? If we fully assure ourselves through our faith.

Ecclus. ii. 12.

Having our hearts sprinkled: why did he not say " having been purified?" because he wished to point out the difference of the sprinklings: the one he says is [the act] of God, the other our own. For the washing and sprinkling the conscience is God's [act]; but *the drawing near with* truth and *in full assurance of faith* is our own. Then he also gives strength to their faith from the truth of Him that promised.

What is *and having our bodies washed with pure water?* With water which makes persons pure, or which has no blood [with it].

Then he adds the perfect thing, charity. *Not forsaking the assembling of ourselves together,* which some (saith he) do, and divide the assemblies; this he forbids them [to do]. For *a brother helped by a brother is as a strong city.*

Prov. xviii. 19. (LXX.)

But let us consider one another to provoke unto love. What is, *Let us consider one another?* For instance if any be virtuous, let us imitate him, let us look on him so as to love and to be loved. For from Love good works proceed.

(2) For the assembling is a great good: since it makes love more warm; and out of love all good things arise. For nothing is good which is not done from love.

[4.] This then let us *confirm*[1] towards each other. *For love is the fulfilling of the law.* We have no need of labours or of sweatings if we love one another. It is a natural pathway, leading towards virtue. For as on the public highway, if any man find the beginning, he is guided by it, and has no need of one to take him by the hand; so is it also in regard to Love: only lay hold on the beginning, and at once thou art guided and directed by it. *Love worketh no ill to his neighbour; thinketh no evil.* Let each man of himself consider himself, how he is disposed toward himself. He does not envy himself; he wishes all good things for himself; he prefers himself before all; he is willing to do all for himself. If then we were so disposed towards others also, all grievous things are brought to an end; there is no enmity; there is no covetousness: for who would choose to over-reach himself? no man: but on the contrary we shall possess all things in common, and shall not cease from assembling ourselves together. And if we do this, the remembrance of injuries would have no place: for who would choose to remember injuries against himself? who would choose to be angry with himself? do we not make allowances for ourselves most of all? If we were thus disposed towards our neighbours also, there will never be any remembrance of injuries.

And how is it possible (you say) that one should so love his neighbour as himself? If others had not done this, thou hadst reason to think it impossible: but if they have done it, it is plain that it is from indolence that it is not done by ourselves.

And besides, Christ enjoins nothing impossible, seeing that many have even gone beyond His commands. Who hath done this? Paul, Peter, all the company of the Saints. Nay, indeed if I say that they loved their neighbours, I say no great matter: they loved their enemies so, as no man would love those who were of one soul with himself. For who of us would choose for the sake of those even that are as his own soul, to go away into Hell, when he was about to depart unto a Kingdom? No man. But Paul chose this for the sake of his enemies, for those who stoned him, those who scourged him. What pardon then will there be for us, what excuse, if we shall not exhibit towards our friends even [what tends] to the very smallest portion of that love which he displayed towards his enemies? _{He. x. 25.}

And before him too, the blessed Moses was willing to be blotted out of God's book for the sake of his enemies who had stoned him. David also when he saw those who had stood up against him slain, saith, *I the shepherd have sinned, but these, what have they done?* And when he had Saul in his hands, he would not slay him, but saved him; and this when he was himself about to be in danger. But if these things were done under the Old [Covenant] what excuse shall we have who live under the New, and do not attain even to the same measure with them? For if, *unless our righteousness exceed that of the Scribes and Pharisees, we shall not enter into the kingdom of Heaven,* how shall we enter in when we have even less than they? See 2 Sam. xxiv. 17. S. Matt. v. 20.

[5.] *Love your enemies,* He saith. Love thou therefore thy enemy: for thou art doing good not to him, but to thyself. How? Thou art becoming equal to God. He, if he be loved of thee, hath reaped no great gain, for he is [but] beloved by a fellow-slave. But thou, if thou love thy fellow-slave, hast gained much, for thou art becoming like unto God. Seest thou that thou art doing a kindness not to him but to thyself? for He appoints the prize not for him, but for thee. ib. 44.

What then if he be evil (you say)? So much greater is the reward. Even for his wickedness thou oughtest to feel grateful to him: even should he be evil after receiving ten thousand kindnesses. For if he were not exceedingly evil, thy reward would not have been exceedingly increased; so that the cause [thou assignest] for not loving him, the saying that he is evil, this same is a cause for loving him. Take away the adversary and thou takest away the opportunity of [obtaining] the crowns. Seest thou not the athletes, how when they have filled the bags with sand, they so exercise themselves? But there is no need for thee to practise this. Life is full of those that exercise thee, and make thee strong. Seest thou not the trees too, the more they are shaken by the winds, so much the more do they become stronger and more firm? We then, if we be long-suffering, shall also become strong. For it is said, *a man who is long-suffering abounds in wisdom, but he that is of a little soul is strongly foolish.* Seest thou how great is his commendation of the one, seest thou how great his censure of the other? *Strongly foolish,* i.e. very [foolish]. Let us not then be meanly contentious¹ one towards another: for this does not arise from enmity, but from having a little soul. Inasmuch as if the soul be strong, it will endure all things easily, and nothing will have power sufficient to sink it but will lead it into the tranquil havens. To which may we all attain, by the grace and loving-kindness of our Lord Jesus Christ, with whom to the Father and also to the Holy Ghost, be glory power honour, now and for ever and world without end. Amen.

¹ μικρο-
ψυχῶμεν

HOMILY XX.

HEB. x. 26, 27.

For if we sin wilfully, after we have received the knowledge of the truth, there remaineth no more[1] *sacrifice for sins, but a certain fearful looking for of judgment, and fiery indignation*[2] *which shall devour the adversaries.*

[1] οὐκέτι
[2] lit. indignation of fire

TREES which have been planted, and have had the advantage of all other due care, and the hands and the labours of the cultivator, and yet yield no return for his labours, are pulled up by the roots, and handed over to the fire. So somewhat of this kind takes place also in the case of our Illumination[3]. For when Christ has planted us, and we have enjoyed the watering of the Spirit, and then shew no fruit; fire awaits us, even that of Hell and flame unquenchable.

[3] i.e. Baptism.

Paul therefore having exhorted them to love, and to the bringing forth the fruit of good works, and having urged them from the kindlier [considerations] (what are these? that we have an entrance into the holy place, *the new way which He hath inaugurated for us*), does the same again from the more gloomy ones, speaking thus. For having said, *not forsaking the assembling of ourselves together, as the manner of some is, but exhorting*[4] *one another, and so much the more, as ye see the day approaching,* this [day] even being sufficient for consolation, he added, *For if we sin wilfully after we have received the knowledge of the truth.* There is need, he means, of good works, yea, very great need, *For if we sin wilfully after we have received the knowledge of the truth, there remaineth no more sacrifice for sins.* Thou wast cleansed; thou wast set free from the charges against

supra ver. 20.
Ib. 25.
[4] encouraging

234 Novatian errors. It is Baptism that cannot be repeated.

Hom. 20. thee, thou hast been made a son. If then thou return to thy former vomit, there awaits thee on the other hand excommunication and fire and whatever such things there are. For there is no second sacrifice.

[2.] At this place we are again assailed by those who take away repentance [a], and by those who delay to come to baptism. The one saying, that it is not safe for them to come to baptism, since there is no second remission: And the other asserting that it is not safe to impart the mysteries [1] to those who have sinned, if there is no second remission.

[1] The Holy Eucharist.

What shall we say then to them both? Why, that he does not take away repentance, nor the propitiation [which is obtained] through repentance, nor does he thrust away him that hath fallen, and cast him down with despair. He is no such enemy of our salvation, but what? he takes away the second Washing. For he did not say, no more [2] is there repentance, or no more is there remission, but *no more* is there a *sacrifice*, that is, there is no more a second Cross [b]. For this is what he means by sacrifice. *For by one sacrifice*, saith he, *He hath perfected for ever them that are sanctified*, not like the Jewish rites. For it is for this cause that he treated so much throughout concerning the Sacrifice, that it is one, and [that it is] one; Not wishing to point out this only, that herein it differed from [and surpassed] the Jewish [rites], but also to make [men] more cautious that they might no more expect another sacrifice after the manner of the Jewish law.

[2] οὐκέτι

supra ver. 14

For, saith he, *if we sin wilfully*. See how he is disposed to pardon. He says *if we sin wilfully*, so that there is pardon for those [who sin] not wilfully. *After the knowledge of the truth:* He either means, of Christ, or of all doctrines. *There remaineth no more a sacrifice for sins*, but what? *a certain fearful looking for of judgment and indignation of fire which shall devour the adversaries*. By *Adversaries* he means not the unbelievers, but those also who practise what is adverse to virtue; or [else he means] that the very same

---

[a] The Novatians, who refused to admit to Penitence and the Sacraments, those who had fallen into deadly sin after Baptism.

[b] Compare Hom. ix. [5.] pp. 119, 120.

fire shall receive them of the household, which [receives] the adversaries too. Then expressing its devouring nature, he, as it were, gave it life, saying, *indignation of fire which shall devour the adversaries.* For just as a wild beast when irritated and very fierce and made quite savage, would not rest till it had laid hold on some one and eaten him up, so that fire too, like a person goaded by indignation, whatever it catch hold of, does not let it go but devours and tears it to pieces.

[3.] Next he adds also the reason of the threat, that it is on good grounds, that it is justly [made]; which very thing contributes to conviction, when [I mean] we shew that [the threat] is made justly.

For, saith he, (ver. 28) *He that hath despised Moses' law dies without mercy, under two or three witnesses. Without mercy,* he says; so that there is no pardon, no pity there: and yet the law is [only] that of Moses; for the most [of it] he ordained.

What is *under two or three?* If two or three have borne witness he means, they [the accused] immediately suffered punishment.

If then under the Old [Covenant], where it is the law of Moses that is set at nought, there is so great punishment, (ver. 29) *Of how much sorer punishment, suppose ye, shall he be thought worthy, who hath trodden under foot the Son of God, and hath counted the blood of the covenant an unholy [a common] thing, and hath done despite unto the Spirit of grace.*

And how does a man *tread under foot the Son of God?* Why (he would say), when partaking of Him in the mysteries, he has wrought sin, has he not trodden Him under foot? has he not despised Him? For just as we make no account of those who are trodden under foot, so also, they who sin have made no account of Christ; and so they have sinned. Thou art[1] become the Body of Christ, and thou givest thyself to the devil, so that he treads thee under foot.

[1] *or* Art thou... dost thou give?

And accounted the blood a common thing, saith he. What is *common?* It is "unclean," or the having nothing beyond the others.

And done despite unto the Spirit of grace. For he that accepts not a kindness, does despite to him that does the kindness. He made thee a son: and thou wishest to become a slave? He came to dwell with thee, and thou introducest besides Him wicked imaginations? Christ was willing to stay with thee: and thou treadest Him down by surfeiting, by drunkenness?

Let us listen, whoever of us partake of the mysteries unworthily: let us listen whoever approach that Table unworthily. *Give not* (saith He) *holy things to the dogs, lest at any time they trample them under their feet,* that is, lest they despise, lest they repudiate [them]. Yet he said not this, but what was more fearful than this. For he constrains their souls by what is fearful. For this also is calculated to convert, no less than consolation is. And he at the same time both points out the difference, and declares the chastisement, and the judgment upon them, as though it were an evident matter. *Of how much sorer punishment, suppose ye, shall he be thought worthy?* Here also he appears to me to hint at the mysteries.

[4.] Next he subjoins a testimony [from the Scripture] saying (ver. 31, 30) *It is a fearful thing to fall into the hands of the Living God.* For it is written: *Vengeance [belongeth] unto Me, I will recompense, saith the Lord.* And again, *The Lord shall judge His people. We will fall,* saith one, *into the hands of the Lord, and not into the hands of men.* But if ye repent not, ye shall *fall into the hands of* God: that is fearful: this other is nothing, to *fall into the hands of men.* When, he means, we see any man punished here, let us not be terrified at the things present, but let us shudder at the things that are to come. *For according to His mercy, so is His wrath*[c]. And, *His indignation will rest upon sinners.*

At the same time too he insinuates somewhat else in these words. For *Vengeance [belongeth] unto Me,* he says, *I will recompense.* This is said in regard to their enemies, who are doing evil, not to themselves who are suffering

---

[c] S. Chrys. may have had in mind the latter part of the verse just cited Ecclus. ii. 18, " for as His majesty is, " so is His mercy," and combined it with the first part of the verse he next cites, Ecclus. v. 6. " For mercy " and wrath come from Him &c."

evil. Here he is consoling them too, all but saying, God He. x. 31. abideth for ever and liveth, so that even if they receive not [their reward] now, they will receive it hereafter. They ought to groan, not we: for we indeed shall fall into their hands, but they into the hands of God. For neither is it he that suffers who suffers the ill, but he that does it; nor is it he who receives a benefit that is benefited, but he that does it.

[5.] Seeing then that we know these things, let us be patient as to suffering evil, forward as to performing kindnesses. And this will be, if we hold wealth and honour in contempt. He that hath stripped himself of those affections, is of all men most generous, and more wealthy even than he who wears the purple. Seest thou not how many evils arise on account of money? I do not say how many arise from covetousness, but merely from our attachment to these things. For instance, if a man has lost his money, he leads a life more wretched than any death. Why grievest thou, O man? why weepest thou? Is it because God has delivered thee from excessive watching? because thou dost not sit trembling and alarmed? Again, if any one chain thee to a treasure, commanding thee to sit there perpetually, and to keep watch for other peoples' goods, thou art vexed, thou art annoyed: And dost thou, after thou hast bound thyself with most grievous chains, vex thyself when thou art delivered from the slavery? assuredly our sorrows and our joys are [matters] of fancy [1]. For we keep guard over [our goods] just as if we had what belonged to others.

[1] προλη-ψεως

Now my discourse is directed to the women. A woman oftentimes will have a garment inwoven with gold, and this she shakes, wraps up in linen, keeps with care, trembles for it, and has no enjoyment of it. For either she dies, or she becomes a widow. Or, even if none of these things happen, yet from her fear lest wearing it out by continual use, she should deprive herself of it, she deprives herself of it in another way, by her sparing it. But she passes it on [you say] to another. But neither is this clear: and even if she should pass it on, the other again also will use it in the same way. And if any one will examine in their

Hom. 20. houses, he will find that the most costly garments and other things of superior excellence, are tended with special honour, as if they were living masters. For she does not use them habitually, but fears and trembles, driving away moths and the other things that are wont to eat them, and laying most of them among perfumes and spices, nor permitting all persons to be counted worthy of the sight of them, but oftentimes carefully putting them in order herself with her husband.

(3) Tell me: was it not with reason that Paul called covetousness *idolatry*? For as great respect as they exhibit towards their idols, so great do these persons also [exhibit] towards their garments, towards their golden [ornaments].
Col. iii. 5.

[6.] How long shall we go on stirring up the mire? how long shall we be rivetted to the clay and the brickmaking? For just as they toiled for the King of the Egyptians, so do we also toil for the devil, and are scourged with stripes that are far more severe. For as much as the soul is more important than the body, so much is anxiety than the weals of scourging. We are scourged every day, we are full of fear, in anxiety, in trembling. But if we be willing to groan, if we be willing to look up to God, He sendeth to us, not Moses, nor Aaron, but His own Word, and compunction. When this [word] has come, and hath taken hold of our souls, He will free from the bitter slavery, He will bring us forth out of Egypt, our earnest devotion that is unprofitable, and toils in vain; from this slavery which brings no gain: For they indeed went forth after having at least received golden [ornaments], the wages for their building work, but we [receive] nothing: and would it were nothing. For indeed we also receive, not golden ornaments, but the evils of Egypt, sins and chastisements and punishments.

Let us then learn to be benefited, let us learn to be spitefully treated, this is the part of a Christian. Let us think lightly of golden raiment, let us think lightly of money, that we may not think lightly of our salvation. Let us think lightly of money and not think lightly of our soul. For this it is which is chastised, this it is which is punished: those things remain here, but the soul departeth yonder.

For what purpose, tell me, dost thou cut thyself to pieces, He. x. 31. without perceiving it?

[7.] These things I say to those who are covetous and over-reaching. And it is well to say also to those of whom they take advantage: Bear their over-reachings in a generous way; they are ruining themselves, not you. You indeed they defraud of your money, but they strip themselves of the good will and help of God. And he that is stripped of that, though he clothe himself with the whole wealth of the world, is of all men most poor: just as he too who is the poorest of all, if he have this, is the wealthiest of all. For *the Lord* (it is said) *is my shepherd, and I shall lack* Ps. xxiii. *nothing.* 1.

Tell me now, if thou hadst had a husband, a great and admirable man, who thoroughly loved thee and cared for thee, and then knewest that he would live continually, and not die before thee, and would give thee all things to enjoy in security, as if they were thine own: wouldst thou then have wished to acquire any possessions? Even if thou hadst been stripped of all, wouldst thou not have thought thyself the richer for this?

Why then dost thou grieve? Because thou hast no property? But consider that thou hast [thereby] had the occasion of sin taken from thee. But is it because thou hadst [property] and hast been deprived of it? But thou hast acquired the good will of God. And how [does it appear] that I have acquired it (you say)? He has said, *Wherefore do ye not rather suffer wrong?* He hath said, 1 Cor. vi. " Blessed are they who bear all things with thankfulness ^d." 7. Consider therefore how great good will thou wilt enjoy, if thou shewest forth those things by [thy] works. For one thing only is required from us, *in all things to give thanks* to God, and [then] we have all things in abundance. I mean, for instance: hast thou lost ten thousand pounds of gold? forthwith give thanks unto God, and thou hast acquired ten times ten thousand, by that word and thy thanksgiving.

---

^d It does not appear what passage of Scripture S. Chrys. referred to: the altered text has, "He hath said: 'In "'every thing give thanks.' He hath "said,'Blessed are the poor in spirit.'"

[8.] For tell me when dost thou account Job blessed? When he had those many camels, and flocks, and herds, or when he uttered that saying: *The Lord gave, The Lord hath taken away?* For it is for this cause also that the Devil causes us losses, not that he may take away our goods only, for he knows that this is nothing, but that through them he may compel us to utter something blasphemous. So in the case of the blessed Job too, he did not earnestly endeavour after this only, to make him poor, but also to prove him a blasphemer. At least when he had stripped him of every thing, observe what he says to him through his wife, *Say some word against the Lord, and die.* And yet, o accursed one! thou hadst stripped him of every thing. 'But (says he) this is not what I was labouring for; for I 'have not yet accomplished that for which I did all. I was 'labouring to deprive him of God's help: for this cause I 'deprived him of his goods too. This is what I wish, that 'other is nothing. If this be not gained also, he not only 'has not been injured at all, but has even been benefited.'

(4) Thou seest that that wicked demon ever knows how great is the loss in this matter?

And see too that he contrives his treacherous assault [on Job] through his wife. Hear this, ye husbands, as many as have wives that are fond of money, and compel you to blaspheme God. Call Job to mind. But let us see if it please you, his great moderation, how he silenced her. *Wherefore* (saith he) *hast thou spoken as one of the foolish women [speaketh]?* Of a truth *evil communications corrupt good manners*, at all times indeed, but particularly in case of calamities: then they who give evil advice have strength. For if the soul is even of itself ready to become indignant and impatient, how much more, when there is also some one to advise it. so to do. Is he not being thrust into a pit? A wife is a great good, as also a great evil. For because a wife is a great [good], observe from what point he [Satan] wishes to break through the strong wall. 'The 'depriving him of his property (saith he) did not take him; 'the loss has produced no great effect:' On this account he says, *If indeed he will bless thee to thy face.* You see whither he was aspiring [1].

If then we bear [losses] thankfully, we shall recover even these things, and if we should not recover them, our reward will be greater. For when he had wrestled nobly, then God restored to him these things also. When He had shewn the devil, that it is not for these things that he serves Him, then He restored them also to him.

[9.] For such is He. When God sees that we are not rivetted to things of this life, then He gives them to us. When He sees that we set a higher value on things spiritual, then He also bestows on us things carnal. But not first, lest we should break away from things spiritual: and to spare us He gives us not things carnal, in order to keep us away from them, even against our will.

Not so (you say) but if I receive [them], I am satisfied, and am the more thankful. It is false, O man, for then especially wilt thou be easy and careless.

Why is it then (you say) that He gives [them] to many? Whence is it evident, that it is He that gives [them]? But who else, you say, gives? Their overreaching, their plundering. How then is it that He allows these things to happen? Just as He also [allows] murders, thefts, and acts of violence.

What then (you will say) as to those who receive by succession an inheritance from their fathers, being themselves full of evils innumerable? And what of this? How is it (you say) that God suffers them to enjoy these things? Surely just as He allows thieves, and murderers, and other evil doers. For it is not now the time of judgment, but of the best course of life.

And what I just now said, that I repeat, that they shall suffer greater punishment, who, when they have even had the enjoyment of all good things, do not even so become better. For all shall not be punished alike; but they who, even after His benefits, have continued evil, shall suffer a greater punishment, while they who have been in poverty, not so. And that this is true, hear what He says to David, *Did I not give thee all thy master's goods?* Whenever then thou seest a young man that has received a paternal inheritance without labours and has continued wicked, be assured that his punishment is increasing, and the vengeance is made more intense. Let us not then emulate these; but if any man has succeeded to virtue, if any man has obtained spiritual wealth, [him let us emulate]. For (it is said) *Woe to them that trust in their riches : Blessed are they that fear the Lord.* To which of these, tell me, wouldst thou belong? Doubtless to those who are pronounced blessed. These therefore emulate, not the other, that thou mayest also obtain the good things which are laid up for them. Which may we all obtain, in Christ Jesus our Lord, with whom to the Father together with the Holy Ghost, be glory, now and for ever, and world without end. Amen.

marginalia: cf. Ps. xlix. 6. Ps. cxxviii. 1.

HOMILY XXI.

HEB. x. 32—34.

But call to remembrance the former days, in which after ye were illuminated, ye endured a great fight of afflictions[1]; *partly, whilst ye were made a gazing stock both by reproaches and afflictions*[2], *and partly whilst ye became companions of them that were so used. For ye had compassion on those who were in bonds* [a], *and took joyfully the spoiling of your goods, knowing that ye have for yourselves* [b] *in heaven a better and an enduring substance.*

[1] παθημάτων
[2] θλίψεσι

THE best Physicians after they have made a deep incision, and by the wound have caused the pains to be more intense, soothing the afflicted part, and giving rest and refreshment to the disturbed soul, proceed not to make a second incision, but rather soothe that which has been made with gentle remedies, and such as are calculated to remove the violence of the pain. This Paul also did after he had shaken and cast down their souls, and pierced them with the recollection of Hell, and convinced them, that beyond all doubt he must perish, who does despite to the grace of God, and after he had shewn from the laws of Moses, that they shall be destroyed and that too in a higher degree; and confirmed it by other testimonies, and had said, *It is a fearful thing to fall into the hands of the Living God:* then, in order that the soul might not despond through excessive fear, and be swallowed up with grief, he soothes

supra ver. 31.

[a] τοῖς δεσμίοις. This is held to be the true reading of the sacred text: τοῖς δεσμοῖς μου was substituted in some MSS. and in the editions of S. Chrys. before the Benedictine, here, but not in the body of the Homily.
[b] ἑαυτοῖς without ἐν is the approved reading of the sacred text, and is found in all the MSS. and Edd. of S. Chrys.

them by his commendations and his exhortation; and he applies [as a remedy] zeal derived from their own conduct. For, he saith, *call to remembrance the former days, in which after ye had been enlightened, ye endured a great fight of afflictions.* Powerful is the exhortation which is derived from deeds [already done]: for he who begins a work ought to go forward and add to it. It is as if he had said, when ye were brought in [1] [to the Church], when ye were in the rank of learners, ye displayed so great readiness of mind, so great nobleness, but now it is no longer so. And he who encourages, does thus especially encourage them from their own example.

[1] ἐνήγεσθε

And he did not simply say, *ye endured a fight* [2] but a *great* [fight]. Moreover he did not say "temptations" but *fight*, which is an expression of commendation and of very great praises.

[2] ἄθλησιν a contest as that of wrestlers.

Then he also enumerates them particularly, amplifying his discourse, and multiplying his praises. How? *Partly* (saith he) *whilst ye were made a gazing-stock by reproaches and afflictions*, for reproach is a great thing, and calculated to pervert the soul, and to darken the judgment. For hear what the prophet saith [c]: *While they daily say unto me, Where is thy God?* And again, *If the enemy had reproached me, I would have borne it.* For inasmuch as the race of men are exceedingly vain-glorious, for this cause are they also easily overcome hereby.

Ps. xlii. 10.
Ib. lv. 12.

And he did not simply say *by reproaches*, but expressed that even with great intensifying, being *made a gazing-stock [a public display]* [3]. For when a person is reproached being by himself, it is indeed painful, but far more so when it is in presence of all. For tell me how great an evil was it, that men who had departed from the meanness of Judaism, and gone over, as it were, to the best course of life, and despised the things of their fathers, should be ill treated by their own people, and have no help !

[3] θεατριζόμενοι

[2.] I cannot say (saith he) that ye even suffered these things and were grieved, but ye even rejoiced exceedingly. And this he expressed by saying, *Whilst ye became companions of them that were so used,* and he brings forward

---

[c] The common editions have the entire text, *My tears have been my meat day and night, while &c.*

the very Apostles themselves. Not only (he means) were ye not ashamed of your own sufferings, but ye even shared with the others who had suffered these things. This too is the language of one who is encouraging and exhorting them. He said not Bear my afflictions, share with me, but respect your own afflictions. HE. x. 34.

Ye had compassion on them that were in bonds[d]. Thou seest that he is speaking concerning himself and the rest who were in prison. Thus ye did not account *bonds* to be bonds: but as noble wrestlers so stood ye: for not only did ye need no consolation in your own [distresses], but ye also even became a consolation to others.

And *ye took joyfully the spoiling of your goods.* O! what *full assurance of faith!* Then he also sets down the motive, not only exhorting them for their struggles, but also that they should not be shaken from the Faith. When ye saw your property plundered (he means) ye endured; for already ye saw Him who is invisible, as though He were visible: which was the effect of genuine faith, and ye displayed your faith by your deeds themselves. supra ver. 22.

Well then, the plundering was perhaps dependent on the force of the plunderers, and no man could have prevented it; so that as yet it is not manifest, that ye endured the plundering for the faith's sake (Although this too is manifest. For it was in your power if you had wished it, not to have been plundered, by not believing). But ye did what is far greater than this; the enduring such things even *with joy;* which was altogether apostolical, and worthy of those noble souls, who rejoiced when they had been scourged. For, it says, *they departed from the presence of the council, rejoicing that they were counted worthy to suffer shame for the Name*[e]. But he that endures *with joy*, shews that he has some reward, and that the matter is no loss but a gain to him. Acts v. 41.

Moreover the expression *ye took unto yourselves*[1] shews their voluntary endurance, because, he means, ye chose and accepted. [1] προσέ- δεξασθε

---

[d] a catena, the Verona editions and perhaps one MS. have "with my bonds."

[e] κατηξιώθησαν ὑπὲρ τοῦ ὀνόματος ἀτιμασθῆναι. The common editions of S. Chrys. as the common text of the New Testament, add αὐτοῦ, "*His* Name," in this and in other places.

HOM. 21.   *Knowing* (he saith) *that ye have for yourselves, a better substance in heaven and an enduring;* instead of saying, firm, not perishing, as this [earthly substance] is.

(2)   [3.] In the next place after having praised them, he says, (ver. 35) *Cast not away therefore your confidence, which hath great recompence of reward.* What meanest thou? he did not say, 'ye have cast it away, and recover it:' but, which tended much more to strengthen them, 'ye have it,' he saith. For to recover again that which has been cast away, requires more labour: whereas not to lose that which is held fast does not. But to the Galatians he says the very opposite: *My children, of whom I travail in birth again, till Christ be formed in you;* and with reason; for they were rather supine in disposition: whence they needed a sharper word; but these were more faint-hearted, so that they rather needed what was more soothing.

Gal. iv. 19.

Cast not away therefore (saith he) *your confidence,* so that they were in great confidence towards God, *which hath* (he saith) *great recompence of reward.* "And when shall "we receive them (some one might say)? behold! all things "[which were to be done] by ourselves have been [done]:" on this account he anticipated them on their own supposition, all but saying, If ye know that ye have in heaven a better substance, seek nothing here.

For ye have need of patience, not of any addition [to your labours], that ye may continue in the same state, that ye may not cast away what has been put into your hands. Ye have no need of anything else, but only so to stand as ye have stood, that when ye have come to the end, ye may receive the promise.

(ver. 36) *For* (he saith) *ye have need of patience, that after ye have done the will of God, ye may receive the promise.* Ye have need of one thing only, to bear with the delay; not, to fight again. Ye are [close] at the very crown (he means); ye have borne all the combats of bonds, of afflictions; your goods have been spoiled. What then? Henceforward ye are standing to be crowned: endure this only, the delay of the crown. O the greatness of the consolation! It is as if one should speak to an athlete who had overthrown all, and had no antagonist, and then was to be crowned, and yet endured not that time, during which the president of the games comes, and places the crown [upon him]; and as if he were unable to endure patiently, was wishing to go out, and escape as though he could not bear the thirst and the heat.

He then also hinting this what does he say? (ver 37) *Yet a little while and He that cometh will come, and will not tarry.* For lest they should say, And when will He come? he comforts them from the Scriptures. For thus also when he says in another place, *Now is our salvation nearer*, he comforts them on the ground that the time which remained was but short. And this he says not of himself but from the Scriptures [f]. But if from that time it was said, *Yet a little while, and He that cometh will come, and will not tarry*, it is manifest that now He is nearer at hand. Wherefore also to wait [for Him] is no small reward.

(ver. 38) *But the just* (he saith) *shall live by faith, and if he draw back, My soul hath no pleasure in him.* This is a great encouragement, when one points out that they have succeeded in the whole matter and are losing it through a little indolence. (ver. 39) *But we are not of them that draw back unto perdition, but of them that believe to the saving of the soul.*

[4.] (ch. xi. 1, 2) *But faith is the substance*[1] *of things hoped for, the evidence of things not seen. For by it the elders obtained a good report.* O what an expression has he used, in saying, *an evidence of things not seen.* For [we say] there is *evidence*, in the case of things that are exceedingly manifest [g]. Faith then is the seeing things not evident (he means), and brings what are not seen to the same full assurance with what are seen. So then neither is it possible to disbelieve in things which are seen, nor, on the other hand can there be faith, unless a man be more clearly convinced with respect to things invisible, than he is with respect to things that are seen. For inasmuch as the

[1] substantiality

---

[f] It is to be observed that the words "He that cometh will come and will not tarry," are from the prophet Habakkuk ii. 3: where the LXX has, ἐὰν ὑστερήσῃ, ὑπόμεινον αὐτόν ("Him" not "it.") ὅτι ἐρχόμενος ἥξει, καὶ οὐ μὴ χρονίσῃ &c. The Apostle interprets this by adding the article: ὁ ἐρχόμενος, the well-known designation of the Messiah.

[g] δήλων. Savil and Morell following some MSS. read ἀδήλων "obscure:" but S. Chrys. means that we use the word ἔλεγχος of a proof which makes things most certain and evident.

objects of hope seem to be unsubstantial, Faith gives them substantiality[1], or rather, does not give it, but is itself their substance[2]. For instance, the Resurrection has not come, nor does it exist substantially, but hope brings it into substantial existence in our soul. This is [the meaning of] *the substance of things.*

If therefore it is an *evidence of things not seen,* why forsooth do you wish to see them, so as to fall away from faith, and from being just[3]? since *the just shall live by faith,* whereas ye, if ye wish to see these things, are no longer believing. Ye have laboured (saith he), ye have struggled: I too allow this, nevertheless, wait; for this is Faith: do not seek the whole *here.*

(3) [5.] These things were indeed said to the Hebrews, but they are a general exhortation [suited] to many also of those who are here assembled. How, and in what way? to those who are fainthearted; to those who are mean-spirited. For when they see the wicked prospering, and themselves faring ill, they are troubled, they bear it impatiently: while they long for the chastisement of the others, and the inflicting vengeance on them; while they wait for the rewards of their own sufferings. *For yet a little time, and He that cometh will come.*

Let us then also say this to the slothful: Doubtless there will be punishment; doubtless He will come, henceforth the events of the[4] Resurrection are even at the doors.

Whence [does] that [appear] (you say)? I do not say, From the prophets; for neither is my discourse now addressed to Christians only; but even should there be a heathen here, I am perfectly confident, and bring forward my proofs, and will instruct him. How (you say)?

Christ foretold many things. If those former things did not come to pass, then neither do thou believe these; But if they all came to pass, why dost thou doubt concerning those that remain? Although it were very unreasonable[5], if nothing had come to pass, to believe concerning those former ones, or when they all have come to pass, to disbelieve these others.

But I will make the matter more plain by an example.

Christ said, that Jerusalem should be taken, and should be so taken as never was any city before, and that it should never be raised up any more: and in fact this prediction came to pass. He said, that there should be *great tribulation*, and it came to pass. He said that like a grain of mustard seed that is sown, so should the preaching [of the Gospel] be extended: and every day we see this running over the world. He said, that they who have left father or mother, or brethren, or sisters, should have both fathers and mothers; And this we see fulfilled in facts. He said, *in the world ye shall have tribulation, but be of good cheer, I have overcome the world*, that is, no man shall get the better of you. And this we see by the events has really come to pass. He said that *the gates of hell shall not prevail against the Church*, and that, although it is persecuted, and that no one shall quench the Preaching [of the Gospel]: and the experience of events bears witness to this prediction also: and yet at that time when He said these things, it was very hard to believe Him. Wherefore? because all was [but] words, and He had not as yet given any proofs of the things which had been spoken. So that they now are become far more credible. He said that *when the Gospel should have been preached among all the nations, then the end shall come*, and lo! now we have arrived at the end: for the greater part of the world hath been preached to, henceforth therefore the end is at hand. Let us tremble, beloved.

HEB.xi.1.

S. Matt. xxiv. 21.

S. John xvi. 33.

S. Matt. xvi. 18.

Ib. xxiv. 14.

[6.] But what, tell me. Art thou anxious about the end of all things? For while it also itself is near, each man's life and his death is much nearer[h]. For it is said, *the days of our years, in them are seventy years; but if [one be] in strength, fourscore years* [&c.] The day of judgment is near. Let us fear. *A brother doth not redeem; shall man redeem?* There we shall repent exceedingly, *but in death no man shall confess unto Him.* Wherefore he saith, *Let us prevent His presence with confession*, that is, His coming. For here [in this life] indeed, whatever we do has efficacy; but there, no longer. Tell me, if a man placed us for a little

Ps.xc.10.

Ib. xlix. 7.
Ib. vi. 5.
Ib.xcv.2.

[h] ἡ δὲ ἑκάστου ζωὴ ἐγγυτέρα πολλῷ καὶ ἡ τελευτή. But Mut. "sed et vitæ finis uniuscujuscunque prope est."

while in a flaming furnace, should we not submit to anything in order to escape, even were it necessary to part with our money, nay to undergo slavery? How many are there that have fallen into grievous diseases, who would gladly have chosen to give up all, to be delivered from them, if the choice had been offered them? If in this world then, a disease which can be but of short duration so afflicts us, what shall we do yonder, when repentance will be of no avail?

[7.] Of how many evils are we now full, without being conscious of them? We bite one another, we devour one another, in wronging, accusing, calumniating, being vexed by the credit of our neighbours.

cf. Gal. v. 15.

And observe their mischievousness[1]. When a man wishes to destroy the character of his neighbour, he says, 'Such an 'one said this of him; O God, forgive me, do not call me to 'a strict account, I must give account of what I have heard¹.' Why then dost thou speak of it at all, if thou dost not believe it? why dost thou repeat it? why dost thou make it credible by its being often reported? why dost thou pass on the story which is not true? Thou dost not believe it, and thou entreatest God not to call thee to strict account? Do not repeat it then, but keep silence, and so free thyself from all fear.

¹ χαλεπόν

But I know not from whence this disease has fallen upon men. We are become tattlers, nothing remains[2] in our mind. Hear the exhortation of a wise man who saith, *Hast thou heard a word? let it die in*[3] *thee, be bold; it will not burst thee.* And again, *A fool heareth a word, and travaileth, as a woman in labour of a child.* We are ever ready to make accusations, prepared for condemning. Even if no other evil thing had been done by us, this were sufficient to ruin us, and to carry us away to Hell, this involves us in ten thousand evils. And that thou mayest know this certainly, hear what the prophet saith, *Thou satest and spakest against thy brother.*

(·1.)
² ἐναπο-
μένει
Ecclus.
xix. 10.
³ ἐναπο-
θανέτω
ib. 11.

Ps. l. 20.

But it is not I, you say, but the other [who told me]. Nay rather, it is thyself; for if *thou* hadst not repeated it, another would not have heard it: or even if he must have

---

¹ Or might it be read, ἀκοῆς λόγον ὀφείλω; "am I responsible for what I "hear, for common reports?"

heard it, yet still *thou* wouldest not have been the person to be blamed for the sin. When we ought to shade over and conceal the failings of our neighbours, thou notwithstanding paradest them under a shew of zeal for goodness. Thou becomest, not an accuser, but a gossip, a trifler, a fool. O what cleverness! without being aware of it, thou art bringing disgrace upon thyself as well as on him. Heb.xi.2.

And consider how great are the evils which arise from this. Thou provokest the wrath of God. Dost thou not hear Paul saying about widows, *they not only* (these are his words) *learn to be idle, but tattlers also and busy-bodies, going about from house to house, and speaking things which they ought not.* So that even when thou believest the things which are said against thy brother, thou oughtest not even in that case to speak of them; much less, when thou dost not believe them. 1 Tim. v. 13.

But thou [forsooth] lookest to thine own interest? thou fearest to be called to strict account by God? Fear then, lest even for thy tattling thou be called to strict account. For here, thou canst not say, 'O God call me not to a strict 'account for [my] light talking:' for the whole matter is light talking. Why didst thou publish it? why didst thou increase the evil? This is sufficient to destroy us. On this account Christ said, *Judge not, that ye be not judged.* S. Matt. vii. 1.

But we pay no regard to this, neither are we brought to our senses by what happened to the Pharisee. He said what was true, *I am not as this Publican*, he said it too in no man's hearing: yet was he condemned. If he were condemned when he said what was true, and uttered it in no man's hearing, what fearful [punishment] shall not they suffer, who like gossiping women, carry about every where [stories] that are false, and which they do not themselves believe? what shall they not have to endure? S. Luke xviii. 11.

[8.] Henceforward let us set *a door and a bolt before* our *mouth*. For innumerable evils have arisen from tattling; families have been ruined, friendships torn asunder, innumerable other miseries have happened. Busy not thyself, O man, about the affairs of thy neighbour. Ecclus. xxviii.25.

But thou art a talkative person and thou hast a weakness [in this respect]? Talk of thine own [faults] to God: thus

<small>Hom. 21.</small> thy defect will be no longer a defect, but an advantage. Talk of thy own faults to thy friends, those who are thorough friends and righteous men, and in whom thou hast confidence, that so they may pray for thy sins. If thou speak of the [sins] of others, thou art nowise profited, neither hast thou gained anything, but hast ruined thyself. If thou acknowledgest thy own [sins] to the Lord, great is thy <small>Ps. xxxii. 5.</small> reward: for one says, *I said, I will confess against myself mine iniquity to the Lord, and Thou forgavest the impiety of my heart.*

Dost thou wish to judge? judge thine own sins. No [1] ἐγκαλεῖ one will accuse[1] thee, if thou condemn thyself: but he will accuse thee, if thou do not condemn thyself: he will accuse thee, unless thou convict thyself; will accuse thee of insensibility. Thou hast seen such an one in anger, irritated, doing something else that is unreasonable? Do thou thyself also at once turn thy thoughts on thy own [faults]: and thus thou wilt not vehemently condemn him, and wilt free thyself from the load of thy past transgressions. If we thus regulate our own conduct, if we thus manage our own life, if we condemn ourselves, we shall probably not commit many sins, and we shall do many good things, being fair and moderate; and shall enjoy all the things that have been promised to them that love God: to which may all attain, by the grace and mercy of our Lord Jesus Christ, with whom to the Father and also to the Holy Ghost, be glory power honour, now and for ever and world without end. Amen.

HOMILY XXII.

Heb. xi. 3, 4.

Through faith we understand that the worlds were framed by the word of God; so that things which are seen were not made of things which do appear. By faith Abel offered unto God a more excellent sacrifice than Cain, by which he obtained witness[1] *that he was righteous, God testifying of his gifts: and by it he being dead yet speaketh*[a].

[1] *was testified of*

The quality of Faith[2] has need of a soul generous and of youthful spirit, and ascending above all things of sense, and passing beyond the weakness of human reasonings. For it is not possible for a man to become a believer, otherwise than by raising himself up above the common customs [of the world].

[2] τὸ τῆς πίστεως

Inasmuch then as the souls of the Hebrews were thoroughly weakened, and though they had begun from faith, yet from their circumstances, I mean, their sufferings, their afflictions, they had afterwards become faint-hearted, and of little spirit, and were shaken from [their position], he encouraged them first indeed from these very same things, saying, *Call to remembrance the former days* [&c.]; supra x. 32. next from the Scripture which saith, *But the just shall live by faith;* ib. 38. afterwards from arguments, saying, *But Faith is the substance of things hoped for, the evidence of things not seen.* supra ver. 1. And now again from their forefathers, those great and admirable men, all but saying; If [under that dispensation] where the good things were close before them, they all were saved by faith, much more are we.

For when a soul finds one that shares the same sufferings

[a] λαλεῖ, with the most approved MSS. of the Epistle; the editions have λαλεῖται; which is the reading of the common texts of the N.T.

with itself, it is refreshed and recovers breath. This we may see also in the case of Faith; this we may see also in the case of affliction: *that there may be comfort for you[b] through our mutual faith.* For mankind are very distrustful, and cannot place confidence in themselves, are fearful about whatever things they think they possess, because they have great regard for the opinion of the many.

[2.] What then does Paul do? He encourages them from [the history of] their fathers; and before doing that from the common notions [of mankind][1]. For tell me, he says, since Faith is calumniated[c] as being a thing without demonstration[2] and as rather matter of deceit, for this cause he points out that the greatest things are attained through faith and not through reasonings. And how does he shew this? tell me[d]. It is manifest, he saith, that God made the things which are out of things which are not[3], things which appear out of things which appear not, things which subsist out of things which subsist not. But whence [does it appear] that He also did this *by a Word?* For reason suggests nothing of this kind, but on the contrary, that things which do appear are [formed] out of things which appear.

On this account especially the philosophers say that "nothing is out of what is not[e];" *sensual* as they are, and committing nothing to Faith. And yet these same men, when they have said anything great and noble, are caught committing it to Faith. For instance, that 'God is without beginning[4], and without origin[5]:' for reason does not suggest this, but the contrary. And consider, I beseech you, their exceeding folly; saying[f] [as they do] that God is without beginning; and yet this is far more wonderful than that [things should be created] out of nothing. For to say, that He is without beginning, that He is without

---

[1] κοινῆς ἐννοίας
[2] ἀναπόδεικτον
[3] ἐξ οὐκ ὄντων i.e. "out of nothing."
[4] ἄναρχος
[5] ἀγέννητος

Hom. 22.
Rom. i. 12.

S. Jude 19.

[b] ὥστε εἶναι παράκλησιν ὑμῖν: the common editions follow MSS. in which the very words of Rom. i. 12 have been substituted.

[c] Thus the sentence is inconsequent, as it stands in the best texts: in the common editions it is altered to, "For "inasmuch as the Faith was at that time "calumniated" &c.

[d] At this place and generally through- out the Homily: the later texts and the common editions insert the words of the Epistle, but not so the best MSS. or the old translation.

[e] "De nihilo nihil" is probably referred to.

[f] λέγοντες, an irregular construction: the common texts substitute λέγουσιν.

origin, produced neither by Himself nor by any other is more full of difficulties[1], than to say that God made the things which are, out of the things which are not. For in this [assertion] there are many [points] which are calculated to persuade: as, that some one made it, that what was made had a beginning, that on the whole it was made. But in the other case, that He is self-existing[2], without origin, that He neither had beginning nor time; tell me, do not these things require faith? But [the Apostle] did not assert this, which was far the greater thing [of the two], but the lesser.

HEB.xi.3.
[1] ἀπορώ-τερον
[2] αὐτόμα-τος

Whence [does it appear], he would say, that God made these things? Reason does not suggest it; no one was present when it was done. Whence does it appear? It is plain that it is the result of faith. *Through faith we understand that the worlds were made.* Why *through faith?* Because *the things that are seen have not been made of things that appear.* For this is Faith.

[3.] Having thus stated the general [principle][3], he afterwards tries[4] it by applying it in the case of particular persons. For a man of credit is equivalent to the world. This at all events he afterwards hinted. For when he had balanced the matter in the case of one or two hundred persons, and then saw that the number was small in amount, he afterwards says, *to whom the world was not equal in worth*[g].

[3] τὸ κοι-νόν
[4] γυμνά-ζει

infra ver. 38.

And observe whom he puts first, him who was ill-treated, and that by a brother. It was their own affliction[5], *For you also* (saith he) *have suffered the same things from your own countrymen.* And by a brother who had been in no respect wronged, but who envied him on God's account; indicating that they also are looked on with an evil eye and envied. He honoured God, and died because he honoured Him: and has not yet attained to a resurrection. But his readiness in God's service is manifest, and his own part[6] has been done, but what is from God has not yet been bestowed on him.

[5] οἰκεῖον τὸ πάθος
1 Thess. ii. 14.
[6] τὰ παρ' αὐτοῦ

And by the *more excellent sacrifice* in this place, he

---

[g] ἄξιος. S. Chrys. takes the word in its primary sense, "of like value," "worth so much as." See Hom. xxvii. [6.] pp. 316 sqq.

means that which is more honourable, more splendid, more necessary.

And we cannot say (saith he) that it was not accepted. He did accept it, and said unto Cain, [*Hast thou*] *not* [*sinned*], *if thou rightly offer, but dost not rightly divide?* So then Abel both rightly offered, and rightly divided. Nevertheless in return for this, what recompence did he receive? He was slain by his brother's hand: and that sentence of condemnation which his father underwent on account of his sin, this he was the first to receive who had conducted himself aright. And what he suffered was so much the more grievous, as it was from a brother, and as he was the first [to die].

And he conducted himself rightly in these respects without having any man to look to. For to whom could he look, when he so honoured God? to his father and his mother? But they had outraged Him in return for His benefits. To his brother then? but he also had dishonoured [God]. So that from himself he found out what was good.

And he that is worthy of so great honour, what does he suffer? He is put to death. And how too was he otherwise *testified of that he was righteous?* It is said, that fire came down and consumed the sacrifices. For instead of [*And the Lord*] *had respect to Abel and to his sacrifices*, the Syriac[h] said, *And He set them on fire.* He therefore who both by word and deed bare witness to the righteous man and sees him slain for His sake, did not avenge him, but left him to suffer.

(2) But your case is not such as this: for how could it be? you who have both prophets and examples, and encourage-

---

[h] The reading of some MSS. and of the editions except Savile's was ὁ κύριος instead of ὁ Σύρος. On this Montfaucon has the note: "This sentence is imperfect. Mutianus' "rendering is, 'On Abel (saith he) He "'looked, and on his sacrifices.' But "in the Syrian language, it has, "'And set [them] on fire.' It would "seem therefore that we should read, "ὁ Σύρος, καὶ ἐνεπύρισεν, εἶπεν. The "Hebrew words are שעה וישע which "(not the Syriac translator, but) "Theodotion renders καὶ ἐνεπύρισεν ὁ "Θεός· 'And God set [them] on fire,' "as may be seen in our edition of the "Hexapla, and is proved by Jerome's "testimony on the passage. For the "Syriac translation is, 'and God was "'well pleased.' So perhaps it might "be an error of Chrysostom." Four of the six MSS. mentioned by Mr. Field [but not the Catena] have Σύρος.

ments innumerable, and signs and miracles accomplished? Heb.xi.5 So that that was faith indeed. For what miracles did he see, that he should believe that he should have any recompence of good things? Was it not from Faith alone, that he chose virtue?

What is, *and by it he being dead yet speaketh?* That he might not cast them into great despondency, he points out that he has in part obtained a recompence. How?[1] 'The influence which is maintained by him[1] is great, he 'means, *and he yet speaketh;* that is, [Cain] slew him, but 'he did not with him slay his glory and honour also. He is 'not dead; therefore neither shall ye die. For by how 'much the more grievous a man's sufferings are, so much 'the greater is his glory.'

[1] ἡ ἐπὶ σκοπὴ ἡ παρ' αὐτοῦ

How does he *yet speak?* This is a sign both of his being alive, and of his being by all men celebrated, admired, counted blessed. For he who encourages others to be righteous, speaks. For no speech has so much effect, as that man's suffering. As then heaven by its mere appearance speaks, so also does he by being had in remembrance. Not if he had made proclamation of himself, not if he had ten thousand tongues, and were alive, would he have been so held in admiration as now he is. That is, these things do not take place with impunity nor as in a chance way, neither do they pass away.

[4.] (ver. 5) *By faith Enoch was translated, that he should not see death, and was not found, because God had translated him.* This man displayed greater faith than Abel. How (you ask)? Because, although he came after him, yet what took place with regard to [Abel] was sufficient to turn him away [from serving God]. How? God foreknew that [Abel] would be killed. For He said to Cain: *Thou hast sinned: do not add thereto*[1]. He was honoured by him, [yet] He did not protect him. And yet neither did this throw him [Enoch] into indifference. He said not to himself, ' What need of toils and dangers? Abel 'honoured God, yet He did not protect him. For what

[1] The words of the Septuagint, Gen. iv. 7, are ἥμαρτες; ἡσύχασον: for which S. Chrys. substitutes the words of Ecclus. xxi. 1. ἥμαρτες; μὴ προσθῇς ἔτι. He combines these two texts (either from confusing them or by way of explanation) in three other places. See Mr. Field's note. The words were addressed to Cain before he killed his brother.

'advantage had he that was departed, from the punishment
'of his brother? and what benefit was it possible he could
'reap therefrom? Let us allow that he suffers severe pun-
'ishment: what is that to him who has been slain?' He
neither said nor thought anything of this kind, but passing
beyond all these things, he knew that if God exist, certainly
there exists a recompencer also: Although as yet they knew
nothing of a resurrection. But if they who as yet know
nothing of a resurrection, and here [in this world] see
things that are contrary [to the idea of recompence for the
righteous], thus pleased [God], how much more should
we? For they neither knew of a resurrection, nor had
they any examples to look to. This very same thing then
made [Enoch] well-pleasing [to God], namely that he had
received no reward. For he knew that [God] *is a rewarder.*
Whence [knew he this]? "For He recompensed Abel," do
you say? So that reason suggested different things [from
what faith suggested], but faith the opposite of what was
seen. Even then (he would say) if you see that you receive
no recompence here, be not disturbed.

How was it *by faith* that *Enoch was translated?* Because
his pleasing [God] was the cause of his translation, and
faith [the cause] of his pleasing [Him]. For if he had not
known that he shall receive a recompence, how could he
have pleased [Him]? *But without faith it is impossible to
please* Him. How? If a man believe that there is a God
and a retribution, he will have the recompence. Whence
then is the well-pleasing?

[5.] It is necessary to *believe that He is*, not 'what He is[k].'
If *that He is* needs Faith, and not reasonings; it is impossible to ascertain by reasoning 'what He is.' If [the doctrine]
that *He is a rewarder* require Faith and not reasonings,
how is it possible by Reasoning to comprehend the [truths]
of His essence[1]? For what Reasoning will be able to attain
to them? For some persons say that the things that exist
are self-caused[2]. Thou seest that unless we have Faith in
regard to all things, not only in regard to the Retribution,
but also in regard to the very being of God, all is lost to us?

[1] τὰ τῆς οὐσίας
[2] αὐτόματα

---

[k] That is what the substance of God is, is not a part of what we must believe in order to please Him: nor can it be ascertained by reasonings.

unrevealed. God punished: yet soon poured forth life. 259

But many seek to know whither Enoch was translated, HE. xi. 6. and for what cause he was translated, and why he did not die, neither he nor Elijah, and, if they are still alive, how they live, and in what form. However to enquire into these matters is superfluous. For that the one was translated, and that the other was taken up, the Scriptures have said; but where they exist, and in what manner they exist, they have not added: For they say nothing more than what is necessary. For this indeed took place, I mean the event of his translation immediately at the beginning, the human soul [thereby] receiving a hope of the destruction of death, and of the overthrow of the devil's tyranny: and that death will be done away; for he was translated, not being dead, but *that he should not see death.*

On this account he added, he was translated being alive, because he was well-pleasing [unto God]. For just as a Father when he has threatened his son, wishes indeed immediately after he has threatened, to relax his threat, but endures and continues resolute, that for a time he may chasten and correct him, allowing the threat to remain firm; so also God, after the manner of men, one may almost say, did not continue resolute, but immediately shewed that death has been done away. And first He allows death to happen, wishing to terrify the father through the son: For wishing to shew that the sentence is fixed in very deed, He subjected to this punishment not wicked men at once, but him even who was well-pleasing to Him, I mean, the blessed Abel; and almost immediately after him, He translated Enoch. Moreover He did not raise the former to life, that they might not at once be full of confidence: but He translated the other being yet alive: having excited fear by the case of Abel, but by this latter exciting a zeal to be well-pleasing unto Him. Wherefore they who say that all things are carried hither and thither by chance[1], and do not expect a recompence, are not well-pleasing [to God]; as neither are the heathen. For *He proves a rewarder of them that diligently seek Him* by works and by knowledge.

[1] αὐτόματα

[6.] Since then we have *a rewarder*, let us do all things (3) that we may not be deprived of the rewards of virtue. For indeed the neglecting such a recompence, the scorning such a reward, is a subject worthy of many tears. For just as to *those who diligently seek Him*, He is a rewarder, so to those who seek Him not, the contrary.

Seek (saith He) *and ye shall find :* but how is it [possible] to find the Lord? Consider how gold is found; with much labour. [*I sought the Lord*] *with my hands* (it is said) *by night before Him, and I was not deceived*, that is, just as we seek any thing which is lost, so let us seek God. Do we not combine our whole attention thereon? Do we not make enquiry of every one? Do we not travel far from home? Do we not promise [rewards in] money?

For instance, suppose that any among us has lost his son, what do we not do? what land, what sea do we not make the circuit of? Do we not reckon money, and houses, and every thing else as secondary to the finding him? And should we find him, we cling to him, we hold him fast, we do not let him go. And when we are going to seek any thing whatever, we busy ourselves in all ways to find the object of our search. How much more ought we to do this in regard to God, just as if we were seeking somewhat indispensable; nay rather, not in the same way, but much more! However since we are weak, at least seek God as thou seekest thy money or thy son. Wilt thou not leave thy home for Him? Hast thou not then ever left thy home for the sake of money? dost thou not [for this] busy thyself about all things? when thou hast found [it], art thou not full of confidence?

[7.] *Seek* (saith He) *and ye shall find.* For things which are sought after need much care, especially in regard of God. For many are the hindrances, many the things that bring on darkness, many those that impede our perception. For just as the sun is manifest, and set forth publicly before all, and we have no need to seek it; whilst if on the other hand we bury ourselves and turn every thing upside down, we need much labour in order to look at the sun; so truly here also, if we bury ourselves in the depth of evil desires, in the darkness of passions and of the affairs of this life, with difficulty do we look up, with difficulty do we raise our heads, with difficulty do we see clearly. He that is buried underground, in whatever degree he sees upwards, in that degree does he come nearer to the sun. Let us therefore shake off the earth from ourselves, let us break through the mist which lies upon us. It is a thick, and a close one, and does not allow us to see clearly. HE. xi. 6.

And how, you say, is this cloud broken through? If we draw to ourselves the beams of *the sun of righteousness.* The *lifting up of my hands* (it is said) *is an evening sacrifice.* With our hands let us also lift up our mind: ye who have been initiated in the mysteries know what I mean [1], perhaps too ye recognize the expression, and comprehend what I am hinting at. Let us raise up our thoughts on high. Ps. cxli. 2.

I myself know many men almost suspended apart from the earth, and beyond measure stretching up their hands, and out of heart because it is not possible to be lifted up into the air, and thus praying with earnestness. Thus I wish you to be always, and if not always, at least very often; and if not very often, at least now and then, at least in the morning, at least in the evening prayers [1]. For, tell me, canst thou not stretch forth thine hands? stretch forth thy will, stretch forth as far as thou wilt, yea even to heaven itself. Even shouldst thou wish to touch the very summit, even if thou wouldst ascend higher still and walk thereon, it is open for thee to do it. For our mind is lighter, and rises higher than any winged creature. And when it has also received the grace which [comes] from the Spirit, O! how swift is it! how quick is it! how does it compass all things! how does it never sink down or fall to the ground! These wings let us provide for ourselves: by means of them shall we be able to fly even across the tempestuous sea of this present life. [1] ἐν ταῖς ἑωθιναῖς, ἐν ταῖς ἑσπεριναῖς

The swiftest birds fly unhurt over mountains, and woods, and seas, and rocks, in a brief moment of time. Such also is our mind; when it has put on its wings, when it has separated itself from the things of this life, nothing can lay hold of it, it is higher than all things, even than the fiery darts of the devil.

[1] The words of the Liturgy which were said throughout the Church Catholic, "Lift up your hearts &c."

Hom. 22. The devil is not so good a marksman, as to be able to reach this height; he does however send forth his darts indeed, for he is void of all shame, yet he does not hit the mark; the dart returns to him without effect, and not without effect only, but it even [falls] upon his own head. For that which has been sent forth by him must of necessity strike [something]. Just then, as that which has been shot out by men, either strikes the person against whom it is directed, or pierces bird, or fence, or garment, or wood, or the mere air, so does the dart of the devil also. It must of necessity inflict a wound; and if it wound not him that is shot at, it necessarily wounds him that shoots it.

And this we may learn from many instances, [I mean] that when we are not wounded, without doubt he is wounded himself. For instance, he insidiously attacked Job: he did not wound him, but was wounded himself. He insidious attacked Paul, he did not wound him, but was wounded himself. In all cases, if we are watchful, we may see this taking place. For even when he wounds, he is wounded; much more then [when he does not wound].

[8.] Let us turn his weapons then against himself, and having fully armed and fortified ourselves with the shield of faith, let us keep guard with all carefulness, so as to be impregnable. Now the dart of the devil is evil concupiscence. Anger is in a special way a fire, a flame; it catches, destroys, consumes; let us quench it, by long-suffering, by forbearance. For just as red-hot iron dipped into water, loses its fire, so an angry man falling in with one that is long-suffering, does no hurt to the patient man, but rather benefits him, and is himself more thoroughly subdued.

For nothing is equal to long-suffering. A man of such a character is never insulted; but just as bodies of adamant are not wounded, so neither are souls such as this. For they are raised above the reach of the darts. The man that is long-suffering is high, and so high as not to receive any wound from the shot. When he is furious, do thou laugh: but do not laugh openly, lest thou irritate him: laugh however in thy mind on his account. For in the case of children, when they strike us passionately, as though forsooth they were avenging themselves, we laugh. If then thou laugh, there will be as great difference between thee and him, as between a child and a man: but if thou art furious thou hast made thyself a child. For men under the influence of anger are more senseless than children. If any one look at a child that is furious [with rage], does he not laugh at him? *The poor-spirited* (it is said) *is mightily simple.* The simple then is a child: and *he who is long-suffering* (it is said) *is abundant in wisdom.* This *abundant wisdom* then let us follow after, that we may attain to the good things promised us in Christ Jesus our Lord, with Whom to the Father and also to the Holy Ghost, be glory, power, honour, now and for ever and world without end. Amen.

_{Heb.xi.6.}

_{Prov.xiv. 29.}

HOMILY XXIII.

HEB. xi. 7.

By faith Noah, being warned of God[1] *of things not seen as yet, moved with fear, prepared an ark to the saving of his house; by the which he condemned the world, and became heir of the righteousness which is by Faith.*

(1) *BY faith* (saith he) *Noah being warned of God.* As the Son of God, speaking of His own coming, said, *In the days of Noah they married and were given in marriage*, on this account the Apostle also recalled to their mind an appropriate image of their own circumstances. For the example of Enoch, was an example only of Faith; that of Noah on the other hand, of unbelief also. And this is a complete consolation and exhortation, when it is found that not only those who believe are approved, but that those also who do not believe meet with the contrary portion.

For what saith he? *By faith being warned of God [having received a divine communication*[2]*].* What is *having received a divine communication?* It is, "It having been foretold to him." But why is the expression *divine communication*[3] used? for in another place also it is said, *and it was divinely communicated*[4] *to him by the Spirit*, and again, *and what saith the divine communication*[3]*?* (Thou seest the equal dignity of the Spirit? for just as God reveals[a], so also does the Holy Spirit.) But for what cause did he

[1] χρημα-τισθείς
[2] χρημα-τισθείς
[3] χρημα-τισμός Ib. ii. 26.
Rom. xi. 4.
[4] ἦν κε-χρηματι-σμένον

S. Luke xvii. 26, 27.

[a] χρᾷ. This word is properly used of quasi-Divine communications made through oracles: the word χρηματί-ζω and χρηματισμὸς have the same meaning. Hence the emphatic character of the words, *of God*, in our Version of the text Rom. xi. 4; and so in the other passage which S. Chrys. cites (S. Luke ii. 26) the Divinity of the Holy Spirit (he says) is implied in the use of the word ἦν κεχρηματισμέ-νον ὑπὸ (not διὰ) τοῦ Πνεύματος, "a divine communication was made by the Spirit."

express himself thus? It is a prophecy that is called a *divine communication.* Heb. xi. 9.

Of things not seen as yet, saith he, that is of the rain.

Moved with fear, prepared an ark. Reason indeed suggested nothing of this sort; For *they were marrying and being given in marriage;* the air was clear, there were no signs [of change]: but nevertheless he was alarmed: *By faith* (he says) *Noah being warned of God of things not seen as yet, moved with fear, prepared an ark to the saving of his house.*

In what sense [is it that he says], *By the which he condemned the world?* He shewed them to be worthy of punishment, since they were not brought to their senses even by the construction [of the ark].

And he became (he says) *heir of the righteousness which is by Faith:* that is, from *this* he was manifested to be righteous, from his believing God. For this is the [mark] of a soul that is sincerely disposed towards Him and judges nothing more thoroughly to be relied on than His words, just as Unbelief is the very contrary. And as to Faith, it is manifest that it works righteousness. For just as we have been warned of God respecting Hell, so was he also warned: and yet at that time he was laughed at; he was reviled and ridiculed; nevertheless he regarded none of these things.

[2.] (ver. 8, 9) *By faith Abraham when he was called to go out into a place which he should after receive for an inheritance, obeyed; and he went out not knowing whither he went. By faith he sojourned in the land of promise, as in a strange country, dwelling in tents, with Isaac and Jacob, the heirs with him of the same promise.* [*By faith:*] for (tell me) whom did he see to emulate [1]? He had for father a Gentile, and an idolater; he had heard no prophets; he knew not whither he was going. For as they of the Hebrews who believed, looked to these [patriarchs] as men who had enjoyed blessings innumerable, he points out that no one of them had obtained anything as yet; all are unrewarded; no one as yet had received his recompences. *He* was banished from his country and his home, and *went out not knowing whither he went.*

And what marvel, if he himself [were so], when his seed

[1] "to endeavour to imitate, or even surpass."

also dwelt in this same way? For beholding the promise proving untrue ¹ (since He had said, *To thee will I give this land, and to thy seed*), he saw his son dwelling there; and again his grandson saw himself dwelling in a land not his own; yet was he nowise troubled. For as to Abraham himself what happened would have been such as we might have expected, on the supposition that the promise was to be accomplished afterwards in his family (although it is said even to himself, *To thee, and to thy seed*, not, " to thee " through thy seed," but *to thee and to thy seed*): still neither he, nor Isaac, nor Jacob, enjoyed the promise. For one of them served for hire, and the other was driven out: and he himself even was failing ᵇ through fear: and while he took some things indeed in war, others, unless he had had the aid of God, would have been destroyed. On this account the Apostle says, *with the heirs of the same promise;* not himself alone, he means; but the heirs also.

[3.] (ver. 13) *These all died in faith*, he says, *not having obtained ᶜ the promises.* At this place it is worth while to make two enquiries, how it is that after saying that [God] *translated Enoch, and he was not found, so that he did not see death*, he now says, *These all* DIED *in Faith*. And again, after saying, *they not having obtained the promises*, he declares that Noah had received a reward, *to the saving of his house*, and that Enoch had been *translated*, and that Abel *yet speaks*, and that Abraham had gained a hold on the land, and yet he says, *These all died in Faith, not having obtained the promises.* What then is it [that is meant]?

It is necessary to solve the first [difficulty], and then the second. *These all* (saith he) DIED *in faith.* The word *all* is used here not because all had died, but because with that one exception *all these had died*, whom we know to be dead.

(2) And the [statement] *not having obtained the promises*, is true: for surely the promise to Noah was not to be this [which is here spoken of]. But further, of what kind of *promises* is he speaking? For Isaac and Jacob did receive

---

HOM. 23.
¹ ἐλεγχομένην
Gen. xii. 7; x.ii. 15.

ᵇ ἐξέπιπτε: i.e. τῆς ὑποσχέσεως, "of the promise," is Mr. Field's interpretation; Mutianus has *pœne exciderat*.
ᶜ κομισάμενοι. This word is used by S. Chrys. throughout this passage without any variation of reading. The text of the Epistle here has λαβόντες, but in ver. 39, οὐκ ἐκομίσαντο.

the promises of the land; but as to Noah and Abel and Enoch, what kind of promises did they receive? Either then he is speaking concerning these three; or if concerning those others also, the promise was not this, that Abel should be admired, nor that Enoch should be translated, nor that Noah should be preserved [d], but these things indeed accrued to them for their virtue's sake, yet they were only a sort of foretastes of things to come. For God from the beginning, knowing that the human race needs much condescension, bestows on us not only the [good] things in the world to come, but also those here; as for instance, what Christ said even to His own disciples, *Whosoever hath left houses, or brethren, or sisters, or father, or mother, shall receive an hundred fold and shall inherit everlasting life.* And again, *Seek ye the kingdom of God, and all these things shall be added unto you.* Thou seest that these things are given by Him in the way of addition, that we might not faint? For just as the athletes have the benefit of careful attention, even when they are engaged in the combat, but do not then have the enjoyment of entire ease, as living under rules, yet nevertheless afterwards they enjoy it entire: so God also does not grant us here to partake of *entire* ease. For even here He does give [some].

[Heb.xi.13.]
[S. Matt. xix. 29.]
[ib. vi. 33.]
[see above p. 112.]

[4.] *But having seen them afar off,* he says [e], *and embraced them.* Here he hints at something mystical: that they received beforehand all the things which have been spoken concerning things to come; concerning the resurrection, concerning the Kingdom of Heaven, concerning the other things, which Christ proclaimed when He came, for these are *the promises* of which he speaks. Either then he means this, or, that they did not indeed receive them, but died in confidence respecting them, and they were [thus] confident through Faith only.

Having seen them afar off: four generations before; for after so many [generations], they went up out of Egypt.

[d] We must probably understand also, 'nor that the Patriarchs should 'live in Canaan:' the argument seems to require this; besides in the statement of the difficulty Abraham's having "got a hold on the land" is mentioned together with the blessings bestowed on Abel Enoch and Noah, as something already given them.

[e] S. Chrys. does not cite nor yet refer to the words καὶ πεισθέντες, *and were persuaded of them.* They are found in the common editions of the Epistle, but are not supposed to be a genuine part of the Sacred text.

And embraced them, saith he, and were glad. They were so persuaded of them as even to *embrace* [or *salute*] *them*, from the metaphor of persons on ship-board beholding from afar the cities [their homes] which they long for: which, before they enter them, they take and appropriate to them by words of greeting.

(ver. 10) *For they looked* (he saith) *for the*[1] *city which hath foundations, whose builder and maker is God.* Thou seest that they received them in this sense, in their already accepting them and being confident respecting them. If then to be confident is to receive, it is in your power also to receive. For these [saints], although they enjoyed not those [blessings], yet still by means of their longing desire saw them. Why now do these things happen? That we might be put to shame, in that they indeed, when things on earth were promised them, regarded them not but sought the future *city* [or *home*]: whereas God again and again speaks to us of *the home*[2] which is above, and yet we seek that which is here. He said to them, I will give you the things of the present [world]. But when He saw, or rather, when they shewed themselves worthy of greater things, then He no longer suffers them to receive these, but those greater ones; wishing to shew us that they are worthy of greater things, because they were not willing to be bound to these. As if one should promise play-things to an intelligent child, not that he might receive them, but by way of exhibiting his philosophy, when he asks for things more important. For this is to shew, that they held off from the land with so great earnestness, that they did not even accept what was given. Wherefore their posterity receive it on this account, for themselves were wort' y of the land.

What is, *the city which hath foundations?* for are not these [which are visible] *foundations?* in comparison of the other, they are not.

Whose Builder and Maker is God. O! what an enconium on that city!

[5.] (ver. 11) *By faith also Sarah herself*, he says. Here he began [speaking] in a way to put them to shame, in case, that is, they should shew themselves more faint-

---

[1] τὴν πόλιν

[2] πόλιν

hearted than a woman. But possibly some one might say, He.xi.12.
How [could it be] *by faith,* when she laughed? Nay while
her laughter indeed was from unbelief, her fear [was] from
Faith, for to say, *I laughed not,* arose from Faith. From Gn.
this then it appears that when unbelief had been cleared xviii. 15.
out, Faith came in its place.

*By faith also Sara herself received strength to conceive
seed even when she was past age*[f]*.* What is, *to conceive
seed*[1]*?* She who was become dead, who was barren, re- [1] εἰς κατα-
ceived power for the retaining of seed, for conception. For βολὴν
her imperfection was two-fold; first from her time of life, τος
for she was quite an aged person; secondly from nature, for
she was barren.

ver. 12. *Wherefore even from one they all sprang, as the
stars of the sky, and as the sand which is by the sea-shore.*
Wherefore (saith he) *even from one they all sprang.* Here
he not only says that she bare [a child], but that she also
became mother of so many as not even faithful wombs [are
mothers of]. *As the stars,* He saith. How then is it that
He often numbers them, although He said, *As the stars of* ib. xv. 5.
the heaven shall not be numbered, so neither shall your seed?
He either means the excess, or else [speaks of] those who
are continually being born. For [in the case] of one family
is it possible, tell me, to number their forefathers, as, such
an one son of such an one, such an one son of such an
one? But here such are the promises of God, so easy of (3)
accomplishment are His undertakings.

[6.] But if the things which He promised as additional,
are so admirable, so beyond expectation, so magnificent,
what will those be, to which these are an addition, to
which these are somewhat over and above? What then
can be more blessed than they who attain them? What
more wretched than those who miss them? For if a man
when driven out from his native country, is pitied by all;
and when he has lost an inheritance is considered by all
men as an object of compassion, with what tears ought he
to be bewailed, who fails of Heaven, and of the good

---

[f] καὶ παρὰ καιρὸν ἡλικίας. The common texts of S. Chrys. add here ἔτεκεν, in accordance with the common editions of the New Testament: but in neither case is it supposed to be genuine.

things there stored up? Or rather, he is not even to be wept for: for a person is wept for, when his calamity is one of which he is not himself the cause; but when of his own choice he has entangled himself in evil, he is not an object[1] of tears, but of wailings[2]; or rather even then of mourning[3]; since even our Lord JESUS Christ mourned and wept for Jerusalem, impious as it was. In very deed we are fit objects for lamentations innumerable, for wailings innumerable. If the whole world should receive a voice, both stones, and wood, and trees, and wild beasts, and birds, and fishes, and, in a word, the whole world, if, I say, it should receive a voice and bewail us who have failed of those good things, its wailing and its lamentation would be in no wise proportioned [to the calamity]. For what language, what intellect, will be able to represent to us that blessedness and virtue, that pleasure, that glory, that happiness, that splendour? *what eye hath not seen, and ear hath not heard, and what hath not entered into the heart of man* (he did not say, that they simply surpass [what we imagine]; but, never hath any man even conceived) *the things which God hath prepared for them that love Him.* For of what kind is it likely that those good things should be, of which God is the Preparer and Establisher? For if immediately after He had made us, when we had not yet done anything, He freely bestowed so great [favours], Paradise, familiar intercourse with Himself, promised us immortality, a life happy and freed from cares; what will He not bestow on those who have laboured and struggled so greatly, and endured so much on His behalf? For our sake He spared not His Only Begotten, for us when we were enemies He gave up His own SON to death; of what will He not count us worthy, now that we are become His friends? what will He not impart to us, now that He has reconciled us to Himself?

[7.] He both is abundantly and infinitely rich; and He desires and earnestly endeavours to obtain our friendship; we do not thus earnestly endeavour. What am I saying, 'do not earnestly endeavour?' We do not wish to obtain His blessings, so much as He wishes it. And that He wishes it more [than we] is proved by what He has done.

---

[1] ἄξιος
[2] θρήνων
[3] πένθους

1 Cor. ii. 9.

For while, for our own selves' sake, we with difficulty think He.xi.12. lightly of a little gold: He, for our sake, gave even His Son, His own [Son]. Beloved, let us make use of the love of God as we ought; let us reap the fruits of His friendship. For *ye are My friends* (He saith) *if ye do what I* S. John *say to you.* How wonderful! His enemies, who were at xv. 14. an infinite distance from Him, whom in all respects He excels by an incomparable superiority, these He has made His friends and calls them friends. What then should not one choose to suffer for the sake of this friendship? For the friendship of men we often risk our lives, but for that of God, we do not even give away our money. Our [condition] does indeed call for mourning, for mourning and tears and wailings, and loud lamentation and beating of the breast. We have fallen from our hope, we are cast down from our high estate, we have shewn ourselves unworthy of the honour of God; even after His benefits we are become unfeeling, and ungrateful. The devil has stripped us of all our good things. We who were counted worthy to be sons; we His brethren and fellow-heirs, are come to be in nothing different from His enemies that openly insult Him.

Henceforward, what consolation shall there be for us? He called us to Heaven, and we have thrust ourselves down to hell. *Swearing and lying and stealing and adultery, are* Hos. iv. *poured out upon the earth.* Some *mingle blood upon blood;* 2. and others do deeds worse than blood-shedding. Many of those that are wronged, many of those that are defrauded prefer ten thousand deaths to the suffering such things: and were they not influenced by the fear of God, would even have killed themselves, being so murderously disposed against themselves. Are not these things then worse than blood-shedding?

[8.] *Woe is me, my soul! for the godly man is perished* Micah *from the earth, and there is none upright among men;* let LXX. us also now cry out, first about our own selves: nay, do you, I beseech you, aid me in my lamentation.

Perhaps some are even disgusted and laugh. For this very cause ought we to make our lamentations the more intense, because we are so mad and beside ourselves, that we do not even know that we are mad, but laugh at things for which we ought to groan. O man! *there is wrath revealed from heaven against all ungodliness and unrighteousness of men; God will come manifestly: a fire will burn before Him, and round about Him will be a mighty tempest. A fire will burn before Him, and consume His enemies on every side. The day of the Lord is as a burning oven*, and no man lays up these things in his mind, but these tremendous and fearful doctrines are more despised than fables, and are trodden under foot. He that heareth, —there is no one: while they who laugh and make sport are—all. What resource will there be for us? whence shall we find safety? *we are undone, we are utterly consumed*, we are become the laughing-stock of our enemies, and a mockery for the heathen and the Demons. Now is the devil greatly elated; he glories and is glad. The angels to whom we had been entrusted are all ashamed and in sadness: there is no man to convert [you]: all means have been used up by us in vain, and we ourselves are regarded by you as idle talkers. It is seasonable in this our day also to call on the heaven, because there is no man that heareth; to take to witness the elements: *Hear, O heaven! and give ear, O earth! for the Lord hath spoken.*

Give a hand, stretch it forth, O ye who have not yet been overwhelmed, to them who are undone through their drunkenness: ye that are whole to them that are sick, ye that are sober-minded to them that are mad, that are giddily whirling round.

Let no man, I beseech you, prefer the favour of his friend to his salvation; and let your chiding and your rebuke look to one thing only,—his benefit. When one has been seized by a fever, even slaves lay hold of their Masters. For when that is pressing on him, throwing his mind into confusion, and a swarm of slaves are standing by, they recognize not the law of Master and Servant, in the calamity of their Master.

Let us collect ourselves, I exhort you: there are daily wars, submersions [of towns], destructions innumerable all around us, and on every side the wrath of God is enclosing us as in a net. And we, as though we were well-pleasing to

Him, are thus in security. We all make our hands ready for unjust gains, none for helping others: all for plundering, none for protecting: each one is in earnest as to how he shall increase his possessions; no one as to how he shall assist him that is in need: each one has much anxious care how he may add to his wealth; no one how he may save his own soul. One and the same fear possesses all, lest (you say) we should become poor; lest we should fall into hell, [as to that] no man is in anxiety and trembling. These are the things that call for lamentation, these are what call for accusation, these are what call for reprobation. He.xi.12.

[9.] These however are not the things I wish to speak of, but I am constrained by my grief. Forgive me: I am forced by sorrow to utter many things, even things which I do not wish. I see that our wound is grievous, that our calamity admits of no comfort, that woes which have overtaken us are beyond the reach of consolation. We are undone. *O that my head were waters and mine eyes a fountain of tears,* that I might lament. Let us weep, beloved, let us weep, let us lament. Jerem. ix. 1.

Possibly there may be some here who say, He talks to us of nothing but lamentation, nothing but tears. It was not my wish, believe me, it was not my wish: [I wished] rather to go through a course of commendations and praises: but now it is not the season for these things. Beloved, it is not lamenting which is grievous, but the doing things which call for lamentations. Sorrow is not the thing to shrink from, but the committing things that call for sorrow. Do not thou be punished, and I will not mourn. Do not die, and I will not weep. If the body, however, lies dead, thou callest on all to grieve with thee, and holdest them to be devoid of sympathy who do not mourn: And when the soul is perishing, dost thou tell us *not* to mourn?

But I cannot be a father, if I do not weep. I am a father full of affection. Hear how Paul exclaims, *My little children, of whom I travail in birth again:* what mother in child-birth utters cries so bitter as he! Would that it were possible for thee to see the very fire that is in my heart, Gal. iv. 19.

and thou wouldest know, that I burn [with grief] more intense than any woman, or girl that suffers untimely widowhood. She does not so mourn over her husband, nor any father over his son, as I do over this multitude that is here with us.

I see no progress. Every thing turns to calumnies and accusations. No man makes it his business to please God; but (says he) 'such an one let us speak evil of or such an 'one.' 'Such an one is unfit to be among the Clergy.' 'Such 'an one does not lead a respectable life.' When we ought to be grieving for our own evils, we judge others, whereas we ought not to do this, even when we are pure from sins. *For who maketh thee to differ* (saith he) *and what hast thou which thou didst not receive? but if thou hast received it, why dost thou glory, as though thou hadst not received it? And thou, why dost thou judge thy brother*, being thyself full of innumerable evils? When thou sayest, Such an one is a bad man, and a spendthrift, and vicious, think of thyself, and examine strictly thy own [condition], and thou wilt repent of the things which thou hast said. For there is not any, no not any, such powerful stimulus to virtue, as the recollecting of our sins.

If we turn over these two things in our minds, we shall be enabled to attain the promised blessings, we shall be enabled to cleanse ourselves and wipe away [what is amiss]. Only let us take serious thought sometime or other; let us be anxious about the matter, beloved. Let us grieve here in reflection, that we may not grieve yonder in punishment, but may enjoy the everlasting blessings, where *pain and sorrow and sighing are fled away*, that we may attain to the good things which surpass man's understanding, in Christ Jesus our Lord, for to Him is glory and power for ever and ever. Amen.

HOMILY XXIV.

HEB. xi. 13—16.

These all died in faith[1], *not having received the promises,* [1 κατὰ πίστιν] *but having seen them afar off, and embraced them, and confessed that they were strangers and pilgrims on the earth. For they that say such things, declare plainly that they seek a country. And truly if they had been mindful of that country from whence they came out, they might have had opportunity to have returned. But now they desire a better country, that is, an heavenly; wherefore God is not ashamed*[2] *to be called Their God, for He hath prepared for them a city.* [2 lit. ashamed of them, to be &c.]

THE first virtue, yea the whole of virtue is to be a stranger to this world, and a sojourner, and to have nothing in common with things here, but to hang loose from them, as from things strange to us; As those blessed disciples did, of whom he says, *They wandered about in sheep-skins, in goat-skins, being destitute, afflicted, tormented*[3]: *of whom the world was not worthy.* [infra ver. 37, 38. ³ill-treated]

They indeed then spake of themselves as *strangers;* but Paul said somewhat much beyond this: for not merely did he call himself a stranger, but said that he was dead to the world, and that the world was dead to him. *For the world* (he saith) *has been crucified to me and I to the world.* [Gal. vi. 14.] But we, being at home[4] and quite alive busy ourselves about all things here as citizens. And the very thing which righteous men were to the world, *strangers* and *dead,* that we are to Heaven. And the very thing which they were to Heaven, alive and as its citizens [whose home and interests were there], that we are to the world. Wherefore [4 πολῖτα.]

we are dead, because we have refused that which is indeed life, and have chosen this life which is but for a time. Wherefore we have provoked God to wrath, because when the enjoyments of Heaven have been set before us, not even so are we willing to separate ourselves from things on earth, but, just like worms, we turn about from the earth to the earth, and again from this to that [1], and in short are not willing to lift up ourselves even for a little while, nor to withdraw ourselves from human affairs; but just as if we were thoroughly immersed in our torpor and sleep and drunkenness, are stupified with imaginations.

[2.] And just as those who are under the power of sweet sleep lie on their bed not only during the night, but even when the very morning has overtaken them, and it is become bright day, and are not ashamed to indulge in pleasure, and to make the season of business and activity a time of slumber and indolence, so truly we also, when the day is drawing near, when the night is far spent, or rather the day, for *work* (it is said) *while it is day;* when it is day we practise all that belongs to the night, sleeping, dreaming, indulging in luxurious fancies; and the eyes of our understanding are closed as well as those of our body; we speak amiss, we talk absurdly; even if a person inflict a deep wound upon us, if he carry off all our substance, if he set the very house on fire, we are not so much as conscious of it.

Or rather, we do not even wait for others to do this, but we do it ourselves, piercing and wounding ourselves every day, lying in unseemly fashion, and stripped bare of all credit, all honour, neither ourselves concealing our shameful deeds, nor permitting others to do so, but lying exposed to public disgrace, to the ridicule, the numberless jests of spectators and passers by.

[3.] Do ye not suppose that the wicked themselves laugh at those who are of like characters to themselves, and condemn them? For inasmuch as God has placed within us a tribunal which cannot be corrupted by bribes, nor ever utterly destroyed, even though we come to the very lowest depth of vice; for this cause even the wicked themselves give sentence against themselves; and if one

---

[1] from this piece to earth o. that

S. John ix. 4.

call them that very thing which indeed they are, they are ashamed, they are angry, they say that it is an insult. Thus they condemn the very things which they practise, even if not by their deeds, yet by their words, by their conscience, nay rather [I may say] even by their deeds. For when they carry on their practices out of sight and in concealment, they exhibit the strongest proof of the opinion which they hold concerning the thing itself. For wickedness is so manifest, that all men are its accusers, even those who follow after it, while such is the quality of virtue, that it is admired even by those who do not emulate it. For even the fornicator will commend chastity, and the covetous man will condemn injustice, and the passionate man will admire patience, and he will blame quarrelsomeness, and the wanton [will blame] wantonness.

He.xi.13.

How then is it (you say) that he pursues these things? From excessive indolence, not because he judges it well [so to do]; otherwise he would not have been ashamed of the thing itself, nor would he have denied it when another accused him. Nay many when they have been caught, not enduring the shame, have even hanged themselves. So strong is the witness within us in behalf of what is good and becoming. Thus what is good is brighter than the sun, and the contrary [things] more unsightly than any thing.

[4.] The saints were *strangers and sojourners*. How and in what way? And where doth Abraham confess himself to be *a stranger and a sojourner?* Perhaps indeed he even himself confessed it[1]: but David both confessed, *I am a stranger*, and what? *as all my fathers were.* For they who dwell in tents, they who purchase even burial places for money, evidently were in some sense strangers, as they had not even where to bury their dead.

(2)

[1] see Gen. xxiii. 4. Ps. xxxix. 12.

What then? Did they mean that they were *strangers* in respect of that land that is in Palestine? By no means: but in respect of the whole world: and this with reason; for they saw therein none of the things which they were wishing for, but every thing foreign and strange to them. They indeed wished to practise themselves in virtue: but here there was much wickedness, and things were quite foreign to them. They had no friend, no familiar acquaintance, save only some few.

Hom. 24. But how were they *strangers?* They had no care for things here. And this they shewed not by words, but by very deeds. How and in what manner?

He said to Abraham, "Leave thy country, that which "seems [thy country] and come to one that belongs to "others:" And he did not cleave to his own [friends and home] but gave it up as unconcernedly as if he were about to leave a foreign land. He said to him, "Offer up thy "son," and he offered him up as if he had not a son; as if he had divested himself of his nature, so he offered him up. The wealth which he had acquired was common to all passers by, and this he accounted as nothing. He was wont to yield up the first places to others: to throw himself into dangers; to suffer troubles innumerable. He built no splendid houses, he enjoyed no luxuries, he had no care about dress, which all belong to the things of this world; but lived in all respects as one whose home is in the City which is yonder; he exhibited hospitality; brotherly love; mercifulness; forbearance; contempt for wealth and for present glory, and for all else.

And his son too was such as himself: when he was driven hither and thither, when war was made on him, he yielded and gave way, as being in a foreign land. For foreigners, whatever they suffer, endure it, as not being in their own country. Even when his wife was taken from him, he endured this also as being in a strange land: and lived in all respects as one whose home was above, displaying sobermindedness and a well ordered life [1]. For after he had begotten a son, he had no more commerce with his wife, and it was when the flower of his youth had passed that he married her, shewing that he did it not from passion, but in subservience to the promise of God.

And what did Jacob? Did he not seek bread only and raiment, which are asked for by those who are strangers indeed, by those that have come to great poverty? When he was driven out, did he not give place just as a stranger? Did he not serve for hire? Did he not suffer afflictions innumerable, every where, just as a stranger would?

[5.] And these things (saith he) they said, like persons *seeking* their *country.* Ah! how great is the difference!

[1] σωφρο-σύνην κοσμι-ότητα

They indeed were in travail-pains each day, wishing to be released from this world, and to return to their own country. But we, on the contrary, if a fever attack us, neglecting every thing, just like little children which sob and cry, are frightened at death.

Nor is it without reason that we are thus affected. For since we do not live here like strangers, nor as if we were hastening to our proper country, but are like persons that are going away to punishment, for this cause we grieve, because we have not used our circumstances as we ought, but have turned the order of things upside down. Hence we lament when we ought to rejoice: hence we shudder, just like murderers or robber chiefs, when they are going to be placed before the judgment-seat, and are thinking over all the things they have done, and for this cause are fearing and trembling.

Not such however were they of old, but they were in haste [to depart]. Nay Paul even groaned [for it]; *And we ourselves also* (he says) *who are in the tabernacle do groan being burdened*. Such was Abraham and they who were with him, *strangers*, saith he, they were in respect of the whole world, and were *seeking a country*.

What sort of *country* was this? Was it that which they had left? By no means. For what hindered them if at least they had wished, from returning again, and becoming settled there? but they sought that [home] which is in Heaven. Thus they were earnestly desirous for their departure hence, and so were they pleasing to God; for *God was not ashamed to be called their God*.

[6.] Ah! how great a dignity! He vouchsafed *to be called their God*. What dost thou say? He is called the God of the earth, and the God of Heaven, and hast thou set it down as a great thing that *He is not ashamed to be called their God?* A great thing and truly great thing this is, and a proof of exceeding blessedness. How? Because He is called God of earth and of heaven in the same sense as [He is called God] of the Gentiles: in that He created and formed them: but [God] of those holy men, not in this sense, but as being a genuine friend.

And I will make it plain to you by an example; as in

Hom. 24. the case of [slaves] in large households, when any of them, who have been placed over the household, are very highly esteemed, and manage every thing themselves, and can use great freedom of speech towards their masters, the Master is called after them, and one may find many instances of persons so called. But what do I say? as we might say the God, not of the Gentiles but of the world, so we might say *the God of Abraham*. But you do not know how great a dignity this is, because neither do we attain to it. For as now the Lord is called [the God] of all Christians, and yet the name goes beyond our deserts: consider how exceeding great it would be if He were called the God of one [individual]! He who is called the God of the whole world is *not ashamed to be called* the God of three men: and with good reason: for the saints would turn the scale, I do not say against the world [1] but against ten-thousand such [worlds]. *For one man who doeth the will of the Lord* [a], *is better than ten thousand transgressors.*

Now that it was in this sense that they called themselves *strangers*, is manifest. But supposing that these [Patriarchs] said that they were *strangers* [only] on account of the strange land [they were in], why did David also [call himself a stranger]? Was not he a king? was not he a prophet? did he not spend his life in his own country? On what account then does he say, *I am a stranger and a sojourner?* In what sense art thou a stranger? *as* (saith he) *all my fathers were*. Thou seest that they too were strangers? We have a country, he means, but not that which is really our country. But in what sense art thou thyself a stranger? As to the earth. Therefore they also [were strangers] in respect of the earth: For *as they were*, he says, so also am I; and as he, so they too.

[1] see on ver. 38, pp. 314 sqq. Ecclus. xvi. 3.

Ps. xxxix. 12.

(3) [7.] Let us now at least become strangers; that God may *not be ashamed of us to be called our God*. For it is a shame to Him, when He is called the God of the wicked, and He Himself also is ashamed of them; just as He is

---

[a] Mr. Field observes that S. Chrys. repeatedly cites Ecclus. xvi. 3. thus; and that while the Greek is simply, *for one is better than a thousand*, the Syriac seems to have read ὅτι κρείσσων εἷς ποιῶν θέλημα &c. So the English version has "for one *that is just*."

glorified when He is [called the God] of the good and the kind, and of them that cultivate virtue. For if *we* decline to be called the masters of our wicked slaves, and give them up; and should any one come to us and say, 'such 'a one does innumerable bad things, he is your slave, is he 'not?' we immediately say; By no means, wiping off the disgrace: for a slave has a close relation to his master, and the discredit passes from the one to the other ᵇ.—But they were so glowing, so full of confidence towards Him, that not only was He *not ashamed to be called* from them, but He even Himself says, *I am the God of Abraham, and the God of Isaac, and the God of Jacob.* HE.xi.16.

Exod. iii. 6.

Let us also, my beloved, become *strangers;* that God may *not be ashamed of us;* that He may not be ashamed, and deliver us up to Hell. Such were they who said, *Lord, have we not prophesied in Thy Name, and in Thy Name have done many wonderful works!* But see what Christ says to them: *I know you not:* the very thing which masters would do, when wicked slaves run to them [for protection], wishing to wipe off the disgrace. *I know you not*, saith He. How then is it that Thou punishest those whom Thou knowest not? I said, *I know not*, in a different sense: that is, "I deny you, and refuse to have any thing "to do with you." But God forbid that we should hear this fatal and terrible utterance. For if they who cast out devils and prophesied, were denied, because they had not a life suitable thereto; how much more we!

S. Matt. vii. 22.

[8.] And how (you ask) is it possible that they should be denied, who have displayed prophetic powers, and have wrought miracles, and cast out devils? It is probable they were afterwards changed, and became wicked; and in consequence of this were nothing benefited, even by their former virtue. For not only ought we to have our beginnings splendid, but the end also more splendid still.

For tell me, does not the Orator take pains to make what comes at the end of his speech splendid, that he may retire with applause? He that administers a public office in a city, does he not make the most splendid display at the

---

ᵇ The sentence is left incomplete: The common editions add, "much more "does God."

close of his administration? The wrestler, if he do not make a more splendid display then, and be the conqueror unto the end, and if after vanquishing all [before] he be vanquished by the last [of his antagonists], is not all of no profit to him? Should the pilot have crossed the whole ocean, yet if he wreck his vessel at the port, has he not lost all his former labour? And what [of] the Physician? Is it not the fact that if, after he has freed the sick man from his disease, yet at the very time when he is on the point of completely curing him, he should destroy him, is it not the fact that he has destroyed his whole [work]? So too in respect of Virtue, as many as have not placed on the end suitable to the beginning, and in unison and harmony with it, are ruined, and utterly undone. Such are they who have sprung forth from the starting place bright and exulting, and afterwards have become faint and feeble. Wherefore they are also deprived of the prize, and not acknowledged by their master.

Let us listen to these things, those of us who are in love with wealth: for this is the greatest of iniquities. *For the love of money is the root of all evils.* Let us listen, those of us who wish to make our present possessions greater, let us listen and at length cease from our covetousness, that we may not hear those words which they [will hear]. Let us listen to them now, and be on our guard, that we may not hear them then. Let us hear now with fear, that we may not then hear with vengeance: *Depart from Me* (saith He) *I never knew you,* no not even then (He means) when ye were making a display of prophecyings, and were casting out devils.

It is probable that in these words He also hints something else, that even at that very time they were wicked; and that at the beginning, grace wrought even by the instrumentality of the unworthy. For if it wrought even through Balaam, much more through the unworthy, for the sake of those who shall profit [by it].

But if even signs and wonders did not avail to deliver from punishment; much more, if a man happen to be in the dignity of the Priesthood[1]: even if he arrive at the highest honour, even if grace work in him to his ordination,

[1] ἀξιώματι ἱερατικῷ

Obedience. The different virtues to be practised in order. 283

even if [it work in him] unto all the other [grades], for   He.xi.16.
the sake of those who need his rule and care[1], he also shall   ¹τῆς προ-
hear, *I never knew thee*, no, not even then when grace was   στασίας
working in thee.

[9.] O! how strict shall the investigation there be as to
purity! How is that, even of itself, sufficient to introduce us
into the kingdom? while the absence of it gives up the man
[to destruction], though he have ten thousand miracles and
signs to exhibit. For nothing is so pleasing to God as an
excellent course of life. *If ye love Me*, saith He, He did not   S. John
say, 'work miracles,' but what? *keep My commandments.*   xiv. 15.
And again, *I call you friends*, not when ye cast out devils,   ib. xv.
but *if ye keep My words*. For those [powers] indeed come   14.
of the gift of God: but the other after the gift of God, of
our own diligence also. Let us endeavour earnestly to become friends of God, and not remain enemies to Him.

These things we are ever saying, these exhortations we
are ever giving, both to ourselves and to you: but nothing
more is gained. Wherefore also I am afraid. And I would
have wished indeed to be silent, so as not to increase your
danger. For when a person often hears, and even so does
not act, this is to provoke the Lord to anger. But I fear
also myself that other danger, the [danger] of silence, if
when I am appointed to the ministering of the word, I
should hold my peace.

What shall we then do that we may be saved? Let us
begin [the practice of] virtue, as we have opportunity: let
us portion out the virtues to ourselves, just as labourers
do their works of husbandry; in this month let us gain
the mastery over evil-speaking, injuriousness, unjust anger;
and let us lay down a law for ourselves, and say, To-day
let us successfully accomplish this thing. Again, in this
month let us school ourselves in the patient endurance of
evil, and in another, in some other virtue: And when we
have got into the habit of this one virtue let us proceed to
another, just as in the things we learn at school, carefully
preserving what we have already gained, and acquiring
others in addition.

After this let us proceed to contempt for riches. First
let us restrain our hands from taking more than is right,

and then let us give alms. Let us not absolutely confound every thing, with the very same hands both slaying and forsooth doing works of mercy. After this, turn we to some other virtue, and from that, to another. *Filthiness and foolish talking and jesting, let it not be even named among you.* Let us be thus far in the right way.

There is no need of spending money, there is no need of labour, none of the sweat of the brow, it is enough to have only the will, and all is done. There is no need to travel a long way, nor to cross a limitless ocean, but to be in earnest, and of ready mind, and to put a bridle on the tongue. Unseasonable reproaches, anger, disorderly lusts, luxuriousness, expensiveness, cast we off; and the desire of wealth also from our soul, perjury and habitual oaths.

If we thus cultivate ourselves, plucking out the thorns which were there before, and casting in the heavenly seed, we shall be able to attain the good things which are promised. For the Husbandman will come and will lay us up in His Garner, and we shall attain to all good things, to the which may we all attain, by the grace and mercy of our Lord Jesus Christ, with Whom to the Father and also to the Holy Ghost, be glory power honour, now and for ever, and world without end. Amen.

HOMILY XXV.

HEB. xi. 17—19.

By faith [Abraham[a]] when he was tried offered up Isaac, and he that had received the promises offered up his only-begotten son, of whom it was said, In Isaac shall thy seed be called: accounting that God was able to raise him up even from the dead; from whence also he received him in a figure.

GREAT indeed was the faith of Abraham. For while in the case of Abel, and of Noah, and of Enoch, there was an opposition of reasonings only [against faith], and it was necessary to go beyond human reasonings; in this case it was necessary not only to go beyond human reasonings, but to manifest also somewhat more. For what was of God[1] seemed to be at variance with what was of God; and faith to be opposed to faith, and command to promise.

[1] τὰ τοῦ Θεοῦ the acts and words of God

I mean this: He had said, *Come forth out of thy country, and from thy kindred, and I will give thee this land.* He gave him none inheritance in it, no not so much as to set his foot on. Seest thou how the things which resulted were at variance with the promise? Again He saith, *In Isaac shall thy seed be called,* and he believed: and again He saith, Sacrifice to Me this child, who was to fill all the world from his seed. Thou seest the opposition between the commands and the promise? He enjoined things that were in contradiction to the promises, and yet not even so was the righteous man staggered, nor did he say that he had been deceived.

Gen. xii. 1, 7. Acts vii. 5.

Gen. xxi. 12.

For you indeed, he means, could not say this, that He has promised ease and gave tribulation. For in our case, the very things which He promised, these also He performs.

[a] Mr. Field's text omits Ἀβραὰμ, and has δεξάμενος for ἀναδεξάμενος.

^{Hom. 25.}
S. John xvi. 33.
S. Matt. x. 38.
S. John xii. 25.
S. Luke xiv. 27, 33.
S. Matt. x. 18.
ib. 36.

How so? *In the world* (He saith) *ye shall have tribulation. He that taketh not his cross and followeth Me, is not worthy of Me. He that hateth not his life shall not find it.* And, *He that forsaketh not all that he hath, and followeth after Me, is not worthy of Me.* And again, *Ye shall be brought before rulers and kings for My sake.* And again, *A man's foes shall be they of his own household.* But the things which pertain to rest are yonder.

With regard to Abraham however, the contrary [was the case]. He was enjoined to do things which were opposed to the promises; and yet not even so was he troubled, nor was he staggered, nor did he think that he had been deceived. But you are enduring nothing except what was promised, and yet you are troubled.

[2.] He heard what was at variance with the promises from Him Himself who had made those promises; and yet he was not disturbed, but did them as if they had been in harmony [therewith]. For in fact they were in harmony; being opposed indeed according to human calculations, but in harmony [when viewed] by Faith. And how this was, the Apostle himself has taught us, by saying, *calculating*[b] *that God was able to raise Him up, even from the dead.* From the same faith (he means) by which he believed that God freely gave what existed not[c], and raised up one that was dead, by the same was he persuaded that He would also raise him up after he had been slain in sacrifice. For it was alike impossible (to human calculation, I mean) from a womb which was dead and grown old and already become useless for child-bearing to give a child, and to raise again [to life] one who had been slain. But his previous faith prepared the way for the things that were to come.

And see; the good things came first, and the hard things afterwards, in his old age. But for you, on the contrary, (he says) the sad things are first, and the good things last. This [is directed] against those who presume to say, 'It is

---

[b] λογισάμενος. The cognate word λογισμὸς is used throughout for our "reasoning," "calculation."

[c] οὐκ ὄντα ἐχαρίσατο, i. e. Isaac. See Rom. iv. 17, *Before God, in whom he believed, who quickeneth the dead, and calleth those things which be not as though they were* (τὰ μὴ ὄντα ὡς ὄντα); and for the next clause, see ib. ver. 19, *He considered not his own body, now dead, nor yet the deadness of Sarah's womb:* to which, so to say, life was restored.

'after death that He has promised us the good things; perhaps He has deceived us.' He points out that *God is able to raise up even from the dead*, and if God be able to raise from the dead, without all doubt He will pay all [that He has promised].

But if Abraham believed so many years before *that God is able to raise from the dead*, much more ought we to believe it. Thou seest (which was the very thing I at first said) that death had not yet entered in, and yet at once He drew them to the hope of the resurrection, yea and led them to such full assurance, that when bidden, they even slay their own sons, and readily offer up those from whom they expected to people the world.

Yea and another thing too he shews by saying, that *God tempted Abraham*. What then? did not God know that the man was noble and approved? For what purpose then He tempt him? [He did it,] not that He might Himself learn it, but that He might shew it to the others, and make his fortitude manifest to all [d]. And here also he points out the cause of trials, that they may not suppose that they suffer these things as being forsaken [of God]. For in their case indeed, it is even unavoidable that they should have trials, because of there being many who persecuted or insidiously attacked them: but in Abraham's case, what need was there to devise trials for him which did not [otherwise] exist? Now this trial as is evident took place by His command. The others indeed happened by His allowance, but this even by His command. If then temptations make men approved in such wise that even where there is not [otherwise] a cause God exercises His own athletes; much more ought we to bear all things nobly.

And here he said emphatically, *By faith, when he was tried, he offered up Isaac*, for there was no other cause for his bringing the offering but that.

[3.] After this he pursues the same thought. No one (he says) could allege, that he had another son, and that he expected that the promise would be fulfilled from him, and that on this account he confidently offered up this one. *And* (his words are) *he offered up his only-begotten*

HE.xi.19.

Gen. xxii. 1.

---

[d] [See S. Cyr. Alex. Glaph. p. 87 A B C]

Hom. 25. [*son*], *he who had received the promises.* Why sayest thou *only-begotten?* what then? of whom was Ishmael sprung? I mean *only-begotten* (he would say) so far as relates to the word of the promise. For for this cause after saying, *Only-begotten,* shewing that is on this account that he says it, he added, *Of whom it was said, In Isaac shall thy seed be called,* [*in*] that is, " from " him. Thou seest how he admires what was done by the Patriarch? *In Isaac shall thy seed be called,* and that son he brought to be slain as a sacrifice.

Afterwards, that no one may suppose he does this in despair, and that in consequence of this command he had cast away that Faith[1], but may understand that this also was indeed of faith, he says that he retained that faith[2] also, although it seem to be at variance with this. But it was not at variance. For he did not measure the power of God by human calculations, but committed all to faith. And hence he was not afraid to say, that God was *able to raise him up, even from the dead.*

From whence also he received him in a figure[3], that is by a pattern[4], by the ram, he means. How? The ram, that is, having been slain, he was saved: so that by means of the ram he received him again, having slain it in his stead. But these things were types: for here it is the Son of God who is slain.

And observe, I beseech you, how great is His love to mankind. For inasmuch as a great favour was about to be bestowed on men, He, wishing to do this, not as a favour, but as if He were a debtor, arranges that a man should first give up his own son on account of God's command, in order that He Himself might seem to be doing nothing great in giving up His own Son, since a man had done this before Him; [nay,] that He might be supposed to do it not of grace, but of debt. For with respect to those whom we love, we wish to do them this kindness in addition to others, [viz.] to appear first to have received some little thing from them, and then in consequence to give them all: and we are more proud of receiving than of giving; and we do not say, We gave him this, but, We received this from him.

[1] conviction
[2] conviction
[3] ἐν παραβολῇ
[4] ἐν ὑποδείγματι, see ch. ix. 9, 23.

Good things of this world given to those who value them not. 289

From whence also (are his words) *he received him in a figure*, i.e. as in a riddle [e] (for the ram was as it were a figure of Isaac) or, as in a type. For since the sacrifice had been completed, and Isaac slain in his intention and will [1], for this cause He bestows him freely on the Patriarch.

He. xi. 19.

[1] τῇ προαιρέσει

[4.] Thou seest, that what I am constantly saying, is shewn in this case also? When we have proved that our mind is made perfect, and have shewn that we disregard earthly things, then are earthly things also bestowed on us; but not before; lest being bound to them already, we should be bound still more by receiving them. Loose thyself from thy slavery first (He saith), and then receive [earthly goods], that thou mayest receive them no longer as a slave, but as a master. Despise riches, and thou shalt be rich; Despise honour, and thou shalt be honoured; Despise the avenging thyself on thine enemies, and then shalt thou attain it; Despise repose, and then thou shalt receive it: that in receiving it thou mayest receive it not as a prisoner, nor as a slave, but as a freeman.

(2)

For just as in the case of little children, when the child eagerly desires childish playthings, we hide them from him with much care, as a ball, for instance, and such like things, that he may not be hindered from things that are necessary; but when he thinks little of them, and no longer eagerly desires them, we fearlessly give them to him, knowing that henceforth no harm can come to him from them, the desire no longer having strength enough to draw him away from things necessary; so God also, when He sees that we are no longer eagerly desirous of the things of this world, thenceforward permits us to use them. For we possess them as freemen and grown men, not as children.

For [in proof] that if thou despise the avenging thyself on thine enemies, thou wilt then attain it, hear what he says, *If thine enemy hunger, feed him; if he thirst, give him drink*, and he added, *for in so doing, thou shalt heap coals of fire on his head*. And again, that if thou despise

Rom. xii. 20.

---

[e] ἐν αἰνίγματι, where one thing is said, and another covertly meant: as the expression is used 1 Cor. xiii. 12, of our present knowledge of the Blessedness of Heaven.

VOL. VII.   U

riches, thou shalt then obtain them, hear Christ saying, *There is no man which hath left father, or mother, or houses, or brethren, who shall not receive an hundred fold, and shall inherit everlasting life.* And that if thou despise glory, thou shalt then attain it, again hear Christ Himself saying, *He that will be first among you, let him be your minister.* And again, *For whosoever shall humble himself, he shall be exalted.*

What sayest thou? If I give drink to mine enemy, do I then punish him? if I give up my goods, do I then possess them? if I humble myself, shall I then be exalted? Yea, saith He, for such is My power, to give contraries by means of contraries. I abound in resources and in contrivances: be not afraid. The 'Nature of things' follows My will: it is not I that follow Nature. I am the Maker of all things: I am not led [or impelled] by them: wherefore also I am able to alter their form and order.

[5.] And why dost thou wonder that [it is so] in these instances? for thou wilt find the same also in all other cases. If thou injure [another], thou art injured [thyself]¹; if thou art injured, then thou art not injured; if thou punish [another], then hast thou not punished [him], but hast punished thyself. For *he that loveth iniquity*, it is said, *hateth his own soul.* Seest thou that thou dost not injure, but hast been injured [thyself]ᶠ? For this cause also Paul saith, *Why do ye not rather endure injury?* Dost thou perceive that this is not to be injured?

When thou insultest [another], then art thou insulted [thyself]. And in some measure people in general know this: as when they say one to another, 'Let us go away, 'do not disgrace yourself.' Why? because the difference is great between thee and him: for however much thou insultest him, he accounts it a credit. Let us consider this in all cases, and raise ourselves above insults. I will tell you how.

ᶠ This reading adopted by Mr. Field, is found only in one MS. followed by Savile and the later editions: the other authorities, including Mutianus' version have, "Seest thou that thou hast not been injured, but injurest?" Perhaps this may be the true reading, S. Chrys. in these words turning his address to those who are suffering worldly wrong: and saying that if they patiently endure, they are not the sufferers, but inflict suffering on their oppressors, though the expression ἀδικεῖς is very strong.

Should we have a contest even with the very person who wears the [imperial] purple, let us consider that in insulting him, we insult ourselves. For [thereby] we ourselves become worthy to be disgraced. Tell me, what dost thou mean? when thou art a citizen of Heaven, and hast the Philosophy that is above, dost thou disgrace thyself with him *that mindeth earthly things?* For though he be in possession of countless riches, though he be in high place of power, he does not as yet know thy Good. Do not in disgracing him, disgrace thyself. Spare thyself, not him. Honour thyself, not him. Is there not some Proverb such as this, He that honoureth[1], honoureth himself? With good reason: for he honours not the other, but himself. Hear what a certain wise man says, *Do honour to thy soul according to the dignity thereof. According to the dignity thereof*, what is this? If he have defrauded [thee] (it means), do not thou defraud [him]. If he has insulted [thee], do not thou insult [him].

[6.] Tell me, I pray thee, if some poor man has taken away dirt which had been thrown out of thy court, wouldst thou for this have had a court of justice to sit? Surely not. Wherefore? Lest thou shouldst disgrace thyself; lest all men should condemn thee. The same also happens in this case. For the rich man is poor, and the more rich he is, the poorer is he in that which is indeed poverty. Gold is dirt, cast out in the court, not lying in thy house, for thy house is Heaven. For this, then, wilt thou have a lawsuit in a Court of Justice, and will not thy fellow Citizens on high condemn thee? will they not cast thee out from their country, thee who art so mean, who art so shabby, as to choose to contend for a little dirt? For if the world were thine, and then some one had taken it [from thee], oughtest thou to pay any attention to it?

Knowest thou not, that if thou wert to put the world [in the scale] ten times over or an hundred times, or ten thousand times, yea and twice as much as that, it is not comparable even to the very smallest portion of the good things that are in Heaven? He then who admires the things that are here has cast a slight on those which are yonder, seeing that he judges these worthy of his earnest regard, though so far

HE.xi.19.

Phil. iii. 19.

[1] *or*, respects [another], respects &c.

Ecclus. x. 28.

(3)

inferior to the other. Nay, rather indeed he will not be able to admire those other. For how [can he], whilst he is overcome by amazement at these earthly things? Let us cut through the cords and entanglements: for this is what earthly things are.

How long shall we be stooping down? How long shall we devise evil one against another, like wild beasts; like fishes? Nay rather, the wild beasts do not attack each other, but [only] animals of a different tribe. A bear for instance does not readily kill a bear, nor does a serpent kill a serpent, having respect for the sameness of race. But thou, with him that is the same race with thee, when thou hast also grounds of duty[1] without number, as, common origin, rational faculties, the knowledge of God, [nay] the force of nature, ten thousand other things besides, him, I say, who is thy kinsman, and partaker of the same nature—him thou killest, and involvest him in evils innumerable. For what, if thou dost not thrust thy sword, nor plunge thy right hand in his neck, other things more grievous than this thou doest, when thou involvest him in perpetual sufferings. For if thou hadst accomplished that other deed, thou wouldst have freed him from anxiety, but now thou encompassest him with hunger, with slavery, with feelings of impatience and indignation, with many sins. These things I say, and shall not cease to say, not [as] preparing you to commit murder: nor as encouraging you to proceed to some crime short of that; but that you may not be confident, as supposing that you will not be brought to punishment. *For* (it saith) *he that taketh away a livelihood* and asketh bread, it saith [g].

[1] δικαιώματα

Ecclus. xxxiv.22.

[7.] Let us at length keep our hands to ourselves, or rather, let us not keep them [to ourselves], but stretch them out in an honourable way, not for unjust gains, but for alms-giving. Let us not have our hand unfruitful nor withered; for the hand which doeth not alms is withered;

[g] καὶ ἄρτον αἰτῶν, φησί. There is great variation in the MSS. of this passage: and possibly the true reading is lost. S. Chrys. partly quotes Ecclus. xxxi. 22. of the Septuagint (xxxiv. 22 of our Version) "He that taketh "away his living slayeth his neighbour, "and he that defraudeth the hireling "of his hire is a blood-shedder." As the text stands we must suppose that he is alluding to sayings which had become proverbial, and that his hearers would supply the words, "is a murderer;" or "is the same."

and that which also grasps more than its due, is polluted <u>He.xi.10.</u> and unclean.

Let no one eat with such hands as these; for this is an insult to the guests that have been invited. For, tell me, if a man when he had made us lie down on tapestry, and a ¹ ταπήτων soft covering of a couch, and fine linen interwoven with gold, in a great and splendid house, and had set by us a great multitude of attendants, and had prepared a table ¹ of ¹ πίνακα silver and gold, and filled it with many dainties of great cost and of all sorts, then urged us to eat, provided we would only endure his besmearing his hands with mire or with human ordure, and so sitting down to meat with us— would any man endure this infliction? would he not rather have considered it an insult? Indeed I think he would, and that he would have straightway started off. But now in fact, thou seest not hands [only] filled with what is indeed filth, but even the very food, and yet thou dost not start off, nor avoid, nor find fault. Nay, if he be a person in place of authority, thou even accountest it a grand affair, and destroyest thine own soul, in eating such things. For covetousness [and unjust gain] is worse than any mire; for it pollutes, not the body but the soul, and makes it hard to be washed clean. Thou therefore, though thou seest him that sitteth at meat defiled with this filth both on his hands and his face, and his house filled with it, nay and his table also full of it (for dung or if there be anything more unclean than that, it is not so unclean and polluted as those viands of his), dost thou feel as if forsooth thou wert highly honoured, and as if thou wert going to enjoy thyself?

And dost thou not even fear Paul who allows us to go without restraint to the Tables of the heathen if we wish it, but does not permit us to go to those of the covetous, even if we wish? For, *if any who is called a Brother*, he 1 Cor. v. saith, meaning by Brother in this place every one who is ¹¹· simply a believer, not him who is devoted to a solitary life. For what is it which makes brotherhood? The Washing of regeneration; the being enabled to call God our Father. So that he that is a Monk, if he be a Catechumen, is not

HOM. 25. a Brother [h], but the believer though he be in the world, is a Brother. *If any man*, saith he, *that is called a Brother.* For at that time there was not even a trace of any one leading a Monastic life, but this blessed [Apostle] addressed all his discourse to persons in the world. *If any*, he saith, *that is called a Brother, be a fornicator, or covetous, or a drunkard, with such an one, no not to eat.* But not so with respect to the heathen : but *If any of them that believe not*, meaning the heathen, *invite you and ye be disposed to go, whatsoever is set before you eat.*

1 Cor. v. 11.

ib. x. 27.

(4) [8.] *If any that is called Brother be* (saith he) *a drunkard.* O! how great is his strictness! Yet we not only do not avoid drunkards, but even go to their houses, in order to partake of what they set before us.

For this cause all things are turned upside down, all things are put into confusion, and overthrown, and ruined. For tell me, if any person of this kind should invite thee to a banquet, thee who art accounted poor and mean, and then should hear thee say, ' Inasmuch as the things set before ' me are [the fruit] of overreaching, I will not endure to ' defile my own soul,' would he not be ashamed? would he not be confounded? would he not feel that he had disgraced himself? This alone were sufficient to correct him, and to make him on the one hand account himself wretched for his wealth's sake, and on the other admire thee for thy poverty, if he saw himself with so great earnestness despised by thee.

ib. vii. 23. But we *are become* (I know not from what cause) *servants of men*, though Paul cries aloud throughout, *Be not ye the servants of men.* Whence then have we become *servants of men?* Because we first became servants of the belly, and of money, and of glory, and of all those other things; we gave up the liberty which Christ had bestowed on us.

What then awaiteth him who is become a servant (tell me)? Hear Christ saying, *The servant abideth not in the*

S. John viii. 35.

[h] It will be observed that the word πιστὸς, "believer," means "one who believes and is baptized:" as opposed to the unbaptized, even though they believed and were so religious as to devote themselves to an ascetic life. Also, that at this time there were those who had given themselves up to an ascetic life and still deferred their Baptism, see S. Greg. Naz. Hom. xl. 18. In the later form of the text, this clause has been altered to " So that "a Catechumen, even though he be a " Monk, is not a brother."

house for ever. Thou hast a declaration complete in itself, that he never at any time entereth into the Kingdom; for this is what *the House* means. For, saith He, *in My Father's House are many mansions. The servant* then *abideth not in the House for ever.* By a servant He means him who is *the servant of sin.* But he that *abideth not in the House for ever,* abideth in Hell for ever, having no consolation from any quarter. _{He.xi.19.} _{S. John xiv. 2.}

Nay, to this point of wickedness are matters come, that they themselves even give alms out of these [ill gotten gains], and also that many receive [these alms]. For this cause has our boldness of speech been broken down, and we are not able even to rebuke any one. But however, henceforward at least, let us flee the mischief which arises from this cause; and ye who have rolled yourselves in this mire, cease from such fatal guilt, and restrain your eager desire for such banquets, if even now we may by any means be able to have God propitious to us, and to attain to the good things which have been promised [us]: which may we all obtain in Christ Jesus our Lord, with whom to the Father and also to the Holy Ghost, be glory, power, honour, now and for ever, and world without end. Amen.

HOMILY XXVI.

HEB. xi. 20—22.

By faith, concerning things to come Isaac blessed Jacob and Esau. By faith, Jacob when he was a dying blessed each of the sons of Joseph, and worshipped¹ leaning on the top of his staff. By faith, Joseph when he died made mention of the departing of the children of Israel, and gave commandment concerning his bones.

¹ or bowed himself, made obeisance

MANY *prophets and righteous men* (it is said) *have desired to see those things which ye see, and have not seen them; and to hear those things which ye hear and have not heard them.* Did then those righteous men know all the things to come? Yea, most certainly. For if it was on account of the weakness of those who were not able to receive Him that the Son was not revealed,—He was with good reason revealed to those who were eminently bright in virtue. This Paul also says, that they knew *the things to come*, that is the resurrection of Christ.

S. Matt. xiii. 17.

Or [it may be said] he does not mean this: but that *By faith, concerning things to come* [means] not [concerning] the world to come, but *concerning things to come* in this world. For how [except by faith] could a man sojourning in a strange land, give such blessings?

But on the other hand he obtained the blessing, and yet did not receive it ª. Thou seest that what I said with regard to Abraham, may be said also of Jacob, that they did not enjoy ᵇ the blessing, but the [substance] of the blessings

---

ª That is, Jacob obtained the blessing from Isaac, but did not himself receive the good things bestowed by the blessing. Therefore the good things to come were not those of this world. This is a reply to the second, the alternative, interpretation suggested.

ᵇ ἀπώναντο. This is the reading of the best MSS. and the oldest translation: There seems no reason to adopt the later reading ἀπώνατο "he did not enjoy."

went to his posterity, while he himself obtained the *things* Hɛ.xi.21.
to come. For we find that his brother had greater enjoyment [of this world than he]. For [Jacob] spent all his time in servitude and working as a hireling, and [amid] dangers, and plots, and deceits, and fears; and when he was asked by Pharaoh, he says, *Few and evil have my days* Gen. *been;* while the other lived in independence and great xlvii. 9. security, and afterwards was an object of terror to [his brother]. Where then did the blessings come to their accomplishment, save in the [world] to come?

Thou seest that from the beginning the wicked had the enjoyment of things here, but the righteous the contrary? Not however all [of them]. For behold, Abraham was a righteous man, and he enjoyed the things of this world as well, though with affliction and trials. For indeed wealth was all he had, seeing all else relating to him was full of affliction. For it is impossible that the righteous man should not be afflicted, though he be rich: for when he is willing to be overreached, to be wronged, to suffer all other things, of necessity he must be afflicted. Wherefore even if he have the enjoyment of wealth, [yet is it] not without grief. Why? you ask. Because he is in affliction and distress. But if at that time the righteous were in affliction, much more now.

By Faith concerning things to come, saith he, *Isaac blessed Jacob and Esau* (and yet Esau was the elder; but he puts Jacob first for his excellence). Thou seest how great was his Faith? Whence did he promise to his sons so great blessings? Entirely from his having faith in God.

[2.] *By Faith, Jacob when he was a dying, blessed each of the sons of Joseph.* Here we ought to set down the blessings entire, in order that both his faith and his prophesying may be made manifest. *And bowed himself*[c], says he, *upon the top of his staff.* Here, he means, he not only spake, but was even so confident about the future things, as to shew it also by his act. For inasmuch as another King was about to arise from Ephraim, therefore it is said,

---

[c] προσεκύνησεν, as Gen. xlvii. 31. The same word also is used in the LXX. in Gen. xxxvii. 7, 9, 10. of Joseph's dreams, where our version has "made obeisance" and "bow down ourselves."

Hom. 26. *And he bowed himself upon the top of his staff.* That is, even though he was now an old man, *he bowed himself* to Joseph, shewing the obeisance of the whole people which was to be [directed] to him. And this indeed had already come to pass, when his brethren *bowed down* to him: but it was afterwards to come to pass through the ten tribes. Thou seest how he foretold the things which were to be afterwards? Thou seest how great faith they had? how they believed *concerning the things to come?*

For some of the things [mentioned] here are examples of patience only as to things present, and of enduring ill-treatment, and of receiving nothing good in the way of recompence; for instance, what is mentioned in the case of Abraham, in the case of Abel. But others are [examples] of Faith, as in the case of Noah, that there is a God, that there is a recompence. (For Faith in this place is manifold [1], both of there being a recompence, and of awaiting it, not under the same conditions [d], and of wrestling before the prizes [are to be given].) And the things also which concern [2] Joseph are of Faith only. That [God] had made a promise to Abraham, that He had engaged His word to him, *to thee and to thy seed will I give this land,* this Joseph had heard: and though he is in a strange land, and does not as yet see the engagement fulfilled, yet not even so did he fail [in faith], but so believed as even to *speak of the going forth* [of the Israelites], *and to give commandment concerning his bones.* He then did not believe himself alone, but led on the rest also to Faith: in order that ever having in mind their going out [of Egypt] (for he would not have *given commandment concerning his bones,* unless he had been fully assured [of this]), they might look for their return [to Canaan].

Wherefore, when some men say, 'See! even righteous 'men had care about their sepulchres,' let us reply to them, that it was for this cause: for he knew that *the earth is the Lord's and all that therein is* [3]. He indeed could not possibly have been ignorant of this, who had lived in so great philosophy, who had spent his whole life in Egypt. And yet if he had wished, it was possible for him to return,

[1] πολύ-τροπος

[2] τὰ κατὰ

Ps. xxiv. 1.
[3] τὸ πλή-ρωμα αὐτοῦ

[d] καὶ τοῦ μὴ ἐπὶ τοῖς αὐτοῖς αὐτὴν ἀναμένειν.

and not to mourn nor vex himself. But when he had even Hᴇ.xi.23. taken up his father thither, why did he enjoin them to carry up from thence his own bones also? Is it not evident that it was for this reason?

But what? tell me, are not the bones of Moses himself (2) laid in a strange land? and those of Aaron, of Daniel, of Jeremiah? and as to those of the Apostles we do not even know where those of most of them are laid. For of Peter indeed, and Paul, and John, and Thomas, the sepulchres are well known; but those of the rest, being so many, are not known anywhere[1]. Let us not therefore lament at all about this, nor be so little-minded. For wherever we may be buried, *the earth is the Lord's and all that therein is.* Beyond all question what must take place, does take place: to mourn however, and lament, and bewail those who are departed, arises from littleness of mind.

[1] οὐδαμοῦ γνώριμοι γεγόνασι Ps. xxiv. 1.

[3.] (ver. 23) *By faith, Moses when he was born, was hid three months of his parents.* Dost thou see that in this case they hoped for the things [which were to be] on the earth after their death[e]? and many things were fulfilled after their death. This is directed against what some say, 'After death these things are done for them, which they 'did not obtain whilst they were alive; nor did they be-'lieve [would be] after their death.'

Moreover Joseph did not say, He gave not the land to me in my life-time, nor to my father, nor to my grandfather, whose excellence too ought to have been reverenced; and will He vouchsafe to these wretched people what He did not vouchsafe to them? He said nothing of all this, but by Faith he both conquered and went beyond all these things.

He has [already] named Abel, Noah, Abraham, Isaac, Jacob, Joseph, all illustrious and admirable men. Again he makes the encouragement greater, by bringing down the matter to ordinary persons. For that those who are regarded with admiration should feel thus, is nothing wonderful, and to appear inferior to them, is not so sad: but to

[e] i.e. they hoped that through their child, when they were dead, the promised blessings upon earth (or in the land of Canaan) would be given. In the next sentence S. Chrys. seems to return to the conduct of Joseph, in order to add an observation, which he had omitted before.

shew oneself inferior even to people whose names are not known, this is the sad thing. And he begins with the parents of Moses, obscure persons, who had nothing so great as had their son. For this cause also in proceeding, he increases the strangeness of what he says by enumerating even women that were harlots, and widows. For *by Faith* (he says) *Rahab the harlot perished not with them that believed not, when she had received the spies with peace.* And he mentions the rewards not only of belief but also of unbelief; as in [the case of] Noah.

But at present we must speak of the parents of Moses. Pharaoh gave orders that all the male children should be destroyed, and none had escaped the danger. From what cause then did these expect to save their child? From faith. What sort of Faith? *They saw* (he saith) *that he was a fair child.* The very sight drew them on to this Faith: thus from the beginning, yea from the very swaddling-clothes, great was the Grace that was poured out on that righteous man, this being not the work of nature. For observe, the child immediately on its birth appears fair and not disagreeable to the sight. Whose [work] was this? not that of nature, but of the Grace of God, which also stirred up and strengthened that barbarian woman, the Egyptian, and took [her] and drew her on.

And yet in truth Faith had not a sufficient foundation in the case of those persons. For what was it to believe from the [mere] appearance [of the child]? But you (he would say) believe from the facts themselves and having many of the pledges of Faith. For *the receiving with joyfulness the spoiling of their goods,* and other such [things], were [evidences] of Faith and of Patience. But inasmuch as these [Hebrews] also had believed, and yet afterwards had become faint-hearted, he points out that even the Faith of those [saints of old] was very long continued [1], as, for instance, that of Abraham, although the circumstances seemed to contend against it.

And (saith he) *they were not afraid of the king's commandment,* and yet nevertheless that was in actual operation [2], but this [their hope respecting their child] was simply a kind of bare expectation. And this indeed was [the act] of his parents; but Moses himself what did he contribute? Heb.xi.26.

[4.] Next the example is again appropriate to their own case, or rather it is greater than that. For, saith he, (ver. 24—26) *by faith Moses when he was come to years, refused to be called the son of Pharaoh's daughter, choosing rather to suffer affliction with the people of God than to enjoy the pleasures of sin for a season*[1]; *esteeming the reproach of Christ greater riches than the treasures of Egypt*[f]; *for he had respect unto the recompence of the reward*. As though he had said to them, 'No one of you has left a palace, yea a 'splendid palace, nor treasures such as these; nor, when he 'might have been a king's son, has he despised this, as Moses 'did.' And that he did not simply leave [these things], he expressed by saying, *he refused*, that is, he hated, he turned away as with aversion. For when Heaven was set before him, it was superfluous to admire an Egyptian Palace.

[1] or to have a temporary enjoyment of sin

And see how admirably Paul has put it. He did not (3) say, "*Esteeming* heaven, and the things in heaven," but what? *the reproach of Christ greater riches than the treasures of Egypt*. For the being reproached for the sake of Christ he accounted better than being thus at ease; and this itself by itself, was his reward.

Choosing rather (he says) *to suffer affliction with the people of God*. For ye indeed suffer on your own account, but he *chose* [to suffer] for others; and voluntarily threw himself into so many dangers, when it was in his power both to live religiously, and enjoy the good things [of the world]:

Than (he saith) *to have a temporary enjoyment of sin*. He called the being unwilling *to suffer affliction with the rest sin:* this, he says, [Moses] accounted to be *sin*. If then he accounted it *sin* not to be willing to *suffer affliction with* the rest, it follows that the suffering affliction must be a great good; since he threw himself into it from the royal palace.

But this he did, seeing some great things before him. *Esteeming the reproach of Christ greater riches than the*

---

[f] Αἰγύπτου. This is the approved reading of the sacred text and of S. Chrys. The common editions have ἐν Αἰγύπτῳ "in Egypt," in each of the three places where the words recur.

treasures of Egypt. What is, *the reproach of Christ?* It is, the being reproached in such ways as ye are, the reproach which Christ endured; Or that he endured for Christ's sake: for *that rock was Christ*[g]; the being reproached as you are.

But what is *the reproach of Christ?* That [because] we repudiate the [ways] of our fathers we are reproached; that we are evil-entreated when we have run to God for help. It was likely that he also was reproached, when it was said to him, *Wilt thou kill me as thou killedst the Egyptian yesterday?* It is *the reproach of Christ* to be ill-treated even to the end, and to the last breath: just as He Himself was reproached and heard, *If Thou be the Son of God,* [said] by those for whom He was being crucified, by those who were of the same tribe [with Himself]. It is *the reproach of Christ* when a man is reproached by those of his own family, when by those whom he is benefiting. For [Moses] also suffered these things from the man who had been benefitted [by him].

In these words he raised them up, by pointing out that even Christ suffered these things, and Moses also, two illustrious persons. So that this is rather *the reproach of Christ* than of Moses, inasmuch as He suffered these things from *His own.* But neither did the One send forth lightnings, nor the other feel any [anger][1], but He was reviled and endured all things, whilst they *wagged their heads.* Since therefore it was probable that they also would hear such things [said to them], and would long for the Recompence, he says that even Christ and Moses had suffered the like. So then ease[2] is [the portion] of sin; but to be reproached, of Christ. For what then dost thou wish? *the reproach of Christ,* or ease?

[5.] (ver. 27) *By faith he forsook Egypt not fearing the wrath of the king; for he endured as seeing Him who is Invisible.* What dost thou say? that he did not fear? And yet the Scripture says, that when he heard, he *was afraid*[h],

---

[g] The later MSS. and common editions add some explanatory words, thus: "he suffered for Christ's sake when he was reviled in the matter of the rock, from which he brought out water: and *that rock* (he says) "*was Christ;*" they omit the clause next following.

[h] See Exod. ii. 14, 15. S. Chrys. is speaking of Moses' flight after killing the Egyptian.

and for this cause provided for his safety by flight, and stole HE.xi.27.
away, and secretly withdrew himself; and afterwards he was
exceedingly afraid. Observe the expressions with accurate
attention: he said, *not fearing the wrath of the king*, with
reference to his even presenting himself again. For it
would have been [the mark] of one who was afraid, not to
engage again in the defence [of his countrymen], nor to
have any hand in the matter. That he did however again
engage in it, was [the conduct] of one who committed all
to God: for he did not say, ' He is seeking me, and is busy
' [in the search], and I cannot endure again to engage in
' those matters.'

Wherefore even his flight was [an act of] faith. Why then
did he not remain (you say)? That he might not cast
himself into a foreseen danger. For this afterwards would
have been [the conduct] of one who tempted [God], to
leap I mean into the midst of dangers, and to say, ' Let us
' see whether God will save me.' This the devil said even
to Christ, *Cast Thyself down*. Thou seest that it is a thing S. Matt.
suited to the Devil, to throw ourselves into danger without iv. 6.
cause and for no purpose, and to try whether God will save
us? For he could no longer be their leader and protector,
when they who were receiving benefits were so ungratefully
disposed [towards him]. It would therefore have been a
foolish and senseless thing to remain there. But all these
things were done, because *he endured as seeing Him who is
Invisible*.

[6.] If then we too at all times see God with our mind,
if we at all times think in remembrance of Him, all things
will appear endurable to us, all things tolerable; we shall
bear them all easily, we shall [be raised] above them all.
For if a person seeing one whom he loves, or rather, having
him in remembrance, is thoroughly roused in spirit, and
elevated in thought, and bears all things easily, while he
delights himself in the remembrance; [surely] one who
has in his thoughts Him who has vouchsafed to love us in
deed, and remembers Him, when will he either feel any
thing painful, or dread any thing fearful or dangerous?
When will he be of cowardly spirit? Never.

For all things appear to us to be difficult, because we do not have the remembrance of God as we ought to have it; because we do not carry Him about alway in our thoughts. For He might justly say to us, 'Thou hast forgotten Me, I 'also will forget thee.' And so the evil becomes twofold, in that we both forget Him and He us. For these two things are involved in each other, but two they are. For great is the effect produced by God's remembrance [of us], and great also is that of His being remembered by us. The result of the one is that we choose things that are good; of the other that we accomplish them, and bring them to their end[1]. For this cause the prophet saith, *I will remember Thee from the land of Jordan, and from the little hill of Hermon.* This saith the people which was in Babylon, Being there, I will remember Thee.

(4) [7.] Therefore let us also, as being in Babylon, [do the same]. For although we are not sitting among warlike foes, yet we are among enemies. For some [of them] indeed were sitting as captives, but others did not even feel their captivity, as Daniel, as the three children; who even while they were in captivity became in that very same country more glorious even than the king himself who had carried them captive. And he who had taken them captive falls down in reverence[1] before the captives.

Dost thou see how great a thing virtue is! when they were in actual captivity he treated them with respect as masters. He therefore was the captive, rather than they. It would not have been so marvellous if when they were in their native country, he had come and done them reverence in their own land, or if they had been rulers there. But the marvellous thing is, that after he had bound them, and taken them as captives, and had them in his own country, he was not ashamed to do them reverence in the sight of all, and to *offer an oblation*[k].

You see that the things which are really splendid, are those which have relation to God, whereas things human are a shadow? He knew not, it seems, that he was leading

---

[1] Probably this is to be understood according to that said Hom. xii. 5. [supra pp. 155,156] of the co-operation of Grace and the human will.

[k] μαναὰ Dan. ii. 46. according to the translation of Theodotion: and the Vatican MS. The Alex. has μαννὰ, as has one MS. of S. Chrys.

away [those who would be] masters for himself, and that He.xi.27.
he had cast into the furnace those whom he was about to
worship. But to them, these things were as a dream.

Let us fear God, beloved, let us fear [Him] : even should
we be in captivity, we are more glorious than all men.
Let the fear of God be present with us, and nothing will
be painful, even though thou speak of poverty, or of disease, or of captivity, or of slavery, or of any other grievous
thing whatever: Nay even these very things will themselves
work together for us unto the contrary [effects]. These
men were captives, and the king worshipped them : Paul
was a tent-maker, and they sacrificed to him as a God.

[8.] Here a question arises: Why, you ask, did the
Apostles prevent the sacrifices, and rend their clothes, and
divert them from their attempt, and say with earnest lamentation, *What are ye doing? we also are men of like* Acts xiv.
passions with you; whereas Daniel did nothing of this kind. 15.

For that he also was humble, and referred [the] glory to
God no less than they, is evident from many places. Most
especially indeed is it evident, from the very fact of his
being beloved by God. For if he had appropriated to
himself the honour belonging to God, He would not have
suffered him to live, much less to be in honour. Secondly,
because even with great openness he said, *And as to me,* Dan. ii.
O King, this secret hath not been revealed to me through 30.
any wisdom that is in me. And again; he was in the den
for God's sake, and when the prophet brought him food, he
saith, *For God hath remembered me.* Thus humble and Bel and
contrite was he. the Dra-
gon, 38.

He was in the den for God's sake, and yet he counted
himself unworthy of His remembrance, and of being heard.
Yet we though presuming to commit atrocities innumerable, yea and being of all men most polluted, if we be not
heard at our first prayer, draw back. In very truth, great
is the distance between them and us, as great as is that
between heaven and earth, or if there be any greater.

What sayest thou? After so many achievements, after
the miracle which had been wrought in the den, dost thou
account thyself so low? Yea, saith he; for what things
soever we have done, *we are unprofitable servants.* Thus S. Luke
xvii. 10.

by anticipation did he fulfil the evangelical precept, and accounts himself nothing. For *God hath remembered me,* he said. His prayer again, of how great lowliness of mind it is full. And again the three children said thus, *We have sinned, we have committed iniquity.* And every where they shew their humility.

And yet Daniel had occasions innumerable for being lifted up [with pride]; but he knew that these also came to him on account of his *not* being lifted up, and he did not destroy his treasure. For among all men, and in the whole world was he celebrated, not for these things only [1], that the king cast himself on his face [before him] and offered sacrifice to him, and that he accounted him to be a God, who was himself honoured as God in all parts of the world: for he ruled over the whole [earth]; (and this is evident from Jeremiah. *Who putteth on the earth,* saith he, *as a garment.* And again, *I have given it to Nebuchadnezzar My servant,* and again from what he [the King] says in his letter [1]). And because he was held in admiration not only in the place where he was, but every where, and was greater than if the rest of the nations had been present and seen him; when even by letters [the King] confessed his submission [2] and the wonderful event. But yet again for his wisdom he was also held in admiration, for it is said, *Art thou wiser than Daniel?* And after all these things he was thus humble, dying ten thousand times for the Lord's sake.

Why then, you ask, being so humble did he not repel either the adoration which was paid him by the king, or the offerings?

[9.] This I will not say, for it is sufficient for me simply to mention the subject of enquiry, and the rest I leave to you, that at least in this way I may stir up your thoughts.

(5) (This however I conjure you, to choose all things for the fear of God, having such examples [before you]; and because in truth we shall obtain the things here also, if we sincerely lay hold on the things which are to come.) For that he did not do this out of arrogance, is evident from his saying, *Thy gifts be to thyself.*

---

[1] The apodosis seems to be, "But yet again for his wisdom &c." which comes after some parentheses.

For besides this also again is another subject of enquiry, how while in words he rejected it, in deed he received the honour, and wore the chain [1] [of gold]. He.xi.27. ¹μανιδκην Dan. v. 29.

Moreover while Herod on hearing the cry *It is the voice of a god and not of a man*, inasmuch as *he gave not God the glory, burst in sunder, and all his bowels gushed out*, this man received to himself even the honour belonging to God, not words only. Acts xii. 22, 23. (see i. 18.)

However it is necessary to say what this is. In that case [at Lystra] the men were falling into greater idolatry, but in this [of Daniel] not so. How? For his being thus accounted of, was an honour to God. For it was on this account that he said in anticipation, *And as to me, not through any wisdom that is in me hath it been revealed, &c.* And besides he does not even appear to have accepted the offerings. For he said (as it is written) that they should offer sacrifice, but it did not appear evident that the act also followed, upon [the command]. But there [at Lystra] they carried it even to sacrificing the bulls, and *they called* the one *Jupiter* and the other *Mercurius*. Dan. ii. 30. Acts xiv. 12.

The chain [of gold] then he accepted, that he might make himself known; the offering however why does it not appear evidently that he rejected it? For in that case too they did not do it, but they attempted it, and the Apostles hindered them; wherefore here also he ought at once to have rejected [the adoration]. And there it was the entire people: here the King. The cause then why he did not divert [him from doing this] [Daniel] expressed by anticipation, [viz.] that [the king] was not making an offering [to him] as to a God, to the overthrow of religious worship, but for the greater wonder. How so? It was on God's account that [Nebuchadnezzar] made the decree; wherefore [Daniel] did not mutilate[2] the honour [offered]. But those others [at Lystra] did not act thus, but supposed them to be indeed gods. On this account they were repelled. ² ἠκρωτηρίαζε

And here it is, after having bowed [to him] in reverence, that he does these things: for he did not do reverence to him as to a God, but as to a wise man.

But it is not even clear that he did make the offering:

Hom. 26. and even if he did make it, yet not that it was with Daniel's acceptance.

And what [shall we say of this], that he called him *Belteshazzar, the name of* his own *god*[1]? Thus [it seems] they accounted their gods to be nothing wonderful, when he called even the captive thus; he who commands all men to worship the image[2], manifold and of various colours, and who adores the dragon[3].

[1] see Dan. iv. 8.
[2] Dan. iii. 1. &c.
[3] Bel and the Dragon 24.

Moreover the Babylonians were much more foolish than those others at Lystra. Wherefore it was not possible at once to lead them on to this. And many [more] things one might say: but thus far these suffice.

If therefore we wish to obtain all good things, let us seek the things that have relation to God. For just as they who seek the things of this world fail both of them and of those others, so they who prefer the things of God, obtain both. Let us then not seek these but those, that also we may attain to the good things which have been promised in Christ Jesus our Lord, with Whom to the Father and also to the Holy Ghost, be glory power honour, now and for ever and world without end. Amen.

HOMILY XXVII.

HEB. xi. 28—31.

By faith, he kept the Passover and the sprinkling of blood, lest he that destroyed the first-born should touch them. By faith they passed through the Red sea, as by dry land; which the Egyptians assaying to do, were drowned[a]. *By faith, the walls of Jericho fell down, after they had been compassed about for seven days. By faith, Rahab the harlot perished not with them that believed not, having received the spies with peace.*

PAUL is wont to establish many things incidently, and is very full[1] of thoughts. For such is the grace of The Spirit. [1] πυκνὸς He does not comprehend a few ideas in a multitude of words, but includes great and manifold thought in brevity of expressions. Observe at least how, in the midst[2] of [2] ἐν τάξει exhortation, and when discoursing about faith, of what a type and mystery he reminds us, whereof we have the reality. *By faith* (he says) *he kept the Passover and the sprinkling of blood, lest he that destroyed the first-born should touch them.*

But what is *the sprinkling of blood*[3]? A lamb was slain [3] πρόσχυ- in every household, and the blood was smeared on the σις door-posts, and this was a means of warding off the Egyptian destruction. If then the blood of a lamb preserved the Jews unhurt in the midst of the Egyptians, and under so great a destruction, much more will the blood of Christ save us, who have had it sprinkled[4] not on our door-posts, [4] ἐπιχρι- but in our souls. For even now also the Destroyer is going ομένους "been about in this depth of night: but let us be armed with that anointed with it."

[a] κατεποντίσθησαν is the reading adopted by Mr. Field, but κατεπόθησαν *swallowed up*, seems to be the reading of his MSS. see his annotation.

Hom. 27. Sacrifice. (He calls the smearing *the pouring on*[1] [or *sprinkling*].) For God has brought us out from Egypt, from darkness, from idolatry.

[1] πρόσχυσιν, the word used by S. Paul, which we translate *sprinkling*.

And yet what was done, was nothing: what was achieved was great. For what was done was blood; but was achieved, was salvation, and the stopping, and preventing of destruction. The angel feared the blood; for he knew of what it was a Type; he shuddered, thinking on the Lord's death; on this account he did not touch the door-posts.

Moses said, Smear ye [the door-posts], and they smeared [them], and were full of confidence. And you, having the Blood of the Lamb Himself, are ye not full of confidence?

[2.] *By faith, they passed through the Red Sea as by dry land.* Again he compares one whole and entire people with another, that they might not say, we cannot be as the saints were.

By faith (he says) *they passed through the Red Sea, as by dry land, which the Egyptians assaying to do, were drowned.* In this place he leads them also to a recollection of the sufferings in Egypt.

How, *by faith?* Because they had hoped to pass through the sea, and for that cause they prayed: or rather it was Moses who prayed. Thou seest that in all cases Faith goes beyond human calculations, and [beyond human] weakness and lowliness also? Thou seest at the same time they believed, and feared the punishment in the blood on the doors, and in the Red sea?

And he evidently shewed this too that it was [really] water, by [the fact of] those that fell into it, and were choked; that it was not a mere appearance: but just as in the case of the lions those who were devoured proved the reality of the facts, and in the case of the fiery furnace, those who were burnt; so in this instance also thou seest that the very same things become to the one a cause of salvation[2] and glory, and to the other of destruction.

[2] πρὸς σωτηρίας

So great a good is Faith. Even when we fall into the greatest perplexity, then are we delivered, even though we come to death itself, even though our condition be utterly desperate. For what else was left [for them]? They were unarmed, compassed about by the Egyptians and the sea;

and of necessity they must either be drowned if they fled, He.xi.32.
or fall into the hands of the Egyptians. But nevertheless
[He] entirely saved them from [such] resourceless dangers.
The same [sea] was spread under the one, just as if it were
land: the others it overwhelmed as sea. In the former case
it forgat its own nature: in the latter it even armed itself cf. Wisd.
against them. xix. 20.

[3.] *By faith, the walls of Jericho fell down, after they
had been compassed about for seven days.* [*By faith;*] for
assuredly the sound of trumpets is not able to throw down
stones, though one blow for ten thousand years, but Faith
can do all things.

Thou seest in all cases that it is not by natural sequence, (2)
nor yet by any law of nature that it was changed, but all
is done contrary to expectation? Accordingly in this case
also all things take place contrary to expectation. For
inasmuch as he had said again and again, that we ought to
trust to the future hopes, he introduced all this argument
with reason, shewing that not now [only], but even from
the beginning all the miracles have been accomplished and
achieved by means of it.

*By faith Rahab the harlot perished not with them that
believed not, having received the spies with peace.* It would
then be disgraceful, if you should prove yourselves more
unbelieving even than a harlot. Yet she [merely] heard
what the men related, and forthwith believed. Whereupon
the end also followed in course: for when all perished, she
alone was preserved. She did not say to herself, I shall
be with my [friends and relatives[1], who are] many. She [1] μετ'
did not say, Can I possibly be wiser than these judicious ἐμῶν
men who do not believe,—and shall I believe? Nothing of
this kind did she say: but believed the things which had
taken place[b], which very thing it was likely that they would
suffer.

[4.] (ver. 32) *And what shall I more say? for the time
would fail me to tell.* From this point he no longer puts
down the names: but having ended with an harlot, and put
them to shame by the quality of the person, he no longer

[b] τοῖς γενομένοις: probably the destruction of the Egyptians and the
Amorites &c. Josh. ii. 10. The common texts have τοῖς λεγομένοις.

enlarges on the histories, lest he should be thought tedious. However he does not set them aside, but runs over them, [doing] very judiciously in both respects, avoiding satiety, and not spoiling the close arrangement [of instances] ; he neither altogether suppressed the mention of them, nor did he cause annoyance by speaking of them; for he effects both points. For when a man is contending vehemently [in argument], if he persist in contending, he wearies out the hearer, annoying him when he is already persuaded, and gaining the reputation of vain ambitiousness. For he ought to accommodate himself to what is expedient.

And what do I say more (saith he) *? for the time will fail me to tell of Gedeon, and of Barak, and of Sampson, and of Jephthae, of David also and Samuel, and of the prophets.*

Some find fault with Paul, because he sets down Barak, and Sampson, and Jephtha in these places. What sayest thou? After having introduced the harlot, shall he not introduce these men? For do not tell me of the rest of their life, but only whether they did not believe and shine forth in Faith.

And the prophets, saith he, (ver. 33) *who through faith subdued kingdoms.* Thou seest that he does not here testify to their life as being illustrious; for this was not the point in question: but the enquiry thus far was about their faith. For tell me whether it was not by faith that they accomplished all?

By faith, saith he, *they subdued kingdoms.* Gedeon and those with him. *Wrought righteousness.* Who? These same. Plainly in this place [by *righteousness*] he means kindness¹.

I think it is of David that he says *they obtained promises.* But what sort of *promises* were these? Those in which He said that his *seed should sit upon* his *throne.*

Stopped the mouths of lions, (ver. 34) *quenched the violence of fire, escaped the edge of the sword.* See how they were in death itself, Daniel encompassed by the lions, the three children abiding in the furnace, the Israelites ͨ,

---

ͨ i. e. " when crossing the Red Sea." Field.

Faith when things contrary. The life of the world to come. 313

Abraham, Isaac, Jacob, in divers temptations; and yet not He.xi.35.
even so did they despair. For this is Faith; when things
are turning out contrarily, then ought we to believe that
nothing is done contrary, but all things in due order.

Escaped the edge of the sword. I think that he is again
speaking of the three children.

Out of [1] *weakness were made strong.* Here he alludes [1] ἀπὸ
to what took place at their return from Babylon. For *out* *from* or *after*
of weakness, is, out of captivity. When the condition of
the Jews had now become desperate, when they were no
better than dead bones, who could have expected that they
would return from Babylon, and not return only, but also
wax valiant, and *turn to flight armies of aliens?* 'But to
'us' some one says [2], 'no such thing has happened.' But [2] i.e. some Hebrew
these are figures of *the things to come.* Christian.

Women received their dead raised to life again. He here tian.
speaks of what occurred in the case of the prophets, Elisha,
[and] Elijah; for these raised the dead.

[5.] (ver. 35) *And others were tortured* [3], *not accepting* [3] ἀποτυμ-
deliverance, that they might obtain a better resurrection. πανισθῆ-
But we have not obtained a Resurrection. I am able however, he means, to shew that they also were cut off, and
did *not accept* [*deliverance*], *that they might obtain a better*
resurrection. For why, tell me, when it was open to them
to live, did they not choose it? Were they not evidently
looking for a better life? And they who had raised up
others, themselves chose to die, in order *to obtain a better*
resurrection, not such as the children of those women [had
obtained] [d].

Here I think he alludes both to John and to James.
For beheading is called "torturing [e]." It was in their power
still to behold the sun. It was in their power to abstain
from reproving [f] [sinners], and yet they chose to die; even
they who had raised others chose to die themselves, *that*
they might obtain a better resurrection.

[d] The children of the widow of Sarepta, and the Shunamite had been brought back to continue this life of temptation and sorrow; it was a *better* kind of *Resurrection* which the Prophets sought to obtain themselves.

[e] ἀποτυμπανισμός. For instances of this meaning of the word see Mr. Field's annot.

[f] ἐλέγξαι, the word used of S. John Baptist reproving Herod, S. Luke iii. 19.

(ver. 36) *And others had trial of cruel mockings and scourgings, yea moreover of bonds and imprisonment.* He ends with these; with things that are more akin [to their own sufferings]. For these [examples] most especially bring consolation, when the distress is from the same cause, since even if you mention something which is more extreme, yet if it does not arise from the same cause, you have effected nothing. For that reason he concluded his discourse herewith, mentioning *bonds, imprisonments, scourges, stonings,* alluding to the case of Stephen, also to that of Zacharias.

Wherefore he added, *They were slain with the sword.* What sayest thou? Some *escaped the edge of the sword,* and some *were slain by the sword.* What is this? which dost thou praise? which dost thou admire? the latter or the former? Yea verily, saith he, [I mention both] : the former indeed, [as being] appropriate to your case, and the latter, because Faith was strong even unto death itself, and it is a type of things to come. For the wonderful qualities of Faith are two, that it both accomplishes great things, and suffers great things, and counts itself to suffer nothing.

And thou canst not say (saith he) that these were sinners and worthless. For even if you put the whole world in the scale against them, I find that they weigh down the beam and are of greater value[g]. What [reward] then were they to receive in this life? Here he raises up their thoughts, teaching them not to be rivetted to things present, but to mind [1] things greater than all that are in this present life, since the whole *world is not worthy* of them. What then dost thou wish to receive here? for it were an insult to thee, shouldst thou receive thy reward here.

[6.] Let us not then mind [2] worldly things, nor seek our recompence here, nor be so mean and beggarly. For if *the* whole *world is not worthy of* them, why dost thou seek after a part of it? And with good reason [is it so], for they are friends of God.

Now by *the world* does he mean here the generality of

[g] The common texts add the explanatory words, "For this cause also he "said, *Of whom the world was not worthy.*"

people, or the creation itself? Both: for the Scripture is Hᴇ.xi.36.
wont to use the word of both. If the whole creation, he
would say, with the human beings that belong to it, were
put in the balance, they yet would not prove of equal value
with these; and that with reason. For just as ten thousand measures of chaff and hay would not be of equal value
to ten pearls, so neither they; for *better is one that doeth* Ecclus.
the will of the Lord, than ten thousand transgressors, mean- xvi. 3.
ing by *ten thousand* not [merely] many, but an infinite p. 280,
multitude. note a.

Consider of how great value is the righteous man. Joshua
the son of Nun said, *Let the sun stand still at Gibeon, the* Josh. x.
moon at the valley of Elom, and it was so. Let then the 12.
whole world come, or rather two or three, or four, or ten,
or twenty worlds and let them say so and do this; yet
shall they not be able. But the friend of God laid his
commands on the creatures of his Friend, or rather he besought his Friend, and the servants yielded, and he below
gave command to those above. Thou seest that they are
made for service fulfilling their appointed course?

This was greater than the [miracles] of Moses. Why
(I ask)? Because it is not so great a thing to command the
sea as [to command] the heavenly [bodies]. For that
indeed was also a great thing, yea very great, nevertheless
it was not at all equal [to the other].

Why was this? The name of Joshua [Jᴇsᴜs], was a type.
For this cause then, and because of the appellation itself,
the creation reverenced him. What then! was no other
person called Jesus? [Yes;] but this man was on this account so called in type; for he used to be called Hoshea.
On this account the name was changed: for it was a prediction and a prophecy. He brought in the people into
the promised land, as Jᴇsᴜs [does] into heaven; not the
Law; as also neither did Moses [bring them in], but remained without. The Law has not power to bring in [to
heaven], but grace has. Thou seest the types which have
been long before sketched out from the beginning? He
laid his commands on the creation, or rather, on the vital [1]   [1] καιρίᾳ
part of the creation, on the very head itself as he stood
below; that so when thou seest Jᴇsᴜs in the form of Man

saying the same, thou mayest not be disturbed, nor think it strange. He, even while Moses was living, turned back wars. Thus, even while the Law is living, He directs [h] all things; but not openly.

(4) [7.] But consider we how great is the virtue of the saints. If *here* they work such [wonders], if *here* they do such things, as the very angels do, what then [will they do] yonder? How great is the splendour they possess?

Possibly each of you might wish to be such as to be able to command the sun and moon. (At this point what would they say who assert that the heaven is a sphere[1]? For why did he not [merely] say, *Let the sun stand still*, but added *Let the sun stand still at the valley of Elom*, that is, he shall make the day longer? This was done also in the time of Hezekiah. The sun went back. This again is more wonderful than that other, to go the contrary way, not having yet gone round his course.)

[1] see above p. 175.

Nevertheless greater things than these shall we attain to, if we will. For what has Christ promised us? Not that we shall make the sun stand still, or the moon, nor that the sun shall retrace his steps, but what? *I and the Father will come unto him*, saith He, *and We will make our abode with him*. What need have I of the sun and the moon, and of these wonders, when the Lord of all Himself takes up His lodging, yea His settled habitation with me? I need these not. For what need I any of these things? He Himself shall be to me for Sun and for Light. For, tell me, if thou hadst entered into a palace, which wouldst thou prefer, to be able to re-arrange some of the things which have been fixed there, or so to gain the familiar friendship of the king, as to persuade him to take up his abode with thee? much rather [wouldst thou choose] the latter than the former.

S. John xiv. 23.

[8.] But in what respect is it wonderful, says some one, that those very things which a [mere] man commands, these Christ also [commands]? But Christ (you say) needs not the Father, but acts of His own authority, you say. Well. Therefore first confess and say, that he needs not the Father, and acts of His own authority: and then

[h] διοικεῖ: so Tertullian in the well known words: Adv. Prax. 16.

I will ask thee, whether His prayer is not in the way of He.xi.36. condescension and economy (for surely Christ was not inferior to Joshua the son of Nun); and that He might teach us. For as, when thou hearest a teacher lisping [1], and saying over the alphabet, thou dost not say that he is ignorant; and when he asks, Where is such a letter? thou knowest that it is not in ignorance that he asks, but because he wishes to lead on his scholar; in like manner Christ also did not make His prayer as needing prayer, but desiring to lead thee on, that thou mayest continually apply thyself to prayer, that thou mayest do it without ceasing, with sobriety, and with great watchfulness.

[1] ψελλί-ζοντος

And by watching, I do not mean, merely the rising at night, but also the being soberly attentive [2] in our prayers during the day. For such an one is called watchful [3]. Since it is possible both in praying by night to be asleep, and in praying by day to be awake, when the soul is stretched out intently towards God, when it considers with whom it holds converse, to whom its words are addressed, when it has in mind that angels are standing by with fear and trembling, while he approaches gaping and scratching himself.

[2] νήφειν
[3] ἀγρυπνος

[9.] Prayer is a mighty weapon if it be made with suitable mind. And that thou mayest learn its strength, shamelessness, and injustice, and savage cruelty, and overbearing rashness, have been overcome by continued entreaty. For, saith He, *Hear what the unjust judge saith.* Again it has overcome sloth also, and what friendship did not effect, this continued entreaty did: and *although he will not give him because he is his friend* (saith He), *yet because of his importunity he will rise and give to him.* And her who was unworthy was made worthy by continued assiduity. *It is not meet* (He saith) *to take the children's bread and to cast it to the dogs. Yea! Lord!* she saith, *for even the dogs eat [what falls] from their masters' table.* Let us apply ourselves to Prayer. It is a mighty weapon if it be offered with intense earnestness, if without vain-glory, if with a sincere mind. It has turned back wars, it has benefitted an entire nation though undeserving. *I have heard their groaning* (saith He) *and am come down to deliver them.* It

S. Luke xviii. 6.
ib. xi. 8.

S. Matt. xv. 26, 27. (5)

Acts vii. 34.

is itself a saving medicine, and has power to prevent sins, and to heal misdeeds. In this the widow who had been left solitary was assiduous.

If then we pray with humility, smiting our breast as the publican, if we utter those very same things which he did, if we say, *Be merciful to me a sinner*, we shall obtain all. For though we be not publicans, yet have we other sins not less than his.

For do not tell me, that thou hast gone wrong in some small matter [only], since the thing of itself has the same nature. For just as a man is equally called a homicide whether he has killed a child or a man, so also is he called overreaching, whether he be overreaching in much or in little. Yea and to remember injuries too, is no small matter, but even a great sin. For it is said, *the ways of those who remember injuries* [*tend*] *to death.* And *He that is angry with his brother without a cause, shall be in danger of hell,* and he that *calleth his brother a fool,* and senseless, and numberless things such as these.

But we partake even of the tremendous mysteries unworthily, and we envy, and we revile. And some of us have even oftentimes been drunk. But each one of these things, even itself by itself, is sufficient to cast us out of the kingdom, and when they even come all together, what comfort shall we have? Much is the penitence whereof we have need, beloved, much the prayer, much the endurance, much the perseverance, that we may be enabled to attain the good things which have been promised to us.

[10.] Let us then ourselves also say, *Be merciful to me a sinner*, nay rather, let us not say it only, but let us also be thus minded; and should another call us so, let us not be angry. He heard the words, *I am not as this Publican,* and was not provoked thereby, but filled with compunction. He accepted the reproach, and he put away the reproach. The other spoke of the wound, and *he sought the medicine.* Let us say then, *Be merciful to me a sinner*, yea and even if another should so call us, let us not be indignant.

But if we say ten thousand evil things of ourselves, and still when we hear them said by others, are vexed, then this is no longer humility, nor confession, but ostentation and vain-glory. Is it ostentation (you say) to call one's self a sinner? Yes, surely. For we obtain the credit of humility, we are admired, we are greatly commended; whereas if we say the contrary of ourselves, we are despised. So that we do this too for the sake of credit. But what is humility? It is when another reviles us, to bear it, to acknowledge our fault, to endure evil speakings. And yet not even would this be [a mark] of humility but of candour. But now as it is we call ourselves sinners, unworthy, and ten thousand other such names, whilst if any other person apply one of them to us, we are vexed, we become quite savage. Thou seest that this is not confession, nor even candour? Thou saidst of thyself that thou art such an one: be not indignant if thou hearest it also said by others, and art reproved [by them]. He.xi.36.

In this way thy sins are made lighter for thee, when others reproach thee: for on themselves indeed they lay a burden, but thee they lead onwards into philosophy. Hear what the blessed David says, when Shimei cursed him, *Let him alone* (saith he) *the Lord hath bidden him, that He might look on my humiliation* (saith he): *And the Lord will requite me good for his cursing on this day.* 2 Sam. xvi. 11, 12.

But thou while saying evil things of thyself even in excess, if thou hearest not from others the commendations that are due to the great [and] the righteous, art wild with rage. Seest thou that thou art trifling with things that are no subjects for trifling? For we even repudiate praises in our desire for other praises, that we may obtain yet higher panegyrics, that we may be more admired. So that when we decline to accept commendations, we do it that we may augment them. And all things are done by us out of regard to appearance, not to truth. For this cause are all things hollow, all impracticable. Wherefore I beseech you now at any rate to withdraw from this mother of evils, vain-glory, and to live according to what is approved by God, that so you may attain to the good things which are to come, in Christ Jesus our Lord, with Whom to the Father be glory, together with His Holy and good Spirit, now and ever and world without end. Amen.

HOMILY XXVIII.

Heb. xi. 37, 38.

They wandered about in sheep-skins, in goat-skins, being destitute, afflicted, tormented (of whom this[a] *world was not worthy); wandering in deserts, and mountains, and dens, and caves of the earth.*

At all times indeed, but especially then when I reflect upon the achievements of the saints, does it come over me to feel despondency concerning my own condition[1], because we have not even in dreams had experience of the [sufferings] among which those men spent their whole lives, not paying the penalty of sins, but always doing rightly and yet always afflicted.

[1] ἀπαγορεύειν τὰ καθ' ἑ.

For consider, I beseech you, Elijah, to whom our discourse has come round to-day, for it is of him that he is speaking in this passage, and in him his examples end: which very [example] was appropriate to their case. And having spoken of what befel the Apostles, that *they were slain with the sword, were stoned*, he goes back again to Elijah, who suffered the same things which they did. For since it was probable that they would not as yet hold the Apostles in so great estimation, he brings his exhortation and consolation from him who had been taken up [into Heaven] and who was held in special admiration.

see 2 Kings i. 8.

For *they went about* (saith he) *in sheep-skins, in goat-skins, being destitute, afflicted, tormented*[2], *of whom this world was not worthy*.

[2] ill treated, κακουχούμενοι

They had not even raiment, he says, owing to the exceeding greatness of their affliction, not a city [a home],

---

[a] οὗτος. Mr. F. observes that S. Chrys. more usually cites the text without οὗτος.

not a house, not a lodging-place; the very same which Christ said, *but the Son of Man hath not where to lay His head.* Why do I say "not a lodging-place?" no, not a standing-place: for not even when they had gained the wilderness, were they at rest. For he said not, In the wilderness they sat them down, but even when they were there, they fled, and were driven thence, not out of the inhabited world only, but even out of that which was uninhabitable. And he reminds them of the places where they were set, and of things which there befel [them]. ^(margin: He.xi.40. S. Matt. viii. 20.)

Then next, he saith, they bring accusations against you on account of Christ. What accusation had they against Elijah, when they drove him out, and persecuted him, and compelled him to struggle with famine? Which very same thing these [Hebrews] were at that time suffering. At least the brethren it is said decided to send [relief] to those of the disciples who were afflicted. *As each person had the means, they determined each one to send relief unto the brethren that dwelt in Judea,* which was [the case] of these also. ^(margin: Acts xi. 29.)

Tormented [or *ill-treated*], he saith; that is, suffering distress, in their journeyings, in their dangers.

But *They wandered about,* what is this? *wandering,* he says, *in deserts and mountains and in dens and the caves of the earth,* just like exiles and outcasts, just like persons taken in the basest [of crimes], just like those who are not worthy even to see the sun, they found no refuge even from the wilderness, but must alway be flying, must be seeking hiding-places, must bury themselves alive in the earth, always be in terror.

[2.] What then, is the reward of so great an exchange[b]? what is the recompence?

They have not yet received it, but are still waiting; and after thus dying in so great tribulation, they have not yet received it. They gained their victory so many ages ago, and have not yet received [their reward]. And you who are yet in the conflict, do you complain?

Do you also consider what a thing it is, and how great, that Abraham should be sitting, and the Apostle Paul,

---

[b] ἀμοιβῆς i. e. the accepting sufferings instead of an easy life.

waiting till thou hast been perfected, that then they may be able to receive their reward. For the Saviour has told them before that unless we also are present, He will not give it them. Just as an affectionate father might say to sons who were well approved, and had accomplished their work, that he would not give them to eat, unless their brethren came. And art thou vexed, that thou hast not yet received thy reward? What then shall Abel do, who was victor before all, and is sitting uncrowned? And what [shall] Noah [do]? And what, they who lived in those [early] times: seeing that they are waiting for thee and for those who shall be after thee?

Dost thou see that we have the advantage of them? For *God* (he says) *has provided some better thing for us.* In order that they might not seem to have the advantage of us from being crowned before us, He appointed that the time of crowning should be one for all; and he that gained the victory so many years before, receives his crown with thee. Thou seest His tender carefulness?

And [the Apostle] did not say, "that they without us "might not be crowned," but *that they without us might not be made perfect,* so that at that time they appear perfect also. They were before us as regards the conflicts, but are not before us as regards the crowns. He wronged not them, but He honoured us. For they themselves also wait for their brethren. For if we are *all one body*, the pleasure becomes greater to this body, when it is crowned altogether, and not partially. For besides in this [respect] also the righteous are worthy of admiration, that they rejoice in the welfare of their brethren, as in their own. So that for themselves also, this is according to their wish, to be crowned along with their own members. To be glorified all together, is [to them] a great delight.

[3.] (Ch. xii. 1) *Wherefore* (he says) *we also being compassed about with so great a cloud of witnesses.* In many places does the Scripture derive its consolation in evils from things which commonly happen to us. As when the prophet says, *From burning heat, and from storm, and rain.* This at least he says here also, that the memory of those holy men, re-establishes and recovers the soul which had

been weighed down by woes, just as a cloud does him who He. xii. 2.
is burnt by the too hot rays [of the sun].

And he did not say, [a cloud] "lifted on high above us," but, *compassing us about*, which was more than the other; so that we are in greater security.

What sort of *cloud? A load of witnesses* ᶜ. With good reason he calls not those in the New Testament only, but those in the Old also, *witnesses* [or *martyrs*]. For indeed they also were witnesses to the greatness of God, as for instance, the Three Children, Elijah, all the prophets.

Laying aside all things. All: what? that is, slumber, indifference, mean reasonings, all human things.

And the sin which doth [so] easily beset us; εὐπερίστατον, that is either, "which easily circumvents us," or "what can "easily be circumvented¹," but rather this latter. For it is easy, if we have the will, to overcome sin.   ¹ περίστα-σιν παθεῖν

With patience (he says) *let us run the race that is set before us.* He did not say, Let us contend as boxers, nor, Let us wrestle, nor, Let us battle: but, which was lightest of all, the [contest] of the foot-race, this has he brought forward. Nor yet did he say, Let us add to the length of the course; but, Let us continue patiently in this [which we have], let us not faint. *Let us run* (saith he) *the race that is set before us.*

[4.] In the next place as the sum and substance of his exhortation, what [he had put] first, this also he puts last, even Christ. ver. 2. *Looking* (saith he) *unto* Jesus *the Author and Finisher of our Faith;* The very thing which Christ Himself also continually said to His disciples, *If* S. Matt. *they have called the Master of the house Beelzebub, how much* x. 25. *more them of His household?* and again, *The disciple is not* ib. 24. *above his Master, nor the servant above his Lord.*

Looking (saith he), that is, in order that we may learn to run. For just as in all arts and games, it is by looking to our masters, that we impress the art upon our mind, receiving certain rules through our sight, so in this case also,

ᶜ μαρτύρων ὄγκον. S. Chrys. connects ὄγκον with μαρτύρων and takes πάντα as a neuter plural; the words of the Apostle, τοσοῦτον ἔχοντες περικείμενον ἡμῖν νέφος, μαρτύρων ὄγκον, ἀποθέμενοι πάντα, he would understand thus, *Seeing we are compassed about with so great a cloud, a load of witnesses, let us lay aside all things &c.*

if we wish to run, and to learn to run well, let us look to Christ, even to JESUS *the author and finisher of our faith.* What is this? He Himself has put the Faith within us. For He said also to His disciples, *Ye have not chosen Me, but I have chosen you;* And Paul too saith, *But then shall I know, even as also I have been known*[1]. He Himself put the Beginning into us, He will Himself also put on the End.

[Sidenote: S. John xv. 16. 1 Cor. xiii. 12. [1] ἐπεγνώ-σθην]

Who, saith he, *for the joy that was set before Him, endured the Cross, despising the shame.* That is, it was in His power, if He so willed, not to suffer at all. For neither had He done any sin, nor was guile found in His mouth; as He Himself also saith in the Gospels, *The Prince of the world cometh and hath nothing in Me.* It lay then entirely in His power, if so He willed, not to come to the Cross. For, *I have power,* He saith, *to lay down My life, and I have power to take it again.* If then He who was under no necessity of being crucified, was crucified for our sake, how much more is it right that we should endure all things nobly!

[Sidenote: 1 S. Pet. ii. 22. S. John xiv. 30. ib. x. 18.]

Who for the joy that was set before Him (he says) *endured the cross, despising*[2] *the shame.* But what is, *Despising the shame?* He chose, he means, that ignominious death. For suppose that He died. Why [should He] also [die] ignominiously? For no other cause, but to teach us to account as nothing the glory which [comes] from men. For this cause though under no obligation He chose it, [even shame], teaching us to be bold against it, and to set it at nought. Why did he say not "pain," but *shame?* Because it was not with pain[3] that He bore these things.

[Sidenote: [2] disregarding [3] λύπης]

What then is the end? *He is set down at the right hand of the throne of God.* Thou seest the prize of the conflict? which very same thing Paul also says in an epistle, *Wherefore God also hath highly exalted Him, and given Him a Name which is above every name, that in the Name of* JESUS *Christ every knee should bow.* He is speaking of that which relates to the flesh[4]. Well then, even if there were no prize, the example would be abundantly sufficient to persuade us to accept all [such] things. But now in fact prizes also are set before us, and these no common ones, but great and ineffable.

[Sidenote: Phil. ii. 9, 10. [4] the human nature]

[5.] Wherefore let us also, whenever we suffer any thing

of this kind, before the Apostles consider Christ. Why? He.xii.2. His whole life was full of insults. For indeed He was continually hearing Himself called mad, and a deceiver, and a sorcerer; and at one time the Jews said, *Nay,* (it saith) *but* S. John *He deceiveth the people.* And again, *That deceiver said* vii. 12. S. Matt. *while He was yet alive, after three days I rise again.* As xxvii. 63. to sorcery too they calumniated Him, saying, *It is by Beel-* ib. xii. *zebub that He casteth out the devils.* And that *He is mad* 24. S. John *and hath a devil. Said we not well* (it saith) *that He hath* x. 20. *a devil and is mad?* ib. viii. 48.

And these things He was wont to hear from them, when He was doing them kindnesses, performing miracles, shewing forth the works of God. For indeed, if He had been so spoken of, when He did nothing, it would not have been at all so wonderful: But [it is wonderful] that when He was teaching what pertained to Truth He was called *a deceiver,* and when He cast out devils, was said to *have a devil,* and when He was overthrowing all that was opposed [to God], was called a sorcerer. For these things they were continually alleging against Him.

And if thou wouldst also know the scornful jests[1] and (3) the ironical jeerings[2], which they used to make against Him [1] σκώμματα (a thing which particularly wounds our souls), hear first [2] εἰρωνείας those which [were drawn] from His family. *Is not this* (it S. Matt. saith) *the carpenter's son, whose father and mother we* xiii. 55. S. John *know? are not his brethren all with us?* Also scoffing at vi. 42. Him from His country, they said that He was *of Nazareth.* And again, *search,* it saith, *and see, for out of Galilee hath* ib.vii.52. *no prophet arisen.* And He endured the being so greatly calumniated. And again they said, *Doth not the Scripture* ib. 42. *say, that Christ cometh from the town of Bethlehem?*

Wouldst thou see also the ironical jeerings which they made? Coming, it saith, to the very cross they worshipped Him; and they struck Him and buffeted Him, and said, *Tell us who it is that smote Thee;* and they brought vinegar S. Matt. to Him, and said, *If Thou be the Son of God, come down* xxvi. 68. ib. xxvii. *from the Cross.* And again, even the servant of the High 40. Priest struck Him with the palm of his hand; and He saith, *If I have spoken evil, bear witness of the evil; but if* S. John *well, why smitest thou Me?* And in derision they put a xviii. 23.

robe about Him; and they spat in His face; and they were continually applying their tests, tempting [and making trial of] Him.

Wouldst thou see also the accusations, those that were made in secret and the open ones, those that came from His disciples? *Will ye also go away?* saith He, and that saying, *Thou hast a devil,* was uttered by those who already believed.

Was not He Himself continually a fugitive, sometimes in Galilee, and sometimes in Judea? Was not His trial great, even from the very swaddling clothes? When He was yet a young child, did not His mother take Him and go down into Egypt? For all these reasons he saith, *Looking unto* JESUS *the Author and Finisher of our Faith, who for the joy that was set before Him endured the cross, despising the shame, and is set down at the right hand of the throne of God.*

To Him then let us look, also to the [sufferings¹] of His disciples, reading the [writings²] of Paul, and hearing him say, *In much patience, in afflictions, in necessities, in persecutions, in distresses, in stripes, in imprisonments.* And again, *Even to this present hour, we both hunger, and thirst, and are naked, and are buffeted, and have no certain dwelling-place, and labour, working with our own hands. Being reviled, we bless; being persecuted, we suffer it; being defamed, we entreat.* Has any one [of us] suffered the smallest part of these things? For, saith he, [we are] *As deceivers, As despised, as having nothing.* And again, *Five times received I of the Jews forty stripes save one; thrice was I beaten with rods, once was I stoned, a night and a day have I been in the deep; in journeyings often, in tribulations, in distress, in famine.* And that these things seemed good to God, hear him saying, *For this I besought the Lord thrice, and He said to me, My Grace is sufficient for thee: for My strength is made perfect in weakness. Wherefore,* he saith, *I take pleasure in infirmities, in afflictions, in necessities, in distresses, in stripes, in imprisonments, that the power of Christ may rest upon me.* Moreover, hear Christ Himself saying, *In the world ye shall have tribulation.*

[6.] ver. 3. *For consider*, saith he, *Him that endured such* He.xii.8. *contradiction of sinners against Himself, lest ye be wearied and faint in your minds.* For if the sufferings of those who are near to us greatly arouse us, how much earnestness will not those of our Master give us! What effect will they not have on us?

And passing by all [else], he expressed the whole by the [word] *Contradiction;* and by adding *such* [*contradictions*]. For the blows upon the cheek, the laughter, the insults, the reproaches, the mockeries, all these he indicated by the [word] *contradiction.* And not these only, but also the things which befel Him during His whole life, [His whole life I mean] as a teacher.

For a great, a truly great consolation are both the sufferings of Christ, and those of His Apostles. For so [surely] did He know that this is the better way of virtue, that He even Himself went that way, who had no need thereof: so [surely] did He know that tribulation is expedient for us, and that it becomes rather a ground and occasion for repose. For hear Him Himself saying, *If a man take not his cross,* S. Matt. *and follow after Me, he is not worthy of Me.* If thou art a ˣ·³⁸· disciple, He means, imitate thy Master; for this is [to be] a disciple. But if while He went by [the path of] affliction, thou [goest] by that of ease, thou no longer treadest the same path, which He trod, but a different one. How then dost thou follow, when thou followest not? how shalt thou be a disciple, when thou dost not go after the Master? This Paul also says, *We are weak, but ye are strong; we* 1 Cor. iv. *are despised, but ye are honoured.* How is it reasonable, ¹⁰· he means, that we should be zealously pursuing opposite things, and yet that you should be disciples and we teachers?

[7.] Affliction then is a great thing, beloved, for it brings to a successful issue those two great things: It wipes out sins, and it makes men firm [and steady].

What then, you say, if it overthrow and destroy? It is (4) not affliction which does this, but our own slothfulness. How (you say)? If we are sober and watchful, if we beseech God that He would not *suffer us to be tempted above that* Ib. x. 13. *we are able*, if we always hold fast to Him, we shall stand nobly, and set ourselves against our enemy. So long as we have Him for our helper, though temptations blow more violently than all the winds, they will be to us as chaff and a leaf borne lightly along. Hear Paul saying, *In all these things* (are his words) *we are more than conquerors*. And again, *For I reckon that the sufferings of this present time are not worthy to be compared with the glory which shall be revealed in us.* And again, *For the light affliction which is but for a moment, worketh for us a far more exceeding and eternal weight of glory.*

Consider what great dangers, shipwrecks, afflictions one close upon another, and other such things whatsoever, he calls *light;* and emulate this [rock of] adamant, who wore this body simply and heedlessly[1]. Thou art in poverty? but not in so great [poverty] as Paul was, who was thoroughly tried by hunger, and thirst, and nakedness. For he suffered this not for one day, but endured it continually. Whence does this appear? Hear himself saying, *Even unto this present hour we both hunger and thirst and are naked.* Oh! how great glory had he already [attained] in the preaching [of the Gospel], when he was undergoing so great [afflictions]! having now [reached] the twentieth year [thereof], at the time when he wrote this. For he saith, *I knew a man fourteen years ago, whether in the body, or out of the body, I know not.* And again, *After three years* (saith he) *I went up to Jerusalem.* And again hear him saying, *It were better for me to die, than that any man should make my glorying void.* And not only this, but again also in writing he said, *We are become as the filth of the world.* What is more difficult to endure than hunger? what than freezing cold? what than insidious attacks made by brethren: whom he afterwards calls *false brethren?* Was he not called the pest of the world? [was he] not [called] an Impostor? one that turned [the world] upside down? was he not cut to pieces with scourging?'

[8.] These things let us take into our mind, beloved, let us consider them, let us hold them in remembrance, and then we shall at no time faint, though we be wronged, though we be plundered, though we suffer evils innumerable. May it be granted us to be approved in Heaven, and all things [are] endurable. May it be granted us to fare well

---

[1] ἁπλῶς καὶ εἰκῇ

there, and of things here no account [need be made]. Heb. xii. 3.
These things are a shadow, and a dream; whatever they may
be, they are nothing either in nature or in duration, while
those other are hoped for and expected.

For what wouldst thou that we should compare with those
fearful things? what with the unquenchable fire? with the
never-dying worm? Which of the things here canst thou
name as equal, in comparison with the *gnashing of teeth*,
with the *chains*, with the *outer darkness*, with the *wrath*,
the *tribulation*, the *anguish*? But as to duration? why
what are ten thousand years to ages boundless and without
end? not so much as one little drop to the boundless ocean.

But [what can we compare] to those good things? There,
however the superiority is [still] greater. *Eye hath not seen* 1 Cor. ii. 9.
(it is said), *ear hath not heard, it hath not entered into the
heart of man*, and these things again shall be during boundless ages. For the sake of these then were it not well to be
cut [by scourging] times out of number, to be slain, to be
burned, to undergo ten thousand deaths, to endure every
thing whatsoever that is dreadful both in word and deed?
For even if it were possible for one to live when burning in
the fire, ought one not to endure all for the sake of attain-
ing to those good things which have been promised?

[9.] But why do I trifle in saying these things to men
who do not even choose to disregard riches, but hold fast to
them as though they were immortal? And if they give a
little out of much, think they have accomplished every
thing? This is not Almsgiving. For Almsgiving is that
of the Widow who emptied out *all* her *living*. But if thou S. Mark xii. 44.
art not capable of contributing so much as the widow did,
yet at least contribute the whole of thy superfluity: keep
what is sufficient, not what is superfluous.

But there is no one who contributes even his superabundance. For so long as thou hast many servants[1], and [1] i.e. "slaves"
garments of silk, these things are all superfluities. Nothing
is indispensable or necessary, without which we are able
to live; these things are superfluous, and are uselessly
superadded[2]. Let us then see, if you will, what we can- [2] ἁπλῶς ἔξω πρόσκειται
not live without. Even if we have only two servants, we
can live. For whereas there are some who live without

Hom. 28. servants [at all], what sort of excuse have we, if we are not content with the two? We can also have a house built of brick of three rooms¹, and this were sufficient for us. For, tell me, are there not some men with children and wife who have but one room²? Let there be also, if you will, two serving boys.

¹ οἰκημά-
των
² οἶκον

[10.] And how is it not a shame (you say) that a gentlewoman³ should walk out with [only] two servants? It is no shame, that a gentlewoman should walk abroad with two servants, but it is a shame that she should go forth with many. Perhaps you laugh when you hear this. Believe me it *is* a shame. Just like dealers in sheep, or like dealers in slaves, you think it a great matter to go out with many servants? This is pride and vain-glory, the other is philosophy and respectability. For a gentlewoman ought not to be known from the multitude of her attendants. For what virtue is it to have many slaves? This belongs not to the soul, and whatever is not of the soul does not shew gentility. When she is content with a few things, then is she a gentlewoman indeed; but when she needs many, she is a servant and inferior to slaves.

³ τὴν ἐλευ-
θέραν

(5) Tell me, do not the angels go to and fro about the world alone, and need not any one to follow them? Are they then on this account inferior to us? they who need no [attendants] to us who do need them? If then the not even needing an attendant at all, is angelic, who comes nearer to the angelic life, she who needs many [attendants], or she who [needs] few? Is not this a shame? For a shame it is to do anything out of place.

Tell me who attracts the attention of those who are in the public places⁴, she who brings many in her train, or she who [brings but] few? And is not she who is alone, less conspicuous even than she who is attended by few? Seest thou that that [first-named conduct] is a shame? Who attracts the attention of those in the public places, she who wears beautiful garments, or she who is dressed in a simple and unstudied way? Again who attracts [the attention of] those in the public places, she who is borne on mules, and with trappings ornamented with gold, or she who walks out simply, and as it may be, with all de-

⁴ the open spaces of the streets where idlers gathered.

corum? Or as to this latter, is it not the case, that we do not even look at her, if we even see her; while as to the other, the multitudes not only force their way to see her, but also ask, Who is she, and Whence [she comes]? And I do not say how great envy is hereby produced. What then (tell me)? is it disgraceful to be looked at or not to be looked at? When is the shame greater, when all stare at her, or when no one [does]? when they inform themselves about her, or when they do not even care [about her]? Thou seest that we do every thing, not for modesty's sake but for vain-glory? He.xii.3.

However, since it is impossible to draw you away from this, I am content for the present that you should learn that this [other conduct] is no disgrace. Sin alone is a disgrace, which no one thinks to be a disgrace, but everything rather than it.

[11.] Let your dress be such as is needful, not superfluous. However, that we may not shut you up into too narrow a space, this I assure you, that we have no need of ornaments of gold, or of lace[1]. And it is not I who say this. For that the words are not mine, hear the blessed Paul saying, and solemnly charging women *to adorn themselves, not with plaitings [of the hair], or gold, or pearls, or costly apparel.* [1] λεπτῶν ὀθονίων 1 Tim. ii. 9.

But with what kind [of apparel] wouldest thou [that they adorn themselves]? tell us, O Paul. For perhaps they will say, that only golden things are costly; and that silks are not costly. Tell us too with what wouldest thou [that they be adorned]? *But having food and coverings*[2], *therewith* (saith he) *we shall be content*[3]. Let our garment be such (he means) as merely to cover us. For for this cause hath God given them to us, that we may cover our nakedness, and this any garment can do, of whatever sort it be, though but of trifling cost. Perhaps ye laugh, ye [women] that wear dresses of silk, for in truth one may well laugh, considering what Paul enjoined and what we practise! [2] σκεπάσματα ib. vi. 8. [3] ἀρκεσθησόμεθα

But my discourse is not addressed to women only, but also to men. For the rest of the things which we have are all superfluous; it is only the poor who possess no superfluities; and perhaps they too [do so only] from necessity: since, if it had been in their power, even they would not have abstained [from them]. Nevertheless, *whether in pretence or in truth*, they have so far no superfluities.

[12.] Let us then wear such clothes as are sufficient for our need. For what is the meaning of a quantity of gold? To persons on the stage these things are suitable, this apparel belongs to them and to women that are harlots, who do every thing in order to be looked at. Let her beautify herself, who is on the stage or the dancing platform. For she wishes to attract all men to her. But a woman who professes godliness, let her not beautify herself thus, but in a different way. Thou hast a means of beautifying thyself far superior to that. Thou also hast a theatre[1]: for that theatre do thou make thee beautiful: clothe thyself with the ornaments that belong thereto. What is thy theatre? Heaven, the company of Angels. I am not speaking of Virgins only, but also of women who are in the world. All as many as believe in Christ have that for their theatre. Let us speak such things that we may please those spectators. Put on such garments as that thou mayest gratify them.

For tell me, if a woman that is a Harlot putting aside her golden ornaments, and her robes, and her laughter, and her witty and unchaste talk, clothe herself with a cheap garment, and having dressed herself in an unstudied manner come in [on the stage], and utter religious words, and discourse of chastity, and say nothing indelicate, will not all [the spectators] stand up? will not this theatre be dispersed? will they not cast her out, as one who does not know how to suit herself to the crowd, and speaks things foreign to that Satanic theatre? So thou also, if thou enter into the Theatre of Heaven clad with her garments, the spectators will cast thee out. For there, there is no need of these garments of gold, but of different ones. Of what kind? of such as the prophet names, *clothed in fringed work of gold, and in varied colours*, not so as to make the body white and glistering, but so as to beautify the soul. For the Soul it is, which is contending and wrestling in that Theatre. *All the glory of the King's daughter is from within*, it saith. With these do thou clothe thyself. For

---

[1] "body of spectators"

so thou both deliverest thyself from other evils innumera- He.xii.3.
ble, and thy husband from anxiety and thyself from care.

For so thou wilt be respected by thy husband, when thou (6)
needest not many things. For every one is wont to be shy
towards those who make requests of him; but when he
sees that they have no need of him, then he lets down his
haughty spirit, and converses with them as with equals.
When thy husband sees that thou hast no requests to make
of him, that thou thinkest lightly of the presents which
come from him, then, even though he be of very haughty
mind[1], he will respect thee more, than if thou wert clad in [1] φρονημ-
golden ornaments; and thou wilt no longer be his slave. ατιῶν
For those of whom we stand in need, we are compelled to
stoop to. If, however, we draw back from making requests,
we shall no longer be regarded as criminals[2], but he knows [2] ὑπόδικοι
that it is from the fear of God that we pay him obedience,
not for what is given by him. For as it is, on the view
that he confers great favours on you, whatever honour he
receives, he still thinks he has not obtained all [that is due
to him]: but in the other case, though he obtain but a little,
he will account it a favour. He does not reproach [thee];
nor will he be himself compelled to be over-reaching on thy
account.

[13.] For what is more unreasonable, than to provide
golden ornaments, to be worn in baths, and in market places?
However, in baths and in market places it is perhaps no
wonder [that they should be worn], but that a woman
should come into Church so decked out is very ridiculous.
For for what possible reason does she come in here wearing golden ornaments, she who ought to come in that she
may hear [the precept] *that they adorn not themselves with* 1 Tim.
gold, nor pearls, nor costly array? With what object then, ii. 9.
O woman, dost thou come? Is it indeed on the view of
battling with Paul, and shewing that even if he repeat
these things ten thousand times thou regardest them not?
Or is it from wishing to put us your teachers to shame as
discoursing on these subjects in vain? For tell me; if any
heathen or unbeliever, after he has heard the passage read
where the blessed Paul says these things, having a believing wife, sees that she makes much account of beautifying

herself, and puts on ornaments of gold, that she may come publicly into Church and hear Paul solemnly charging [the women] that they adorn themselves, neither with *gold*, nor with *pearls*, nor with *costly array*, will he not indeed say to himself, when he sees her in her little room[1], putting on these things, and arranging them beautifully; 'why is my 'wife staying within in her little room? why is she so slow? 'why is she putting on her golden ornaments? where has 'she to go to? Into the Church? For what purpose? To 'hear, *not with costly array;*' will he not smile, will he not burst out into laughter? will he not believe that our religion[2] is a mockery and a deceit? Wherefore, I beseech [you], let us leave golden ornaments to processions, to theatres, to shopwindows[3]. But let not the image of God be decked out with these things : let the gentlewoman be adorned with gentility, and gentility is the absence of pride, and of boastful display.

Nay even if thou wish to obtain glory from men, thou wilt obtain it thus. For the wife of a man who is rich we shall not wonder at so much, when she wears gold and silk (for this is the common practice of them all), as when she is dressed in a plain and simple garment made merely of wool. This all will admire, this they will applaud. For in that adorning indeed of ornaments of gold and of costly apparel, she has many to share [the admiration] with her. And if she surpass one, she is surpassed by another; Yea, even if she surpass all, she must yield the palm to the Empress herself. In this other case, however, she outdoes all, even the very wife of the Emperor. For she alone in the midst of wealth, has chosen the [dress] of the poor. So that even if we desire glory, here too the glory is greater.

[14.] I say this not only to widows, even those that are rich; for in that case the necessity of widow-hood seems to cause this: but to those also who are under [the authority of] a husband.

'But, you say, I do not please my husband [if I dress 'plainly].' It is not thy husband that thou wishest to please, but the multitude of poor women, or rather [thou dost] not [wish] to please them, but to make them pine [with envy], and to give them pain, and make their poverty greater. How many blasphemous speeches are uttered HE.xii.3. because of thee! 'Let there be no such thing as poverty' (say they). 'God hates those that are become poor.' 'God 'loves not those who are in poverty.' For that it is not thy husband whom thou wishest to please, nor for this cause that thou deckest thyself out, thou shewest plainly to all by what thou thyself doest. For as soon as thou hast passed over the threshold of thy chamber[1], thou immedi- [1] θαλάμου ately puttest off all, both the robes, and the golden ornaments, and the pearls; and at home of all places thou dost not wear them.

But if thou really wishest to please thy husband, there are ways of pleasing him, by gentleness [I mean], by meekness, by propriety of conduct. For believe me, O woman, even if thy husband be infinitely debased in his habits[2], [2] κατωφερής these are the things which will more effectually win him, gentleness, propriety, freedom from haughtiness and expensiveness and extravagance. For as to the profligate, even if thou devise ten thousand such things, thou wilt not restrain him. And this they know who have had such husbands. For however thou mayest beautify thyself, he being a profligate will go off to a courtesan; while [the husband] that is chaste and regular thou wilt gain not by these means, but by the opposite: yea by these thou even causest him pain, clothing thyself with the reputation of a lover of the world. For what if thy husband out of respect, and that as a sober-minded man, does not speak, yet in his heart he will condemn thee, and will not rid himself of[3] ill-will[4] and feelings of jealousy. Wilt thou not drive [3] or conceal, περιστελεῖται away all pleasure for the future, by exciting ill-will against thyself? [4] φθόνους

[15.] Possibly you are annoyed at hearing what I have (7) said, and are indignant, saying, 'He irritates husbands still 'more against their wives.' It is not to irritate your husbands that I say this, but I wish that these things should be done by you of your own accord, for your own sakes, not for theirs; [I say them] not to free them from envy, but to free you from the parade of this life.

Dost thou wish to appear beautiful? I also wish it, but with beauty such as God seeks for, which He *the King* Ps. xlv. 11.

336 *The beauty which pleases God, and is permanent.*

Hom. 28. *greatly desires.* Whom wouldst thou have as a Lover?
see Hom. God or men? shouldest thou be beautiful with that beauty,
xiv. [8.]
pp. 183, God will *desire thy beauty;* but if with that other apart
184. from this, He will abominate thee, and thy lovers will be
profligates. For no man who loves a married woman is a
good man. Consider this even in regard to the adorning
that is external. For the other adorning, I mean that of
the soul, attracts God; but this, [attracts only] profligates.
Seest thou that it is for you that I care, about you that I
am anxious, that ye may be beautiful, really beautiful,
splendid, really splendid, that, instead of profligate men, ye
may have for your Lover God the Lord of all. And she
who hath Him for her Lover, to whom will she be like?
She has her place among the choirs of Angels. For if one
who is beloved of a king is accounted happy above all, what
will her dignity be who is beloved of God with much love?
Though thou put the world [in the balance against it],
there is nothing that is equivalent to that beauty.

This beauty then let us cultivate; with these embellishments let us adorn ourselves, that [so] we may pass into the Heavens, into the spiritual chambers, into the nuptial chamber that is undefiled. For as to this beauty, it is liable to be destroyed by any thing; and when it lasts well, and neither disease nor anxiety impair it (which is impossible), it does not last for twenty years. But that other is ever blooming, ever in its prime. *There,* there is no change to fear; no old age approaching brings a wrinkle with it, no disease coming vehemently down withers it; no desponding anxiety disfigures it; but it is far above all these things. But as to this [earthly beauty], before it appears it takes flight, and if it appears it has not many admirers. For those of well-ordered minds do not admire it; and those who do admire it, admire with wantonness.

[16.] Let us not therefore cultivate this [beauty], but that other: to that let us cleave, that with bright torches we may pass into the bridal chamber. For not to virgins only has this been promised, but to virgin souls. For had it been the [privilege] of virgins absolutely, those five would not have been shut out. This then belongs to all who are virgins in soul, who have been freed from worldly imaginations: for these imaginations corrupt our souls. If therefore we remain unpolluted, we shall depart thither, and shall be accepted. *For I have espoused you*, saith he, *to one husband, to present you a chaste virgin unto Christ.* These things he said, not with reference to Virgins, but to the whole body of the entire Church. For the uncorrupt soul is a virgin, though she have a husband: she is a virgin as to that which is Virginity indeed, that which is worthy of admiration. For this of the body is but the accompaniment and shadow of the other: while that is the True Virginity. This let us cultivate, and so shall we be able with cheerful countenance to behold the Bridegroom, to enter in with our torches bright, if the oil should not fail us; if by melting down our golden ornaments we procure such oil as makes our lamps bright. And this oil is kindness towards men.

<small>He, xii. 3.</small>
<small>2 Cor. xi. 2.</small>

If we impart what we have to others, if we make oil therefrom, then will it stand forth to protect us, and we shall not at that time say, *Give us oil, for our lamps are going out*, nor shall we beg of others, nor shall we be shut out when we are gone to them that sell, nor shall we hear that fearful and terrible voice, while we are knocking at the doors, *I know you not*. But He will acknowledge us, and we shall go in with the Bridegroom, and having passed into the spiritual Bride-chamber we shall enjoy good things innumerable.

<small>S. Matt. xxv. 8.</small>
<small>ib. 12.</small>

For if here the bride-chamber is so bright, the rooms so splendid, that none is weary of contemplating them, much more will it be so there. Heaven is the chamber[1], and the bride-chamber[2] better than Heaven: into this shall we enter. But if the Bride-chamber is so beautiful, what will the Bridegroom be?

<small>[1] θάλαμος</small>
<small>[2] νυμφών</small>

And why do I say, "Let us put away our golden orna-"ments, and impart to those that need?" For if ye ought even to sell yourselves, if ye ought to become slaves instead of free women, that so ye might be enabled to be with that Bridegroom, to enjoy that Beauty, [nay] merely to look on that Countenance, ought you not with ready mind to welcome all things? A king upon the earth we look at and admire, but when [we see] a king and a bridegroom both, much more ought we to welcome him with eagerness. In very deed these things are a shadow, while those others are a reality. And a King and a Bridegroom in Heaven! To be counted worthy also to go before Him with torches, and to be near Him, and to be ever with Him, what ought we not to do? what should we not perform? what should we not endure? Wherefore, I entreat you, let us conceive some desire for those blessings, let us long for that Bridegroom, let us be virgins as to the true Virginity. For it is the virginity of the soul which the Lord seeks after. With this let us enter into Heaven, *not having spot, or wrinkle, or any such thing;* that we may attain also to the good things which have been promised to us, of which may we all be partakers through the grace and mercy of Jesus Christ our Lord, with Whom to the Father together with the Holy Ghost, be glory power honour, now and ever, and world without end. Amen.

Eph. v. 27.

HOMILY XXIX.

Heb. xii. 4—6.

Ye have not yet resisted unto blood, striving against sin. And ye have forgotten the exhortation which speaketh unto you as unto children, My son, despise not thou the chastening of the Lord, nor faint when thou art rebuked of Him. For whom the Lord loveth, He chasteneth: and scourgeth every son whom He receiveth [1].

[1] or accepteth

THERE are two kinds of consolation, apparently opposed to one another, but yet contributing great strength each to the other; both of which he has here put forward. The one, I mean, is, when we say that persons have suffered much: for the soul is greatly refreshed, when it has many witnesses of its own sufferings, and this was the very thing that he introduced above, saying, *Call to mind the former days, in which, after ye had been illuminated, ye endured a great fight of afflictions.* The other is when we say, 'Thou hast suffered no great thing.' The former, when [the soul] has been exhausted refreshes it, and makes it recover breath: the latter, when it is becoming indolent and supine, turns it again [2] and pulls it down from its pride. Thus in order that no pride may spring up in them from that testimony [to their sufferings], see what he does. *Ye have not yet* (he says) *resisted unto blood, combating against sin.* And he did not at once go on with what follows, but after having shewn them all those who had stood [their ground] *unto blood*, and next brought in the glory of Christ, His sufferings [a], he then easily pursued his discourse.

supra x. 32.

[2] ἐπιστρέφει, or, turns, converts to God

[a] τὸ καύχημα τοῦ Χριστοῦ τὰ παθήματα, or "our glory—our boast—the sufferings of Christ."

HOM. 29. This he says also in writing to the Corinthians, *There hath*
1 Cor. x. *no temptation taken you, but such as is common to man,* that
13.
is, small. For this is calculated to arouse and raise up the
soul, when [I mean] it considers that it has not reached the
entire height [of trial], and encourages itself from the things
which have already befallen it.

What he means is this: Ye have not yet submitted to
death; your loss has extended only to money, to reputation,
to being driven from place to place. Christ however shed
His blood for you, while you have not [done it] even for
yourselves. He contended for the Truth even unto death,
fighting on your behalf; while ye have not yet entered
upon dangers that threaten death.

And ye have forgotten the exhortation. That is, And ye
have slackened your hands, ye have become faint. (*Ye have
not yet,* he said, *resisted unto blood, combating against sin.*
¹ σφόδρα Here he indicates that sin is both very vigorous¹, and is
πνέουσαν
itself armed. For the [expression] *Ye have resisted [stood
firm against],* is used with reference to those who stand [in
fight].

[2.] *Which* (saith he) *speaketh unto you as unto sons,
My son, despise not thou the chastening of the Lord, nor
faint when thou art rebuked of Him.* He has drawn his
encouragement from the facts themselves; over and above
he adds also that which is drawn from arguments, from
this testimony.

Faint not (saith he) *when thou art rebuked of Him.* It
follows that these things are of God. For this too is no
² τὸ τοιαῦ- small matter of consolation, when we come to know that it
τα δυνη-
θῆναι   is God's work that such things have power², He allowing
2 Cor. xii. [them], even as also Paul says; *He said unto me, My grace
9.
*is sufficient for thee: for My strength is made perfect in
weakness.* He it is who allows [them].

*For whom the Lord loveth He chasteneth, and scourgeth
every son whom He receiveth.* Thou canst not affirm that
there is any righteous man without affliction: even if he
appear to be so, yet *we* know not his other afflictions. So
that of necessity every righteous man must pass through
affliction. For it is a declaration of Christ, that the wide
and broad way leads to destruction, but the strait and nar-

row one to life. If then it is possible to enter into life by that means, and is not possible by any other, it follows that all have entered in by the narrow [way], as many as have departed unto life.

ver. 7. *Ye endure for chastisement*[1][b] (he saith); not for punishment, nor for vengeance, nor that we may [simply] suffer affliction. See, from those very things from which they supposed they had been deserted [of God], from these he says they may be confident, that they have not been deserted. It is as if he had said, Because ye have suffered so many evils, do you suppose that God has left you and hates you? If ye did not suffer, then it were right to suspect this. For if *He scourgeth every son whom He receiveth*, he who is not scourged, perhaps is not a son. What then, you say, do not bad men suffer distress? They suffer indeed, for how should they not? He did not say, Every one who is scourged is a son, but every son is scourged. For in all cases He scourges His son: what is wanted then is to shew, whether any son is not scourged. But thou wouldest not be able to say: why, there are many wicked men also who are scourged, for instance, Murderers, Robbers, Sorcerers, Plunderers of tombs. These however are paying the penalty of their own peculiar wickedness, and are not scourged as sons, but punished as being wicked: but ye as sons.

[3.] Then next, [he] again [argues] from the general custom. Thou seest how he brings up arguments from all quarters, from facts in the Scripture, from its words, from our own notions, from examples in ordinary life. ver. 8. *But if ye be without chastisement* [&c.] Thou seest that he said what I just mentioned, that it is not possible to be a son without being chastened. For just as in families, fathers care not for bastards, though they learn nothing, though they be not distinguished, but fear for their legitimate sons, lest they should be indolent, [so here]. If then not to be chastised is [a mark] of bastards, we ought to rejoice at chastisement, if this be [a sign] of legitimacy. *God dealeth with you as with sons;* for this very cause.

HE. xii. 7.

[1] εἰς παιδείαν

(2)

---

[b] εἰς παιδείαν ὑπομένετε is the reading of the best MSS. &c. of S. Chrys. as it is the approved reading of the Epistle. The later texts have the later reading εἰ π. ὑπ.

HOM. 29. ver. 9. *Furthermore, we have had fathers of our flesh which corrected us, and we gave them reverence.* Again, [he reasons] from their own experiences, from what they themselves

supra x. 32. suffered. For as in that other place he says, *Call to mind the former days,* so here also, God (he saith) *dealeth with you as with sons,* and ye could not say, We cannot bear it: yea, *as with sons* tenderly beloved. For if those others reverence their *fathers of the flesh,* how shall not you reverence your heavenly Father?

However it is not from this alone, that the difference arises, nor from the persons, but also from the cause itself, and from the fact. For it is not on the same grounds that He and they inflict chastisement: but they [did it] with a view to *what seemed good to them,* that is, fulfilling [their own] pleasure oftentimes, and not in all cases looking to what was expedient. But here, it is not possible to say that. For not for any interest of His own does He do this, but for you, and for your benefit alone. They [did it] that ye might be useful to themselves also, yea oftentimes too without any reason; but here there is nothing of this kind. Thou seest that this also brings consolation? For we are most closely attached to those [earthly parents], when we see that it is not for any interests of their own that they either command or advise us: but that their earnestness is, wholly and solely, on our account. For this is genuine love, and love in reality, when we are beloved though we be of no use to him who loves us, [when he loves us] not that he may receive, but that he may impart. He chastens, He does every thing, He uses all diligence, that we may become capable of receiving His benefits. (ver. 10) *For they verily* (he saith) *for a few days chastened us according to what seemed* [*good*] *to them, but He for our profit, that we might be partakers of His holiness.*

What is, *of His holiness?* It is, of His purity, so as to become worthy of Him, to the utmost of our capacity. He earnestly desires that ye may receive, and He does all in order that He may give you: do ye not earnestly endeavour

Ps. xvi. 2. that ye may receive? *I said unto the Lord* (saith one) *Thou art my Lord, for of my good things Thou hast no need.*

Furthermore, he saith, *we have had fathers of our flesh*

which corrected us and we gave them reverence: shall we not much rather be in subjection to the Father of spirits, and live? (To the Father *of spirits,* that is, either of spiritual gifts, or of prayers, or of the incorporeal powers.) If we die thus, then *we shall live. For they indeed for a few days chastened us according to what seemed [good] to them,* for what seems is not always profitable, but *He with a view to what is profitable.* He.xii.10.

[4.] It follows therefore that chastisement is *profitable;* that chastisement is a *participation of holiness.* Yea and this in a very eminent degree: for when it casts out sloth, and evil desire, and love of the things of this life, when it makes the soul collected, when it causes us to condemn all things here (for this is [the character of] affliction), is it not holy? does it not draw down the grace of the Spirit? (3)

Let us consider the righteous, from what cause they all shone brightly forth. Was it not from affliction? and, if you will, let us enumerate them from the first and from the very beginning: Abel, Noah himself; for it is not possible that he who was the only one in that so great multitude of the wicked, should not be afflicted; for it is said, *Noah being* alone *perfect in his generation, pleased God.* For consider, I beseech you, if now, when we have innumerable persons whose virtue we may emulate, fathers, and children, and teachers, we are thus distressed, what must we suppose that he suffered, alone among so many? But should I speak of the circumstances of that strange and wonderful rain? or should I speak of Abraham, his wanderings coming one upon another, the carrying away of his wife, the dangers, the wars, the famines? Should I speak of Isaac[c], what fearful things he underwent, driven from every place, and labouring in vain, and toiling for others? Or of Jacob? for indeed to enumerate all his [afflictions] is not necessary, but it is reasonable to bring Gen. vi. 9.

---

[c] The common texts substitute Jacob for Isaac here, omitting the following clause where Jacob is mentioned (as they also in the preceding sentence have "temptations" instead of "famines"); to correct the apparent inaccuracies of the text. But Mr. Field shews from other passages of S. Chrys. that he really means Isaac, having in view Gen. xxvi. 18—22, 27.

before you the testimony, which he himself [gave] when discoursing with Pharoah; *Few and evil are my days, and they have not attained to the days of my fathers.* Or should I speak of Joseph himself? or of Moses? or of Joshua? or of David? or of Elijah? or of Samuel? Or wouldest thou [that I speak] of all the prophets? wilt thou not find that all these were made illustrious from their afflictions? Tell me then, dost *thou* desire to become illustrious from ease and luxury? but this would be impossible.

Or should I speak of the Apostles? Nay but they even went beyond all men [in sufferings]. Even Christ saith this, *In the world ye shall have tribulation.* And again, *Ye shall weep and lament, but the world shall rejoice.* And, *Strait and narrow is the way*[d] *that leadeth unto life.* The Lord of the way hath said, that it is *narrow and strait;* and dost thou seek the *broad* [way]? How is this not unreasonable? In consequence thou wilt not arrive at life, seeing thou goest another [way], but at destruction, for thou hast chosen the [path] which leads thither.

Wouldst thou that I mention and bring before you those [that have lived] in luxury? Let us ascend from the last to the first. The rich man who is burning in the furnace; the Jews who lived for the belly, *whose god is their belly;* those who were ever seeking ease in the wilderness, were destroyed, as also those in Sodom, on account of their gluttony; and those in the time of Noah, was it not because they chose this soft and dissolute life? For *they luxuriated,* it saith, *in fulness of bread.* It speaks of those in Sodom. But if *fulness of bread* wrought so great evil, what could we say of all other delicacies? Esau, was not he in ease? And what of those who being of *the sons of God,* looked on women, and were carried down precipitately [to ruin]? and what of those who were maddened by inordinate lust? and all the kings of the nations, of the Babylonians, of the Egyptians, did they not come to an evil end? Are they not in torment?

[5.] And as to things now, are they not of the same character? Hear Christ saying, *They that wear soft clothing are in kings' houses,* but they who do not [wear] such

---

[d] S. Chrys. seems to have read this text without the words ἡ πύλη.

things, are in Heaven. For the soft garment relaxes even the austere soul, breaks it and enervates it: yea, even if it meet with a body rough and hard, it speedily by such delicate treatment makes it soft and weak. ^{HE.xii.10.}

For, tell me, from what other cause do you suppose it is, that women are so weak? Is it from their sex only? By no means: but from their way of living, and their bringing up. For their avoiding exposure[1], their inactivity, their baths, their unguents, their multitude of perfumes, the delicate softness of their couches, makes them in the end such as they are.

[1] "to the heat," σκιατροφία

And that thou mayest understand [that it is so], attend to what I say. Tell me; take from a garden only one of the trees that stand in the uncultivated[2] part and are beaten by the winds, and plant it in a moist and shady place, and thou wilt find it very unworthy of that [stock] from which thou didst originally take it. And that this is true, [appears from the fact that] women who are brought up in the country are stronger than men who live in towns: and many such would they overcome in wrestling. For when the body becomes more effeminate, it follows of necessity that the soul also shares the fruits of the evil, since, for the most part, the condition of its energies is in accordance with that of [the body]. For in illnesses we are different persons owing to our bodily weakness, and when we become well, we are different again. For just as in the case of a string when the tones[3] are weak and relaxed, and not well stretched out, the excellence of the art is also destroyed, being obliged to subserve to the ill condition of the strings: so in the case of the body also, the soul receives from it many hurts, many necessities[4]. For when it needs much nursing, the other endures a bitter servitude.

[2] ἐν τῇ ἐρήμῳ "dry and open part"?

[3] φθόγγοι

[4] ἀνάγκας

[6.] Wherefore, I beseech you, let us make it strong by work, and not nurse it as an invalid[5]. Not to men only but to women also have I to address my discourse. For why dost thou, O woman, continually enfeeble[e] [thy body] with luxury and make it exhausted[e]? Why dost thou ruin thy strength with fat? this fat is flabbiness not strength.

[5] νοσηλεύωμεν

(4)

^e ἐκπλύνεις .... ἐξίτηλον lit. "washest out," and "faded" as when colours are washed out of dresses.

Hom. 29. Whereas, if thou break off from these things, and manage thyself in a different way, then will thy personal beauty also improve according to thy wish, when strength and a good habit of body are there. If however thou beset it with ten thousand diseases, then will there not be any bloom of complexion, nor good state of health. For thou wilt always be in low spirits. And you know that as when the air is smiling it makes a beautiful house look splendid, so cheerfulness of mind also when added to a fair countenance, makes it still better: but if [a woman] is in low spirits and in pain of any kind, she becomes more ill-looking. Low spirits however are produced by diseases and pains; and diseases are produced from the body being made too delicate by your great luxury. So that even on this account you will flee from luxury, if you take my advice.

'But, you will say, luxurious living is attended with plea-'sure.' Yes, but not so great as the annoyances that attend it. And besides, the pleasure extends no further than the palate and the tongue. For when the table has been removed, or the food swallowed, thou wilt be like one that has not partaken [of it], or rather much worse, in that thou bearest thence heavy loads, and distention, and headache, and a sleep like death; nay oftentimes too, sleeplessness from repletion, and obstruction of the breathing, and eructation. And thou heapest perhaps ten thousand imprecations on thy belly, when thou oughtest to curse thy immoderate eating.

[7.] Let us not then fatten the body, but listen to Paul saying, *Make not provision for the flesh, for lusts.* Just as Rom. xiii. 14. if one should take food and throw it into a drain, so is he who throws it into his belly: or rather it is not so, but [1] ἐργάζε- much worse. For in the one case he uses[1] the drain without harm to himself: but in the latter the diseases which he generates besides are innumerable. For what nourishes is a sufficiency which also can be digested: whereas what is over and above our need, not only does not nourish, but even spoils the other. But no man sees these things, owing to a sort of prejudice and unseasonable pleasure.

Dost thou wish to nourish thy body? Take away what is superfluous; give what is sufficient, and as much as can be digested. Do not load it, lest thou overwhelm it. A sufficiency is both nourishment and pleasure too. For nothing is so productive of pleasure, as food well digested: nothing so [productive of] health: nothing [so productive of] acuteness of the faculties, nothing tends so much to keep away disease. For a sufficiency is both nourishment, and pleasure, and health; but what is more than that is injury to the health, and unpleasantness and disease. For the same [evils] which famine produces, those also does repletion cause; or rather, evils more grievous. For the former indeed within a few days carries a man off and sets him free; but the other eating into and putrefying the body, gives it over to long disease, and then to a most painful death. But *we*, while we account famine a thing greatly to be deprecated, yet run eagerly after repletion, which is more distressing than it.[He.xii.10.]

Whence is this disease? whence this madness? I do not say that we should waste ourselves away, but that we should take so much food as also gives us a pleasure, that is pleasure indeed; and so much as can nourish the body, and make it in good order for us, and well adapted for the energies of the soul, well joined and fitted together. But when it comes to be waterlogged[1] by luxury, it cannot when the flood-wave comes on, keep fast the very nails[2] themselves, as one may say, and joints which hold the frame together. For the flood-wave coming in upon it breaks up and scatters away the whole.

[1] ὑπέραν-τλον
[2] γόμφους

Make not provision for the flesh (he says) *for lusts.* He said well. For luxury is fuel for unreasonable lusts; even should a luxurious person be the most philosophical of all men, of necessity he must be somewhat affected by wine, by eating, he must needs be relaxed, he must needs make the flame greater. Hence [come] fornications, hence adulteries. For a hungry belly cannot generate lustful desire, or rather that which has had just a sufficiency. But that which generates unseemly lusts, is that which is relaxed[3] by luxury. And just as land which is very moist and a dung-hill which is thoroughly wetted and retains much dampness, generates worms, while that which has been freed from such moistness bears abundant fruits, when it [Rom. xiii. 14.]

[3] πλαδῶσα "wet and soft"

has nothing immoderate: even if it be not cultivated, it yields grass, and if it be cultivated, fruits: [so also do we.]

Let us not then make our flesh useless, or unprofitable, or hurtful [to us], but let us plant in it useful fruits, and fruit-bearing trees; let us not enfeeble them by luxury, for they too put forth worms instead of fruit when they are become rotten. So also implanted desire, if thou moisten it above measure, generates unreasonable pleasures, yea the most exceedingly unreasonable possible. Let us then by all means remove this pernicious evil, that we may be enabled to attain to the good things which have been promised us in Christ Jesus our Lord, with whom to the Father, together with the Holy Spirit, be glory now and ever and world without end. Amen.

HOMILY XXX.

Heb. xii. 11—13.

No chastisement for the present seemeth to be joyous[1]*, but* [1 *of joy*]
grievous[2]*, nevertheless afterward it yieldeth the peace-* [2 *of grief*]
able fruit of righteousness to them which have been exercised thereby. Wherefore lift up the hands which hang down, and the feeble knees: and make straight paths for your feet, lest that which is lame be turned out of the way, but let it rather be healed.

They who drink bitter medicines, first submit to some unpleasantness, and afterwards feel the benefit. For of this character is virtue, of this is vice. In the latter there is first the pleasure, then the despondency: in the former first the despondency, and then the pleasure. But there is no equality between them. For it is not the same, to be first grieved and afterwards pleased, and to be first pleased and afterwards grieved. How so? because in the latter case the anticipation of the despondency that is to come makes the present pleasure less: but in the former the expectation of the pleasure to come cuts away the vehemency of the present despondency; so that the result is that in the one instance we never have pleasure, in the latter we never have grief. And the difference does not lie in this respect only, but in others also. As how? That the circumstances of duration are not equal, but the one is far greater and more ample [than the other]. And in this respect too, it is still more so in things spiritual.

From this consideration then Paul attempts to console them; and again takes up the universal judgment of men, for no one is able to stand against this; nor to contend with the common decision when one asserts that which is acknowledged by all.

Ye are suffering, saith he. For such is chastisement; such is its beginning. For *all chastisement for the present seemeth to be not of joy but of grief.* Well said he, *seemeth not.* Chastisement he means is not grievous but *seemeth* so. *All chastisement:* not this and that, but *all,* both human and spiritual. Thou seest that he argues from our common notions? *seemeth* (he saith) *to be of grief,* so that it is not [really so]. For what sort of grief is that which brings forth joy? Just as that is not pleasure which brings forth despondency.

Nevertheless afterwards, it yieldeth the peaceable fruits of righteousness to them which have been exercised thereby. Not "fruit" but *fruits*[1], a great abundance.

[1] καρπούς

To them (saith he) *which have been exercised thereby.* What is *to them which have been exercised thereby?* to them that have endured for a long while, and been patient. And he also made use of an expression of favourable sound[2]. It follows that chastisement is exercise, making the athlete strong, and invincible in combats, irresistible in wars.

[2] εὐφήμῳ

If then *all chastisement* be of this character, this also will be such: so that we ought to look for good things, and for the end to be sweet and peaceful. And be not astonished if, being itself hard, it has sweet fruits; since in trees also the bark is almost destitute of all quality[3], as it were, and rough; but the fruits are sweet. But he took it from the common notion. If therefore we ought to look for such things, why do ye vex yourselves? Why, after ye have endured the painful, are ye desponding as to the good? The distasteful things which ye had to endure, ye endured: do not then be desponding as to the recompence.

[3] ἄποιος

He speaks as to runners, and boxers, and warriors[a]. Seest thou how he arms them, how he encourages them? "Walk straight," saith he. Here he speaks with reference to their thoughts; that is to say, not doubting. For if the chastisement be of love, if it begin from loving care, if it

---

[a] These words refer to ver. 13, *Wherefore lift up the hands which hang down, and the feeble knees, and make straight paths for your feet, lest that which is lame be turned out of the way, but let it rather be healed,* which is inserted in the text of the common editions.

end with a good result (and this he gives proof of, both by facts and by words, and by all considerations), for what cause are ye dispirited? For such are they who despair, who are not strengthened by the hope of the future. "Walk straight," saith he, that your lameness may not be increased, but brought back to its former condition. For he that runs when he is lame, galls the sore place. Thou seest that it is in our power to be thoroughly healed? HE.xii.14.

[2.] ver. 14. *Follow peace with all men, and holiness, without which no man shall see the* LORD. The very thing which he also said above, *Not forsaking the assembling of yourselves together*, this he hints at in this place also. For nothing so especially makes persons easily vanquished and subdued in temptations, as the being separated from each other. For, tell me, Separate a body of soldiers in war, and the enemy will not have need of any trouble at all, but will take them prisoners, coming on them separately, and so in this way the more helpless. supra x. 25.

Follow peace with all men, and holiness[1] (saith he) [*with all men*]. Therefore with the evil-doers as well? *If it be possible*, he says, *as much as lieth in you, live peaceably with all men*. For thy part (he means) *live peaceably*, so long as thou dost no harm to religion: but in whatever respects thou art ill-treated, bear it nobly. For the bearing with evil is a great weapon in trials. Thus Christ also made His disciples strong by saying, *Behold I send you forth as sheep in the midst of wolves: be ye therefore wise as serpents, and harmless as doves*. What dost Thou say? are we *among wolves*, and dost Thou bid us to be *as sheep*, and *as doves?* Yea, saith He. For nothing so shames him that is doing us evil, as our bearing nobly the things which are brought upon us: and not avenging ourselves either by word or by deed. This both makes us ourselves more philosophical, and procures us a greater reward, and also benefits them [that wrong us]. But such an one has been insolent? Do thou bless [him]. See how much thou wilt gain from this: thou hast quenched the evil, thou hast procured to thyself a reward, thou hast made him ashamed, and thou hast thyself suffered nothing serious.

[1] *the sanctification*
Rom. xii. 18.
S. Matt. x. 16.

[3.] *Follow peace with all men, and holiness*. What does

he mean by *holiness*[1]? chaste, and orderly living in marriage. If any person is unmarried (saith he) let him remain pure, let him marry: or if he be married, let him not commit fornication, but let him live with his own wife: for this also is *holiness*. How? Marriage is not *holiness*, but marriage preserves the holiness which [proceeds] from our Faith, not permitting a man to join himself to a harlot. For *marriage is honourable*, not holy. Marriage is pure: it does not however also give holiness, except by preventing the defilement of that [holiness] which has been given by our Faith.

Without which (saith he) *no man shall see the Lord*. Which same thing he also says in the [epistle] to the Corinthians. *Be not deceived: neither fornicators, nor adulterers, nor idolaters, nor effeminate, nor defilers of themselves with mankind, nor covetous persons, nor thieves, nor drunkards, nor revilers, nor extortioners, shall inherit the kingdom of God.* For how shall he who has become the body of a harlot, how shall he be able to be the body of Christ?

[4.] *Looking diligently*[2] *lest any man come short of the grace of God; lest any root of bitterness springing up trouble you, and thereby many be defiled: lest there be any fornicator or profane person.* Dost thou see how every where he puts the common salvation into the hands of each individual? *Exhorting one another daily* (saith he) *while it is called To-day*. Do not then cast all [the burden] on your teachers; do not [cast] all upon them who have the rule over you: ye also (he means) are able to edify one another. Which also he said in writing to the Thessalonians, *Edify ye one the other, even as also ye do*. And again, *Comfort one another with these words*. This advice we now also give to you.

[5.] If ye be willing, ye will have more success with each other than we can have. For ye both are with one another for a longer time, and ye know more than we of each other's affairs, and ye are not ignorant of each other's failings, and ye have more freedom of speech, and love, and intimacy; and these are no small [advantages] for teaching, but great and opportune introductions for it: ye will be more able than we both to reprove and to exhort. And not this only, but because I am but one, whereas ye are many; and ye will all be able, how many soever ye be, to be teachers. Wherefore I exhort you, do not *neglect this gift.* Each one of you has a wife, has a friend, has a servant, has a neighbour; him let him reprove, him let him exhort.

 For how is it not absurd, with regard to [bodily] nourishment, to make associations for messing together, and for drinking together, and to have a set day whereon to club with one another, as they say, and to make up by means of the association what each person being alone by himself falls short of—as for instance, if it be necessary to go to a funeral, or to a dinner, or to assist a neighbour in any matter—and not to do this for the purpose of instruction in virtue? Yea, I entreat you, let no man neglect it. For great is the reward he receives from God. And that thou mayest understand, he who had the five talents entrusted to him, is the teacher: and he who had the one [talent] is the learner. If the learner should say, I am a learner, I am in no risk, and should hide the reason[1], which he received of God, that common and simple [reason], and give no advice, should not speak plainly, should not rebuke, should not admonish, if he is able, but should bury it in the earth, for in very deed that heart is earth and ashes, which hides the gift of God: if then he hides it either from indolence, or from wickedness, it will be no defence to him to say, 'I had but one talent.' Thou hadst one talent. Thou oughtest then to have brought one besides, and to have doubled the talent. If thou hadst brought one in addition, thou wouldst not have been blamed. For neither did He say to him who brought the two, Wherefore hast thou not brought five. But He accounted him worthy of the same [rewards] with him who brought the five. Why? Because he gained as much as he had. And, because he had received fewer than he who had been entrusted with the five, he was not on this account negligent, nor did he use the smallness [of what was entrusted to him, as an excuse] for idleness. And thou oughtest not to have looked to him who had the two; or rather, thou oughtest to have looked to him, and as he having two imitated him who had the five, so oughtest thou to have emulated him who had the two. For if

Heb. xii. 16.

1 Tim. iv. 14.

[1] τὸν λόγον, includes "word," and "doctrine."

for him who has means and does not impart to others, there is punishment in store, how shall there not be the very greatest punishment for him who is able to advise and exhort in any way, and does it not? In the former case the body is nourished, in the latter the soul; there thou preventest the death that is temporal, here that which is eternal.

[6.] But I have no [skill of] speech[1], you say. But there is no need of [skill of] speech nor of eloquence. If thou see thy friend about to be guilty of fornication, say to him, It is an evil thing which thou art going after; art thou not ashamed? dost thou not blush? it is a wrong thing. 'Why, does he not know (you say) that it is wrong?' Yes, [he knows it], but he is dragged on by his lust. They that are sick also know that it is bad to drink cold water, nevertheless they need persons who shall hinder [them from it]. For he who is actually suffering, will not easily be able to help himself in his sickness. There is need therefore of thee who art in health, in order to [forward] his cure. And if he be not persuaded by thy words, watch for him as he goes away, and hold him fast; Peradventure he will be ashamed.

'And what advantage is it (you say), when he does this 'for my sake, and because he has been held back by me?' Do not be too minute in thy calculations. For a while, by whatever means thou canst, withdraw him from his evil practice; let him be accustomed not to go off to that pit [of destruction], whether through thee, or by any other means whatever. When thou hast accustomed him not to go, then by taking him after he has gained breath a little thou wilt be able to teach him, that he ought to do this for God's sake, and not for man's. Do not wish to make all right at once, since thou wilt not be able: but do it gently and by degrees.

If thou see him going off to drinking, or to parties where there is nothing but drunkenness, in this instance [also] do the same; and again on the other hand intreat him, if he observe that thou hast any failing, to help thee and set thee right. For in this way, he will even of himself, bear reproof, when he sees both that thou needest reproofs as

[1] λόγου

well, and that thou helpest him, not as one that had done every thing right, nor as a master, but as a friend and a brother. Say to him, I have done thee a service, in reminding thee of things expedient [for thee]: do thou also, whatever failing thou seest me have, pull me up ¹, set me right. If thou see me irritable, if avaricious, restrain me, bind me by exhortation. HE.xii.16. ¹ ἀναχαί-τισον

This is friendship; thus *brother aided by brother becomes a fortified city*. For it is not eating and drinking which makes friendship: such friendship even robbers have and murderers. But if we are friends, if indeed we have a regard for one another, let us in these respects contribute to help one another. This leads us to a friendship that is profitable: those things let us hinder which lead to Hell. Prov. xviii. 19.

[7.] Wherefore neither let him that is reproved be indignant: for we are men and we have failings; nor let him who reproves do it as laughing over him and making a display, but privately, with gentleness. He that reproves has need of greater gentleness, that thus he may persuade [them] to bear the cutting. Do you not see surgeons, when they burn, when they cut, with how great gentleness do they apply their treatment? much more ought those who reprove others to act thus. For reproof is sharper even than fire and knife, and makes [men] start. On this account surgeons take great pains to make them bear the cutting quietly, and apply it as tenderly as possible, even giving in ² a little, then giving time to take breath. ² ἐνδι-δόντες

So ought we also to offer reproofs, that they who are reproved may not start away. Even if then it be necessary to bear to be insulted, yea even to be struck, let us not decline it. For those also who are cut [by the surgeons] utter numberless cries against those who are cutting them; they however heed none of these things, but [look] merely to the health of the patients. So indeed in this case also we ought to do all things that our reproof may be effectual, to bear all things, looking to the reward which is in store.

Bear ye one another's burdens, saith he, *and so fulfil the law of Christ.* In this way then, both by reproving and bearing with one another, shall we be able to complete our Gal. vi.2.

Hom. 30. edifying [one another]. And thus will ye make the labour light for us, in all things taking a part with us, and stretching out a hand, and becoming sharers and partakers, both in each other's salvation, and each one in his own. Let us then endure patiently, both in bearing *one another's burdens,* and in reproving: that we may attain to the good things promised in Christ Jesus our Lord, with Whom to the Father and also to the Holy Ghost, be glory might honour, now and for ever and world without end. Amen.

HOMILY XXXI.

HEB. xii. 14.

Follow peace with all men, and holiness[1] *without which no one shall see the* LORD.

[1] or, the sanctification

MANY things there are which are characteristic of Christianity: but more than all, and better than all, Love towards each other, and Peace. For this cause Christ also saith, *My peace I give unto you.* And again, *By this shall all men know that ye are My disciples, if ye love one another.* For this cause Paul too saith, *Follow peace with all men, and holiness,* that is, purity [a], *without which no man shall see the* LORD.

S. John xiv. 27. ib. xiii. 35.

Looking diligently lest any man fail of the grace of God. Just as if they were travelling together on some long journey, in a large company, he says, Take heed that no man be left behind: I do not seek this only, that ye should arrive yourselves, but also that ye should look diligently after the others.

Lest any man (he saith) *fail of the grace of God.* (He means the good things to come, the faith of the gospel, the most excellent course of life: for they all are of *the Grace of God.*) Do not tell me, It is [but] one that perisheth. Even for one Christ died. Hast thou no care for him *for whom Christ died?*

1 Cor. viii. 11.

Looking diligently, he saith, that is, searching carefully, considering, thoroughly ascertaining, as is done in the case of sick persons, and in all ways examining: thoroughly

---

[a] σεμνότητα, properly a disposition and conduct which creates respect or reverence: so specially (here as in other places) chastity. see Hom. xxx. [3.], above p. 352.

ascertaining, *lest any root of bitterness springing up trouble you* (This [expression] is found in Deuteronomy; and he derived it from the metaphor of plants. *Lest any root of bitterness*, he saith); which he said also in another place when he writes, *A little leaven leaveneth the whole lump.* Not for his sake alone do I wish this, he means, but also on account of the harm arising therefrom. That is to say, even if there be a root of this kind, do not suffer any shoot to come up, but let it be cut off, that it may not bear its proper fruits, that so it may not defile and pollute the others also. For he saith, *Lest any root of bitterness springing up trouble you; and by it many be defiled.*

And with good reason did he call sin *bitter:* for in very deed nothing is more bitter than sin, and they know it, who after they have committed it pine away from [the working of] their conscience, who endure much bitterness. For being exceedingly bitter, it perverts even the very reasoning faculty itself. Such is the nature of what is bitter: it is unprofitable.

And well said he, *root of bitterness.* He said not, "bitter," but *of bitterness.* For it is possible that a bitter root might bear sweet fruits; but it is not possible that a root and fountain and foundation of bitterness, should ever bear sweet fruit. For [in this case] all things are bitter, they have nothing sweet, all are bitter, all unpleasant, all full of hatred and abomination.

And by this (he saith) *many be defiled.* That is, Cut away the lascivious persons.

[2.] ver. 16. *Lest there be any fornicator: or profane person, as Esau, who for one morsel of meat sold his birthrights*[1].

And wherein was Esau a *fornicator?* He does not say that Esau was a fornicator. *Lest there be any fornicator* he says, then, *follow after holiness: lest there be any, as Esau, profane;* that is, gluttonous, without self-control, worldly, selling away things spiritual.

Who for one morsel of meat sold his birthrights, that is, who on account of his own slothfulness sold this honour which he had from God, and for a little pleasure, lost the greatest honour and glory. This [he said] as exactly suit-

[1] πρωτο-τόκια birthright privileges

able to their case. This [was the conduct] of an abominable, He.xii.17. of an unclean person. So that not only is the fornicator unclean, but also the glutton, the slave of his belly. For he also is a slave [though] of a different pleasure. He is forced to be overreaching, he is forced to be rapacious, to behave himself unseemly in ten thousand ways, being the slave of that passion. And oftentimes too does he blaspheme. In this way he accounted *his birthright privileges* to be nothing worth. That is, providing for temporary refreshment, he went even to the [sacrifice of his] *birthrights*. So henceforth *the birthright* belongs to us, not to the Jews. And at the same time also this is added to their calamity, that the first is become last, and the second, first: the one, for courageous endurance; this other last for indolence.

[3.] ver. 17. *For ye know* (saith he) *how that afterwards, when he would have inherited the blessing, he was rejected. For he found no place of repentance, though he sought it carefully with tears.* What now is this? doth he indeed exclude repentance? By no means. 'But how, you say, was 'it that *he found no place of repentance?*' For if he condemned himself, if he made a great wailing, why did he *find no place of repentance?* Because it was not really a case of repentance. For just as the grief of Cain was not of repentance, and the murder proved it; so also in this case, his words were not those of repentance, and the murder afterwards proved it. For even he also in purpose of mind slew Jacob. For *Let the days of mourning for my father,* he saith, Gen. *come, and I will slay my brother Jacob.* His *tears* had not xxvii. 41. power to give him *repentance*. And [the Apostle] did not say "by repentance" simply, but even *with tears, he found no place of repentance*. Why now? Because he did not repent in the manner in which he ought, for this is repentance, he repented not as it behoved him.

For how is it that he [the Apostle] came to say this? how did he exhort them again after they had become *sluggish?* supra vi. how, when they were become *lame;* how, when they were supra *paralysed* [b]? how, when they were *relaxed* [b]? for this is the ver. 13. beginning of a fall. He seems to me to glance at some ib. 12. amongst them who were fornicators, but not to wish at

[b] [παραλυθέντας ... παρειμένους, as in ver. 12.]

(2)

that time openly to reprove them: but feigns ignorance that they might correct themselves. For it is right at first indeed to pretend ignorance: but afterwards, when they continue [in sin], then to add reproof also, that so they may not become utterly shameless. Which very thing Moses also did in the case of Zimri and the daughter of Cosbi.

For he found (saith he) *no place of repentance*, he found not repentance; or that he sinned beyond[1] repentance. There are then sins too great for repentance. His meaning is, Let us not fall by a fall that is incurable. So long as the matter is [one of] lameness, it is easy to become upright: but if we turn out of the way, what will be left? For it is to those who have not yet fallen that he thus discourses, striking them with terror, and says that it is not possible for him who is fallen, to obtain consolation; but to those who have fallen, that they may not fall into despair, he says the contrary, speaking thus, *My little children, of whom I again travail in birth, until Christ be formed in you.* And again, *Whosoever of you are justified by the Law, are fallen from Grace.* Lo! he testifies that they had fallen away. For he that standeth, hearing that it is not possible to obtain pardon after having fallen, will be more earnest, and more cautious about his standing: if however thou use the same severity towards one also who is fallen, he will never rise again. For what hope will he have to shew forth the change?

But he not only wept (you say), but also *sought earnestly*. He does not then exclude repentance; but makes them careful, that they may not fall.

[4.] As many then as do not believe there is a Hell, let them call these things to mind: as many as think to sin without being punished, let them take account of these things. Why did Esau not obtain pardon? Because he repented not as he ought. Wouldest thou see perfect penitence? Hear of the repentance of Peter after his denial. For the Evangelist in relating to us the things concerning him, says, *And he went out and wept bitterly.* For this cause even such a sin as that was forgiven him, because he repented in the manner he ought. Although the Victim

---

[1] μείζονα "committed sins too great for repentance"

Gal. iv. 19.

ib. v. 4.

S. Matt. xxvi. 75.

(3)

had not yet been offered, nor had The Sacrifice as yet been made, nor was sin as yet taken away, it still had the rule and sovereignty. He.xii.17.

And that thou mayest learn, that this denial [arose] not so much from sloth, as from his being forsaken of God, who was teaching him to know the measures of human [power], and not to contradict what was said by his Master, nor to be more highminded than the rest, but to know that it is not possible that anything should be done without God, and that *Except the Lord build the house, they labour in vain who build it:* for on this account also Christ said to him alone, *Satan desired to sift thee as wheat,* and I allowed it not, *that thy faith may not fail.* For inasmuch as it was likely that he would be high-minded, as being conscious to himself that he loved Christ more than they all, for this cause *he wept bitterly.* And the rest that he did after his weeping is of the same character. For what did he not do? After this he exposes himself to dangers innumerable, and by many means evinces his courage and presence of mind. Ps. cxxvii. 1. S. Luke xxii. 31, 32.

Judas also repented, but in an evil way: for he hanged himself. Esau too repented, as I said; or rather, he did not even repent; for his tears were not [tears] of repentance, but rather of pride and wrath. And this was proved by what followed. The blessed David repented, thus saying, *Every night will I wash my bed: I will water my couch with my tears.* And the sin which had been committed long ago, after so many years, after so many generations he bewailed, as if it had recently occurred. Ps. vi. 6.

[3.] For he who is penitent ought not to be angry, nor to be fierce, but to be contrite, as a condemned person, as not having boldness of speech, as one on whom sentence has been passed, as one who ought to be saved by mercy alone, as one who has shewn himself ungrateful toward his Benefactor, as unthankful, as reprobate, as worthy of punishments innumerable. If he considers these things, he will not be angry, he will not be indignant, but will mourn, will weep, will sigh, and will lament night and day.

He that is penitent ought never at any time to hand over his sin to oblivion, but on the one hand to beseech God not to remember it, while on the other he himself never at

362 *Knowledge, Confession, remembrance of sins necessary.*

HOM. 31. any time forgets it. If we remember it, God will forget it. Let us exact punishment from our own selves; let us accuse our own selves; thus shall we propitiate the Judge. For sin when confessed becomes less, but not confessed [becomes] worse. For if sin add to itself shamelessness and ingratitude, how will he be at all able to guard himself from again falling into the same [evils], who does not know that he sinned the first time?

Let us then not deny [our sins], I beseech you, nor be shameless [about them], that we may not have to suffer punishment even against our will. Cain heard God say, *Where is Abel thy brother? And he saith, I know not; am I my brother's keeper?* Thou seest how this made his sin the more grievous? But his father did not act thus. What then? When he heard, *Adam, where art thou?* he saith, *I heard Thy voice, and I was afraid, because I am naked, and I hid myself.* A great good it is to acknowledge our sins, and to bear them in mind continually. Nothing so effectually cures a fault, as a continual remembrance of it. Nothing makes a man so slow to wickedness.

Gen. iv. 9.

ib. iii. 9.
ib. 10.

[6.] I know that conscience starts back, and endures not to be scourged by the remembrance of evil deeds; but do thou hold tight thy soul and place a halter on it. For just like a horse ill broken in [1], so does it bear impatiently [what is put upon it], and is unwilling to persuade itself that it has sinned: all this however is the work of Satan [2]. But for ourselves let us persuade it that it has sinned; let us persuade it that it has sinned, that it may also repent, in order that having repented it may escape torment. How dost thou claim to obtain pardon for thy sins, tell me, when thou hast not yet confessed them? assuredly he is an object of compassion and kindness that hath sinned. But thou who hast not yet persuaded thyself [that thou hast sinned], how dost thou claim to be pitied, when thou art thus without shame for some things [3]?

[1] δυσήνιος
[2] σαταvι-κόν
[3] ἐπὶ τίσιν

Let us persuade ourselves that we have sinned. Let us say it not with the tongue only, but also with the mind. Let us not call ourselves sinners, but also count over our sinful deeds, going over them each specifically [4]. I do not say to thee, Make a parade of thyself, nor accuse thyself

[4] κατ' εἶ-δος, see above p. 124.

before others: but [I tell thee] to be persuaded by the pro- Hᴇ.xii.17.
phet when he saith, *Reveal thy way unto the Lord.* Confess Ps.xxxvii.
these things before God. Confess before the Judge thy 5.
sins with prayer; if not with tongue, at least in memory,
and thus earnestly beg to find mercy.

If thou keep thy sins continually in thy remembrance,
thou wilt never bear in mind any wrongs done thee by thy
neighbour. I do not say, if thou art persuaded that thou
art thyself a sinner; This does not avail so to humble the
soul, as do our sins [taken] themselves by themselves, and
examined specifically [1]. Thou wilt have no remembrance [1] κατ'
of wrongs [done thee], if thou hast these things continually εἶδος
in remembrance; thou wilt feel no anger, thou wilt revile
no man, thou wilt have no high thoughts, thou wilt not be
again involved in the same [sins], thou wilt be more vehement towards what is good.

[7.] Thou seest how many excellent [effects] are pro- (4)
duced from the remembrance of our sins? Let us then
write them in our minds. I know that the soul does not
endure a recollection which is so bitter: but let us constrain and force it. It is better that it should be gnawed
with the remembrance now, than at that time with the
vengeance.

Now, if thou remember them, and continually present see p.210.
them before God, and pray for them, thou wilt speedily
blot them out; but if thou forget them now, thou wilt
then be reminded of them even against thy will, when they
are brought out publicly before the whole world, displayed
before all, both friends and enemies, and Angels. For surely
He did not say to David only, *What thou didst secretly, I* 2 Sam.
will make manifest to all, but even to us all. Thou wert xii. 12.
afraid of men (saith he) and respected them more than
God; and when God was seeing thee caredst not, but
wert ashamed before men. For it saith [c], "the eyes of men,
"this is their fear." For this cause thou shalt suffer punishment in that very point; for I will reprove thee, setting
thy sins before the eyes of all. For that this is true, and
that in that day the sins of us all are [to be] publicly dis-

[c] This seems to be alleged as a citation from Holy Scripture, but it does not appear what passage S. Chrysostom had in view.

played, unless we now do them away by continual remembrance, hear how cruelty and inhumanity are publicly exposed, *I was an hungred* (saith He) *and ye gave Me no meat.* When are these things said? Is it in a corner? Is it in a secret place[1]? By no means. When then? *When the Son of Man is come in His glory,* and *all the nations* are gathered together, when He has separated the one from the other, then will He speak in the audience of all, and will *set* them *on His right hand* and *on* His *left: I was an hungred and ye gave Me no meat.*

See again the five virgins also, hearing in the presence of all, *I know you not.* For the five and five do not intimate the number of five only, but those virgins who are wicked and cruel and inhuman, and those too who are not such. So also he that had buried his one talent, heard in the presence of all, even of those who had brought the five and the two, *Thou wicked and slothful servant.* But not by words alone but by deeds also does He then convict them: even as the Evangelist also saith, *They shall look on [Him] whom they pierced.* For the resurrection shall be of all at the same time, both of sinners and of the righteous. At the same time shall He be present to all in the judgment.

[8.] Consider therefore who they are who shall then be in dismay, who in grief, who dragged away to the fire, whilst the others are crowned. *Come* (He saith), *ye blessed of My Father, inherit the kingdom which hath been prepared for you from the foundation of the world.* And again, *Depart from Me into the fire which hath been prepared for the devil and his angels.*

Let us not merely hear the words but depict them also before our sight, and let us imagine Him to be now present and saying these things, and that we are led away to that fire. What heart shall we have? what consolation? And what, when we are cut asunder? and what when we are accused of rapacity? what excuse shall we have to utter? what specious argument? Not any: but of necessity bound with chains, bending down, must we be dragged to the mouths of the furnace, to the river of fire, to the darkness, to the never-dying punishments, and must not entreat any one [to help us]. For it is not, it is not possible, it saith, to pass across from this side to that: for *there is a great gulf betwixt us and you*, and it is not possible even for those who wish it to go across, and stretch out a helping hand: but we must needs burn continually, there being no one to aid us, even should it be father or mother, or any whosoever, yea though he have much boldness toward God. For, it says, *A brother doth not redeem; shall man redeem?* Hᴇ.xii.17. S. Luke xvi. 26. Ps. xlix. 8.

Since then it is not possible to have one's hopes of salvation in another, but [it must be] in one's self after the loving kindness of God, let us do all things, I entreat you, so that our conduct may be pure, and our course of life the best, and that we may not incur any stain even from the beginning. But if we have incurred it, at all events let us not sleep after the stain, but continue always washing away the pollution by penitence, by tears, by prayers, by works of mercy[1].

What then, you say, if I have it not in my power to do works of mercy[1]? But thou hast *a cup of cold water*, however poor thou art. But thou hast *two mites*, in however deep poverty thou art; but thou hast feet, so as to go to visit the sick, so as to enter into a prison; but thou hast a roof, so as to receive strangers. For there is no pardon, no not any for him who does not perform works of mercy.

These things we say to you continually, that we may effect if it be but a little by the continued repetition: these things we say, not caring so much for those who receive the benefits, as for yourselves. For ye give to them indeed things here, but in return you receive heavenly things: which may we all obtain, in Christ Jesus our Lord, with whom to the Father, together with the Holy Ghost, be glory, now and ever, and world without end. Amen.

---

[1] ἐλεημοσύνην ἐργάζεσθαι S. Matt. x. 42. S. Mark xii. 42.

HOMILY XXXII.

Heb. xii. 18—24.

For ye are not come unto a fire[a] *that might be touched and that burned, and unto blackness, and darkness, and tempest, and the sound of a trumpet, and the voice of words, which voice they that heard entreated that the word should not be spoken to them any more*[1]. *(For they could not endure that which was commanded, And if so much as a beast touch the mountain, it shall be stoned. And, so terrible was the sight, that Moses said, I exceedingly fear and quake.) But ye are come unto Mount Sion, and unto the city of the Living God, the Heavenly Jerusalem; and to myriads of Angels, in festive gathering*[b], *and to the Church of the first-born which have been enrolled in Heaven; and to God the Judge of all; and to the spirits of just men made perfect: and to* JESUS *the Mediator of the New Covenant: and to the blood of sprinkling that speaketh better things than*[2] *Abel.*

[1] that not a word more should be spoken to them

[2] in comparison of

WONDERFUL indeed were the things in the Temple, the Holy of Holies; and again awful were these things also that were done at Mount Sina, *the fire, the darkness, the blackness, the tempest.* For, it says, *God appeared in Sina,* and long ago were all these things celebrated[c]. The New Covenant however, was not given with any of these things, but has been given in simple discourse by God[d].

cf. Deut. xxxiii. 2.

See then how he makes the comparison in these points

---

[a] ὑμεῖς is omitted in Mr. Field's text as by some critical editors of the New Test. It is not referred to by S. Chrys.

[b] πανηγύρει. See below p. 367. This word is connected with the preceding μυρίασιν ἀγγέλων by S. Chrys. as appears from his interpretation. So the Latin Vulgate has *et multorum millium angelorum frequentiam, et ecclesiam primitivorum &c.*

[c] ᾔδετο. e.g. Ps. xviii, lxviii. Habak. iii. as well as Exod. xix.

[d] παρὰ Θεοῦ. The reading of the common edition is Χριστοῦ: which was that of Mutianus.

also. And with good reason has he put them after [the other]. For when he had persuaded them by [arguments] innumerable, when he had also shewn the wide difference between the covenants, then afterwards, the one having been already condemned, he easily enters on these points also.

And what says he? *For ye are not come unto a fire which might be touched, and that burned, and unto blackness, and darkness, and tempest, and the sound of a trumpet, and the voice of words; which they that heard entreated that the word should not be spoken to them any more.*

These things, he means, are terrible; and so terrible that they could not even bear to hear them, that not even *a beast* dared to go up; (But they are not such as the things that come hereafter[1]. For what is Sina to Heaven? And what the *fire which might be touched* to God who cannot be touched? for *God is a consuming fire.*) [They were terrible;] for it is said, *Let not God speak, but let Moses speak unto us*. And so fearful was that which was commanded, *Though even a beast touch the mountain, it shall be stoned; Moses said, I exceedingly fear and quake.* What wonder as respects the people? he himself who entered into *the thick darkness where God was*, saith, *I exceedingly fear and quake.*

[2.] *But ye are come unto Mount Sion and to the city of the Living God, the heavenly Jerusalem: and to myriads of angels in festive gathering, and to the Church of the first-born which have been enrolled in Heaven, and to God the Judge of all, and to the spirits of just men made perfect, and to* JESUS *the Mediator of the New Covenant, and to the blood of sprinkling, that speaketh better [things] than Abel.*

Instead of *Moses*, there is JESUS. Instead of the people, *myriads of angels.*

Of what *first-born* does he speak? Of the faithful.

And to the spirits of just men made perfect. With these shall ye be, he means.

And to Jesus the mediator of the New Covenant, and to the blood of sprinkling that speaketh better [things] in comparison of Abel. Did then the [blood] *of Abel* speak? Yea, he saith, *and by it he being dead yet speaketh.* And

HE.xii.24.

[1] τὰ μετὰ ταῦτα

infra ver. 29.

Exod. xx. 19.

Ib. 21.

supra xi. 4.

HOM. 32. again God saith, *The voice of thy brother's blood crieth unto*
Gen. iv. 10. *Me.* Either this latter [is the meaning] or that [former];
because it is still even now celebrated: but not in such
way as that of Christ. For this has cleansed all men, and
sends forth a voice more clear and more distinct, in proportion as the testimony it has is greater, namely that by
facts.

ver. 25—29. *Take heed that ye refuse not Him that speak-*
[1] χρημα- *eth. For if they escaped not, who refused him that spake*[1]
τίζοντα
that made *on earth, much more shall not we escape, if we turn away*
a revela- *from Him that speaketh from Heaven. Whose voice then*
tion: see
above *shook the earth: but now hath He promised, saying, Yet*
p. 264. *once more I shake not the Earth only, but also Heaven.*
And this [word], *Yet once more, signifieth the removing of*
those things that are shaken, as of things which have been
made, that those which cannot be shaken may remain.
Wherefore we receiving a Kingdom which cannot be moved,
let us have grace whereby we serve God acceptably with
reverence and godly fear. For our God is a consuming
fire.

[3.] Fearful were those other things, but far more admirable and more glorious are these. For here there is not
darkness, nor *blackness*, nor *tempest*. It seems to me that
by those words he hints at the obscurity of the Old [Testa-
[2] τὸ συνε- ment], and the overshadowed and veiled[2] character of the
σκιασμέ-
νον καὶ Law. And besides, the Giver of the Law in fire appears
συγκεκα-
λυμμένον terrible, and apt to punish those who transgress.
(2) But what are *the sounds of the trumpet?* Probably it is
as though some King were coming. This at all events will
1 Cor. xv. also be at the Second Coming. *At the last trump* we
52. must all be raised. But it is the trumpet of His voice
which effects this. At that time then all [the things]
were objects of sense, and sights, and sounds; now all are
objects of the understanding, and invisible.

See Exod. And, it says, *there was much smoke.* For since God is
xix. 18. said to be fire, and thus appeared in the bush, He indicates
the fire even by the smoke. And what is *the blackness*
and the darkness? He again expresses its fearfulness.
Is. vi. 4. Thus Isaiah also says: *And the house was filled with smoke.*
And what is the object of *the tempest?* The human kind

Voice *to them through* darkness, *to us through veil of flesh.*

were indolent. It was therefore needful that they should be thoroughly aroused by these things. For no one [was] so dull as not to have had his thoughts [raised] up, when these things were done, and promulgated as the Law[1]. HE.xii.19.

[1] νομοθετουμένων Exod. xix. 19.

Moses spake, and God answered him by a Voice[e]: for it was necessary that the Voice of God should be uttered. Inasmuch as He was about to promulgate His Law through Moses, on this account He makes him worthy of confidence. They saw him not, because of the thick darkness: they heard him not, because of the weakness of his voice. What then? *God answered by a voice,* [as it were] addressing an assembled multitude[2]: yea and his name shall be called[f].

[2] δημηγορῶν

They entreated (he saith) *that the word should not be spoken to them any more*[3].

[3] that not a word more should be spoken to them

From the first therefore they were themselves the cause of God's being manifested through the Flesh[4]. Let Moses speak with us, it is said, and *Let not God speak with us.* They who make comparisons elevate the one side the more, that they may shew the other to be far greater. In this respect also our [privileges][5] are more gentle and more admirable. For they are great in a twofold respect: because while they are glorious and greater, they are more accessible. This he says also in the Epistle to the Corinthians: *with unveiled countenance,* and, *not as Moses put a veil over his face.* They, he means, were not counted worthy of the [privileges] that we [are]. For of what were they thought worthy? They saw *darkness, blackness;* they heard *a voice.* But thou also hast heard a voice, not through darkness, but through flesh. Thou hast not been disturbed, neither hast thou been troubled, but thou hast stood and held discourse with the Mediator.

Exod. xx. 19.
[4] φανῆναι διὰ τῆς σ.
[5] τὰ ἡμέτερα
2 Cor. iii. 18.
ib. 13.

And on another view, by the *darkness* he indicates the invisibleness[6] [of God]. *And darkness* (it saith) *was under His feet.*

[6] τὸ ἀόρατον
Ps. xviii. 9.

Then even Moses was afeard, but now no one is.

---

[e] S. Chrys. says this referring to, without expressly citing, the φωνῇ ῥημάτων of the text.
[f] ἀλλ' ὄνομα αὐτοῦ καλέσεται. Mr. Field with hesitation adopts here the reading of the Catena καλέσεται, in the sense here given. The MSS have καλέσαι and (excepting one) not any stop after it. S. Chrys. probably has in view the fact of Moses being called up to the top of the Mount, Exod. xix. 20.

As the people *then* stood below, so also do we. They were not below, but below Heaven. The son is near to God, but not as Moses[g].

There was a wilderness, here a city.

[4.] *And to myriads of angels in festive gathering.* Here he indicates the joy, the delight, in place of the *blackness* and the *darkness*, and the *tempest.*

And to the church of the first-born which have been enrolled in Heaven, and to GOD *the Judge of all.* They did not draw near, but stood afar off, even Moses: but *ye are come near.*

Here he makes them fear, by saying, *And to God the Judge of all;* not of the Jews alone, and the faithful, but even of the whole world.

And unto the spirits of just men made perfect. He means the souls of those who are approved.

And unto JESUS *the Mediator of the New Covenant: and unto the blood of sprinkling,* that is, of purification, *which speaketh better things than Abel.* And if the blood speaks, much more does He who was slain as a victim live. But what does it speak? *The Spirit also* (saith he) *speaketh with groanings unspeakable.* How does He speak? whensoever, it means, He falls into a sincere mind, He raises it up and makes it speak.

[5.] *See that ye refuse not Him that speaketh;* that is, that ye reject[1] [Him] not. *For if they escaped not who refused Him that spake*[h] *on earth.* Whom does he mean? Moses, I suppose [you say]. What he means, however, is this: If they, having *refused Him* when He gave laws *on earth, did not escape,* how shall we refuse Him, when

[1] ἀπογνῶ-τε

---

[g] This passage, Mr. Field observes, is difficult and probably corrupt. S. Chrysostom seems to mean, that we are like the people in that we are still here below, not in heaven: for they were "below" only in the sense of being below the mountain and heaven to which Moses had been called up. At the same time as being sons of God we are near to Him with a special nearness—a spiritual and so most intimate nearness—of the soul, not like that bodily nearness with which Moses was called to draw near.

If, however, "the Son" be understood of the Only-Begotten, it may be supposed that there is some latent connection of thought, as, that in His nearness His people also are brought near to the Father in a manner far more intimate than was granted to Moses.

[h] χρηματίζοντα. The word is used of God's speaking: See above, Hom. xxiii. [1], p. 264. S. Chrysostom's argument seems to oblige us to understand in the next clause something equivalent to " you say," which words have been inserted for clearness sake. The supposition that Moses was meant by τὸν χρηματίζοντα, is mentioned only to be rejected.

He gives laws from Heaven? He declares here not that He [who gave the old Law] was a different [Being]; God forbid. He does not set forth One and Another, but He is shewn to be terrible, when uttering His Voice *from Heaven*. It is He Himself then, both This [that speaks now], and That [that spake of old]: but This [that speaks now] is terrible. For he expresses not a difference of Persons but of [the manner of] giving [the Law]. Whence does this appear? *For if they escaped not who refused Him that spake on earth, much more shall not we escape, if we turn away from Him [that speaketh] from Heaven.* What then? is this [last mentioned] another than the one [before named]? [If so], how is it that he says, *whose voice then shook the earth?* For it was the *voice* of Him who *then* gave the Law, which *shook the earth. But now hath He promised, saying, Yet again once for all I shake not the earth only, but also the heaven. And this word Yet again once for all, signifieth the removing of the things which are shaken, as of things which have been made.* All things therefore will be clean taken away, and will be compacted anew unto a better [state]. For this is what he intimates here. Why then dost thou grieve when thou sufferest in a world that abideth not; when thou art afflicted in a world which will very shortly have passed away? If our Rest were [to be] in the latter period of the world, then one ought to be afflicted in looking to the end.

That (saith he) *the things which are not shaken may remain.* But of what sort are *the things which are not shaken?* The things to come.

[6.] Let us then do all with a view to this, that we may attain that [rest], that we may enjoy those good things. Yea, I pray and beseech you, let us labour earnestly for this. No one builds in a city which is going to fall down. Tell me, I pray you, if any one had said that after a year, this city would fall, but such a city would not [fall] at all, wouldst thou have built in that which was about to fall? So I also now say this, Let us not build in this world; it will fall a little while hence, and all things [here] will be destroyed. But why do I say, It will fall? Before its fall

(3)

He.xii.27.

comp. S. Iren. pp. 330, 338. 403 O.T.

we ourselves shall be destroyed, and suffer what is fearful; we shall be removed from them.

Why build we upon the sand? Let us build upon the rock: for whatsoever may come on, that building remains impregnable, nothing will be able to destroy it. With good reason. For to all such attacks that region is inaccessible, just as this is accessible. For earthquakes, and fires, and inroad of enemies, take it away from us even while we are alive: and oftentimes destroy us together with it.

And in case it even remains, disease speedily removes us, or if we stay, suffers us not to enjoy it fairly. For what pleasure [can there be], where there are sicknesses, and false accusations, and envy, and treacherous attacks? Or should there be none of these things, yet oftentimes if we have no children, we are disquieted, we are impatient, not having any to whom we may leave our houses and all our other things; and thenceforward we pine away as labouring for others. Yea oftentimes too our inheritance passes away to our enemies, not only after our death, but even while we are yet alive. What is more miserable then than to labour for our enemies, and ourselves to be gathering sins together in order that they may have rest? And many are the instances of this that are to be seen in our cities. And yet [I say no more,] lest I should grieve those who have been deprived of their property. For I could have mentioned some of them even by name, and have had many histories to tell, and many houses to point out to you, which have received for owners the enemies of those who had laboured upon them: Nay not houses only, but slaves also and the whole inheritance have oftentimes devolved upon personal enemies. For such are things human.

But in Heaven there is none of these things to fear; lest [I mean] after a man is dead, his enemy should come, and succeed to his inheritance. For *there* there is neither death nor enmity; the tabernacles of the saints are permanent abodes; and among those saints is exultation, joy, mirthfulness. For *the voice of joy* (it is said) is *in the dwellings of the righteous.* They are eternal, having no end. They do not fall down through age, they do not change their owners, but stand continually in their best estate. With

good reason. For *there* there is nothing corruptible, no- He.xii.27.
thing perishable, but all is immortal, and such as cannot be
impaired. On this building let us exhaust all our wealth.
We have no need of carpenters nor of labourers. It is the
hands of the poor that build houses of this kind; the lame,
the blind, the maimed; These build those houses. And
wonder not; seeing that they procure even a kingdom for
us, and give us confidence towards God.

[7.] For mercifulness [1] is as it were a most excellent art, [1] or *cha-rity*, ἐλε-
and a protector of those who labour at it. For it is dear ημοσύνη
to God, and ever stands near Him, readily asking favour in see above
behalf of whomsoever it will, if only it be not wronged by p. 365.
us; And wronged it is, when we perform it by means of see p.
ill-gotten gain. So, if it be pure, it gives great confidence 295.
to those who offer it up. It intercedes even for those who (4)
have offended, so great is its power, even for those who
have sinned. It breaks the chains, disperses the darkness,
quenches the fire, kills the worm, drives away the gnashing
of teeth. To it the gates of Heaven are opened with great
security: And just as when a Queen is entering, no one of
the guards stationed at the doors will be so bold as to inquire
who she is, and whence [she comes], but all straightway
receive her; so also in truth [do they welcome] mercifulness. For a queen indeed she is, making man like unto
God. For, saith He, *ye shall be merciful, as your Heavenly* S. Luke
Father is merciful. vi. 36.

She is winged and buoyant, having golden pinions, with
a flight which greatly delighteth the angels. There, it is
said, are *the wings of a dove covered with silver, and her back* Ps. lxviii.
with the yellowness of gold. Just as some dove golden and 13.
yet living, she flies, with gentle look, and mild eye. Nothing is better than that eye. The Peacock is beautiful, but
in comparison of her, he is a jackdaw. So beautiful and
worthy of admiration is this bird. She continually looks
upwards; she is surrounded abundantly with God's glory:
she is a virgin with golden wings, decked out, with a fair
and a mild countenance. She is winged, and buoyant, standing by the royal throne. When we are being judged, she
suddenly flies in, and shews herself, and rescues us from
punishment, sheltering us with her own wings.

> 374 *Mercifulness and abundant almsgiving recommended.*

Hom. 32.   Her, God would have, rather than sacrifices. Much does He discourse concerning her: in such wise does He love her. *He will relieve* (it saith) *the widow* and *the fatherless* and the poor. God loves to be called from her. *The Lord is pitiful and merciful*[1], *long-suffering, and of great mercy* and true. The mercy of God is over all the earth. She hath saved the race of mankind: For unless God had pitied us, all things would have perished. *When we were enemies,* she *reconciled* us, she gained the innumerable blessings [which we have]: she persuaded the Son of God to become a slave, and to empty Himself [of His glory][1].

Ps. cxlvi. 9.
ib. cxlv. 8.
see Ps. cxlv. 9.
see Rom. v. 10.
Phil. ii. 7.
[1] κενῶσαι ἑαυτὸν

Her let us earnestly emulate, beloved, by whom we have been saved; her let us love, her let us prize before wealth, and [if we are] without wealth let us have a merciful soul. Nothing is so characteristic of a Christian, as mercifulness. There is nothing which both unbelievers and all men so admire, as when we are merciful. For oftentimes we are ourselves also in need of this mercy, and say to God *Have mercy upon us, after Thy great goodness.* Let us begin first ourselves: or rather it is not we that begin first. For He has Himself already shewn forth His mercy towards us: yet at least let us follow second. For if men pity a merciful man, even if he has done innumerable wrong things, much more does God.

Ps. li. 1.

[8.] Hear thou the prophet saying, *But I* (his words are) *am as it were an olive tree full of fruit in the house of God.* Let us become such: let us become *as an olive tree:* let us be laden on every side with the commandments. For it is not enough to be as an olive tree, but to be also full of fruit. For there are persons who in doing alms give little, [only once] in the course of the whole year, or in each week, or who give away a mere chance matter. These are indeed olive trees, but not fruitful ones, but even withered. For in that they shew compassion they are olive trees, but in that they do it not liberally, they are not fruitful olive trees. But let us be full of fruit.

ib. lii. 8.

I have often said and I say now also: the greatness of the charity[2] is not shewn by the measure of what is given, but by the disposition of the giver. You know what hap-

[2] ἐλεημοσύνης

supra p. 17.

---

[1] [ἐλεήμων, akin to ἐλεημοσύνη, which S. Chrysostom is here describing.]

pened in the case of the Widow. It is well continually to bring this example [forward,] that not even the poor man may despair of himself, when he looks on her who threw in the two mites. Some contributed even hair in the fitting up of the temple, and not even these were rejected. But if when they possessed Gold, they had brought hair, they [would have been] accursed: but if, having this only, they brought it, they were accepted. For this cause Cain also was blamed, not because he offered worthless things, but because they were the most worthless he had. *Accursed (it saith) is he which hath a male, and sacrificeth unto God a corrupt thing.* He did not speak absolutely, but, *he that hath* (he says) and spareth [it]. If then a man have nothing, he is freed from blame, or rather he has a reward. For what is of less value than two farthings, or more utterly worthless than hair? what than a pint of meal? but nevertheless these were approved equally with the calves and the gold. For *a man is accepted according to that he hath, not according to that he hath not.* And, it saith, *according as thy hand hath, do good.*

^{HE.xii.27.}
^{Ex. xxxv. 23.}
^{Mal. i. 14.}
^{2 Cor. viii. 12.}
^{Prov. iii. 27.}

Wherefore, I entreat you, let us readily empty out what we have for the poor. Even if it be little we shall receive the same reward with them who have cast the most; or rather, more than those who cast in ten thousand talents. If we do these things we shall obtain the unspeakable treasures of God, if we not only hear, but practise also, if we do not praise [charity], but also exhibit [it] by our deeds. Which may we all attain to, in Christ Jesus our Lord, with Whom to the Father and also to the Holy Ghost, be glory might honour, now and for ever and world without end. Amen.

HOMILY XXXIII.

HEB. xii. 28, 29.

Wherefore we receiving a Kingdom that cannot be moved, us have grace [or *gratitude*]^a, *whereby we serve*^b *God acceptably with reverence and godly fear. For our God is a consuming fire.*

2 Cor. iv. 18.

JUST as in another place he says, *for the things which are seen are temporal, but the things which are not seen are eternal;* and from this frames his exhortation with regard to the evils which we endure in this present life, the very same he does in this place also, and says, let us continue steadfast; *let us have thankfulness,* i. e. let us give thanks unto God. For we ought not only not to be vexed and desponding on account of our present condition, but even to feel very great gratitude to Him, on account of the things to come.

Whereby we serve God acceptably, that is to say, 'for 'thus is it possible to serve God acceptably,' [viz.] by giving thanks in all things. *Do all things* (he saith) *without murmurings and disputings.* For whatever work a man performs with murmuring, he cuts away and loses his reward; just as the Israelites—how great a penalty they paid for their murmurings. Wherefore he saith, *Neither murmur ye* [&c.] It is not therefore possible to *serve* Him *acceptably* without a sense of gratitude towards Him for all things, both for our trials, and the alleviations of them. That is, let us utter nothing hasty, nothing disrespectful,

Phil. ii. 14.

1 Cor. x. 10.

---

^a χάριν ἔχωμεν. S. Chrys. understands the expression in this sense: which it has elsewhere: as in S. Luc. xvii. 9: 2 Tim. i. 3.

^b λατρεύομεν is the reading of all the MSS., the common texts have λατρεύωμεν.

but let us be subdued that we may be reverential. For this is *with reverence and godly fear*.

Chap. xiii. 1, 2. *Let brotherly love continue. Be not forgetful of hospitality*[1], *for hereby some have entertained angels unawares.* See how he enjoins them to preserve what they had: he does not add other things thereto. He did not say, "Be loving as brethren," but, *Let brotherly love continue.* And again, he did not say, "Be hospitable," as though they were not so, but, *Be not forgetful of hospitality,* for this was likely to happen owing to their afflictions.

For for this cause[2] (he says) *some have entertained angels unawares.* Thou seest how great was the honour, how great the gain!

What is *unawares*[3]*?* They entertained them without knowing it. On this account his reward also was great, because he entertained them, not knowing that they were Angels. For, if he had known it, it would have been nothing wonderful. Some say that he here alludes to Lot also.

[2.] ver. 3—5. *Remember them that are in bonds, as bound with them, them that suffer affliction as being yourselves also in the body. Marriage is honourable in all, and the bed undefiled; but fornicators and adulterers God will judge. Let your conversation be without covetousness: being content with such things as ye have.*

See how large is his discourse concerning chastity. *Follow peace,* he said, *and holiness; Lest there be any fornicator or profane person;* and again, *Fornicators and adulterers God will judge.* In every case, the prohibition is [accompanied] with a penalty. *Follow peace with all men,* he says, *and holiness without which no man shall see the Lord: But fornicators and adulterers God will judge.*

And having first set down *Marriage is honourable in all men, and the bed undefiled,* he shews that it is with reason that he added what follows. For if marriage has been conceded, justly is the fornicator punished, justly does the adulterer suffer vengeance.

In these words he prepares himself to combat[4] with the heretics. He did not say again, Let no one be a fornicator; but having said it once for all, he then went on as

---

Margin notes:
He.xiii.5.
[1] φιλοξε-νίας see below [5.]
[2] διὰ τοῦ-το, or διὰ ταύτης, thereby
[3] ἔλαθον
supra xii. 14.
ib. 16.
[4] ἀποδύ-εται πρὸς

with a general exhortation, and not as directing himself against them.

Let your conversation be without covetousness, he says. He did not say, Possess nothing, but, *Let your conversation be without covetousness*: that is, let it shew forth the philosophical character of your mind. And it will shew it, if we do not seek superfluities, if we keep only to what is necessary. For he says above also, *And ye took joyfully the spoiling of your goods.* He gives these exhortations, that they might not be covetous.

Being content (he says) *with such things as ye have.* And then here also is the consolation ; *For He Himself* (saith he) *hath said, I will never leave thee nor forsake thee*; (ver. 6) *so that we may boldly say, the Lord is my helper, and I will not be afraid what man shall do unto me.* Again consoling encouragement in their trials.

[3.] ver. 7. *Remember them that have the rule over you.* This he was labouring to say above : for this cause he said, *Follow peace with all men.* He gave this exhortation also to the Thessalonians, to *hold them in honour very exceedingly.*

Remember (saith he) *them that have the rule over you*[1], *who have spoken unto you the word of God, whose faith imitate, considering the end of their conversation.* What kind of consequence is this? Nay truly it is a very excellent one: for he saith, beholding their life, *imitate their faith.* For from a pure life [cometh] faith.

Or else by *faith*, he means stedfastness. How so? Because they believe in the things to come. For they would not have shewn forth a pure life, if they had questioned about the things to come, if they had doubted. So that here also he is applying a remedy to the same [evil][2].

ver. 8, 9. JESUS CHRIST *the same yesterday and to-day and for ever. Be not carried aside with diverse and strange doctrines. For it is good that the heart be established with grace, not with meats, which have not profited them that have walked therein.*

(2) In these words, *Jesus Christ the same yesterday and to-day and for ever, yesterday*, means all the time that is past: *to-day*, the [time] present : *for ever*, that also which is to come and which has no limit. That is to say : Ye

have heard of an High Priest, but not an High Priest who ceases [to be one]. He is always the same. As though there were some who said, 'He is not [any longer in being], 'another will come,' he says this, that He that was *yesterday and to-day,* is *the same also for ever.* For even now the Jews say, that another will come; and having deprived themselves of the true [Christ] will fall into the hands of Antichrist. HE.xiii.15.

Be not carried aside (saith he) *with diverse and strange doctrines.* Not *with strange doctrines* only, but not even with *diverse ones.*

For it is a good thing that the heart be established with grace, not with meats which have not profited them that have been occupied [c] *therein.* Here he gently hints at those who introduce the observance of *meats.* For by Faith all things are pure. Of Faith then there is need, not of *meats.*

For (ver. 10) *we have an altar whereof they have no right to eat which serve*[1] *the Tabernacle.* Not as the Jewish [ordinances], are those among us, as it is not lawful even for the High Priest to partake of them. So that since he had said, "Do not observe[2] [such and such things]," and this seemed to be [the language] of one who is throwing down his own building, he again turns it round. What, have not we then observances as well (saith he)? Yea we have, and we observe them very earnestly too, not allowing even to the priests themselves to partake of them.

[1] *perform the service of*
[2] παρατηρεῖτε, see Gal. iv. 10.

[4.] (ver. 11, 12) *For the bodies of those beasts whose blood is brought into the Holy Place by the High Priest for sin, are burned without the camp. Wherefore* JESUS *also, that He might sanctify the people with His own blood, suffered* (he saith) *without the gate.* Thou seest the type shining forth? *For sin,* he saith, and *suffered without the gate.* ver. 13. *Let us therefore go forth to Him without the camp bearing His reproach,* that is, suffering the same things; having communion with Him in His sufferings. He was crucified without as a condemned person: neither let us then be ashamed to *go forth out* [of the world].

ver. 14, 15. *For we have here no continuing city* (saith he)

[c] οἱ περιπατήσαντες, i. e. "that have walked in them:" "lived in the observance of rules respecting them."

Hom. 33.

[¹ His human Nature.]

but we seek that which is to come. By Him therefore let us offer unto God the sacrifice of praise continually, that is, the fruit of lips giving thanks to His Name.

By Him, as by an High-Priest, according to the flesh[1].

see p. 376. *Giving thanks* (saith he) *to His Name.* Let us utter nothing blasphemous, nothing hasty, nothing overbold, nothing

supra xii. 28.
presumptuous, nothing desperate. This is *with reverence and godly fear.* For a soul in tribulations becomes des-

[² ἀπαναισχυντεῖ "loses respect"]
ponding, and reckless[2]. But let not us [be such]. See here he again says the very same thing which he said before, *not forsaking the assembling of ourselves together,* for so shall we be able to do all things with reverence. For oftentimes even out of respect for men, we refrain from doing many evil things.

(ver. 16) *But to do good and to communicate forget not.*

(3) "It is not [merely] with reference to the brethren that are "present, but to those also who are absent that I speak. "But if others have plundered your property, display your "hospitality out of such things as ye have." What excuse then shall we have henceforward, when they, even after the spoiling of their goods, were thus admonished?

[5.] And he did not say, *Be not forgetful* of the enter-

[³ Love of the stranger, φιλοξενία]
taining of strangers[d], but *of hospitality*[3]: that is, do not merely entertain strangers, but [do it] with love for the strangers. Moreover he did not speak of the recompence that is future, and is in store for us, lest he should make them more supine, but of that which has been already given. For *thereby some have entertained angels unawares.*

But let us see in what sense *Marriage is honourable in all and the bed undefiled.* Because (he means) it preserves the believer in chastity. In this place he also alludes to the Jews, because they accounted the woman after child-

[⁴ τὴν λεχώ: Edd. τὴν κοίτην]
birth[4] polluted: and also whosoever comes from the bed, it is said, is not clean[5]. Those things are not polluted[6]

[⁵ See Lev. xv. 18.]
which arise from nature, O thou ungrateful and senseless Jew, but those which arise from our own will[7]. For if

[⁶ βδελυρά]
marriage is honourable and pure, why forsooth dost thou

[⁷ τῆς προαιρέσεως]
think that one is polluted even by it?

---

[d] S. Chrys. here reverts to v. 2. and goes over again the portion on which he has already commented.

Let your conversation (saith he) *be without covetousness:* inasmuch as many after having exhausted[e] their property, afterwards wish to recover it again under the name of alms, for this cause he says, *Let your conversation be without covetousness,* that is, that we should be [desirous] of what is necessary[1] and indispensable. What then (you say)? supposing we should not have a supply even of these? This is not possible; indeed it is not. *For He hath Himself said,* and He doth not lie, *I will never leave thee, neither will I ever forsake thee. So that we confidently say, The Lord is my Helper, and I will not be afraid what man shall do unto me.* Thou hast the promise from Himself: do not doubt henceforward. He has Himself promised; make no question. But this, *I will never leave thee* [&c.] he says not concerning money only, but concerning all other things also. *The Lord is my Helper, and I will not be afraid what man shall do unto me;* With good reason.

Hɛ.xiii.8.

[1] τῆς χρείας ὦμεν

This then let us also say in all our temptations; let us smile with contempt on human things, so long as we have God favourable to us. For just as, when He is our enemy, it is no gain, even if all men should be friends to us, so when He is our friend, even if all men together war against us, there is no harm. *I will not be afraid what man shall do unto me.*

[6.] *Remember them that have the rule over you, who have spoken unto you the word of God.* In this place I think that he is speaking about assistance also[2]. For this is [implied in the words] *who have spoken unto you the word of God.*

[2] ἐπικουρία: see 1 Tim. v. 17 &c.

Whose faith follow considering the end of their conversation. What is, *considering*[3]? Continually revolving, examining it by yourselves, reasoning [on it], investigating accurately, testing it as you choose. *The end of their conversation,* that is, their conversation to the end: for *their conversation* had a good end.

[3] ἀναθεωροῦντες

Jesus Christ the same yesterday and to-day and for ever. Do not think that then indeed He wrought wonders, but

---

[e] κενῶσαι. This word is used commonly by S. Chrys. for giving away one's whole property in charity, and probably that is its meaning here.

HOM. 33. now works no wonders. He is [still] the same. This is, *Remember them that have the rule over you*[f].

Be not carried aside with diverse and strange doctrines. Strange, that is, different from those ye heard from us; [*Diverse*] that is of all sorts: for they have no stability, but are different [one from another]. For manifold [1] is the subject of meats especially.

For it is good that the heart be established with grace, not with meats. These are the *diverse;* these the *strange*[2] [doctrines]: especially as Christ has said, *not that which entereth into the mouth defileth the man, but that which cometh out.* And observe that he does not make bold to say this openly, but as it were by a hint [3]. *For it is well that the heart be established with grace, not with meats.*

Faith is all. If that establishes [it], the heart stands in security. It follows that Faith establishes: consequently reasonings shake. For Faith is contrary to reasoning.

By which they (saith he) *have not been profited, who have walked therein.* For what is the gain (he means) from the observance [g] [of them], tell me. Does it not rather destroy? Does it not make such an one to be under sin? If it be of obligation to observe [them], it is necessary to observe ourselves [h].

By which (saith he) *they have not been profited which have walked therein.* That is, who have always diligently kept them.

There is one observance, abstaining from sin. For what profit is it, when there are some so polluted, as not to be able to partake of the sacrifices? So that it did not save them at all; and yet they were very earnest about the observances. But because they had not faith, not even thus were they in any wise profited.

[7.] In the next place he takes away [4] the sacrifice from the type, and directs his discourse to the prototype, saying, *The bodies of those beasts whose blood is brought into the sanctuary by the High Priest, are burned without the camp* [&c]. It follows that those former things were a

---

[1] *or* "intricate and complicated," πολύπλοκον
[2] *foreign to us*, S. Matt. xv. 11.
[3] ἐν αἰνίγματι
[4] ἀναιρεῖ

[f] That is, Remember them, because of the continual presence and working of Christ in His Church.
[g] παρατήρησις: see Gal. iv. 10, Ye *observe* (παρατηρεῖσθε) *days* &c.
[h] ἔστι παρατηρεῖσθαι, potius sibi cavendum est: is Mr. Field's translation; "to be guarded," as we say.

type of these latter, and thus Christ fulfilled all by suffer- He.xiii.16.
ing *without* [the city].

In this place too he shews plainly that He suffered of His own accord, by intimating[i] that those things were not accidental, but even the [Divine] arrangement itself was of a suffering *without*. [He suffered] without, but His Blood was borne up into Heaven. Thou seest then that we par- (ƀ) take of Blood which has been carried into the Holy Place, the True Holy Place; of the Sacrifice of which the High Priest alone had the privilege. We therefore partake of the Truth [the Reality]. If then we partake not of *reproach* [only] but of sanctification[k], the *reproach* is the cause of the sanctification. For just as He was reproached, so also are we. If we go forth *without* therefore, we have fellowship with Him.

But what is, *Let us go forth to Him?* Let us have fellowship with Him in His sufferings; let us bear His reproach. For He did not simply bid us dwell *outside the gate*, but as He was reproached as a condemned person, so also we.

And *by Him let us offer a sacrifice to God*. Of what kind of sacrifice is he speaking? *The fruit of lips giving thanks to His Name*. They [the Jews] brought sheep, and calves, and gave them to the Priest: let *us* bring none of these things, but [let us bring] thanksgiving. This *fruit* let *our lips* put forth.

For with such sacrifices God is well pleased. Let us give such a sacrifice to Him, that He may offer [it] to The Father. For in no other way it is offered except through the Son, or rather also through a contrite mind. All these things are said for the sake of those that are weak. For that the thanks belong to the Son is evident: for otherwise, how is there equal honour [to Him with the Father]? *that all men* (He saith) *should honour the Son even as they honour the Father*. Wherein is the honour equal? *The fruit of lips giving thanks to His Name* [1]. S. John v. 23.

[1] That is, "to the Name of the Son."

[8.] Let us bear all things thankfully, be it poverty, be it disease, be it any thing else whatever: for He alone knows

---

[i] δεικνὺς ὅτι οὐκ ἐκεῖνα ἁπλῶς ἦν, ἀλλὰ καὶ αὐτὴ ἡ οἰκονομία ἔξω πάθους ἦν.

[k] ἁγιασμοῦ. The effect of the sprinkling with Blood. see ch. ix. 12, 13 &c. x. 10, 14.

the things that are expedient for us. *For we know not what we should pray for as we ought.* We then who do not know even how to ask for what is fitting, unless we have received of[1] the Spirit, let us take care to offer up thanksgiving for all things, and let us bear all things nobly. Are we in poverty? let us give thanks. Are we in sickness? let us give thanks. Are we falsely accused? let us give thanks: when we are suffering affliction, let us give thanks.

This makes us to be near to God: then we even have God for our debtor. But when we are in prosperity, it is we who are debtors and liable to be called to account. For when we are in prosperity, we are debtors to God: and oftentimes these [prosperous circumstances] result in being a judgment upon us, while those other are a payment of the penalty[2] of sin. Those [afflictions] draw down mercy, they draw down kindness upon us: while these on the other hand lift up even to an insane pride, and lead also to slothfulness, and make a man fancy great things concerning himself; they puff up. On this account the prophet also said, *It is good for me, Lord, that Thou hast afflicted[3] me, that I may learn Thy judgments.* When Hezekiah had received blessings and been freed from calamities, his heart was lifted up on high; when he fell sick, then was he humbled, then he became near to God. *When He slew them,* it saith, *then they sought Him diligently, and turned, and were early in coming to[4] God.* And again, *When the beloved waxed gross and fat, then he kicked.* For *the Lord is known when He executeth judgments.*

[9.] Affliction is a great good. *Narrow is the way,* so that affliction [by compression][1] thrusts us into the narrow [way]. He who is not pressed by affliction will not be able to enter in. For he who presses himself by affliction in the narrow [way], is he who also enjoys ease; but he that spreads himself out[5], does not enter in, and also suffers from being so to say wedged in[6]. See how Paul enters into this narrow way. He *keeps under* his *body,* so as to be able to enter. On this account, in all his afflictions, he still continued giving thanks unto God. Hast thou been

---

[1] θλῖψις, literally "pressing:" probably S. Chrys. had in mind a word of the text which he does not cite. τεθλιμμένη ἡ ὁδός.

deprived of thy property? this hath lightened thee of the most of thy wideness. Hast thou fallen from glory? this is another sort of wideness. Hast thou been falsely accused? have the things been believed that have been said against thee, of which thou art nowise conscious to thyself? *Rejoice and leap for joy.* For *blessed are ye* (saith He) *when men reproach you, and say all manner of evil against you, falsely, for My sake. Rejoice and be exceeding glad, for great is your reward in Heaven.*

Why marvellest thou, if thou art grieved, and wishest to be set free from temptations? Paul wished to be set free, and oftentimes entreated God, and did not obtain [his prayer]. For the *thrice for this I besought the Lord,* is oftentimes; *and He said unto me, My grace is sufficient for thee, for My strength is made perfect in weakness.* By *weakness,* he here means "afflictions." What then? As soon as he heard this he received it with thankfulness, and says, *Wherefore I take pleasure in infirmities;* that is, I am pleased, I rest in my afflictions. For all things then let us give thanks, both for comfort, and for affliction [m]. Let us not murmur: let us not be unthankful. *Naked came I out of my mother's womb, naked also shall I depart.* Thou didst not come forth glorious, do not seek glory. Thou wast brought into life naked, not of money alone, but also of glory, and good character.

Consider how great evils have oftentimes arisen from wealth. For *It is easier* (it is said) *for a camel to go through the eye of a needle, than for a rich man to enter into the kingdom of Heaven.* Thou seest to how many good things wealth is a hindrance, and dost thou seek to be rich? dost thou not rejoice that the hindrance has been overthrown? So narrow is the way which leadeth into the Kingdom. So broad is wealth, and full of bulk and swelling out. For this cause He saith, *Sell that thou hast,* that that way may receive thee. Why dost thou regret thy wealth? For this cause He took it away from thee, that He might set thee

---

[m] [see above, pp. 197, 239, 241, 384. S. Chrysostom in his bitter banishment finished his last prayer "with his usual "thanksgiving, 'Glory to God for all "'things,' and sealed it with a final "Amen." Dr. Bright Hist. of Church between A.D. 313 and 451 chapter ix. end, p. 255 and Dr. Bright's note b. on the same page.]

Hom. 33. free from slavery. For true fathers also, when a son is corrupted by an attachment to some mistress, and after having given him much exhortation, they do not persuade him to part from her, send the mistress into banishment. Of the same kind also is abundance of wealth. It is then because the Lord hath care for us, and to deliver us from the harm [which arises] therefrom, that He takes away the wealth from us.

Let us not then esteem poverty to be an evil: sin is the only evil. For neither is wealth a good thing by itself: to be well-pleasing to God is the only Good. Poverty then let us seek, this let us pursue: so shall we lay hold on Heaven, so shall we attain to all the other good things. Which may we all attain by the grace and loving-kindness of our Lord Jesus Christ, with Whom to the Father and also to the Holy Ghost be glory power honour, now and ever and world without end. Amen.

HOMILY XXXIV.

Heb. xiii. 17.

Obey them that have the rule over you, and submit yourselves. For they watch for your souls, as they that must give account, that they may do it with joy, and not with grief[1], for this is unprofitable for you.

[1] lamenting, στενάζοντες

ANARCHY [the having no ruler][a] is an evil, and the occasion of many calamities, and the source of disorder and confusion. For just as, if from a chorus thou take away the leader, the chorus will not be in tune and in order; and if from a division of an army thou remove the commander, the movements of the host will no longer be made in time and order, and if from a ship thou take away the steersman, thou wilt sink the vessel; so too if from a flock thou remove the shepherd, thou hast overthrown and destroyed all.

Well then, the having no ruler is an evil, and a cause of ruin. But no less an evil also is the disobedience of those that are under rule. For it comes again to the same. For a people which does not obey a ruler, is like one which has none: and perhaps even worse. For in the former case they have at least an excuse for their disorderliness, but in this latter [they have it] no longer, but are even punished.

But perhaps some one will say, that there is also a third evil, when the Ruler is a bad one. I myself too know it, and no small evil it is, but even a far worse evil than anarchy. For it is better to be led by no one, than to be led by one who is evil. For the former indeed are oftentimes

---

[a] It will be observed that S. Chrysostom uses "rulers" (ἄρχοντες) and the cognate words, of spiritual rulers.

saved, and oftentimes are in peril[1], but the latter will be altogether in peril, being led into the pit [of destruction].

How is it then that Paul says, *Obey them that have the rule over you, and submit yourselves?* Having said above, *whose faith follow, considering the end of their conversation,* he then said, *Obey them that have the rule over you and submit yourselves.*

What then (you say), when he is wicked should we obey him?

Wicked? in what sense dost thou use the word? If in regard to Faith indeed, flee and avoid him; not only if he be a man, but even if he be an angel come down from Heaven. But if it be in regard to life, be not over-curious. And this instance I do not allege from my own mind, but from the Divine Scripture. For listen to Christ saying, *The Scribes and the Pharisees sit on Moses' seat.* Having previously spoken many fearful things concerning them, He then says, *They sit on Moses' seat: all therefore whatsoever they tell you to do, do; but do not ye after their works.* They have (He means) the dignity of office, but they are of unclean life. Do thou however attend, not to their life, but to their words.

For as regards their characters, no one would be harmed [thereby]. How is this? Both because their characters are manifest to all, and also because not even if he be ten thousand times as wicked, will he ever himself teach what is wicked. But as respects Faith, [the evil] is not manifest to all men, and the wicked [ruler] will not shrink from teaching it.

For further, the [warning], *Judge not that ye be not judged* concerns life, not faith: At all events what follows makes this evident. For *why* (saith He) *beholdest thou the mote that is in thy brother's eye, but considerest not the beam that is in thine own eye?*

All things therefore (saith He) *which they bid you to do, do ye* (But to do belongs to works not to Faith) *but do not ye after their works.* Thou seest that [the discourse] is not concerning doctrines, but concerning life and works?

[2.] Paul however previously commended them[2], and then says, *Obey them that have the rule over you, and submit*

---

[1] "suffer" ἐκινδύνευσεν

supra ver. 7.

S. Matt. xxiii. 2.

ib. 2, 3.

ib. vii. 1.

ib. 3.

[2] i.e. the rulers, see ver. 7.

yourselves, for they watch for your souls, as they that shall He.xiii.17. *give account.*

Let those who rule also hear, and not only those who are under their rule; that just as the subjects ought to be obediently disposed, so also the rulers also ought to be watchful and sober. What sayest thou? He watches; he imperils his own head; he is subject to the punishments of thy sins, and for thy sake is amenable to what is so fearful, and art thou slothful, and affectedly indifferent, and at ease? For this cause he says, *That they may do this with joy, and not with lamentation*[b] : *for this is unprofitable for you.*

Seest thou that the ruler, when he is despised, ought not to avenge himself, but his great revenge is to weep and to lament? For neither is it possible for the physician, if he be despised by his patient, to avenge himself, but to weep and lament. But if [the ruler] lament (he means), God inflicts vengeance on thee. For if when we lament for our own sins we draw God to us, shall we not much more [do this], when we lament for the arrogance and scornfulness of others? Thou seest that he does not suffer him to be led on to reproaches? Thou seest how great is his philosophy? He ought to lament, even he that is despised, that is trodden under foot, that is spit upon.

Be not thou confident on the notion that he does not avenge himself on thee, for this lamenting is worse than any revenge. For when of himself he profits nothing by his lamenting, he calls on the Lord: And just as in the case of a teacher and tender of children, when the child does not listen to him, one is called in who will treat him more severely, so also in this case.

[3.] Oh! how great is the danger! what should one say to those wretched men, who throw themselves upon so great an abyss of punishments? Thou hast to give an account of all over whom thou rulest, women and children and men; into so great a fire dost thou put thy head. I marvel if it be possible that any of the rulers should ever be saved,

---

[b] στενάζοντες. It will be observed that S. Chrys. dwells much on this word: and also that he understands the "do this" of "watching for souls;" not as the English version might lead us to understand it, of the "giving account."

when in the face of[1] so great a threat, and of the present indifference, I see some still even running on, and throwing themselves upon so great a burden of authority.

For if they who are dragged by force[c] have no refuge or defence, if they discharge their duty ill and are negligent; since even Aaron was dragged by force, and yet was imperilled[d]; and Moses again was imperilled, although he had oftentimes declined; and Saul having been entrusted with another kind of rule, after he had declined it, was in peril, because he had managed it amiss; how much more they who take so great pains to obtain it, and throw themselves upon it? Such an one much more deprives himself of all excuse and pardon. For men ought to fear and to tremble, both because of their own conscience, and because of the burden of the office; and neither when dragged to it should they once for all decline, nor, when not dragged throw themselves upon it, but should even flee, foreseeing the greatness of the dignity, and when they have been seized, again shew their godly fear[c]. Let there be nothing out of measure. If thou hast perceived it beforehand, retire; convince thyself that thou art unworthy of the office. Again, if thou hast been seized, in like manner be thou reverential[2], in all circumstances displaying rightmindedness[3].

[4.] (ver. 18) *Pray also for us* (he saith); *for we trust that we have a good conscience towards all*[4], *wishing to live honestly*.

Thou seest that he used these expressions of apology, as writing to persons who had been grieved with regard to him, as to those who turned away from him, who were disposed towards him as towards a transgressor, not enduring even to hear his name? Inasmuch then as he was asking from those who hated him, this, which all others ask from those who love them [their prayers for him], on that account he here introduces this; saying, *We trust that we have a good conscience*. For do not tell me of the accusa-

---

[c] Those who are ordained against their will by actual force; as frequently occurred in the age of S. Chrysostom.

[d] κινδυνεύω seems here as elsewhere in writers of this age to imply actual suffering as well as danger; so in this discourse. [1.]

[e] εὐλάβειαν. That is by submitting to the will of God thus manifested, and receiving ordination.

tions [against us]. Our conscience, he says, in nothing H E. xiii. 22.
hurts¹ us; nor are we conscious to ourselves that we have ¹ κατα-
plotted against you. *For we are persuaded,* saith he, *that* βλάπτει
we have a good conscience towards all, not towards the
Gentiles only, but also towards you. We have done no- ² καπηλεί-
thing with deceitfulness², nothing with hypocrisy: for it Chrys. on
was probable that these calumnies were reported respecting 2 Cor.
him. *For they have been informed concerning thee* (it is Acts xxi.
said) *that thou teachest apostacy.* Not as an enemy, he ²¹.
means, nor as an adversary do I write these things, but as
a friend. And this he shews also by what follows.

(ver. 19) *But I beseech you the more earnestly to do this,
that I may be restored to you the sooner.* This was [the
language] of one who loved them exceedingly, his thus
praying, and that not simply, but with all earnestness, that
so, he says, I may come to you speedily. It is [the mark]
of one who is conscious to himself of nothing [wrong], to
be earnestly desirous to come to them, and to entreat them
to pray for him.

For this cause, having first asked their prayers, he then
himself also prays for all good things on them. (ver. 20)
But the God of peace, he saith (be ye not therefore at
variance one with another), *Who brought again from the
earth the Shepherd of the sheep* (this is said concerning the
resurrection) *the Great [Shepherd]* (another addition: In
this place again, he confirms even to the end, his discourse
concerning the Resurrection to them) *in the blood of the
everlasting covenant, our Lord Jesus Christ,* (ver. 21) *make
you perfect in every good work, to do His will, working in
you that which is well-pleasing in His sight.*

Again he bears high testimony to them. For that is
made *perfect* which having a beginning is afterwards completed. And he prays for [blessings] on them which is
the act of one who tenderly loves them. And while in the
other Epistles, he utters his prayer in the prefaces, here
he does it at the end. *Working in you,* he saith, *that which
is well-pleasing in His sight through* JESUS *Christ, to whom
be glory for ever and ever. Amen.*

[5.] ver. 22. *And I beseech you, brethren, suffer the word
of exhortation for indeed I have written my letter to you in*

few words. Thou seest that what he wrote to no one [else], this he writes to them? For (he means) I do not even trouble you with long discourse.

I suppose that they were not at all unfriendly disposed towards Timothy: and that for this cause he also put him prominently forward [f]. For (ver. 23) *ye know,* saith he, *that our brother Timothy is set at liberty* [1], *with whom, if he come shortly, I will see you. Set at liberty,* he says, from whence? I suppose that he had been cast into prison: or if not this, that he was *released* [and gone] from Athens. For this also is mentioned in the Acts [2].

ver. 24, 25. *Salute all them that have the rule over you, and all the saints. They of Italy salute you. Grace be with you all. Amen.*

[6.] Thou seest [g] how he shews that virtue arises [3] neither wholly from God, nor yet from ourselves alone? First [h] by saying, [*may He*] *make you perfect in every good work;* Ye have virtue indeed, he means, but need to be made complete. What is *good work and word* [or *doctrine*] [i]? So as to have both life and doctrines right. *According to His Will, working in you that which is well-pleasing in His sight.*

In His sight, he says. For this is the highest virtue, to do that which is well-pleasing in the sight of God, according as the Prophet also says, *And according to the cleanness of my hands in His eye-sight.*

And having written thus much, he said this was little, in comparison with what he was going to say. According as he says also in another place, *As I wrote to you in brief: whereby when ye read, ye may understand my knowledge in the mystery of Christ.*

And observe his wisdom. He says not, *I beseech you, suffer the word of* admonition, but *the word of exhortation* [4], that is, of consolation, of encouragement. No one, he

---

[f] By saying that he would come with Timothy, as if Timothy were his superior; see the further comment, in the next section.
[g] S. Chrys. here recurs to verse 21.
[h] Here as elsewhere S. Chrys. does not expressly mention any "secondly,"
but after treating the remaining verses recurs to the subject in speaking on the words "Grace be with you;" and there indicates a second evidence.
[i] See 2 Thess. ii. 17. *Stablish you in every good word and work.* Probably S. Chrys. had this in his mind.

means, can be wearied out at the length of what has been said (Was it this then which made them turn away from him? By no means: he does not however wish to express this to them): that is, even if ye be of little spirit, for it is the special property of such persons not to endure a long discourse.

Ye know that our brother Timothy is set at liberty, with whom if he come shortly I will see you. This is sufficient to persuade them to submit themselves, if he is ready to come with his disciple.

Salute them that have the rule over you, and all the saints. See how he honoured them, in that he wrote his Epistle to them [the people], and not to those [their rulers].

They of Italy salute you. Grace be with you all. Amen. Which was for them all in common.

But how does *Grace* come to be *with* us? If we do not do despite to the benefit bestowed on us, if we do not become indolent in regard to the Gift. And what is *the Grace?* Remission of sins, Cleansing: this is *with* us. For who (he means) that has done despite [to it] can keep the Grace, and does not destroy it? For instance; He freely forgave thee thy sins. How then shall the *Grace be with* thee, whether it be the good favour, or the effectual working, of the SPIRIT? If thou draw it to thee by thy good actions. For the cause of all good things is this, the continual abiding with us of the *grace* of the Spirit. For this guides us to all [good things], just as when it flies away from us, it ruins us, and leaves us desolate.

[7.] Let us not then drive it from us. For on ourselves depends, both its remaining, and its departing: For the one results, when we mind heavenly things, the other, when [we mind] the things of this life. *Which the world* (saith He) *cannot receive, because it seeth It not, neither knoweth It.* Thou seest that it is not in the power of a worldly soul to have It? Great then is the earnestness we need, that so It may be held fast by us, that so It may direct all our concerns, and do them in security, and in much peace.

For just as a ship sailing with favourable winds, cannot be hindered nor sunk, so long as it enjoys a prosperous and steady breeze, but also after the coming on [of the wind] it causes great admiration on account of its progress, both to the mariners, and to the passengers, giving rest to the one, and not letting them toil on at their oars, and setting the others free from all fear, and affording to them the most delightful spectacle of her own course, so too a soul fortified by the Divine Spirit, is far above all the billows of this life, and more vehemently than such a ship, cuts its way along the course which leads to Heaven, inasmuch as it is not sent along by wind, but having all its clean sails filled by the Paraclete Himself: and He casts out of our minds all that is slackened and relaxed.

For just as the wind if it fall upon a slackened sail, would not have any effect; so neither does the SPIRIT endure to continue in a soul that is remiss; but there is need of much tension, [yea] of much vehemence, so that our mind may be inflamed, and our conduct under all circumstances on the stretch, braced up. For instance when we pray, we ought to do it with much intentness[1], stretching forth the soul toward Heaven, not with cords, but with vehement earnestness. Again when we do works of mercy, we have need of intentness, lest by any means, thought for our household, and the care for children, and anxiety about one's wife, and fear of poverty, entering in, should slacken our sail. For if we put it on the stretch on all sides by the hope of the things to come, it receives well the impulse[2] of the SPIRIT; and none of those perishable and wretched things will fall upon it, yea, and if any of them should, it in no respect harms it, but is speedily thrown back by the tightness, and is shaken off and falls down.

For this cause then we have need of much intentness. For we too are sailing over a great and a wide sea, full of many monsters, and of many rocks, and producing for us many storms, and from the midst of serene weather raising up against us a most violent tempest. It is necessary then if we would sail with ease, and without danger, that we stretch our sails, that is, our will and resolution: for this is sufficient for us. For Abraham also, when he had stretched forth his affections towards God and set before Him his completed resolution[3], what else had he need of? Nothing:

[1] tension
[2] ἐνέργειαν
[3] [προαίρεσιν]

but *he believed God, and it was counted unto him for right-* He.xiii.25.
eousness. But Faith [comes] of a sincere will [1]. He offered Gen. xv. 6.
up his son, and though he did not slay him, he received a [1] [προαι-
recompence as if he had slain him, and though the work ρέσεως]
was not done the reward was given.

Let our sails then be in good order [2], not worn out with [2] καθαρὰ
age (for every thing *that is decayed and waxen old is nigh* supra viii. 13.
to destruction [3]), not pierced through with holes, that so
they may bear the impulses of the SPIRIT. *For the natural* 1 Cor ii. 14.
man [4], it is said, *receiveth not the things of the Spirit.* For [3] ἐγγὺς
just as the webs of spiders could not receive a blast of wind, ἀφανι-
so neither will the soul devoted to this life, nor the natural σμοῦ
man ever be able to receive the grace of the SPIRIT: for our [4] ψυχικὸς
reasonings differ nothing from them [5], preserving a connec- [5] the cob-
tion in appearance only but being destitute of all power. webs.

[8.] Our condition, however, is not such, if we are sober
and watchful: but whatever may fall upon [the Christian],
he bears all, and is raised above all, stronger than any
whirlpool [6]. For suppose there be a spiritual man, and that [6] ἴλιγγος
innumerable calamities befal him, yet is he overcome by
none of them. And what do I say? suppose that poverty
come upon him, disease, reproaches, revilings, mockings,
stripes, every sort of infliction, every sort of mocking, and
slanders, and revilings: yet, just as though he were outside
the world, and set free from the feelings of the body, so
will he laugh all to scorn.

And in proof that my words are not mere boasting, I
think that many [such] exist even now; for instance, of
those who have embraced the life of the desert. This however, you say, is nothing wonderful. But I say that of those
also who live in cities, there are such men who are unsus-
pected. If thou wish however, I shall be able to exhibit
some among those of old. And that thou mayest learn,
consider Paul I pray thee. What is there fearful that he
did not suffer, and that he did not submit to? But he bore
all nobly. Him let us imitate, for so shall we be able to
land in the tranquil havens with much merchandise.

Let us then stretch our mind to Heaven, let us be held
fast by that desire, let us clothe ourselves with the spiritual fire, let us gird ourselves round with its flame. No man

Hom. 34. who bears flame on him fears those who meet him. Be it wild beast, be it man, be it snares innumerable, so long as he is armed with fire, all things stand out of his way, all things retire. The flame is intolerable, the fire cannot be endured, it consumes all.

With this fire let us clothe ourselves, and offer up glory to our Lord JESUS Christ, with whom to the Father, together with the Holy Ghost, be glory might honour, now and ever and world without end. Amen.

Thanks be to God.

INDEX.

A.

ABRAHAM how *received not the promises, having patiently endured received the promise,* 139. his patience, 139. and great-heartedness, 139, 278, 285 sqq. and intense resolve of his affection Godward, 394, 395. learn from his hospitality, 149. exceeding superiority of Melchisedek to, and thus to the Jewish polity too, 154, 160 sqq. fortitude of manifested by God to all men, 287. his faith to the end, 288. enjoyed things of the world, with affliction, 297. and affliction made him bright, 343.

Affliction, [*see* suffering, pain, punishment,] afflicting ourselves here benefit of, 197. came to Abraham and must come to every righteous person, 279, 340, 341. a great good, 301, 327, 384. wipes out sins, makes people firm and steady, 327. makes GOD our debtor, 384. casts out sloth and ill desire and collects the soul, 343. brings forth joy, 350. for a time, 371. helps to pay the penalty of our sins, 71, 384. thrusts into the narrow way, 384.

Age full, 109. how to be attained, 109. him of, who holds the Faith and a right life, 117.

Aid each can others in the way of salvation, 352—356, and not seek for himself only, 357.

Almsgiving, 124, 136, 137. can exhaust Hell-fires, 16. saves from, 373. of the very poor yea of the beggar surpasses that of rich, 17, 29, 30. in, GOD estimates will, 17, the most essential ingredient in medicine of Repentance, 123. causes our prayer to be heard, 144. God looks at our purpose, 149, 374, 375. not worthiness of recipients, 149. cleanses after sins, 158, 159, 365. blessing of, 225. hand withered that is without, 292. guilt of giving and receiving from ill-gotten gains, 295, 373. what is, 329. we ought to give superfluities in, 329. the oil for our lamps, 337. cf. 374. gives earthly, receives heavenly, 365. Heaven's gates open to, 373. might of, 374. some do it but scantly, 374. some their all, 381 and note e., in doing, we must be intent, lest anxiety for wife and children intervene, 394. false receiving of, 381. *see* Poor, Poverty.

Alphabet, 117, 317.

Angels minister to our salvation, 35, 36. the SON's servants, our fellow-servants, 36. great the interval betwixt us and, 36. manifold examples of ministry of, 36. their ministry to us an encouragement, 36. Law given through, how, 38, 39. entrusted with charge of nation, 39. with care of us mourn over our badness, 272. are by us in the night, 186. in Church especially, 196. and in fear when Christians pray, 317. were our enemies, reconciled by Christ, 208. Cherubim dwell on earth, 202. despise us their fellow-citizens if enslaved to gold, 291. do not need attendants when they go through the world, 330. the Theatre of Christians, 332. with, is that soul, whose Lover God is, 336. Angelic work yea Christ's work to do all for salvation of brethren, 35.

Anger how guarded against, 74. a fire a flame; forbearance quenches it as iron red-hot dipped in water is quenched, 262.

Animals do not readily attack their fellows of the same species, 292.

Antichrist the Jews having rejected Christ will fall into hands of, 379.

Apostles received nothing in writing, 179. tombs of but four known (*see* Tombs), 299.

Arians, 33, 110. their formula *there was when He was not,* 11. as by an

instrument, 21. God needed not an Helper, 34.
Arius, 20, 21, 34.
Armour some parts of Christian, explained, 74. shield of faith, 262. girdle of truth, 216.
Article definite, force of, 34.
Athlete example of an, 72, 232, 246, 247, 267. Christ's, 287. chastisement strengthens, 350.

B.

BABYLONIANS of less understanding than they of Lystra, 308.
Baptism sins forgiven in, 67. cleanses the soul, 228. repentance after, is of grace, 93. after comes repentance, 183. necessary, 118. one, 118, 119, 120, 121, 122, 124, 127, 234. if not so, how careless we should get, 120. if more than one, an endless number, 121. a Cross, 119. our death and rising, 120. gifts in, 121. a grace once for all, 120. the whole is Grace, 119. called "the Seal," 169. enlightening, 169. peril of delaying to the end of life, 169. they who do so alluded to, 234, 294 note. great loss thence even if one does receive Baptism, 170 sqq. shame that accrues to these when they behold others' sweats and Rewards, 171. bears sons, 176. our Lord's Passion, 200. if without fruit, punishment, 233. makes Brotherhood, because God then our Father, 293.
Baptized the, called Enlightened, 172.
Bastards not worth punishing, 341.
Beatitudes, 98.
Begging a disgrace, 147.
Beginning value of, 122, 124. and hardness, 124.
Bitterness root of, difference between and a bitter root, 358.
Brother in S. Paul meant not a monk but a believer, 203, 294.

C.

CAIN, what S. Chrysostom thought the fault of his sacrifice, 375.
Carnal tempers what, 221.
Catechumens, 169, 172. know Christ and the Faith, 172. not a *brother* in S. Paul's sense, even if he be a Monk, 293.
Chance they who attribute all to, are not pleasing to God, 259.

Charity praise of, 44—46. his work on referred to, 45. loves not in order to be loved in turn but for God, 45. wears itself out for Jews heathen heretics, 46. pitying those who have done not well but wrong, 135.
Chastisement is exercise, bearing sweet fruit, 350.
Children in a passion if they strike us we do but laugh, 262. if ourselves in a passion we become, 263. an intelligent, will sometimes decline playthings longing for what is higher, 268. playthings kept back if too eagerly longed for, given freely if not so, 289.
CHRIST His Sufferings, 65, 66. from the Jews, 325. from disciples, 326. in babyhood, 326. from scorning, 325, 327. an aid to patience, 6, 327. an honour, 52. a glory, 339. far far greater than creation, 52. we are to have fellowship with, 379, 383. calls His Cross *glory*, 51, cf. 53: His Death called a *taste* because it held Him not long, 51. smote the devil, 54. and death, 56: His Resurrection, 6, 25, 51, 120, 391. to prove, one aim of S. Paul in Epistle, 6, 7, 391. known to those of old, 296: His appointment as Priest, 102: His weeping at prayer not told in Gospels, 102: sometimes spoken of from the Divine, sometimes from the Human, 13, in Spirit and flesh, 13 init., not ἄναρχος or alien from God (according to some), 20. acts of His own authority, 316, 317, calls His own coming in the flesh Exodus, S. Paul Eisodos (coming in) 31,.*Apostle* as sent, 69. became Priest when He took flesh, 162, 163, 175, One Priest because undying, 166. one act of, 168, 209, 212. Godhead and Manhood in, 167, 175, our One Sacrifice, 169, 176, 189. [see Sacrifice]: all heavenly, 176. died once, 209. died for all even though all accepted not, 210. suffered because He willed, 324, 383. and gladly, 324. His enemies are Jews, unbelievers, carnal, 221. Jews' contumelies to, 325. many of His words already come to pass, 249. gives His Gifts in ways contrary to natural course, 290. because nature's Maker, 290. His Death our Safeguard, 310. why He chose death of the Cross, 324. prayed, not needing prayer but to teach us, 317. if we suffer we must look to, 325, 326, 327. has implanted in us of His

INDEX. 399

Beauty and Comeliness, 13. we one with, 79. we read not that He laughed, 195. to be looked to as a Master that we may learn how to do, 323, 324. gave us the Faith, 324. gave the beginning, will put on the end, 324.
CHRIST's Blood, 340. mixed up with the very substance of peoples' souls, rendering them vigorous and pure, 201. sprinkled in our souls, 309. we have 310. partake of, 383. has cleansed all, 368. purifies us, 192, 200, 201, flowed from the Body which had been framed by the SPIRIT 201, carried into Heaven, 383.
CHRIST's Body framed by the Holy Spirit, 191, 201.
CHRIST GOD, 23, 65, 67, 167, 175, though Priest sits, stands not, 25, 168, 174, 175, 220, 226.
Christian shines out most brightly in poverty, 29. the crucified, has Charity, 45. the crucified, the mourner, 195, how to fight, bravely, not inviting war, not interfering, 73. to be ready to pour out his blood as though it were water, 73. his constant daily warfare, 73, 74. different parts of his armour explained, 74, 75. mercifulness his special characteristic, 374. his super-human might 395. should arm himself with desire of Heaven a fire which none may withstand, 395, 396.
Christianity, danger of fulfilling as a custom, 128.
S. *Chrysostom* rejoices that things will not always abide as they are, 34. thought that miraculous gifts were less at the date of the Epistle to the Hebrews 41. refers to an already-published writing of his on charity, 45. speaks from necessity, would from pleasure too if he knew his hearers were earnest, 47. would fain have been silent lest he increase their peril but fears to be silent, 283. will examine the careless ones, will not tell them *when*, 47, 48. prays and exhorts others to pray that no untimely deaths may befal 59. threatens to punish hired mourners brought into Christian funerals and to suspend those who bring them, 59. cannot preach the Resurrection while Christians thus contradict, 56, 59. calls himself a good-for-nothing, yet must use his authority, 66, 61. begs them to bear with him if severe 60. would fain only loose, yea not need power of loosing, 61. longs to praise, 62, 273. speaks of the want of Bible-knowledge among his people, 110 sqq. the discouragement in his teaching from their inattention, 47, 114. and risk through repetition of making the account of some heavier at the Judgement, 115. expects that his people will bring forth fruit suddenly, 137. thought that the sky did not move and is not spherical, 175, 316. addresses not Christians only but even heathen if any present on the truth of Christ's words 248, 249. thought that Pharisee spake his prayer in no man's hearing, 251. elsewhere thought otherwise 318. apologizes for what he says, as constrained to say it, 273. calls himself a father, 273. attests his inmost grief, 273, 274. always has to repeat same things, 283. knew not how to rebuke owing to the sin of alms out of ill-gotten gains, 295. wants his people to help him by helping each other on, 352 sqq. 356, 357.
Church bonds of, if any despise, put on by authority, the Day of Judgement will teach him, 61. if any burst, he answers it to Christ 61. Laws of, *see* Laws. Church, Heaven 177. [*see* service.]
Clergy who are over us we must obey, 387, 388. even if bad, so their faith be sound, 388. must be sober and watchful; if despised must weep, God punishes, 389. their terrible responsibility, 389. and account, 389. peril in throwing themselves upon dignity, they ought to flee; then if seized, to submit, 390.
Club the, in S. Chrysostom's time, 353.
Comfort the duty of giving, 83.
Commands easiness of God's, 172, 173. *see* Will.
Compunction God's gift 113, to prayer 238. Publican filled with when Pharisee's words came to him, 318.
Confession, the Faith 69, 91, 118. of sins 319. *see* sins, Priest, Repentance.
Conscience must be compelled to own sins, that it may repent and escape torment, 362.
Consulate its transitoriness 125.
Contrition, an ingredient of Repentance, 123. what, 123.
Cornelius the centurion his offering, 144.
Covenants both of God though not in like manner, 37.

Covetous 355. they who overreach ruin themselves not others, 239. sin of going to their entertainments, 293, 295. a poor man who refused to go for his own soul's sake would shame, 294.
Covetousness worse than mire, 293.
Creation a less thing then preservation, 24. transfiguration of, so easy, 34. fulfills its appointed course, 315. reverenced Joshua for the name he bore, 315.
Credibility, those who handed to us Gospel Truth accredited as not forgers, 40, 41. what has already come to pass accredit those yet to come, 248, 249.
Creed. see confession.
Cross our Master calls *glory*, 51. why He chose, 324. fruit of how great, 51. our, 327.
Crowning, time of, one ; of conflict of each, manifold, 322.

D.

DANGER to run needlessly into, tempting God, 303.
Daniel why he did not refuse the *oblation* and *sweet odours*, 305 sqq. he was humble, 305—307.
Deacon's warning and searching cry at Holy Communion, 214, 215. after the whole sacrifice is completed, 215. meaning of, 216.
Death of Christ, smote the devil, 54. death's death, 56. once only, 120, 209. our purification, 201. how death undone to us, 209. its terror, 55. untimely, S. Chrysostom prays and exhorts prelates and all to pray that no, may befal, 59. day of each person's, nearer than end of all things, 249. death's death hope given of in Enoch's translation, 259.
Desire implanted, 28. but capable of most grievous abuse, 348. evil, cast out by chastisement, 343. hides sight of God, 260. *see* Lust.
Despair we may not, 83. even after deepest wickedness, 158.
Devil smitten in Christ's death, 54. and brought to nought, 55, 56. aims to make us speak against God, 240. overthrow of, hope given in Enoch's translation, 259. if he wound not, wounded, 262. wounded in his attack on Job, wounded in his attack on S. Paul, 262. his dart concupiscence, 262. glories at our evil state, 272.

Disobedience peril of, 38.
Dives received (ἀπέλαβες *received* not as a gift but *in return*) here the reward of his good deeds, 71.
Docetae alluded to, 54.
Doctrines which concern the soul must be contended for, 73. cf. 388.
Dress, a lady sometimes had a precious garment inwoven with gold, 237, 238. beautiful and costly, belong to the stage, 332. by, S. Paul set at nought in the very Church itself, 334. *see* Lady, lace, silk.
Drunkards, we go to their houses though S. Paul forbids us, 294.
Drunkenness sin of, 318.

E.

ENOCH not discouraged by what had befallen Abel, 257. and knew that he had received a Recompence, 258.
Envy no one envies himself, 230. Hebrews obnoxious to, 255. we give way to, 318.
EUCHARIST, 261. the Sacrifice, 169. daily, 213. therein the purifying Blood entereth the soul springing up like a fountain in our souls, 201. many partake once or twice a year, many often, the solitaries yearly or after two years, 213 cf. 214. Lent the preparation for the Easter-Eucharist, 214. frequent receiving right if prepared, seldom receiving too frequent if unprepared, 214. peril of unworthy receiving, 214, 235, 236. the Deacon's warning cry at, 214, 215, 216. the beauty of ornament that fits to approach, 216. the beauty of Eunuchs who stand by the Majesty, 216, 217. may be a cause of disease, even as food when the system is disordered, 214. a Royal Table, sweet Ointment, 214. forty days' preparation, one week's care after, 214. in, a person becomes the Body of Christ, 235. unworthy partaking of, 318.
Eunuchs spiritual, to stand before King, 216, 217.
Evil-speaking earns praise to the receiver if he requite it not, more abundant disgrace to the giver, 15. terrible harm we do by, 250, 251. rife, 274. vain prayer uttered by one while repeating gossip, 250. if Pharisee condemned though he spake truth, what we when we utter lies, 251.

Ezra gathered the scattered Scriptures, 111.
Eyes what we see with, more readily retained than what we hear, 177. sometimes injured from a bad habit of body, 214. of the soul, how to make beautiful and keen of sight, 217. evil desires passions affairs of this life darken, 260.

F.

FAINTHEARTEDNESS, 249, 253. sometimes produces unbelief, 134. springs from unbelief, 229. hinders a promise of its fruit, 139. makes one no ready hearer, 151. loss from at the last, 282. at last came on the Hebrews, 300. danger of to soul in tribulation, 380.
Faith to need absolute proof of God's Providence or care, want of, 84. insufficient without a right Life, 87. necessary to salvation, 87. cf. 228, 382. must be very sure, 228. in it we trust the Holy Ghost, 228. contrary to reasoning, 382. the very essence of things of hope, 247, 218. comes of a sincere will, 395. needs a generous soul, 253. saves, 253. its might 310, 312, 313, 314. can do all, 311. is all, 382. a pure life springs of, 378. makes all things pure, 379. mutual aid from, 254. accused by some as being without proof and defended by S. Paul, 254. knowledge concerning God belongs to 254, 255. of Abel, 256, 257. of Enoch, 264. of them of old, 298. of Joseph, 298, 299. manifoldly, 298. in retribution necessary, 258. holds nothing more to be relied on than God's words, 265.
FAITH the, 69, 89, 91, 92, 116, 117, 118, 142, 172, 245. handed down that we may not have to engage with every heresy, 110. known to Catechumens, 172. CHRIST gave, 324. imparts holiness, 352. the, and right life make of full age, 117. we are to endure so long as the, is not touched, 351. cf. 72. who misteach, we must shun, 388. cf. on Galatians, p. 16.
Father his desire to remit punishment seen in God also, 259. as he lets approved children wait for the others, so God orders that the saints wait for us, 322. sends away from a son an evil companion, if the son persist after he is warned, 386.
Filth, like a Host who gives a splendid entertainment and sits down with his hands well smeared with the veriest, such is the covetous Host, 293.
Fire no longer consumes but bears to Heaven Christian sacrifices, 144. of Spirit to burn up desire of wealth, 144. the ardent desire for Heaven the Christian's, 395.
Flesh taken of sits on high and is worshipped by Angels Archangels Cherubin Seraphin, 64.
Food, mischief of immoderate eaters, 346—348. what can be digested nourishes, 346, 347. repletion worse than famine 347.
Forerunner impliesthem who follow, 142.
Foregiveness of others ingredient of Repentance, 123, 124.
Form of a slave, man ; form of God, (GOD, 23.
Freewill its proneness to ill, 155. its reality, 155. it is aided by God, 156, 392.
Friends favour of must be risked to obtain his salvation, 272. real, help one anothers' souls 354, 355.
Funerals Hymns and psalmody at proclaim Triumph, 57. unseemly grief at, 57. those who tear their hair and behave unseemly ought to be long while shut out of Church, 57, 58. the part of madmen, 58. harmful, 58. a scandal and makes Resurrection disbelieved 56, 59. psalms cxvi, xxiii, xxxii, sung at, 58. hired mourners if admitted to Christian funeral shall be punished, those who admit them treated as idolaters, 59. daily, hourly, 157.

G.

GARDEN untilled part of, 345.
Garments precious laid among perfume and spices to preserve from moths, 238.
Gifts, some receive not because of impure life, some lest it should harm their souls, 41, 43. diversity of 42. if householder knows to whom to entrust, God more, 42, 43. how to comfort ourselves that we have not, 42, 44. must use thankfully the little ones we have, 43. the greatest, Charity, offered to all, 44, 45.

402 INDEX.

Glory, from men we must account as nothing, 324. obtained by simplicity, 334.
Glutton overreaching, 359.
GOD His Peace surpasses mind much more does He, 18. Reverence and faith needed to hear or speak of, 18. when our human language fails, then we must praise Him for His Greatness, 18. of, we know somewhat yet understand not, 18, 19. or conceive and cannot utter, 19. not enclosed by space, 25. spoken of as though man, 69. wonderful in His works, in His Love to man more wonderful, 46. through uncertainty would keep us watchful, 48. teaches patience, 138. His condescension in swearing Who ought to be believed without, 140, 141. cf. 165. everywhere present, 173. by remembering we forget wickedness, 184, 185. we must remember specially at night and at day-break, 184, 185. and so have Him our helper, 185. remembrance of Him uplifts us to endure and be brave, 303. and makes hard things easy, 304. several result of His remembering us, and we Him, 304. commands nothing impossible, 205. what philosophers knew of His Being, belonged to Faith, not to reason, 254, 255. Being of, Faith assures; truths of His Essence neither Faith nor reasoning may attain, 258. inflicted punishment of death, as He threatened, as a Parent shewed mercy immediately in translating Enoch undying, 259. they who attribute all to chance are not pleasing to, 259. a Rewarder, 259, 260. how to be sought, 260. evil desires, passions, cares obstruct sight, 260. how to lift ourselves towards, 261. His manifold gifts at creation, 270. His Gift of His Son, 270, 271. the God and Friend of holy people, 279, 280. will be ours if we will be strangers to the world, 281. obedience makes us friends of, 283. gives not full rest here but some refreshment, 267. wished to seem a Debtor even in giving up His own Son, 288. a glory to, to be called God of the good; a shame to, to be called God of the wicked, 280, 281. gives earthly things if our hearts be not set on them, 288. with fear of Him bitter things not painful, 305. the friend of, besought God his Friend and the creatures yielded, 315. if we hold fast to, we shall stand against the foe and temptation, 327, 328. the Lover of holy souls, 336. chastens as sons tenderly beloved, 342. gave Law gives too the Gospel, 371. our example in mercifulness, 374. if our friend, temporal things matter not, 381. alone knows what is good for us, 384.
GOD the FATHER angry for dishonour done to His SON, 35.
GOD the FATHER and the SON Each subsist, 19.
GOD the FATHER GOD the SON GOD the HOLY GHOST unity of, 22.
GOD the SON from the Father, 19, 21. absolutely Equal to the Father, 20, 36. has absolute Power, 21. Equal Honour, 383. gift of Redemption enhanced by being through, 25. what means *sitting*, 25, 26. Who disdained not to become Man neither disdained He the lowly expressions, 26. teaches us thereby lowliness, 27. marked off from creatures, 33. *sent* i. e. made flesh, 36. no minister 36. assumed what is of us and united it to Himself, 49. suffered though God is incapable of suffering, 65, 66. why called a *sword*, 88. passes through inner heart, to judge, 89. severity of, 90. tender aid given by, 91. sympathy of, 66, 91, 92. appointed Priest, 102. His obedience, 103. His learning it, 141. prayed yet raised Himself from the dead, 103. prayed for us, 103. emptied Himself and glorified Himself, 104. *mediated by an oath*, 140. and all the power of the Spirit dwell in His Flesh, 191.
GOD the SON GOD, 24. who is worshipped, 32. who beholds all, 91. who stands not as High Priest but is on the Throne, 93. Who in the Gospels swears by Himself, 139. *see also* CHRIST GOD.
GOD the HOLY GHOST, 144. argument against objectors to His Godhead, 9, 10. God Who reveals, 264. grace of, shews Its might as It will, 11. mighty, 261, 309, 393. *see* Grace. His inspiration of and care for preservation of Scriptures, 110, 111. received in Baptism, 118. S. Paul's words words of, 127. might of in Body of the Word, 191. whose Body of (*ἐκ*), 191. framed by, 201. His Presence hallows men, 216. we trust to in matters of faith, 228. somewhat that S. Chrysostom said, the words of, 213. waters us, Christ having

planted us, 233. we know not how to pray save by, 384.
Gold is but dirt, 291.
Gold-embroidered linen, 293. ornaments, 331, 332, 333, 334. we must part with for others' need that we may enjoy His Beauty, 337.
Gossip grievous sins of, 250, 251. idle excuse that it was another that told us, 250, 251. if we must, to speak of our sins to God and our friends, 251, 252.
Grace Throne of, now will then be Throne of Doom, 93. Repentance after Baptism is of, 93. of the Spirit, 261, 309, 343, 393, 394, 395. compared to wind filling sails and wafting ship, 393, 394. even of old time wrought through the unworthy, 282. prevents, our diligence follows, 283. fills up our work, 392. poured on Moses in his baby-hood, wrought in Pharaoh's daughter, 300. surpasses the Law in that it can bring to Heaven, 315.

H.

HAIR *see* Temple.
Hand withered that doth not alms, 292. filthy that grasps beyond its due, 293.
Heaven, 84—86. not to be reached negligently, 87. we lose by seeking first things of time, 112, 113. the glory beyond words, 126. through hope we now there, 141. offerings presented by Christians borne unconsumed to, 144. who wishes may be in, may be heaven, 202, 203. as S. Paul and others did, 204. there calm, 203. there good things abide, 372, 373. the Patriarchs alive to, dead to the world, we alive to the world, dead to Heaven, 275, 276. Theatre of, 332. Beauty of; how much more His Beauty, 337. the homes that are there the Poor build us, 373.
Hebrews Epistle to, written to Jews (he thought) in Palestine and Jerusalem, 3. mode in, compared to that in Epistle to Romans, 101, 105, 153, 154, 247. Galatians, 105, 108, 130, 131. 1 Corinthians, 107, 369, 2 Corinthians, 376, Thessalonians, 378, others, 391. and his discourse at Athens, 106: had been Christians long time, 7, 106. babes, 109. had been better once, 105, 107, 108, 300.

their Faith and Patience, 300. S. Paul apologizes to them, 390. place of his prayer here at end, in other Epistles at beginning, 391.
Hell, 82, 101, 145, 169, 170, 230, 233, 243, 265, 271, 281, 295, 318. terror of, 15, 16. none afraid of, 273. some believe not that there is, 360. we must often think of lest we suffer it, 16. alms-giving will quench, 16. everlasting, 83, 216, 329. terrible beyond thought, 329, 364, 365. due punishment for evil-speaking, 250. we must hinder in friends what leads to, 355. there none may aid. 365.
Heretics, 103, 109, 164, 377. the Faith handed down to us our preservative against, 110. *see* Arius, Manichaeus, Marcellus, Marcion, Paul, Novatians &c.
Highmindedness to no purpose, 27. danger of, 41, 43, 156, 157. S. Peter's special danger of, as knowing that he loved Christ more than all, 361. prosperity sometimes produces, 384. constant memory of our sins does away with, 363.
Hope, its stay, 70, 76, 132, 141, 142, 165. that of each covenant contrasted, 178. of future bears through despondency, 349.
Human things their transitoriness, 125. a shadow, 304. nought if God our friend, 381. hope a help even in, 142. the whole of virtue to be loose from, 275, *see* Temporal things.
Humility aid from listening to our Lord's words on, 115. not true, to call ourselves sinners and be angry when so called, 318, 319. what, 319.

I. J.

JACOB faith of, 278, 298. gain through affliction, 343, 344.
JESUS in the form of Man, 315.
Jews had power in their own land to act independently of their rulers, 4, 5. their priests ceasing to be priests, 101. S. Paul proves that far superior to, and to their polity is the uncircumcised Melchizedek, 154. times of, under Ezra and Malachi referred to, 181. their law, old, 182. Jewish captives glorious even in captivity, 304. having deprived themselves of Christ will fall into hands of Anti-christ, 379. Jews,

heathens, heretics, true charity wears itself out for, 46.
Jews Christian, how well-nigh worn out when S. Paul wrote to them, 5, 6, 8, 9. cf. 377. had long believed and borne, 7. compared to Elijah in their troubles, 321. exhorted to perseverance in that whereunto they had attained, 377. their enemies Christ's enemies, 35.
Ill we are apt to suspect, good not so, 148. our will readily inclines to side of, 153. we often abstain from out of respect to men, 380.
Image and Express Image contrasted, 23.
Indolence the reason why the bad become not better, 277. why we imitate not the Saints, 230.
Injure they who, injure themselves, 290.
Injuries remembrance of, a great sin, 123, 124, 318. will go if we ever remember our sins, 363. bearing will help us and the injuring party too, 351.
Insult who, insult themselves, 290, 291.
Joshua reverenced, as a very special type of Christ, 315. availed more than did Moses, 315. even while Moses was living, 316.
Joy never unmixed here, 197. the true, how to be attained, 197. endurance with, Apostolical, 245. fruit of grief, of chastisement, 350.
Isaac only-begotten in respect to the promise, 288. praise of, 278, 297. his toils and gain therefrom, 343.
Judge the Judge of words as well as of actions, 186. propitiated if we accuse ourselves for our sins, 362. confess to, 363.
Judgement, 95. the Throne of grace now, becomes then Throne of, 93. day of, 144, 272. near, 249. the Judge will be there, 364. sins of all publicly displayed then except we do them away by continual remembrance of them, 363, 364. in that Day the poor man will deliver thee, 145. proof that end of world is nigh, 248, 249. end of all at hand, day of each person's death yet nearer, 249. we shudder at end, as if going to Judgement, 279. special account then taken of purity, 283. Judgements mentioned in his day 272.
Judgement common of all indisputable, 349, 350.
Jugglers' sleights, 204.

L.

Lace a superfluity, 331.
Lady walking with few attendants attracts less notice, 330, 331. to dress simply, 331 sqq. such an one has her Husband's respect, 334, 335.
Lamb paschal, type of our deliverance, 309, 310.
Laughing evil habit of, in Church and at prayers, 195—197. Sarah rebuked for, 196. her denial of it was from her faith, 269. right use of and misuse of, 197. women do not laugh, save in times of relaxation, in presence of their husbands, 196. we laugh at children who strike us in a passion, 262, 263. when we ought to mourn bitterly, 271, 272.
Law has less might than grace, 315. superiority of Christian things over those of, 369, 370. the Same who gave gave the Gospel, 371.
Laws Ecclesiastical, 60. written in hearts belong not to Jews but to Christians, 179 sqq.
Lent forty days' preparation for Easter Communion, 214. loss if insufficient, 216.
Longsuffering tames anger, 262.
Lose not to, of less toil than afterward to recover the let-go, 246.
Lost a thing, with what earnestness sought, 260.
Love the perfect thing, 229. from, all good things, 230. nought good which is not from, 230. assembling ourselves increases, 228, 229, 230. a natural path leading to virtue, 230. as self what, 230. of enemies and the bad, praise of, 231.
Lungs, reason given why they be placed under the heart, 74.
Lust, not pleasure, a mere shadow of pleasure, 74. he who is possessed by, worse than one in a fever, 193. evil desire hinders our seeing when we would find God, 260. generated by over-eating, 347.
Luxury brings to an ill end, 344. enfeebles body and soul, 345, 346. produces low spirits, 346. food for lusts, 347.

M.

Man spoken of sometimes from the lower, sometimes the higher part, so Christ, 13. Image of God, 23.
Man young, old ; see young, old.

Manichaeans, 109, 115. the modernest heresy, 110.
Marcellus, 19, 21, 22, 33. taught as did Sabellius, 110.
Marcion, 22, 33, 115. the first heresy, 110.
Marriage, 380. not it, but want of moderation in, hurts, 98, 99.
Martyrs whole-burnt-offerings, body and soul, 143.
Mary Virgin some deemed that God the Son had His beginning from, 110 [*see* S. Cyril Alex. de recta fide 11 a, 20 fin. 21 a, 44 e, Quod Unus est Christus 717 b, contra Nest. i. 4 (p. 21, O.T.), Apol. contra Theod. cap. i. 206 e.], the heresy of Paul of Samosata, 110.
Matter self-existent some people say that it is, 258.
Mediator not the owner of that in regard to which he mediates, 199.
Medicine of Repentance, what its ingredients, 122, 123. a, if removes disease utterly at once, has strength; if needed continually is weak, 211. not needed where no stroke, 213. bitter, gives first unpleasantness then benefits, 349.
Mercifulness untold beauty of, 373. might of, 374. specially belongs to a Christian, 374. God first shewed forth, 374. *see* Almsgiving.
Milk the lowlier doctrines, 104, 107, 108. cf. 89.
Mind how the grace of the Spirit gives it wings, 261. winged it soars above the devil's darts, 261, 262.
Miracles they who wrought and prophesied and were denied: it was probably the want of perseverance, 281. perhaps too they were wicked while they wrought, 282.
Money, the degradation of those who give themselves to, 193, 194. peril of love of, 237, 238, 240, 242, 282. and slavery to care of choice treasures, 237, 238. address to Mammon, 195. value for, a worse than Egyptian bondage, 238. gold mere dirt, 291. angels woul despise them who love, 291.
Monks or solitaries, not for them alone Christ's precepts but for people living in the world, 57, 98. saints in life and in faith, 134. might of their life, 395. some wanted to eat only, 135. when beggars, called impostors, 148. sometimes communicate yearly or at intervals of two years, 213.

Moses compared with Christ, 67, 68. a part of *the house*, 68. his faithfulness, 69. grace poured on in his very babyhood, 300. cared not for Palace of Egypt when Heaven is before him, 301. his flight was of faith, 303. less than Joshua, 315, 316. fled from dignity yet imperilled in discharge of it, 390.
Mourners hired forbidden even to come to a Christian funeral and threatened, 59. *see* Funerals.

N.

Night some spend in prayer some in deeds of evil, 186. prayer at, 317.
Novatians alluded to, 234.

O.

Obedience makes friends of God, 283. aids others too, 294. lack of, worse than anarchy, 387. punishment follows, 389.
Of (ἐξ) the Father, 19, 21, 26, 54.
Oil for lamps is kindness, 337 cf. 374.
Old age exceeding disgrace of a wicked, 95 sqq. depends not on years but on virtue, 97. of sin, repentance frees from, 119, 183. impairs not beauty of soul, 336. man, an Emperor if he have all his in subjection, 97.
Olympic games interest excited by, 184, herald's cry at, 215, 216.
τὸ ὅμοιον κατὰ πάντα (similarity in all respects), 22.
Oppression deeds of and of defrauding so great that many would gladly have parted with life, 271. see 292.
Orator his special pains at the end of his speech, 281.

P.

Pain here, 72, 286, 363.
Painting, the outline a shadow, with the colours an image, 210, 211.
Passion patience disarms, 262, 263. if in a, we become very children, 263.
Passions some are useful, 28.
Patience, 133, 140 note, 237. Christ's Sufferings an aid to, 6, 50. needed while things are still in process of *being subjected* to our King, 50. of fisherman and husbandman, 137. of Abraham, 139. why God teaches it us, 138. lost at very end when com-

bat even over, 246, 247. disarms passion, 262, 263. of the Hebrews, 300. need of much, 318.

Patriarchs strangers to the whole world, 268, 275, 277, 278. and lived as foreigners, 278. their faith very persevering, 300.

Paul S. Apostle of Gentiles, 1. Jews ill-disposed to, 1. why not sent to Jews, 2. once a Jew himself and holding with them, has greater force thereby, 2. why he wrote to them, 3, 4, 6. his love for them, 3, 4, 5. for each, 133. his history after close of Acts, 3. his trade alluded to, 11. (like his Master) leads up by little steps, then down, 11, 12, 20 cf. 6, 174. his way of speaking of the SON compared with S. John's 24, 25. (like his Master) does not *utter* all but leaves to conscience of hearers, 38. is not particular in use of his phrases, 39. cites Holy Scripture anonymously to those who were familiar with it, 49. his example as an athlete, 72. transposes his thoughts, 79. [cf. S. Irenæus iii. 7. 2 p. 217, O.T.] his mode here and in the Epistle to the Romans compared, 101, 105, 153, 154, 247. here and in Epistle to the Galatians, 105, 108, 130, 131, 246. and in Epistles to Corinthians, 107, 369, 376, to Thessalonians 378. and discourse to Athenians, 106. leads his hearers on even to the very hard, 105. by little and little, 150, 165. mixes praise and blame, 130, 131, 132, 133, 138, 243, 244. his praise of them, 134. passes not away, 126. words of, words of the Holy Ghost, of Christ, 127. his fear of failing, 128. mixes lowly and lofty, 174. expands Prophet Jeremiah, 182. and others lived in Heaven while here, 204. praises of, 230, 231. his travail-pangs, 273. did not call himself a stranger only but dead to the world, 275. allows not to eat with the *covetous*, 293, 294. nor *drunkards* yet we disobey, 294. his use of term *brother*, 293, 294. not a trace of monastic life in his time, 294. his great wealth of thought, 309. his absolute uncare for troubles when now in twentieth year of preaching, 328. commanding simplicity of attire utterly disobeyed in the very Church, 333, 334. ever gave thanks in all his afflictions, 384, 385. his apology to the Hebrews, 390, 391. his deep love for them and prayers and asking their prayers, 390, 391. we must imitate in his surmounting all suffering and trial for Heaven's love, 395.

Paul of Samosata, 21, 33, 34, 110. taught that God the Son had His beginning from the holy Virgin, 110. his followers called Jews, 33 and note.

Peacock beauty of, 373.

Perseverance need of when near the goal, 89, 94 sqq. need of, 90, 282, 318. from examples, 281, 282. want of probably cost those who had prophesied and cast out devils, their crown 281.

S. Peter, a common person may be as, 224. praise of, 230. his tomb known, 299. his penitence perfect, 360. God left that he might learn not to contradict the Master, 361. his special temptation to be high-minded, 361. his courage afterwards, 361.

Photinus, 19. taught same with Sabellius, 110.

Physicians taste food for the sick man first, 52. why they say that the lungs are placed under the heart, 74. parts of bodies that have grown callous yield not to hands of, 78. mix up medicines of many ingredients, one the essence of the medicine, 123. after deep incisions use gentle remedies, 243. if he go not forward to the end, his early success but loss, 282. if despised cannot avenge himself on his patient, 389.

Playthings sometimes offered to an intelligent child, to shew how he cares for higher things, 268. withheld if too eagerly desired, 289.

Pleasure diminished if disappointment be expected to follow, 349, that brings forth despondency no pleasure, 350.

Poor the, a fellow freeman, 145. will stand by thee in the Day of Doom thy Advocate, 145. neglected while a dead body without feeling is richly adorned, 145. if he beg, called Impostor, 146—148. ought to be helped, for we always eat, our children constantly beg of us, 147. ought to be helped without enquiry for we too say *Remember not my sins*, 147, 148. the Saints of old poor yet very mighty, 222, 224. who feed feed Christ, 225. many of, bitterly defrauded and oppressed, 271, 292. the rich most truly, 291. if a Poor man asked to an entertainment by one who overreached therefore refused, the other would feel shame, 294. none too, to give the *cup of cold water*, the *two mites*, to visit *sick*, prisoners, 365. build us our houses in Heaven, 373. offerings of, accepted equally with that of Gold, 375. yea of ten thousand talents, 375.

Poverty not, but caring to be despised for, renders us despicable, 29. the Christian shines out more in than in riches, 29. it affords too more pleasure, 29. we may not be impatient of, 30. very many blessings of, 222, 239. makes bold, 223. leads by the hand to Heaven, 223. great independence of, 223. Christ called perfection of virtue, 223, 224. its ill-omened sound, 224. if voluntary, gives great might, 224, 225. and trust towards God, 225. every one afraid of, 273. not painful with the fear of God, 305. luxurious habits make, hated, 335. to be sought, 386.

Praise to repudiate, one form of pride, 319.

Prayer intense, one ingredient of Repentance, 123, 124. heard through alms, 144. no marvel if not heard, when we neglect those who beg of us, 147. night-long ($παννυχὶs$) 186. a great weapon, 185. special need of night and morning, 185, 261. a certain uttered in the act of tale-telling, 250. intense, 261, 317, 394. we sin-stained, if not heard at our first, draw back, 305. watching in, what, 317. a mighty weapon, 317. made worthy one unworthy, 317. some yawn and scratch themselves at, 317. laugh during, 195, 196. prevents sins, heals misdeeds, 318. cf. 365. need of, 318. ordinarily asked of them who love us, 399.

Priest our, not visible, under old Covenant not visible, 227. in offerings of Christians, each his own, 143, 144.

Priests, their aid towards forgiveness, 123. the, offer up the prayer of all, 196. if a man call himself a, enquire as not giving but receiving from him, 148, 149. wicked, grace works through, for sake of their flock, themselves condemned, 282, 283. may not be silent, 283. grave responsibility of, 389 sqq. *see* Clergy.

Promises in what respect they of old received, in what sense received them not, 267, 296, 297. received by trusting thoroughly, 268. Christ's not that we shall have power to stay the sun and moon but that He and the Father will dwell in us, 316.

Proof continued after a person is satisfied wearies him, 312.

Proverb a, 291.

Psalm xxiii, xxxii, cxvi. sung at funerals, 58. vi. said every day, 196.

Punishments, 101. *there* not here, 70, 236, 274. given with blessing here that *there* may be no account, 71. instances, 71. evil of being without alluded to, 29. in store for the wicked, 83. to the soul too, 88 [*see* Soul]. much spared us, 122. use of, 157. we must exact from ourselves, 362. greater to those who have enjoyed good things here without becoming better, 241. will come, 248. as in dread of, we grieve at leaving this life, 279. if we deny our sins, 362. if clergy are disobeyed and weep, we incur, 389.

Purity of itself admits to the kingdom, its absence takes to destruction, 283.

R.

Race foot-, S. Paul uses as his simile as being the easiest of the contests, 323.

Reasoning faith opposed to, 254, 382. our reasonings differ not from spiders' webs, 395. reasoning-power given to each is a talent, 353.

Repentance, 124. after Baptism yet remains to us, 234. a propitiation, 234. after Baptism is of grace, 93. sets free from old age of sin, and makes strong, restores not to the former brightness, 119. if used aright will blot out all sins, 122. in deepest peril can establish in safety, 122. medicine of, contains about nine ingredients, almsgiving the most essential, 122, 123. necessity of strict, 158, 318. its might, 159. restores lost beauty so as even the King may desire it, 183, 184. even from deepest deformity, 183. ours a weak, 216. here of use, *there* of none avail, 249, 250. why unavailing Esau's, 359 sqq. Cain's, 359. Judas, 361. sins too great for, 360. S. Peter's, 360. King David's, 361, 363. does not forget sins, 361, 362, *see* sins.

Repetition use of, 115, 365.

Reproach, apt to pervert the soul and darken the judgement, 244. deep trial of when in presence of many,

244. Christ endured 302. we must accept, thus we put away, 318. makes our sins lighter for us, 319. S. Paul does not allow the Clergy if despised to use, but to weep, 389.

Reproof profitable to endure, 60, 61. bitterer than fire and knife; we must take lessons from surgeon in using, 355. patience in giving, 356. looking to the reward in store, 355. not always immediate, 360.

Rest God gives not full here, 267. not here, 371.

Resurrection preaching to heathen of no avail while Christians by unseemly grief at funerals contradict, 56, 61. they believe it not who give way to mad sorrow at loss of theirs, 58. some believe that some rise that others do not, 228. aids to those who believe not, 70. a deceit not to believe, 83. disbelief of, 110. that there is, a part of our Confession, 91. though not yet here hope gives it an existence in our soul, 248. at the doors, 248, Abel and those of his time knew not of a, 258. yet of old the hope of it given, 287. of all together, 364.

Resurrection Christ's, 6, 25, 51, 120, 391.

Rewards, there, 69, 70, 237, 248, 314. cf. 302. to receive here an insult, 314. if we are good only for, we shall never be good, 170. differences of, 172. given to thankfulness, 239, 241. who believe not in, please not God, 259. we may not despond of, 350.

S.

SABBATH-RESTS three, 77. the first, God's; the second, Palestine: 77. the third, Heaven, 78, 84, 91. the proof of this, 81, 82.

Sabbath-day meet occupations for, what, 82.

Sabellius, 20, 21, 22. taught that Father Son Spirit are but one, 110.

Sacrifice the Cross the One, 189, 213. cf. 169, 176, 202, 221, 234, 309, 310, 361. ours the memorial of that One, 213. our, 383. Deacon's cry *Holy things for the holy* uttered after completion of, 215. *see* Eucharist.

Sacrifices shewed weakness by needing repetition, 212, 219. the weakness of shewn, and they abolished, ere Christ came, 218, 219.

Sacrifices of Christians, 143. all their rites heavenly, 176. their own souls, 143. shadowed out in Old Testament too, 143. the Martyrs body and soul, 143. voluntary poverty is also a whole-burnt-offering, 144. those of Cornelius, 144.

Saint every Christian a, in faith, 134.

Saints if put in scale against whole world avail more, 280, 314 sqq. some say "we cannot be as the" 310. friends of God, 279 sqq., 314, 315. how great their virtue, 316. gladly wait for us, 321, 322. made to shine by means of affliction, 343, 344.

Salvation each can aid others in the way of, 352—356. has even more advantage thereto than the teacher has, 352.

Saul declined the Kingdom yet escaped not peril for managing it amiss, 390.

Scripture Holy Old and New Testament of One and the Same, 10. uses human expressions of God, 69. food, 108. experience of makes *of full age,* 109, 110. no one attends to, 110. some do not know existence of, 110, 111. Holy Ghost provided for preservation of, 110, 111. Scripture testimonies to, 111. may not be known without learning, 111, 112. people's ignorance of, 112. what the Reader in Church gives out when he goes to the desk to read, 112. when dispersed God inspired Ezra to gather them, 111. to be heard with fear, 127. Old Testament shadows out Christian sacrifices, 143. say no more than is needed, 259.

Scripture Holy texts commented on or explained.

Ps. vi. 7	217
xxv. 7	95
xxxii. 4	129
xl. 1	144
xlv. 10 (forget)	184
11 (desire thy beauty)	183, 336
13	332
lii. 8	374
lxviii. 13	373
lxxvii. 2	260
ciii. 5	119
Prov. xiv. 29	232, 263
xxiv. 11	136
Isa. i. 16-18	158
Mal. i. 14	375
S. Matt. v. 42	147
vii. 7	260
14	344
22	281

INDEX. 409

x. 38	327
xviii. 18	60
xxiii. 2, 3	388
xxv. 2	364
8	337
15	353
S. Mark xii. 44	329
S. Luke vi. 36	148
x. 30 sqq.	135 sqq.
xvi. 9	16
. 25	71
S. John viii. 35	295
xvi. 33	93
Rom. xii. 1	143
xiii. 14	346, 347
1 Cor. v. 11	293, 294
vi. 9, 10	352
vii. 23	294
ix. 26	94
x. 13	340
2 Cor. iv. 17 (light affliction)	328
xi. 2	337
xii. 9	385
Gal. vi. 2	355, 356
Eph. vi. 14, 17	74, 75
Phil. ii. 6, 7 (form of slave, form of God)	23
Col. i. 20	208
1 Tim. ii. 9	331, 333, 334

Servants two are enough, 329, 330. a lady walking out should not be attended by many, 330. Angels do not have, 330.

Sepulchres see Tombs.

Sermons applause at, 115.

Service in Church every day, 215. increases love, 228, 229, 230. benefit of being together, 351, 380.

Seventy the, translated (by ordering of the Holy Ghost) Scriptures into Greek, 111.

Shame in the wicked their own witness against themselves, 277. before men not before God, 363.

Sheep treatment of unsound, 215.

Silence peril of to ministers of the word, 283.

Silk a superfluity, 331.

Sin a very plague, 193. in Heb. xi. 25 holding back from *affliction*, 301. to, belongs ease, 302. causes some to pine away from its bitterness, 358. easily overcome if we have the will, 323. the sole disgrace though no one thinks so, 331. the sole evil, 386. it is a duty to keep another from grave sin even if need be by force, after in other ways and by begging his help for oneself, 354, 355. King David long bewailed his, 361. may be hindered even from a lower motive, by degrees leading up to a higher, 354. abstaining from, a due observance, 382.

Sins the lesser not even a *spot or wrinkle* but far worse, 15. not small, 318. recoil on the doer, 14, 15. parent of unbelief, 79. notwithstanding, hope remains so long as *to-day* lasts, 82. we may not despair after, 83, 158, 159. he who would look for pardon for sins of youth must not go on in them when old, 95. those who have grown old through, repentance frees, 119. all can be blotted out by a right repentance, 122. must be confessed one by one, 124, 362. affliction wipes out, 327. confession lessens, 362. we must remember our, 124, 184, 361, 362, 364. if we remember, God forgets, 362. remembering helps cure, 362. great help of remembering, 274, 362, 364. punishment if we deny, 362. pity if we confess, 362. called *thorns*, 128—130. not enough to remove, treatment also needed, 129. if we cut out, we may enjoy the good things innumerable, 13. difficulty of cleansing away, 158. but almsgiving and standing up for the wronged do it, 158, 159, cf. 123. if we begin, God cleanses, 158. from of ignorance none is free, 189. we ought to mourn over others', 190. and keep silence as to them, 252. to tell our own to God and our friends, 251, 252. prevented or healed by prayer, 318. one enough to cast us out of the kingdom and they are many, 318. to acknowledge, not humility but candour, 319. some too great for Repentance, 360. remembering always our, does away remembrance of others' wrongs, 363. we must offer to God, 210, 363. penitence tears prayers deeds of mercy wash away, 365. by mourning our, we draw God to us, 389.

Sins putting away, what, 212.

Sinners, if others call us we must not be angry, 319, 320, cf. 361.

Slave-dealers, 330.

Slaves good the Master sometimes called after, 280, 281. two suffice for a family who are willing to part with superfluities, 329, 330.

Sleep some indulge in the day, we spiritually, 276.

Son force of word, 12, 13, 26, 32, 54, 68, 169. the SON and sons contrasted, 52, 53, 54.

Soul punished, 88, 238. suffers, 83. in its vigour when a person is in old age, 94. when one is young it is attacked by fevers, 95. purified by Blood of Christ, 192. its eye how to make quick and beautiful, 217. mingled with soul increases love, 229. might of a great, 232. in calamity more apt to become impatient, 240, reproach a severe trial of the, 244. and scorning and jests, 325. covetousness pollutes, 293. eating at the banquets of the overreaching destroys, 293. and defiles, 294. stretched out in prayer to God, 317. wrestles in Theatre of Heaven, 332. the well-adorned, has GOD for its Lover, her place with the choirs of Angels, 336. virgin if pure even though married, 332, 336, 337. it the Lord seeks after, 338. exhausted, how refreshed, 339, 340. made collected through affliction, 343. enervated through luxury, 345. if body effeminate soul shares it, 345. must be forced to the remembrance of its sins, 363. in tribulation liable to despondency, 380. must be braced to receive the abidance of the SPIRIT, 394, 395.

SPIRIT Holy, *see* GOD the HOLY GHOST.

Starvation no one died of, except of his own will, 148.

Strangers Patriarchs to this world, 268, 275, 277, 278, 280. King David, 280. we to our own country, 275, 279. if we to the world God would be called our God, 280, 281.

Substance no word will express, even of Angel or man, far less of GOD, 23.

Suffering perfects, 52, 72, 104. and is a cause of salvation, 52. cf. 104. we are to rejoice in our own, as paying the penalty of our sins here, 71. helps to wipe them out, 327. use of, 157, 327. it is only our own which moves us, 157. amid, we may be calm within, as is the sky when outwardly overcast, 203. of Abel preaches beyond all speech, 257. in which they of old passed their whole lives we have no dream of, 320, 326. all can be borne if so be we be approved in Heaven, 338, 329.

Suicide, some oppressed long for death and only the fear of God holds them from, 271.

Surgeons their mingled gentleness and unflinchingness, 355.

Suspect we are apt to, 148.

Swearing, 284.

T.

Talents teacher has five, learner has one, 353. the earth wherein single talent is buried, the bad heart, 353.

Teacher of grammar must make the boy master the things to be learnt, 115. if he say over the alphabet, it is not to teach himself, 317.

Teacher has five talents but learner has one, 353. if he teaches a child and the child listens not, one is called in who punishes the child, 389

Tears aid to wash away sins, 197, 365. one ingredient in medicine of repentance, 123, 124, 158. not of, but of wailing and mourning are they worthy who of choice fail of the things to come, 270, 271. S. Chrysostom calls to, 273. of Christ, 196.

Temple its magnificence, 207. its wonders, 366. and from being One, 207. as the Jewish, was for the whole world, so is Christ *our* Priest in the Temple of Heaven, 208. offering even of hair accepted for, 375.

Temporal things we seek first and lose both them and Heaven, 112, 113. God gives when He sees us prefer spiritual, not when rivetted to these 241, 289, 290. given as a refreshment, 267. often possessed not as His gift but from overreaching, 241. Patriarchs of old loved their Home cared not for these, 268. so magnificent, 269. who seek lose them and Divine; who prefer Divine obtain both, 308. soon go, 371 sqq. when we mind, the grace of the SPIRIT goes, 393. *see* Human things.

Temptation different species of conduct under, 72. terrible onslaught of, on the young man to be met by ascetic practises, 98. the noblest had to pass through, 133. stronger in time of calamity, 240. shall be as chaff if we hold fast to God, 328.

Thanksgiving we must bear all with, that we may attain the true joy, 197, 383, 384, 385. as S. Paul did, 384, 385. thank God both for comfort and afflictions, 385. brings untold blessings, 239, 241. without we cannot serve God, 376. our offering, 383. offered through a contrite mind, 383. due to GOD the SON, 383.

Thoughts some beyond power of expression, 19, 23.

Through or *by* (διὰ) not limited to the Son but used of the Father too, 52. cf. on Galatians, pp. 4, 5.
To-day, 26, 79, 80, 82, 90, 378, 379.
Tombs why they of old cared for their, 298, 299. of SS. Peter, Paul, John, Thomas known, of the rest unknown, 299. where'er any one's may be the earth is the Lord's, 299.
Tongue why given us, 14.
Trial without, we cannot know ourselves, 42, 43. life full of people who cause, and thus strengthen, 232. God exercises His own athletes with, 287. in, bearing with evil a great weapon, 351.
TRINITY *see* GOD the FATHER GOD the SON GOD the HOLY GHOST.
Truth our girdle, 216.

U. V.

Vain-glory mother of evils, 319. we act for, 331.
Virgin souls, uncorrupt even though married, 332, 336, 337. earthly virginity a mere shadow of that, 337. the True, 338.
Virtue like bitter medicine, 349.
Virtues to be practised one by one, taking care in acquiring new to not let go the former, 283, 284.
Unbelief, 265, 269. arises sometimes from faintheartedness, 134.

W.

Wants who has few, to be preferred, 28, 330 sqq.
Water taken lessens not fountain; so works remain to doer, 15. a fevered person drinking much, need not be highminded, 27. quenches red-hot iron, so forbearance anger, 262.
Wealth peril of love of, 282. peril of, 385, 386. *see* Money, Poor, Poverty, Covetous.
Wicked sometimes receives here the reward of his few good deeds, *there* utter punishment, 71. instances hereof, 71. God wills that His children shew pity and compassion to the, 136. laugh at and condemn those like themselves, 276. and thereby judge themselves, 277.
Wickedness, by remembering God we forget, 184, 185. of alms from ill-gotten gains, 295.
Wife a great good and great evil, 240.
Will with, nothing difficult, 173. not even to overcome sin, 323. inclines readily to ill, 155. immense power of, not apart from action, 204, 205. two kinds of, 219, 220. alone needed, 284. of it comes Faith, 395.
Wine need of moderation in, 99.
Women race of in towns weakened through delicate habits, 345. living in country stronger than men in towns, 345.
Words when human fail to express of God, Him must we praise, 18. thoughts that may not be expressed by, 19, 23. our, bare: God's not so, 24.
Works good or ill, the doer first reaps fruit of, 15, who holds the Faith and does right, *of full age*, 117. dead, a grievous pollution, 193. our work and God's act combine 229. God's grace preceding, our work following, 283. good, need of, 233. aid from, 210. the wealth of, 216. of teachers, their power, 229. ill, 234.
World to be one day transfigured, 34. avails not weighed against the saints, 280, 314 sqq. nor against the soul's beauty, 336.

Y.

Yawning at prayers, 317.
Yonder, Heaven, 69, 86, 88, 112, 202, 278, 291, 316. are the Rewards, the punishments, 70. the Rewards, 69. the Rest, 286.
Young man has excuse only in things that need experience, not effort and and striving, 97, ascetic practices his safeguard against violent temptation, 98.

INDEX OF TEXTS.

GENESIS.

i. 3	23
iii. 9	362
10	362
16	84
18, 19	84
iv. 4	256
7	256
9	362
10	368
vi. 2	344
5 (?)	69
9	343
xii. 1	285
7	266, 285
xiii. 15	66
xv. 5	269
6	395
xviii. 15	269
21	69
xxi. 12	285
xxii. 1	287
xxvii. 41	359
xxviii. 20	222
xlvii. 9	297, 344

EXODUS.

ii. 14	302
iii. 6	281
vi. 9	151
xix. 18	368
19	369
20	39
xx. 19	367, 369
21	367
xxxv. 23	375

NUMBERS.

xi. 12	43
xvii. 12	272

DEUTERONOMY.

vi. 7	111
xxviii. 23	180
cf. xxix. 18	358
xxxii. 9	10
15	384
cf. xxxiii. 2	366

JOSHUA.

x. 12	315, 316

2 SAMUEL.

xii. 8	241
12	363
xvi. 11, 12	319
xxiv. 17	231

1 KINGS.

xviii. 18	222

JOB.

i. 21	240, 385
ii. 4	55
5	240
9	240
10	240
xxxiv. 3	109

PSALMS.

i. 2	111
ii. 4, 5	35
8	10
11	127
iv. 4	185
5	143
vi. 5	249
6	123, 124, 196, 361
7	217
vii. 12	88
ix. 16	384
x. 13	79
xi. 5	290
xii. 4	79
xiv. 1	79
2	69
xvi. 2	342
4	184
xvii. 3, 4	184
xviii. 9	369
24	392
xix. 5	182
xxiii. 1	239
4	58

INDEX OF TEXTS.

xxiv. 1	298, 299
xxv. 7	95
18	71
19	71
xxxii. 4	129
5	122, 252
7	58
xxxiv. 11	112
12	112
13	14
13, 14	112
xxxvi. 1, 2	79
xxxvii. 5	363
xxxviii. 7	74
xxxix. 12	277, 280
xl. 1	144
6, 7.	143
xlii. 6	304
10	244
xlv. 10, 11	183
11	183, 335
13	332
xlix. 6 [a]	242
7	16, 249
8	305
l. 3	272
14	143
20	250
23	143
li. 1	374
10	23, 158
16	219
17	123, 143
lii. 8	374
lv. 12	244
lxiii. 6	184
lxv. 9	128
lxviii. 13	373
lxxvii. 2	260
lxxviii. 34	384
lxxxii. 8	93
xc. 2	24
10	249
xciv. 7	79
xcv. 2	249
xcvii. 3	272
cii. 9	123
ciii. 5	119
cx. 1	93
cxii. 2	261
9	224
cxvi. 7	58
cxviii. 15	372
cxix. 71	384
103	111
cxxi. 3	155
4	155
cxxvii. 1	361
cxxviii. 1	242
cxxxii. 12	312
cxlv. 8	374
cxlvi. 9	374

PROVERBS.

iii. 21	38
27	375
viii. 22	32
x. 4	222
xii. 28	318
xiv. 29	232, 263
xvi. 6	123
xviii. 3	79
17	122
19	229, 355
xxi. 13	144
xxiv. 11	136
xxvii. 17	229
xxx. 8	222

ECCLESIASTES.

i. 2	197
ii. 4	197
6, 7	197
ix. 16	222
xii. 8	197

ISAIAH.

i. 2	69, 272
12	219
16	158
16, 17	112
17	159
17, 18	158
iv. 6	322
v. 2	129
6	128
vi. 4	368
xi. 9 [b]	182
xxvi. 12	71
xxxv. 10	84, 274
xl. 2	71
xliii. 25	184
26	122, 184
cf. xlviii. 10	222
liii. 9	167
lvii. 17, 18.	124
lxv. 17	181

JEREMIAH.

iii. 3	194
iv. 14	158
vi. 20	143
vii. 4	207

[a] See the same form of citation in S. Chrysostom on Romans p. 459.
[b] The reference Hab. ii. 14 in page 182 is an error for this.

INDEX OF TEXTS.

viii. 4 122
ix. 1 273
xxvii. 6 306

EZEKIEL.

xvi. 49 344
xxviii. 3 306
xxxii. 11 220

DANIEL.

ii. 30 . . . . . 305, 307
46 304
iv. 8 308
v. 17 306

HOSEA.

iv. 2 271
vi. 6 143
xii. 10 9

AMOS.

v. 23 143
vi. 6 136
viii. 11 . . . . . 108, 128

MICAH.

vi. 2 70
8 143
vii. 1, 2 271

MALACHI.

i. 14 375
iv. 1 272

WISDOM.

iv. 8, 9 96

ECCLESIASTICUS.

i. 22 . . . . . . 28, 74
ii. 12 229
18 236
iii. 30 123
v. 6 236
ix. 15 111
x. 28 291
xvi. 3 . . . . . 280, 315
xix. 10 250
11 250
xx. 29 224
xxviii. 3 123
25 251
xxxiv. 22 292

SONG OF THREE CHILDREN.

6 306

HIST. SUSANNAH.

42 42

BEL & DRAGON.

24 308
38 305

S. MATTHEW.

i. 20 191
21 66
iv. 6 303
v. 3 222
11, 12 385
20 . . . . . 108, 231
22 . . . . 14, 28, 318
42 147
44 231
vi. 24 195
33 . . . . . 112, 267
vii. 1 . . . 134, 251, 388
3 388
6 236
7 260
14 . . . . . 344, 384
22 281
23 282
24 141
viii. 20 . . . . . 222, 321
x. 9, 10 222
16 351
18 286
24 323
25 323
36 286
38 . . . . . 286, 327
42 365
xi. 8 344
xii. 24 325
xiii. 3 31
6 129
17 296
22 129
41, 42 166
55 325
xv. 11 382
19 158
26, 27 317
xvi. 18 249
24 72
xviii. 15 60
16 60
17 60
18 60
20 228

INDEX OF TEXTS. 415

xix. 21	. . . . .	223, 385
23	. . . . . .	223
24	. . . . . .	385
29	. . . . .	267, 290
xx. 18, 19	. . . . .	103
26	. . . . . .	290
xxi. 40	. . . . . .	38
43	. . . . . .	35
44	. . . . . .	35
xxii. 29	. . . . . .	111
xxiii. 2, 3	. . . . . .	388
12	. . . . . .	290
xxiv. 14	. . . . . .	249
21	. . . . . .	249
xxv. 8	. . . . . .	337
12	. . . . .	337, 364
26	. . . . . .	364
31, 32	. . . . .	364
33	. . . . . .	364
34	. . . . . .	364
34-36	. . . . .	225
40	. . . . . .	14
41	. . . . . .	364
42	. . . . . .	364
45	. . . . . .	14
xxvi. 28	. . . . . .	201
38, 39	. . . . .	103
41	. . . . . .	72
68	. . . . . .	325
75	. . . . . .	360
xxvii. 39	. . . . . .	302
40	. . . . .	302, 325
63	. . . . . .	325
xxviii. 19	. . . . . .	67

S. MARK.

ii. 5	. . . . . .	67
vi. 18	. . . . . .	222
xi. 25	. . . . . .	123
xii. 42	. . . . .	365, 375
44	. . . . . .	329

S. LUKE.

i. 2	. . . . . .	40
ii. 26	. . . . . .	264
vi. 25	. . . . . .	196
36	. . . . .	148, 373
x. 20	. . . . . .	224
30	. . . . . .	135
34	. . . . . .	135
35	. . . . . .	135
37	. . . . . .	135
xi. 8	. . . . . .	317
15	. . . . . .	41
41	. . . . . .	123
xii. 42	. . . . . .	42
xiii. 34, 35	. . . . . .	35
xiv. 27	. . . . . .	286

xvi. 9	. . . . .	16, 86
11	. . . . . .	42
25	. . . . . .	71
26	. . . . . .	365
xvii. 10	. . . . .	27, 305
26, 27	. . . . .	264
xviii. 6	. . . . . .	317
11	. . . . .	251, 318
13	. . . . . .	318
xix. 27	. . . . . .	35
xxi. 2	. . . . . .	17
xxii. 19	. . . . . .	213
31, 32	. . . . .	361

S. JOHN.

i. 1	. . . . . .	24
3	. . . . . .	24
4	. . . . . .	24
10	. . . . . .	32
11	. . . . . .	302
15	. . . . . .	13
17	. . . . . .	39
ii. 19	. . . . . .	103
iii. 20	. . . . . .	79
34	. . . . .	33, 191
iv. 24	. . . . . .	143
v. 21	. . . . . .	166
22	. . . . .	21, 166
23	. . . . . .	383
vi. 42	. . . . . .	325
67	. . . . . .	326
vii. 12	. . . . . .	325
42	. . . . . .	325
52	. . . . . .	325
viii. 12	. . . . . .	22
18	. . . . . .	199
35	. . . . . .	294
42	. . . . . .	101
48	. . . . .	325, 326
ix. 4	. . . . . .	276
x. 18	. . . . .	103, 324
20	. . . . . .	325
xi. 5	. . . . . .	51
26	. . . . . .	139
xii. 23	. . . . . .	51
25	. . . . . .	286
49	. . . . . .	101
xiii. 16	. . . . . .	6
34	. . . . .	45, 199
35	. . . . .	45, 357
xiv. 2	. . . . .	6, 295
15	. . . . . .	283
17	. . . . . .	393
23	. . . . .	203, 316
26	. . . . . .	180
27	. . . . . .	357
28	. . . . .	101, 104
30	. . . . .	52, 324
xv. 14	. . . . .	271, 283

xv. 16	324
22	128
26	199
27 (?)	199
xvi. 20	344
28	31
33	93, 249, 286, 326, 344
xvii. 11	228
19	210
20	198
21	45
24	198, 217
xviii. 23	325
xix. 37	364
xx. 23	176

ACTS.

i. 11	36
ii. 5, 9, 10	207
36	11, 32
46	41
iii. 6	222, 225
26	66
iv. 32	228
v. 20	36
41	245
vii. 5	285
34	317
51	218
53	38
x. 4	144
xi. 29	321
xii. 5	228
22, 23	307
xiii. 26	66
41	196
xiv. 12	307
15	305
xv. 10	182
xvii. 30, 31	106
xviii. 17	4
xix. 6	118
xx. 24	56
xxi. 20	3
20, 21	1
21	3, 391
xxii. 18	2
19, 20	2
21	1, 2
xxiii. 5	5

ROMANS.

i. 12	254
18	128, 272
27	39
iii. 8	170
31	117
v. 10	374
14	48
15	51
20	8, 209
vi. 1, 2	120
4	119
5	119
6	119
9	120
viii. 3	92, 164, 182
7	221
15	56
18	328
24	70
25	70
26	370, 384
32	51
34	166
35	204
37	328
38, 39	204
ix. 3	3
15	156
16	155, 156
19	156
xi. 4	264
13, 14	1
xii. 1	143
5	79
18	351
20	289
xiii. 10	230
11	9, 228, 247
14	98, 173, 346, 347
xiv. 10	274
xv. 4	111
25	4

1 CORINTHIANS.

i. 17	3
ii. 9	18, 86, 270, 329
11	215
14	395
iii. 2	108
3	107
10	116
12	116
22	36
iv. 7	274
10	327
11	328
11-13	326
13	328
v. 5	71
6	358
11	293, 294
vi. 7	239, 290
9, 10	352
vii. 7	205, 219
14	134
23	294
29	30, 99, 228

INDEX OF TEXTS. 417

vii. 31	. . . . . . 30, 99
viii. 6	 53
11	 357
ix. 15	 328
26	. . . . . . 72, 94
27	. . . . . 128, 384
x. 4	 302
10	 376
11	 111
12	 128
13	. . . . 72, 327, 340
27	 294
xi. 30	 71
xii. 7	. . . . . . 41, 42
18	 41
31	. . . . . . 28, 44
xiii. 1, 2	 44
3	 45
5	 230
12	 324
xv. 32	 197
33	 240
52	 368
58	 155
xvi. 4	 4

2 CORINTHIANS.

i. 22	 119
iii. 13	 369
18	 369
iv. 17	 328
18	. . . . . 204, 376
v. 4	 279
vi. 2	 93
4, 5	 326
8	 326
10	. . . . . 222, 326
16	 201
viii. 5	 134
12	 375
x. 5	 39
xi. 2	 337
24-26	 326
26	 328
xii. 2	 328
8, 9	 385
8-10	 326
9	 340
10	 385

GALATIANS.

i. 4	 104
6	. . . . . 108, 131
18	 328
ii. 8	 1
9	 4
10	 4
iii. 4	. . . . . 105, 131
19	 38

iv. 18	 28
19	. . 122, 246, 273, 360
20	 108
v. 4	 360
7	. . . . . 105, 131
10	. . . . . 105, 130
vi. 2	 355
10	. . . . . 135 twice
14	 275

EPHESIANS.

ii. 6	 53
7	 52
13	 63
iii. 3, 4	 392
6	 79
iv. 29	 14
v. 3	 284
4	. . . . . 195, 284
5	. . . . . 59, 195
27	. . . . 13, 183, 338
30	 79
vi. 11	 203
12	 73
14	. . . . . . 73, 74
17	 74
18	 98

PHILIPPIANS.

i. 18	 332
ii. 6, 7	 23
7	 374
9, 10	 324
14	 376
iii. 19	. . . . . 291, 344
20	 202
iv. 5, 6	. . . . . . 9, 228
7	 18

COLOSSIANS.

i. 20	. . . . . 151, 208
iii. 5	 238
16	 111

1 THESSALONIANS.

ii. 14	. . . . . . 4, 255
iv. 13	 57
18	. . . . . . 43, 352
v. 11	. . . . . . 43, 352
13	 378
14	 83

2 THESSALONIANS.

i. 6, 7	 39
iii. 10	 146
13	 146

1 TIMOTHY.

ii. 6	104
9	331, 333, 334
iv. 14	353
15	111
v. 5	318
11	220
13	251
14	219, 220
20	59
vi. 8	331
10	282

2 TIMOTHY.

i. 7	56
ii. 12	83
25, 26	137
iii. 12	71
16	111
iv. 6	3
16	3

HEBREWS.

i. 1, 2	150
2	20
5	9
6, 5, 7, 10	49
10	21
13	9, 50
14	63, 174
15	174
ii. 1	6
14	63, 64
18	69
iii. 6	67, 76
12	6, 7, 82
13	352
iv. 14	106
v. 1	106
5	106
6	106, 226
7	106
8	141
11	107, 132
11, 12	89
12	7, 114, 128, 131, 154
13	117
vi. 9	62, 105
10	6
12	7, 359
19	165, 187, 191
20	150
vii. 11	178
16	177, 190, 226
8	177, 182
19	177, 178, 182, 190, 226
viii. 3	168
7	37, 182, 190
10	162
13	37, 226, 395
ix. 10	164
11	226
12	226
24	191
x. 5	226
12	168
14	234
20	187, 191, 233
22	245
25	233, 351
31	243
32	89, 253, 339, 342
34	4, 300
37	5
38	253
xi. 1	253
4	367
13	138
34	314
37, 38	275
38	255
39, 40	139
xii. 8	
12	5, 90, 359
12, 13	6
13	359
14	377, 378
16	377
28	380
29	367
xiii. 2	149
4	352
7	388
9	109
13	7
16	143
23	3

S JAMES.

v. 13	57
15	123

1 S. PETER.

ii. 22	324

S. JUDE.

19	254

INDEX OF GREEK WORDS.

Those marked † belong to the Epistle itself.

A.

ἄγγελος ὁ (Malachi) 181
ἀγέννητος 254
† ἅγια, ἅγια τῶν ἁγίων 187
ἅγια τὰ, τοῖς ἁγίοις 215 note
ἁγιάζω 210 note f
ἁγιασμοῦ 383 note k
ἀγνοέω 189
ἀγνώμων 170
ἄγρυπνυς 317
ἠδικήθης 290 note
† ἀδόκιμος 128 note
ἀεί 80
† ἀθέτησις 212 note h
† ἄθλησιν 244
αἰνίγματα,-τι 189, 289, 382
αἰνίττεσθαι 80 note
αἴτιον 152
† αἰῶνας 11 note
ἀκαταλύτου 163
ἀκμὴν 132
ἀκοῆς λόγον ὀφείλω 250 note
† ἀκροθίνια 153
ἄκρον καὶ ἠκριβωμένον 108
ἠκρωτηρίαζε 307
ἀλήθεια 152
ἄλλως 59
ἄλφα 117
ἅμα ἦλθε 192
ἀμετρίας, ἐξ 110
ἀμοιβῆς 321 note
ἀνάγκας 345
† ἀναθεωροῦντες 381
ἀναιρεῖ 382
ἀνακαγχάζω 197
ἀναμένειν, καὶ τοῦ μὴ ἐπὶ τοῖς αὐτοῖς αὐτὴν 298
ἀναπόδεικτον 254
ἄναρχος 20 note, 152, 254
ἀναχαίτισον 355
ἀνενεγκεῖν 210 note d
ἄνεσις 302
ἄνομος 163

ἀντιδιαστολαὶ κυρίαι 169
ἀντίρροπος 210
† ἀντίτυπα 207, 208, 212
ἄξιος † 255 note, 270
ἀόρατον τὸ 369
ἀπαγορεύειν τὰ καθ' ἕ 320
ἀπαναισχυντεῖ 380
ἀπάντων ὑπὲρ 209
† ἅπαξ 189, 207, 209
ἀπαράλλακτος 19, 23
ἀπαρρησίαστος 170, 222
ἀπαυγάσματος καὶ διὰ τοῦ τῆς οὐσίας τὴν ἐγγύτητα ἔδειξεν 22
ἀπίθανον 248
ἀπιστῶ οὐκ 224
ἁπλῶς καὶ εἰκῇ 328
ἁπλῶς ἔξω πρόσκειται 329
† ἀπὸ 313
ἀπογνῶτε 370
ἀποδύεται πρὸς 377
ἄποιος 350
† ἀπόκειται 209
ἀπολαβεῖν ὀφείλουσα 212
ἀπέλαβες 71, see too in Gal. iv. init. p. 63 O.T.
ἀπολαύων 134
† ἀπολελυμένον 392
ἀποξύσωμεν 183 note
ἀπορώτερον 255
† ἀποτυμπανίσθησαν,-σμὸς 313 and note e
ἁπτόμεθα τοῦ πράγματος 205 note
ἀπώναντο 296 note
ἆρα οὖν 156
ἀρκεσθησόμεθα 331
ἄρτον αἰτῶν 292 note
† ἀρχὴ τοῦ λόγου 116
† ἀρχῆς τῆς, τὸν λόγον 114 note, τὰ στοιχεῖα 114
ἀρχῆς ἐξ 118
ἄρχοντες 387 note
ἀσκέω 94
ἀσυγκρίτως 13
αὕτη 213

INDEX OF GREEK WORDS.

τὸν αὐτὸν, τὸ αὐτὸ 213
αὐτόματος,-τα 255, 258
ἀφιέναι 190

Β.

βδελυρὰ 380
βεβίασται τὸ σόν 181
βιωτικαὶ 57
βουλήσεις 155 note d
βούλομαι ... θέλω 219 see too in Eph. i. 4. p. 105 O.T.
βουνοὶ ... ὄρη 70 note

Γ.

γεγενημένην ἐκ 392
γνήσιον τὸ τῆς υἱότητος 11
γνήσιος 12
γόμφους 347
γυμνάζει 255

Δ.

δεῖξαι 118
δημηγορῶν 369
διὰ ταύτης 377
δι' οὗ 52
διακωδωνίζει 150
διαμωκῶνται 197
διάνοια *thought* 18 νοεῖ ἡ διάνοια 19
διαπορθμεύω 40 note c, 199
διαστολῇ ἐν τῇ 181
δικαίωμα τῆς βοηθείας 136
δικαιώματα 292
δινεῖσθαι 175 note
διοικεῖ 316 note
† διορθώσεως 191
δουλείαν 306
δυνάμεις 41
δυνηθῆναι, τὸ τοιαῦτα 340
δυσειδία 194 note l
δυσήνιος 362

Ε.

† ἐγγὺς ἀφανισμοῦ 395
ἐγγυτέρα ἡ ἑκάστου ζωὴ πολλῷ καὶ ἡ τελευτή 219 note
ἐγκαλεῖ 252
ἔθνος 2
εἰδεχθεῖς φύσει 194
κατ' εἶδος 124, 362, 363
εἰκὼν 22, 152 and note b
εἰρωνείας 325
ἐκ 191
ἐκλύω 195
ἐκπλύνεις 345 note

ἔκτισις 71, 384
ἐκτραχηλίσῃς 173
† ἐκφέρουσα 129
† ἔλαθον 377
ἐλέγξαι,-χομένην 266, 313 note f
ἐλεημῶν,-οσύνη 135, 373, 374 and note, cf. 123 note
—— ἐργάζεσθαι 365
ἐλευθέρα, ἡ 330
ἕλκων 215
ἐμβάλλει 155
ἐμπλατύνων ἑαυτὸν 384
† ἐμφανίζεται 208 note a
ἐμφέρεσθαι 152
ἐν 222
ἐν 110 note, 124
ἐναποθανέτω 250
ἐναπομένει 250
ἐνδιδόντες 355
ἐνεδρευόντων 115
ἐνέργειαν 394
ἐνεστηκότα 190
ἐνήγεσθε 244
ἐνηργεῖτο ἐκεῖνο 300
ἐννοίας κοινῆς 254
† ἐν πᾶσιν 390
ἐνταῦθα 176, 183
ἐντεύξει 185
ἐντιθέντα 164
ἐντρεπτικῶς 119
ἐξ αὐτοῦ 19 note a, ἐξ οὗ 26 note k
† ἐξ ἑνὸς 53
ἐξ ἡμῶν τὰ 49
ἐξέπιπτε 266 note b
ἐξευτελίζων 190 note
ἐξίτηλον 345 note
ἐπαπορήσας 148
ἐπειδὴ 140
ἐπιθέτης 146
ἐπικουρία 381
ἐπιλαβώμεθα 384
ἐπισημαίνεται 192
ἐπισκοπὴ ἡ παρ' αὐτοῦ 257
† ἐπισκοποῦντες 352
ἐπιστρέφει 339
ἐπιτρίμματα 194
ἐπιχριομένους 309
ἐργάζεται 346, 365
ἐργαστηρίων, ταῖς προσθήκαις ταῖς ἐπὶ τῶν 334
ἐρήμῳ ἐν τῇ 345
† ἐρχόμενος ὁ 247 note f
† ἐσχάτου τῶν ἡμερῶν 8 note
εὐγνωμοσύνην 390
εὐλάβειαν 390 note c
† εὐπερίστατον 323 text and margin
εὑρεῖν 79
εὐφήμῳ 350
† ἐφάπαξ 192
ἑωθιναῖς ... ἑσπεριναῖς 261

INDEX OF GREEK WORDS.

H.

† ἡγουμένων 378
ἵδετο 366 note
ἡμέτερον,-ρα 180, 195, 228, 334, 369

Θ.

θάλαμας,-μου 335, 337
† θεατριζόμενοι 244
Θεὸς ὁ 34 note d: Θεοῦ τοῦ τῆς ἀξίας 175, τὰ 285, τὰ ὑποκάτω 188
θεραπεύει 101
θεωρία 190: ἐθεώρησε 151, 178 note, 190
θηριομάχοις 194
θλίβεται σφηνούμενος 384: θλῖψις, -εσι † 243, 384 note
θρήνων 270
θῦμα καὶ ἱερεῖον 210
θυσία 142

I.

ἱερατικῷ ἀξιώματι 282
ἱερεῖον 142, 210
† ἱερέων 160
ἴλιγγος 395 (see also on Romans, Mr Simcox's Index p. 528)
Ἰουδαῖοι (followers of Paul of Samosata) 33 note d

K.

καθάπτεται μᾶλλον αὐτοῦ συμφερόντως 182
καθαρὰ 395
καθέστηκε 190
καθ'ὃν 190
καιρίῳ 315
† κακουχούμενοι 320
καπηλείας 391
† καρποὺς 350
κατὰ τὰ 298
καταβλάπτει 391
† καταβολὴν σπέρματος εἰς 269
κατεπόθησαν 309 note
† κατασκεύασας 67,-εσκεύασται 208
καταφρονεῖ 79
κατηφεῖν 124
κατόρθωμα 156
κατωφερὴς 335
καύχημα τὸ, τοῦ χριστοῦ τὰ παθήματα 339 note
κενῶσαι (to give our all) 381 note, ἑαυτὸν 374

κήρυξ 90 note, 185,-γμα 72
ἐκινδύνευσεν 388, 390 note d
κοίνον τὸ 255, κοινῆς ἐννοίας 254
κοινωνία 149
κοιτωνίσκῳ 334
κομισάμενοι 266 note c
κοσμικαὶ καὶ κοσμικοὶ 57
κοσμιότητα 278
κρατητικὸν 200
κρείσσων εἰς ποιῶν θέλημα 280 note
κυβερνῶν 24

Λ.

ἔλαβες 71
† λέγεσθαι ἐν τῷ 79, λέγοντες 254 note f
† λειτουργία 177
λεπτῶν ὀθονίων (lace) 331
λιπαίνει 175
† λογισάμενος 286 note b
λογιστικὸν τὸ 193
λόγος 18, λόγου 354, τὸν λόγον 353
λουτροῦ διὰ 119
λύπης 324

M.

μαναὰ, μαννὰ 304 note k
μανιάκην 307
† μαρτύρων ὄγκον 323 note
μάχαιρα 88
μείζονα 360
μέλλων ὁ ἢ 48
† ἐμεσίτευσεν 140
μέσον τὸ 53
μετὰ ταῦτα τὰ 367
μετ' ἐμῶν 311
† μετριοπαθεῖν 100
μικροψυχῶμεν 232
μοναζόντων ἀνδρῶν 148
μονομάχος 194 note k

N.

νήφειν 317, νήψατε 118
νομοθετουμένων 369
νοσηλεύωμεν 345
νοῦς, νοέω, ἔννοια 18, 19
νυμφῶν 337
† νωθροὶ 132 note

O.

ὀβολοὶ 43
† ὅθεν 69, 200
οἰκεῖον τὸ πάθος 255

INDEX OF GREEK WORDS.

οἰκείως ἔχειν 123
οἰκημάτων 330
οἶκον 330
οἴκοθεν 133
ὀλιγοψυχίαν 139, 151
† ὁμολογία 91
ὄνομα αὐτοῦ καλέσεται 369
† ὁρκωμοσίας 165
οὐδαμοῦ γνώριμοι γεγόνασι 299
† οὐκέτι 233, 234
οὐκ ὄντα ἐχαρίσατο 286 note c
οὐσία 248, οὐσίας τὰ τῆς 258
οὐσίωσις 13 note f

Π.

ἔπαθέ τι 302
† παθημάτων 243
† παιδείαν εἰς 311
παννυχίς, χίζω 186 and note
† παντελὲς, εἰς τὸ 166
† παραβολῇ ἐν 288
παραβύστῳ ἐν 364
παραγίνηται 176
† παρακαλεῖτε 83,-κλήσεως 392
† παραπλησίως 92
παρ' αὐτοῦ τὰ 255, τὰ παρ' ἑαυτοῦ εἰσάγει 155
παρατήρησις,-εῖτε,-εῖσθαι 379, 382 notes g and h
παραφθέγγονται 186
† παροξυσμὸν εἰς 229
πένθους 270
† περιπατήσαντες οἱ 379 note
περιστελεῖται 335
πίνακα 293
ἐπιστεύθη 40 note f
† πίστις 116 note, † κατὰ πίστιν 275
πίστεις καὶ ἐλεημοσύναι 123 note
πίστεως τὸ τῆς 253
πιστὸς 294 note
πλαδῶσα 347
πλήρωμα αὐτοῦ 298
πνέουσαν σφόδρα 340, ποῦ ἔπνει 240
πνεῦμα (Divine Nature of Son) 13 note e
† ποιήσας 68 note
ποιοῦμεν, *offer* 212
† πόλιν 268
πολῖται 275
πολιτισμὸς 195
πολλάκις 43 note h
πολὺ παρετείνετο 300
πολύπλοκον 382
πολύτροπος 298
πρεσβυτέρα 3 note c
προαιρέσει, σεως,-σιν 289, 380, 394, 395
προβληθέντος 155 note e

† προείρηται 81 note
προελέσθαι καὶ βουληθῆναι 156
τὰ προκείμενα 144, 176, προκειμένου 155 note e
προλήψεως 237
πρὸς 390
προσεδέξασθε 245
προσήκοντα καιρὸν 219
προσκυνεῖ 304, † προσεκύνησεν 297 note
προστασίας τῆς 283
† πρόσχυσις 309, 310
πρόσωπα δυὸ δεικνὺς καὶ Θεὸν καὶ ἄνθρωπον 33, † προσώπῳ τῷ 208
ᾗ οἷς προεφητεύετο 189
† πρωτοτόκια 358
πυκνὸς 309

Ρ.

ῥομφαία 88
ῥοπὴ 156 note g

Σ.

† σαββατισμὸς 81
σατανικὸν 362
σεμνότητα 357 note
σκάμματα 72
σκεπάσματα 331
σκηνοῦν ἐκεῖ, παρὰ τὸ 188
σκιατροφία 345
σκώμματα 325
† στενάζοντες 387, 389 note
στοιχεῖ 161
† συγκεκραμένους 80 note
σύγκρισιν ἡ κατὰ 101
συνεσκιασμένον καὶ συγκεκαλυμμένον τὸ 368
σύρος ὁ 256 note
συστρέφον 122
ἐσφαγμένος 176
σφαιρίζειν 204
σχέσει καὶ οἰκειώσει 202
σωτηρίας πρὸς 310
σωφροσύνην 278

Τ.

τὰ 326
τάξει ἐν 309
ταπήτων 293
τελειότης 107, 108
τελείωσιν μετὰ 88 note
† τετραχηλισμένα 89
τίκτουσα 129
τικτόμενος διαφθείρει 193

INDEX OF GREEK WORDS.

† τινα 106 note, ἐπί τίσιν 362
τόπῳ ἀποκλειόμενος 202
τότε 93
† τρίβολος 130
τρόπῳ 162
τύπος 152, † 177, † 208

Υ.

ὕθλος 175
υἱῷ ἐν 9 διὰ τοῦ υἱοῦ 9 διὰ τοῦ ὑ ἐν τῷ πνεύματι τῷ ἁγίῳ 10 note b μετὰ τοῦ ὑ σὺν τῷ πνεύματι τῷ ἁγίῳ ib.
ὑπέραντλον 347
ὑπερβαίνειν 172
ὑπέρβατον καθ' 79
ὑπόδειγμα,-τι,-τα 198, † 202, 288
† ————λατρεύουσι 176
ὑπόδικοι 333
ὑποπτεύειν 167
ὑπόστασις 19 and note d, 22 note h, † ἀρχὴν τῆς 79, κατὰ 33 note c
ἐνυπόστατος 19

Φ.

φανῆναι διὰ τῆς σαρκὸς 369
φανταστικὸν 100
φθόγγοι 345
φθόνους 335

φιλανθρωπίαν 312
† φιλοξενίας 377, 380
φιλοσοφεῖν μυρία 56
φιλοσοφίας (of monastic practice) 148
φρονῶμεν 314 φρονεῖν μείζω 314 ἀνθρώπινα φρονεῖ 157
φρονηματιῶν 333

Χ.

χαλεπὸν 250
χαμαιτυπεῖα 186
χαρακτήρων 153
χάρις 120, † χάριν ἔχωμεν 376 note a
χορεύω 195
χρείας τῆς ὥμεν 381
† χρηματισμὸς,-σθείς,-σμένον,-ζόντα 264 and note, 368, 370 note h

Ψ.

ψελλίζοντος 317
ψυχικὸς 395

Ω.

ὠρθοίζον πόδς 384

PRINTED BY THE SOCIETY OF THE HOLY TRINITY,
HOLY ROOD, OXFORD

NEW EDITION OF THE WORKS

OF

S. CYRIL

ARCHBISHOP OF ALEXANDRIA

EDITED BY

P. E. PUSEY, M.A.

OF all the Greek Fathers who have left us writings, S. Gregory Nyssa and S. Cyril of Alexandria would seem to have been the worst edited. Of the latter, the one and only edition is that of John Aubert, published in seven tomes at Paris in 1638. To his great diligence we owe what we have, while no successor has ever taken up his work with the skill of the unwearied Benedictine Editors. Cardinal Mai a few years back collected with great diligence many fragments of lost works of S. Cyril from the stores of the Vatican. Migne in his great Patrology republished Aubert's edition, with some pains, and gathered into it from every printed source, whatever of his had been subsequently edited: so that Migne's edition of S. Cyril is the Repertorium of all of his that has been published in Greek or Latin. But Migne's own object was the formation of a vast Theological Library, an enterprise too great of itself to admit of more than a careful use of his printed material.

This new Edition of the Works of S. Cyril of Alexandria was begun at Dr. PUSEY's desire, who since 1856 has undertaken the whole expense of procuring collations, and of the long journeys necessary to examine the less-known libraries. The text will be carefully collated with the best MSS.

The first five volumes, viz., the two on the Twelve Minor Prophets, and three on S. John, &c., have been printed by the Delegates of the Clarendon Press; who allow copies to be supplied to subscribers. The Remainder are being printed at Dr. PUSEY's expense.

The volumes already issued are as follows:—

Vols. I. and II., containing the COMMENTARIES UPON THE TWELVE MINOR PROPHETS.

Vol. III., of the series, containing the first part of the COMMENTARY ON S. JOHN, Chapter i.—viii. 19.

Vol. IV., a continuation of the COMMENTARY ON S. JOHN, and containing viii. 20—xvii. 21.

Vol. V., completing the COMMENTARY ON S. JOHN, and containing also general fragments (except those on S. Matthew, S. Luke, the Psalms, and a few others), as well as those upon S. Paul's Epistles. At the end are S. Cyril's replies to questions addressed to him from Monasteries in Palestine.

Vol. VI., containing the first portion of S. CYRIL's chief Dogmatic Works, contains—

    LIBRI V. CONTRA NESTORIUM.
    EXPLANATIO XII. CAPITUM.
    DEFENSIONES XII. CAPITUM.
    SCHOLIA DE INCARNATIONE UNIGENITI.

This is one of the volumes in defence of the Doctrine of the Incarnation, explaining that the union of God the Son with His Human Body and Soul is of such kind, that the action or suffering of His Human Body and Soul is His own. S. Cyril states and enforces this, supporting his statements by Holy Scripture against extracts from different sermons of Nestorius. The twelve chapters are concise statements of the Doctrine of the Incarnation which Nestorius was required to sign, and of these S. Cyril gave a brief explanation for the Council of Ephesus, and an ampler defence against the attacks severally of Theodoret, and Andrew, Bishop of Samosata. From their attacks we get the chapters explained in language guarded on all sides. The *Scholia* is a most simple explanation of the Doctrine *ad populum*.

Vol. VII. Part 1 contains—

    DE RECTA FIDE TRES TRACTATUS.
    QUOD UNUS EST CHRISTUS DIALOGUS.
    APOLOGETICUS AD IMPERATOREM.   [*just ready*]

The other half, containing the EPISTLES, *will be kept till last, to allow of the most complete researches possible being made.*

The *De Recta Fide* consists of three treatises: the first to the Emperor, setting forth the Doctrine of the Incarnation; the second and third to the ladies of the Imperial family, in which different points of our belief thereon are proved and illustrated from Holy Scripture.

The same is done in a different way in the form of a Dialogue in the *Quod Unus;* in which S. Cyril set himself to shew how, since our Lord is One, GOD and Man, even the more human things, even the being forsaken on the Cross, and the fear at the Passion, He made His own.

The last little treatise is a defence of himself to the Emperor, on his conduct at the Council, and contains material for its History.

The volumes to be issued are :—

Vol. VII., Part 2—EPISTLES.

The larger number of these are letters arising out of the Council of Ephesus and the troubles immediately following. They are of great interest as historical documents, and as aiding to throw light on some points of S. Cyril's character. It is intended also that the collection shall include letters of others to him.

This part will follow vol. x.

Vol. VIII. The GLAPHYRA.

This is a treatise on the Pentateuch, shewing how in very much of its history, CHRIST was seen. The very ample citations from it in mediaeval writers, shew how much this work was appreciated.

Vol. IX. The THESAURUS.

This Work comprises proofs, dialectically treated, of our Belief in the Three Persons of the Holy Trinity.

Vol. X. The Treatises DE TRINITATE AD HERMEIAM, &c.

Teaching about the Three Persons of the Holy Trinity, in the form of a Dialogue. It was one of S. Cyril's earlier works, though not published at first and perhaps revised previously to its publication.

The price to Subscribers is fixed at 12s. per volume.

The volumes in this Prospectus do not exhaust the Writings of S. Cyril, nor does the Editor propose to stop here. Still it is thought better not in any way to pledge Subscribers to any further portion of his works, the editing of which must, amid advancing years, be at least a matter of uncertainty and irregularity.

Subscriptions to be paid to Messrs. JAMES PARKER and Co., BROAD-STREET, OXFORD, who will supply the volumes as due.

OXFORD
August 1877.

[1877.

WORKS, SERMONS, &c.

By the REV. E.B. PUSEY, D.D.

SERMONS.

8vo., *Cloth*, 6s. *each*.

PAROCHIAL SERMONS, Vol. I. For the Season from ADVENT to WHITSUNTIDE. With a Preface.

PAROCHIAL SERMONS, Vol. II.

PAROCHIAL SERMONS, Vol. III. Reprinted from the "Plain Sermons by Contributors to the 'Tracts for the Times.'" [Revised edition.]

PAROCHIAL SERMONS, on Various Occasions.

SERMONS preached before the UNIVERSITY of OXFORD between 1859 and 1872. With a Preface.

LENTEN SERMONS, preached chiefly to Young Men at the Universities, between 1858 and 1874.

SERMONS at a Mission and Retreat, at the Consecration of S. SAVIOUR'S LEEDS. 1845. Together with Eight Sermons by the Rev. JOHN KEBLE, C. MARRIOTT, W. U. RICHARDS, I. WILLIAMS, and a Preface by Dr. PUSEY.

ELEVEN ADDRESSES DURING A RETREAT OF THE COMPANIONS OF THE LOVE OF JESUS, engaged in Perpetual Intercession for the Conversion of Sinners. 8vo., cloth, 3s. 6d.

SINGLE UNIVERSITY SERMONS.

THE HOLY EUCHARIST, A COMFORT to the PENITENT. Preached 1843. Twenty-second Thousand. 8vo., 1s.

THE PRESENCE of CHRIST in the HOLY EUCHARIST. Preached 1853. 8vo., 1s.

ENTIRE ABSOLUTION of the PENITENT. Two Sermons. Preached 1846. 8vo., 1s. each.

JUSTIFICATION. Preached 1853. 8vo., 1s.

ALL FAITH the GIFT of GOD. REAL FAITH ENTIRE. Two Sermons. Preached 1855. 8vo., 2s.

PATIENCE and CONFIDENCE the STRENGTH of THE CHURCH. Preached 1841. 8vo., 1s.

EVERLASTING PUNISHMENT. Preached 1864. 8vo., 6d.

MIRACLES of PRAYER. Preached 1866. 8vo., 1s.

WILL YE ALSO GO AWAY? Preached 1867. With Preface and Appendix. 8vo., 1s.

THIS IS MY BODY. Preached 1871. 8vo., 1s.

THE RESPONSIBILITY of INTELLECT in MATTERS of FAITH. Preached 1872. With an Appendix on Bishop Moberley's Strictures on the Athanasian Creed. 8vo., 1s.

SINFUL BLINDNESS AMIDST IMAGINED LIGHT. Preached 1873. 8vo., 6d.

CHRISTIANITY WITHOUT THE CROSS A CORRUPTION OF THE GOSPEL OF CHRIST. Preached 1875. With a Note on "Modern Christianity, a Civilized Heathenism." 8vo., 6d.

GOD and HUMAN INDEPENDENCE. 1876. 8vo., 6d.

The OCCASIONAL PAROCHIAL SERMONS can be had also separately, as follows.

THE DAY OF JUDGEMENT. Preached at Brighton, 1839. 6d.

CHRIST THE SOURCE AND RULE OF CHRISTIAN LOVE. Preached at Bristol, 1840. 1s.

THE PREACHING OF THE GOSPEL A PREPARATION FOR OUR LORD'S COMING. Clifton, 1841. 1s.

GOD IS LOVE. WHOSO RECEIVETH ONE SUCH LITTLE CHILD IN MY NAME RECEIVETH ME. Two Sermons preached at Ilfracombe, 1844. 1s. 6d.

THE BLASPHEMY AGAINST THE HOLY GHOST. Preached at Margaret Chapel, 1845. 1s.

DO ALL TO THE LORD JESUS. At Margaret Chapel, 1845. 6d.

CHASTISEMENTS NEGLECTED, FORERUNNERS OF GREATER. Preached at Margaret Chapel, 1847. 1s.

THE DANGER OF RICHES. SEEK GOD FIRST AND YE SHALL HAVE ALL. Two Sermons at Bristol. 1850. 1s. 6d.

THE CHURCH THE CONVERTER OF THE HEATHEN. Two Sermons preached at Melcombe Regis, 1838. 6d.

THE GLORY OF GOD'S HOUSE. A Sermon preached at Grove Church, 1832. 6d.

Four of the LENTEN SERMONS may also be had separately; namely,

LIFE THE PREPARATION FOR DEATH. Preached at Great S. Mary's, Cambridge. Lent, 1867. 6s.

OUR PHARISAISM. Preached at S. Paul's, Knightsbridge. Ashwednesday, 1868. 6s.

REPENTANCE, FROM LOVE OF GOD, LIFE-LONG. Preached at S. Mary's, Oxford. Lent, 1857. 1s.

THE THOUGHT OF THE LOVE OF JESUS FOR US, THE REMEDY FOR SINS OF THE BODY. Preached at S. Mary's, Oxford. Lent, 1861. 6d.

"BLESSED ARE THE MEEK." A Sermon, preached at the Opening of the Chapel of KEBLE COLLEGE, on S. Mark's Day, 1876. 8vo., 1s.

WORKS.

The MINOR PROPHETS; with a COMMENTARY Explanatory and Practical, and Introductions to the Several Books. 1 volume 4to. £1. 11s. 6d.

The Parts may be had separately.

PART I. contains HOSEA—JOEL, INTRODUCTION. 5s.
 II.—JOEL, INTRODUCTION—AMOS vi. 6. 5s.
 III.—AMOS vi. 7 to MICAH i. 12. 5s.
 IV.—MICAH i. 13 to HABAKKUK, INTRODUCTION. 5s.
 V.—HABAKKUK, ZEPHANIAH, HAGGAI. 5s.
 VI.—ZECHARIAH, MALACHI. 6s.

DANIEL THE PROPHET. Nine Lectures delivered in the Divinity School of the University of Oxford. With Copious Notes. *Third Edition.* 1876. 8vo., cloth, 10s. 6d.

ON THE SACRAMENTS.

The DOCTRINE OF HOLY BAPTISM, as taught by Holy Scripture and the Fathers. (Formerly "Tracts for the Times," No. 67.) 8vo., cloth, 5s.

The DOCTRINE of the REAL PRESENCE, as contained in the Fathers from the death of S. John the Evangelist to the 4th General Council. 1855. 8vo., cloth, 7s. 6d.

The REAL PRESENCE, the doctrine of the English Church, with a vindication of the reception by the wicked and of the Adoration of our Lord Jesus Christ truly present. 8vo., 6s.

ON THE CLAUSE "AND THE SON," in regard to the EASTERN CHURCH and the BONN CONFERENCE. A LETTER to the Rev. H. P. LIDDON, D.D., Ireland Professor of Exegesis, Canon of S. Paul's. 8vo., cloth, 5s.

AN EIRENICON. Vol. I. LETTER to the AUTHOR of "THE CHRISTIAN YEAR," "The Church of England a Portion of Christ's One Holy Catholic Church, and a Means of Restoring Visible Unity." 8vo., cloth, 6s.

——————————— Vol. II. FIRST LETTER to the VERY REV. J. H. NEWMAN, D.D., "The Reverential Love due to the ever-blessed Theotokos, and the Doctrine of her 'Immaculate Conception.'" 8vo., cloth, 6s.

——————————— Vol. III. SECOND LETTER to DR. NEWMAN, "Healthful Re-union as conceived possible before the Vatican Council." (Formerly entitled, "Is Healthful Re-union Impossible?") 8vo., cloth, 6s.

The ROYAL SUPREMACY not an Arbitrary Authority, but limited by the laws of the Church of which Kings are members. Ancient Precedents. 8vo., 6s.

The COUNCILS of the CHURCH, from the Council of Jerusalem to the close of the 2nd of Constantinople, A.D. 581. 6s.

LETTER to the LORD BISHOP of LONDON, in Explanation of some Statements contained in a Letter by the Rev. W. Dodsworth. 16mo., 1s.

RENEWED EXPLANATIONS in consequence of Mr. Dodsworth's Comments on the above. 8vo., 1s.

The CHURCH of ENGLAND leaves her Children Free to whom to Open their Griefs. A Letter to the Rev. W. U. Richards. 8vo. with Postscript, 5s.

MARRIAGE with a DECEASED WIFE'S SISTER, together with a SPEECH on the same subject by E. Badeley, Esq. 3s. 6d.

GOD'S PROHIBITION OF THE MARRIAGE WITH A DECEASED WIFE'S SISTER (Lev. xviii. 6) not to be set aside by an inference from His limitation of Polygamy among the Jews (Lev. xviii. 18). 8vo., 1s.

COLLEGIATE AND PROFESSORIAL TEACHING AND DISCIPLINE, in answer to Professor Vaughan. 5s.

CASE AS TO THE LEGAL FORCE OF THE JUDGEMENT OF THE PRIVY COUNCIL in re Fendal v. Wilson; with the Opinion of the Attorney-General and Sir Hugh Cairns, and a Preface to those who love God and His truth. 8vo., 6d.

DEVOTIONAL WORKS, Edited by DR. PUSEY.

A GUIDE for PASSING ADVENT HOLILY. By AVRILLON. Translated from the French, and adapted to the use of the English Church. Fcap. 8vo., cloth, 5s.

A GUIDE for PASSING LENT HOLILY. By AVRILLON. Translated from the French, and adapted to the use of the English Church. Fcap. 8vo., cloth, 5s.

The SUFFERINGS OF JESUS. Composed by FRA THOMÉ DE JESU, of the Order of Hermits of S. Augustine, a Captive of Barbary, in the Fiftieth Year of his Banishment from Heaven. Translated from the original Portuguese. In Two Parts, Fcap. 8vo., cloth, 7s.

The LIFE of JESUS CHRIST in GLORY. Daily Meditations from Easter Day to the Wednesday after Trinity Sunday. By NOUET. Fcap. 8vo., cloth, 5s.

The YEAR of AFFECTIONS; or, Sentiments on the Love of God, drawn from the Canticles, for every Day in the Year. By AVRILLON. Fcap. 8vo., cloth, 5s.

The FOUNDATIONS of the SPIRITUAL LIFE. (A Commentary on Thomas à Kempis.) By SURIN. 4s. 6d.

The SPIRITUAL COMBAT, with the PATH of PARADISE; and the SUPPLEMENT; or, the Peace of the Soul. By SCUPOLI. (From the Italian.) 3s. 6d.
———————Cheap Edition, in wrapper, 6d.
———————————fine paper, limp cloth, 1s.

MEDITATIONS and select PRAYERS of S. ANSELM. Fcap. 8vo., cloth, 5s.

PARADISE for the CHRISTIAN SOUL. By HORST. Two Vols. Fcap. 8vo., cloth, 6s. 6d.

OF DEVOUT COMMUNION. 1s. "*From the Paradise.*"

LITANIES in the words of Holy Scripture. Royal 32mo., 6d.

ADVENT READINGS from the FATHERS. Fcap. 8vo., cloth, 3s. 6d.

LENT READINGS from the FATHERS. Fcap. 8vo., cloth, 3s. 6d.

MANUAL for CONFESSORS, by M. l'Abbé GAUME. Translated from the French. (Prepared for publication in conjunction with the late BISHOP FORBES.) 8vo., cloth, 6s.

Other WORKS published by the Rev. E. B. PUSEY, D.D.

THE FIFTY-THIRD CHAPTER OF ISAIAH ACCORDING TO THE JEWISH INTERPRETERS.

I. Texts, edited from Printed Books and MSS. by AD. NEUBAUER. Post 8vo., £1.

II. TRANSLATIONS by S. R. DRIVER and AD. NEUBAUER. With an Introduction to the Translations by the REV. E. B. PUSEY, D.D. Regius Professor of Hebrew, Oxford. 10s.

TRACT XC. On certain Passages in the XXXIX Articles, by the Rev. J. H. NEWMAN, M.A., 1841 ; with Historical Preface by E. B. PUSEY, D.D. ; and Catholic Subscription to the XXXIX Articles considered in reference to TRACT XC., by the Rev. JOHN KEBLE, M.A., 1851. 8vo., sewed 1s. 6d.

TRACTATUS DE VERITATE CONCEPTIONIS BEATISSIMÆ VIRGINIS pro Facienda Relatione coram Patribus Concilii Basileæ, Anno Domini MCCCCXXXVII., Mense Julio. De mandato Sedis Apostolicæ Legatorum, eidem Sacro Concilio præsidentium. Compilatus per Reverendum Patrem, FRATREM JOANNEM DE TURRECREMATA, Sacræ Theologiæ Professorem, Ordinis Prædicatorum, Tunc Sacri Apostolici Palatii Magistrum. Postea Illustrissimum et Reverendissimum S. R. Ecclesiæ Cardinalem, Episcopum Portuensem. Primo impressus Romæ, apud Antonium Bladum, Asulanum, MDXLVII. Small 4to. (830 pp.), cloth, 7s.

Card. de Turrecremata, an Ultramontane, was commissioned, as he says, by the Papal legates, to prepare the case *against* the Immaculate Conception of the B. V., for the Council of Basle. He was summoned to Florence, and his treatise was never presented. Had it been, the Council would, probably, never have made its decree. The carefulness of De Turrecremata's quotations was owned by the chief controversialist on the other side, De Alva. The work was probably suppressed. It existed in no English Library. It was reprinted from the copy in the Mazarine Library at Paris, in the hope that the subject might be reconsidered in the Vatican Council. The Theologians, who examined the subject, previously to the decree of Pius IX, used only the slovenly work of De Bandelis, a remarkable contrast with the careful work of De Turrecremata. The present edition was prepared with great care by the Rev. W. STUBBS, Regius Professor of Modern History.

SERMONS FOR THE CHRISTIAN YEAR.

By the REV. JOHN KEBLE, Author of "THE CHRISTIAN YEAR."

Volumes already published, 8vo. Cloth 6s. each.

SERMONS for ADVENT to CHRISTMAS.
— CHRISTMAS and EPIPHANY.
— LENT to PASSION-TIDE.
— HOLY WEEK.
— EASTER to ASCENSION DAY.
— ASCENSION DAY to TRINITY SUNDAY
— SAINTS' DAYS.   [inclusive.

[To complete THE CHRISTIAN YEAR, other Sermons are being selected for the Season of Trinity, &c.]

VILLAGE SERMONS on the BAPTISMAL SERVICE. By the Rev. JOHN KEBLE. 8vo., cloth, 5s.

Edited by P. E. PUSEY, M.A.

THE THREE EPISTLES (ad Nestorium, ii., iii., et ad Joan. Antioch.) OF S. CYRIL, ARCHBISHOP OF ALEXANDRIA. With an English Translation. 8vo., in wrapper, 3s.

(The Text has been revised from the extant MSS. of any value.)

To Subscribers only, 10 vols., 8vo., cloth, 12s. per volume.

A NEW EDITION OF SOME WORKS OF S. CYRIL, ARCH-BISHOP OF ALEXANDRIA. Vols. I. and II., containing the COMMENTARIES UPON THE TWELVE MINOR PROPHETS; Vols. III., IV., V., containing COMMENTARY on S. John, Extant Fragments on S. Paul's Epistles and of other doctrinal works, Answers to Questions addressed him from the Monasteries:
Vol. VI. containing THE THREE EPISTLES; THE BOOKS AGAINST NESTORIUS; EXPLANATION AND DEFENCES OF THE TWELVE CHAPTERS AND THE SCHOLIA (*A Brief Treatise on the Doctrine of the Incarnation in Simple Language.*)
Vol. VII. part 1. FOUR TREATISES ON THE INCARNATION, in October.

The ten volumes embrace only the portion proposed to be issued first: but the labour of collating has not been confined to them.

NEW AND CHEAPER ISSUE
OF
THE LIBRARY OF THE FATHERS
OF THE HOLY CATHOLIC CHURCH,

ANTERIOR TO THE DIVISION OF THE EAST AND WEST.

Translated by Members of the English Church.

	£	s.	d.
S. ATHANASIUS AGAINST THE ARIANS. 2 vols. 'n one (With very full illustrative notes on the history of the times, and the faith in the Trinity and the Incarnation. The most important work published since Bishop Bull.)	0	10	6
——————————HISTORICAL TRACTS S. Athanasius is *the* historian of the period. ——————————The FESTAL EPISTLES . . The work recently recovered in the Syriac translation.	0	10	6
S. AUGUSTINE'S CONFESSIONS, with notes . . Containing his early life and conversion. The notes illustrate the Confessions from S. Augustine himself.	0	6	0
——————————SERMONS ON THE NEW TESTAMENT. 2 vols. . . . . Clear and thoughtful expositions of Holy Scripture to the poor of Hippo, with rhetorical skill in fixing their attention.	0	15	0
——————————HOMILIES on the PSALMS. 6 vols. . . . . Full of those concise sayings on Christian doctrine and morals, which contain so much truth accurately expressed in few words.	2	2	0
——————————On the GOSPEL and FIRST EPISTLE of S. JOHN. 2 vols. . . . At all times, one of the favourite works of S. Augustine.	0	15	0

	£	s.	d.
S. AUGUSTINE'S PRACTICAL TREATISES Chiefly on the doctrines of grace.	0	6	0
S. CHRYSOSTOM'S HOMILIES on the GOSPEL of S. MATTHEW. 3 vols.	1	1	0
————————HOMILIES on the GOSPEL of S. JOHN. 2 vols.	0	14	0
————————HOMILIES on the ACTS of the APOSTLES. 2 vols. S. Chrysostom, besides the eloquence of his perorations, is remarkable for his care in developing the connection of Holy Scripture.	0	12	0
————————HOMILIES on S. PAUL'S EPISTLES, including the Homilies on the EPISTLE to the HEBREWS, (to be published in July.) 7 vols.	2	12	6
S. CHRYSOSTOM'S HOMILIES TO THE PEOPLE OF ANTIOCH. The celebrated Homilies, where S. Chrysostom employed the fears of the people at the Emperor's displeasure to call them to repentance.	0	7	6
S. CYPRIAN. The TREATISES of S. CYPRIAN and the EPISTLES of S. CYPRIAN, with the TREATISES of S. PACIAN. S. Cyprian, besides his great practical wisdom, states the doctrines of grace as carefully as if he had lived after the Pelagian heresy. He was a great favourite of Dean Milner. He is a witness of the early independence of the several Churches.	0	10	0
S. CYRIL (Bishop of Jerusalem), CATECHETICAL LECTURES on the CREED and SACRAMENTS.	0	7	0
S. CYRIL (Archbishop of Alexandria), COMMENTARY upon the GOSPEL of S. JOHN. Vol. 1. Profound and accurate on the Doctrine of the Incarnation.	0	8	0

WORKS published by the Rev. E. B. PUSEY, D.D. 11

S. EPHREM'S RHYTHMS on the NATIVITY, and
on FAITH 0 8 6
From the Syriac. A very devout writer of the mystical
school, and full on the doctrine of the Incarnation.

S. GREGORY the GREAT, MORALS on the BOOK
of JOB. 4 vols. 1 11 6
Called the Magna Moralia, from the depth of the
observations on human nature of one who lived in
close communion with God.

S. IRENÆUS, the WORKS of 0 8 0
Translated by the late Rev. JOHN KEBLE.

S. JUSTIN the MARTYR, The WORKS of . 0 6 0

TERTULLIAN'S APOLOGETICAL and PRACTICAL
TREATISES 0 9 0
The treatises, especially the Apologetic, have, over
and above, much historical information on early
Christianity. They are full of those frequent sayings
of deep practical truth, for which his name is almost
proverbial.

The following Homilies of S. Chrysostom are about to be reprinted, as revised by Mr. Field's Text.

S. CHRYSOSTOM'S HOMILIES on S. PAUL'S EPISTLE to the ROMANS. 1 vol. Revised by the Rev. W. H. Simcox. *Ready.*

―――――――GALATIANS and EPHESIANS. 1 vol.

―――――――PHILIPPIANS, COLOSSIANS, and THESSALONIANS. 1 vol.

The Homilies on the Corinthians and the Pastoral Epistles may still be had in the original bindings at the following prices :―

S. CHRYSOSTOM'S HOMILIES on S. PAUL'S £ s. d.
EPISTLES to the CORINTHIANS. 2 vols. . 0 18 0

―――――――TIMOTHY, TITUS, and PHILEMON. 1 vol. 0 7 6

In Preparation,

The FIVE BOOKS against NESTORIUS, together with the SCHOLIA on the INCARNATION.

ORIGINAL TEXTS.

	s.	d.
S. AUGUSTINI Confessiones (This edition has been revised with the use of some Oxford MSS. and early editions.)	0 7	0
S. CHRYSOSTOMI in Epist. ad Romanos	0 9	0
———————————ad Corinthios I.	0 10	6
———————————ad Corinthios II.	0 8	0
———————————ad Galatas et Ephesios	0 7	0
———————————ad Phil., Coloss., Thessal.	0 10	6
———————————ad Tim., Tit., Philem.	0 8	0
———————————ad Hebræos	0 9	0

(For this edition all the good MSS. of S. Chrysostom in public libraries in Europe were collated, and the Rev. F. Field having employed his great critical acumen upon them, the English edition of S. Chrysostom is, so far, the best extant, as Sir H. Savile's was in his day.)

THEODORETI Commentarius in omnes B. Pauli Epistolas, Edidit C. MARRIOTT. Pars I. continens Epistolas ad Romanos, Corinthios, et Galatas . 0 8 0

———————————Pars II. ad Ephes., Philip., Coloss., Thess., Heb., Tim., Tit., et Philem. . . . 0 6 0
(In this edition gaps were supplied, and the Text improved, by aid of two Paris MSS., the one of the beginning of the tenth, the other of the eleventh century (which were brought to Paris from Constantinople after the time of Sirmondus). Dr. Cramer's "Catenæ" also furnished some good readings, in addition to those of Nosselt in Schulze's edition of his works.)

www.ingramcontent.com/pod-product-compliance
Lightning Source LLC
Chambersburg PA
CBHW032003300426
44117CB00008B/880